Crash Bank Wallop

PAUL MOORE

Crash Bank Wallop

The Memoirs of the HBOS Whistleblower

CO-AUTHOR MIKE HAWORTH

ASSISTANT EDITOR GUY MANKOWSKI

Crash Bank Wallop

First published in Great Britain 2015

This paperback edition published 2015

New Wilberforce Media Ltd

1

ISBN 978 0 9934 518 0 5

Printed and bound in Great Britain by Clays Ltd, St Ives plc

www.crashbankwallop.co.uk

THANK YOUS

Paul Moore

> *"I called to the Lord in my distress; he answered and freed me. The Lord is at my side; I do not fear. What can man do against me? The Lord is at my side as my helper: I shall look down on my foes. It is better to take refuge in the Lord than to trust in men: it is better to take refuge in the Lord than to trust in Princes."*

First and foremost, I give thanks to the Lord my God for everything that has happened and for giving all of us involved the Faith, Hope and Charity that has made this book what it is. We believe that is a very important book and is the start of something big.

As Job, the famous character in the Old Testament Bible who had so much patience, said, "The Lord giveth and he taketh away. Blessed be the Lord our God." We truly do get transformed by trouble. What at first appeared to be a total disaster has, in the end, turned out to be Amazing Grace. Blessed Mother Teresa was also right when she said, "If I lose my reputation, that's at least one less thing I've got to worry about!"

So far as the human race is concerned, there are a large number of people who have been involved in helping to make this book what it is and whom I really want to thank.

You can find the full list of all these kind, amazing people here:

www.crashbankwallop.co.uk/library/thankyous.1

Special, heart and soul-felt thanks I give to my darling wife, Maureen, whom I love even more now than I did when I fell in love with her on the top of that mountain in Chile on Christmas Day 1988. She has simply been a rock. Without her, I would be nothing and this book would never have happened. She was right. It was all part of God's plan for my life. I also want to thank our wonderful children, Emily Jane, Daniel Thomas and Oliver Clive. It's been a difficult time for them but they have come through and are better people for it. What a group they are, a midwife, a business person and a drama genius. Wow, what a great mix and I look forward to the rest of my life to developing our relationships together from one of parent and children to one of adults and friends.

I also want to thank my mother and father (may he rest in peace) for making me the person that I was and am. Once again, without them, none of this would ever have happened. My mother at 88 years old is a truly amazing and kind person. I'm so proud you're proud of me mum!

Finally, I want to thank Mike Haworth and Guy Mankowski.

Mike, you are truly a beautiful person and an incredible editor, rewriter and co-author of this book. It was your idea when you approached me in 2011. You have made this book a wonderful and readable story with so many lessons in it for the world. Without you this book would not be what it is.

Guy, when you approached me after the talk I gave with Ian Foxley at Ampleforth College at Easter 2014, offering to help me to write the book, little did I know just how important your input would turn out to be. As a report writer by profession, I just didn't know how to write texture and flavour into the text. You taught me how to do this and your creative writing coaching was unbelievably valuable as was your early editing. You are a great writer yourself and Mike and I would love to work with you to publish your upcoming books through our new venture New Wilberforce Media.

Mike Haworth

A huge thank you to Paul Moore for friendship and giving me the opportunity to work on producing his memoirs. Also my appreciation to Maureen, Emily, Daniel and Oliver for their cooperation and ever-open door into their family home. A heartfelt thanks to my wife Karen for her unwavering and unconditional support, our children Elliot, Katy, Joshua and Jack for many months putting up with an "absent father", and Elliot for his outstanding contribution to the project. Also my parents Martin and Margaret for their love and dependable backing, and for inspiration from my late and dear Grandma Spencie.

REVIEWS

In praise of … Paul Moore

"Among the many dishonoured bankers of HBOS, here's one who deserves some praise. Had it not been for whistleblower Paul Moore, James Crosby would probably still have his knighthood and the surrendered third of his pension; and he almost certainly would not have stepped down in 2009 as deputy head of the Financial Services Authority.

"Mr Moore was head of risk at HBOS between 2002 and 2004, during which time his queries about sales practices earned him expletive-laden threats. Shortly after warning senior directors that the bank was lending a dangerous amount, he was dismissed by Mr Crosby. When HBOS collapsed, he testified to the Treasury select committee and then to the parliamentary commission on banking. On both occasions, his evidence was key.

"Had there been more alarm-raisers like Mr Moore, and more senior managers willing to listen, HBOS might still be with us, and billions might have been saved."

The Guardian, Editorial
Wednesday 10 April 2013

Crash Bank Wallop – Book Reviews

"Even at the distance of just over a decade the story of arrogance and disregard for customers at a major bank is breathtaking. I know what it cost Paul Moore to blow the whistle on HBOS. His actions precipitated what remains to date the only clear case of a bank executive being brought to book for the behaviour that led to the crash of 2008. Paul's account of the crisis and his own tribulations should be required reading for bank management and non-executives."

Paul Mason

Channel 4 News, Economics Editor

"This is the long-awaited full exposure of the rottenness, deceit and corruption of the malign gang that took over a successful British bank and drove it to ruin in a few short years. This gang has never been properly held to account or been brought to justice whilst Paul Moore, the brave ethical whistleblower who valiantly tried to warn us of impending disaster, has never been compensated for his sacrifice."

Barry Sheerman MP

Member of Parliament for Huddersfield

"Moore's book provides a thought-provoking insight into how greed, vanity, ego and corporate hubris can bring such devastating consequences to a major company but also to the individual who stands up to their superiors for what they believe is right, and in doing so pays a significant personal price. A must read not only for those involved in business but for anyone with an interest into the darker side of human nature!"

Michael Woodford

Former Chief Executive Officer & Whistleblower, Olympus Corporation

"In Crash Bank Wallop, Paul Moore reveals how, under an egotistical chief executive whose impatience for growth led to corners being cut, HBOS had spun out of control. The bank was paying no more than lip service to risk management, capital and liquidity management, corporate governance, regulation and treating customers fairly.

"As Head of Group Regulatory Risk, Moore's job was to alert the Board to risks that might bring the bank down. But, after he identified predatory and dangerously flawed sales practices at the bank, his senior colleagues' response was to suppress his report, fire him and then seek to smear him via a report commissioned from an accountancy firm that also happened to be the bank's auditors. They then sought to buy his silence.

"Three years later, the bank imploded, only surviving thanks to a government bailout and a rescue takeover, and Moore spoke out about the criminal dishonesty he had seen to become the HBOS whistleblower. Today he can feel almost entirely vindicated – though the banking culture remains far from being fully reformed.

"The book shines a bright light on the wilful blindness, toxic culture, sales-mad groupthink and audit failures that led to HBOS's collapse.

"Moore is remarkably candid – he admits his own foibles and idiosyncrasies including his lack of political nous and occasional naiveté – but he is also fair."

Ian Fraser

Author, Journalist and Broadcaster

"When Paul Moore first talked to me about blowing the whistle on HBOS, the full enormity of the insight he offered was hard to understand. Years later, whenever anyone talks about doing a report on whistleblowers, Paul's name is at the top of the list of people to go to. The consequences for him have often been tough, the consequences for those he talks about have perhaps not yet been fully realised. He had a front-row seat to the disastrous show that was the financial crash. But his lips don't witness what his eyes haven't seen. So this is his highly personal account of what he saw and what he thinks about it. Crash Bank Wallop may cause some little earthquakes of its own."

Danny Savage

BBC News, North of England Correspondent

AND finally for now

"This was a colossal failure of leadership right at the top of HBOS and it had direct and catastrophic consequences for the whole bank which went down spectacularly. It was already a ship holed below the waterline, even before the liquidity crisis finally killed it off. .....This could be the worst banking failure, certainly of any size, that we have seen in British history. .....The scale of impairment on the balance sheet of HBOS was colossal, and unprecedented. .....On almost all fronts...this bank was fundamentally unsound, and it was made unsound by decisions taken right at the top by the most senior management."

Andrew Tyrie MP

Member of Parliament for Chichester, Chairman of the UK Treasury Select Committee and Parliamentary Commission on Banking Standards, BBC, 5 April 2013

DRAMATIS PERSONAE

(Positions where relevant as at 12 October 2015)

Maureen **Emily Jane** **Daniel Thomas** **Oliver Clive**	Paul Moore's wife and children.
James Crosby	HBOS Group Chief Executive Officer, September 2001 to early 2006; Appointed a Non-Executive Director of the Financial Services Authority in January 2004, became its Deputy Chairman in November 2007 and resigned this role on 11 February 2009.
Andy Hornby	Chief Executive Officer of HBOS Retail Division, 2001-2005; HBOS Chief Operating Officer, 2005-2006; HBOS Group Chief Executive Officer, 2006-2008.
Lord Dennis Stevenson	First and only Chairman of HBOS Group, 2001-2008.
Mike Ellis	HBOS Chief Financial Officer and Head of Group Finance and Risk.
Jo Dawson	HBOS Head of Advisory Sales in Retail and later appointed HBOS Group Risk Director on Paul Moore's dismissal.
Phil Hodkinson	Product development actuary at Allied Dunbar; Chief Executive Officer of HBOS Insurance and Investment Division; HBOS Group Finance Director.

James Davies	Deputy Head of Risk for HBOS Insurance and Investment Division; Joint Deputy Head of HBOS Group Regulatory Risk (with Tony Brian).
Dr Andrew Smith	Head of HBOS Group Financial and Operational Risk.
David "Whacker" Walkden	Chief Operating Officer of HBOS Retail Division. Head of Risk reported to him.
Tony Hobson	Chairman of HBOS Group Audit Committee.
Charles Dunstone	Chairman of HBOS Retail Risk Control Committee; Founder and Chief Executive Officer Carphone Warehouse.
Harry Baines	HBOS General Counsel and Company Secretary.
Jack Cullen	HBOS Retail Division Head of Risk.
Andrew Tyrie MP	Member of Parliament for Chichester; Member of the UK Treasury Select Committee from 2001 and became Chairman from June 2010; Chairman of the Parliamentary Commission on Banking Standards.
George Mudie MP	Member of Parliament for Leeds East; Member of the UK Treasury Select Committee from 2001; Retired in March 2015.
John Benger	Clerk to the Treasury Select Committee.

John Griffith-Jones	Senior Partner at KPMG; first Chairman of Financial Conduct Authority.
Peter Hamilton	Head of Legal Department at Allied Dunbar; Senior Barrister at 4 Pump Court.
Clive Howard	Solicitor at Russell, Jones & Walker (now Slater & Gordon).
Frank Skillern Jr	Chief Executive Officer at Acuma (part of American Express).
Marcus Sephton	KPMG Partner and now Consultant to KPMG.
Kirstie Caneparo	Manager of the Financial Services Authority's team responsible for close and continuous regulatory supervision of HBOS Group.
Guy Bainbridge	KPMG Audit Partner.
Steve Kaplan	Personal Coach to Paul Moore.
Bill Casey	Therapist to Paul Moore.
Adam Bates **Roger Meads** **Giles Williams**	KPMG Investigators.
Arthur Selman	HBOS Head of Group Regulatory Risk and then; HBOS Public Policy Unit.
Dougie Ferrans	Chief Executive Officer of Insight Investment Management, part of HBOS.

Howard Posner	Chief Executive Officer of Halifax General Insurance.
Mike Gardener	Lead Relationship Manager of HBOS Group Regulatory Risk.
David Fisher	HBOS Group Human Resources Director.
Irene Grant	Human Resources Director of HBOS Group Regulatory Risk.
John Maclean	HBOS Board Non-Executive Director.
Andy Sheppard **Andy Gordon**	Specialist Regulatory Consultants.
John Edwards **Ray Milne** **John Spellman** **Keith Abercrombie**	Halifax Financial Services and Clerical Medical.
Rupert Dorey **Marcus Evans** **Tim Hughes** **Stephen Joyce** **Charlie Martin** **Jo Parkinson** **Stuart Price** **Jason Prior** **Stuart Prosser** **Roger Statham** **Glynn Thompson** **Robert Toone**	Close friends and/or neighbours of Paul Moore.

CONTENTS

PREFACE

Imagine getting a birthday card from your 17-year-old son with the words, “Everyone has flaws” hand-written inside it? Not “Happy birthday Dad” or “Have a fun-tastic day”. No. This is the language of the dark, lonely world of the whistleblower, where anniversaries are rarely occasions for celebration. Paul Moore and his long-suffering family know the territory only too well.

His son’s touching message of hope for the future, continued like this: “I like to look past the flaws and see the good in people, and there’s a lot more good in you than you give yourself credit for. I truly am proud of you and everything that you stand for, which is mainly integrity and truth. Just stay true to yourself and keep on doing what you’re doing. It’ll all work out eventually.”

Paul was fired more than a decade ago from Halifax Bank of Scotland (HBOS) for warning his bosses about their toxic sales culture. The isolation and rejection he’s experienced since has regularly left him wishing he was dead.

I’m a journalist, and I first approached Paul about

writing his memoirs in the spring of 2011. It's taken until now to bring his story to print, the process repeatedly halted by the post-traumatic bouts of depression that have engulfed him as a direct consequence of what happened at HBOS. For me this quote from an anonymous whistleblower perfectly sums up Paul's situation:

> *"We say in this nation that we are looking for people with honesty, integrity, drive and dedication, and then when we find such people, we take them out and whip them."*

Snitch, grass, squealer, Cassandra. Call them what you want but Paul and his ilk are all the same: ordinary people acting on their conscience and speaking out against injustice or corruption. They come from all walks of life and challenge authority simply because they believe it's the right thing to do. Yet most of the time they are ignored, ridiculed and then cast out into the wilderness.

Why is that so, and how has society created an environment where turning a blind eye is often considered the better part of valour?

Paul was one of the top 40 executives at HBOS in the highly paid and key role of Head of Group Regulatory Risk. He was sacked at the end of 2004, and although that might seem an old story, many of the same problems he uncovered still exist. Paul's "explosive" evidence to the UK House of Commons Treasury Select Committee into the collapse of HBOS during the banking crisis of 2008, sent shockwaves to the very top of the British Establishment, causing a global media frenzy.

His is not only a truly unique inside story of a disaster waiting to happen and how he sacrificed a lucrative career to expose the truth but also a shocking insight into the existence and prevalence of breathtaking corporate greed and arrogance. Yet Paul's story does not end there.

Paul offers simple, sensible solutions to solve austerity and the world's woes. Through a grass-roots force for change, he hopes to make finance fair for all.

When Paul started at HBOS he was filled with optimism. The bank's strategy at first seemed like a good idea – lower price, simplified products and broader access for all. But the quid pro quo of that was having to have a supermarket-style approach of stack them high, sell them cheap, growth at all costs. In banking that doesn't work because at the essence of a bank is prudence. Prudence both in terms of the people who put their money into the bank – the depositors and the shareholders – as well as prudence in terms of who that money is provided to.

HBOS brought in a former supermarket executive to run its retail operation. It set demanding targets and wanted another 11 per cent sales growth. It didn't consider the consequences of that.

In all his time in finance Paul has never known a discussion by strategic policymakers within banks about the impact of their decisions on the wider economy. They consider sometimes if the economy will impact the bank but not the other way round.

All too often automated credit risk management systems – computers in other words – are relied upon to make decisions but like any mathematical model they're only as good as the mathematical model. The head of global research for one of the biggest mathematical model providers for banking, once told Paul directly: "One of the major causes of the crisis [2008 banking crisis] was excessive reliance on mathematical models the assumptions for which could not be validated."

The banking and financial system was – and still is to a great extent – all about selling: whether it was credit or corporate bond funds or creditor insurance (PPI) – systematic mis-selling was often taking place.

The way the current banking system works in the existing corporate law and regulation environment allows no room for change. Essentially it will always default to business as usual.

Paul says: "Banks don't do what they're supposed to do, which is fuel ordinary families and business, because the vast majority of their lending has been property-based lending. The numbers are staggering. Incentives are all about sales, it doesn't matter what it says in the competence framework about ethics."

One of HBOS's main stated requirements of its top leaders was "courage". This was to speak up about things even if it might lead to unpopularity or criticism. But when Paul spoke up, which his role in the bank required him to do, look what happened. The HBOS ethics statement said one thing and did another.

Paul believes that the monetary system of fractional reserve banking (or high street banking) demands a thorough overhaul.

"You can calculate capital until the cows come home but it never saves you from a financial banking crisis caused by major conduct of business failures, caused by bad cultures and bad corporate governance," he says. "After the crisis we missed a great chance to micro-analyse the decision-making processes in boardrooms, such as what made Royal Bank of Scotland decide to buy ABN Amro or why banks made loans to skint people. We would have had the foundation of facts on which to rebuild how we think about the economy. An economy without ethics ultimately destroys wealth and creates poverty."

Change is always possible even when the odds appear to be stacked against it. The English politician William Wilberforce (1759 – 1833) took on the entire Establishment with his campaign for the abolition of the slave trade. Success was achieved by bringing home to the general population the horrors of slavery and the trade itself. This was done in various ways but, probably, the most potent was by publishing two key books: one by a freed slave called Equiano which sold 20,000 copies off the street in one month alone; and the other by John Newton, the ex-slave ship master who became an Anglican clergyman and wrote the famous hymn Amazing Grace.

In a sense, Crash Bank Wallop is also about exposing the horrors of the slavery of greed and the damage it does to others and ourselves, including the bankers who did wrong. Here is the simple message put forward by Wilberforce – or Wilber as he was known to friends –

following the publication of Equiano and Newton's books:

> *"You may choose to look the other way, but you can never say again that you did not know."*

When Paul looks back at his time at HBOS he recalls: "My intentions and 90 per cent of my actions were all focused on helping that organisation to be the best it could be. I never hated anyone, I never wanted to do anyone down. Sometimes people made me angry like any other human being but I wanted to help HBOS to be the best and still beat the market place, and ordinary customers to get good financial services. Being financially well organised is very important for peoples' lives. Service, truth and fairness: people need this hard-wiring into their systems like it was 50 years ago."

Paul's wife Maureen has been his "rock" throughout the whole HBOS saga and beyond.

She told me: "Once I'd heard after many years some of the struggles he's had with superiors when he's trying to get his point across, I came to the conclusion that there are certain things I'm not going to be able to change because that's who he is. That inevitably comes with some positive things but also some negatives. So I could always see that he was not going to be able to get on with everyone because he does not comply with the norms of everyone.

"That's where the blindness of Paul's character would come into play: his naivety of people being independent professionals. They might come to you privately and say words of encouragement but not when they are in the public aspect. They just don't have the guts to speak up and be independent. They're all individually good people but when they're out for their goals, well.

"I always say you never know who you work for and where their interests lie. If they are interested in being part of a gang and increasing their financials, their power, their position and status then people will do everything and anything. They will step over many, many of the lines of dignity of a human being to achieve that.

"It wasn't really Paul himself but his job that was the threat to these people [at HBOS]. But Paul would work always with the hope and naivety of thinking that he would eventually prove his point and therefore he would be recognised.

"What he was trying to get across was a difficult message. I don't believe people want to hear bad news and most people don't accept it. I've always felt that Paul's message has been truthful and honest and I've always believed that if you do what you can you can't do anything more and that if you can look at yourself in the mirror the following day then you are going to be fine. Paul's messages in the long-run have always been about that. Nothing in this world to me is of any loss if you don't lose your soul."

Not long after the international media storm that followed Paul's blowing of the whistle, a plain brown envelope dropped through his letterbox. The package was from "an anonymous admirer" and contained a genuine brass Metropolitan Police whistle. Delicately engraved in Latin along its side, were the words, "It is sweet and honourable to speak up for your country".

The first time I met with Paul, he produced the shiny whistle from his jacket pocket and gave it a blast. It prompted a few smiles in the coffee shop we were sat in close to Paddington Railway Station in London. Of course, for Paul its resonance goes far deeper than simple amusement.

On the one hand it is a constant reminder of the turmoil he and his family have suffered since 2004. On the other, it's come to symbolise his on-going pursuit of Truth and Justice. Paul has never found out who sent him that whistle but its single note is setting the tone for a powerful cacophony for change.

Paul says: "I think that even then, deep down in my heart and my soul, I had a dream about helping to build a better world… and I suppose the truth is that I have always felt that calling throughout my working life in financial services. I suppose it was what I was made for."

I'll leave the final word to the great theoretical physicist Albert Einstein:

> *"In matters of truth and justice, there is no difference between large and small problems, for issues concerning the treatment of people are all the same."*

Mike Haworth
2015

In writing my memoirs, I am only too conscious of the fact that I am about to make some very serious and, at times, personal criticisms of people at HBOS. Therefore, right at the outset, there are some important preliminary remarks I wish to make.

Firstly, whatever the failures of the top leadership at HBOS whom I mention, I want to make it absolutely clear that the vast majority of the people working at HBOS and, especially those working at the front line were good, honest and competent people trying to do the very best for the customers, the shareholders and the bank. The same could be said, no doubt, of all the other banks that have engaged in such scandalous misconduct. Virtually everybody that I worked with at HBOS knew the difference between right and wrong and wanted to do what was right. They told me so in their droves.

Secondly, even those people at the very top of the organisation, whom I criticise severely in the text, may very well have thought, subjectively, that what they were doing was right. They almost certainly felt and thought that they had good intentions and that what they were doing was "the greatest good for the greatest number of people". But, the truth is that they weren't. The famous phrase, "The road to Hell is paved with good intentions", springs to mind here.

Objectively and based on the evidence, what they did was, at best, incompetent in the extreme or, at worst, something more serious. That's for you the reader to judge based on the evidence and comments I put to you in this book. What is beyond doubt is that they failed miserably to listen to the siren calls and this was a very serious mistake.

I am a devoted Christian and don't believe in hatred or revenge but I do believe in the importance of accountability and helping people who have done wrong to face that reality and make proper amends to the people they have harmed, just as Jonathan Aitken has done in relation to his fall from grace over his perjury.

In the Christian worldview (as well as from the perspective of the other great faiths of the world or, even a purely humanist / ethical perspective), forgiveness races towards repentance at Godspeed. Very sadly, as yet, we have not really witnessed any serious repentance or making of amends by those who have caused such harm to so very many people both directly and indirectly. We certainly have not seen key people being held to account either under the regulatory regime or the criminal law or, as yet, under the civil law.

Those top executives, non-executives, statutory auditors, regulators and political leaders who caused the banking crisis (many of whom gained enormous wealth in the process), seem to have acted with impunity at the same time as causing huge harm to society. It's no wonder, ordinary people are still so angry.

The United Nations estimated that the banking crisis drove more than 100 million people around the world back into poverty. The "morbidity" statistics (i.e. the number of extra people who become seriously ill) of people in poverty increases exponentially. This also increases the "mortality" statistics exponentially (i.e. the number of extra people who die as a result of poverty). I am not an actuary or an expert in these matters but some people have said that the banking crisis caused more deaths than any single conflict since the Second World War and I can believe that. And, of course, this ignores the general misery caused to all of us by the extreme recession and required austerity around the world which was the direct consequence of the banking crisis.

What makes the whole debacle even more galling to the ordinary person is how, as a direct result of the banking crisis which was caused by the greedy, global asset prices dropped allowing those very same people to buy them up and become even wealthier. In other words, the rich have profited by their own wrongdoing. If the politicians had any guts they would have imposed a one-off wealth tax on these gains.

So far as the ordinary staff at HBOS are concerned, what happened there caused nearly 40,000 job losses and the decimation of the personal savings of so many staff who invested in HBOS shares as they were encouraged to do by the HBOS leadership, right up until the bitter end. And, this ignores the vast number of clients to whom products were mis-sold whether that was too much credit, too much PPI or too much anything else. We know, for example, that the current total bill for compensation for PPI mis-selling at Lloyds Banking Group is now close to £13 billion. This is outrageous. It is these stakeholders for whom we should have the greatest empathy.

Finally, I am also only too conscious of the fact that I am very likely to come across in this book as being self-righteous and vengeful. I have tried not to but, like everyone else, I'm only human and, the nature of the story itself is bound to involve this risk inherently and, there's nothing I can do about that.

Of course, there are always two sides to every story and I know that certain things that I did at HBOS and elsewhere were wrong. I share more with you about my rather unusual personality and weaknesses later, just as I did when I was interviewed by Michael Buerk on the BBC Radio 4 programme called *The Choice*. On that programme, he asked me whether I had a strong moral streak running through me and I remember hesitating before I answered that "hostage to fortune" question, "Well…, yes, I suppose I do, but, at the same time as saying that, I wouldn't want any of the listeners to think that I haven't sinned because I have." No one is perfect and, as my family could tell you, I am very far from perfect.

What I can tell you is that I truly believe in forgiveness and reconciliation and I have tried to reconcile personally with former HBOS Chief Executive Officers James Crosby and Andy Hornby, along with John Griffith-Jones the ex-Senior Partner at KPMG and current Chairman of the Financial Conduct Authority. Understandably, they were not ready at the times that I tried. But, if they do read this book, I would like once again to offer them the opportunity to sit down with me personally and talk things through.

In fact, I believe that they will only be healed from what must have been a terribly traumatic experience for them and their families and friends by coming to terms with what they've done and doing everything they can to make amends rather than trying to escape and hide from the truth. Good can always come from bad, as Jonathan Aitken has demonstrated so powerfully since his revelation and confessional moment whilst in prison after his fall from grace. And, as the most famous person in world history is reported to have said, "The Truth will set you free". Of course, the truth is not always itself free. I know that.

Paul Moore
2015

CHAPTER 1

The Last Tango in Halifax

> "Accept whatever befalls you, in crushing misfortune be patient; for in fire gold is tested, and worthy men in the crucible of humiliation."
>
> Book of Sirach

It was Guy Fawkes Day when the plotters lit the fuse. The fireworks went off a few days later and blew my life apart.

That bonfire night Friday, I'd been looking forward to the weekend; shutting off from work, having some time with the family and enjoying a few pints at the village pub.

It had been a really tough year at the bank – probably the most testing of my 20-year career – but things seemed to be looking up. Or so I thought.

I had been working from home that 5 November day and the mid-afternoon telephone call from the office came out of the blue. I answered almost immediately, and from that moment my life was to change forever.

"Hello, Paul Moore."

There was a brief silence before a female voice responded. It was my boss James Crosby's secretary.

"Paul, James wants to see you in Halifax on Monday, 2pm."

Her tone was unusually brusque. I normally exchanged a bit of banter with the "girls" from the secretarial pool but that clearly wasn't going to happen today.

I explained that I had other meetings already set up in Leeds for Monday. "Cancel them," was the blunt reply, and then she hung up.

Crosby was the Chief Executive of Halifax Bank of Scotland (HBOS), the UK's fastest-growing bank. If he wanted to see his group head of risk, then there was no argument because Crosby always came first.

Tall, clean shaven and bespectacled he'd read mathematics at Oxford, was highly intelligent, and at 48 considered young within the financial community to be in such an exalted position. He was the stereotypical egghead with a rapidly receding hairline. My grandfather would have said, "Grass doesn't grow on busy patches." Maybe that's why I'm bald too.

Crosby was also charismatic and had a sense of humour. Most people would say that the Yorkshireman was fun to be with. I never really got to know him well.

Nevertheless his reputation as a successful and astute operator went before him and he pretty much commanded absolute power at HBOS. Along with his old pal Lord Dennis Stevenson, the bank's Chairman, Crosby had ganged around him an obedient management team that mimicked his flamboyant style and drove his hard-sell culture all the way down the line.

I placed the phone back on its base, swivelled round on my black-leather office chair to face the computer and started emailing those who needed to know that

Monday's meetings were now cancelled.

The past four months, in particular, at HBOS had been demanding to say the least. Under its customer slogan, "Always giving you extra", the bank was growing exponentially and its sales and lending practices had been coming under intense scrutiny from the regulatory authorities. As the bank's Head of Group Regulatory Risk (GRR), I had the job of ensuring that HBOS adhered to all the necessary regulatory requirements.

Although initially surprised at the terseness of the call from Crosby's secretary, I wasn't at all worried about the prospect of meeting him. In fact, I'd a good idea what he wanted to talk to me about: his newly created post of Group Risk Director. With a seat on HBOS's main Board, the new appointee would have a voice on the top table hopefully strong enough to slow the dangerously rapid expansion of Crosby's self-proclaimed New Force In Banking.

Since taking up my high-profile role at the beginning of the year, my department had been at the epicentre of a series of major investigations into HBOS's aggressive sales policies, prompted by the concerns of industry regulator the Financial Services Authority (FSA).

During the summer I'd reported to a meeting of the bank's main Board, held in the City of London, on the findings of an FSA-ordered review into whether HBOS's "sales culture" had got out of hand and was a risk to the organisation itself and the regulatory system.

It had and it was.

All the top brass were there including Lord

Stevenson, Crosby and his heir apparent Andy Hornby, who had moved to HBOS in 2001 from supermarket chain Asda to head up the Retail Division (the Halifax part of the bank). I told the Board that the FSA was right to be concerned as we'd found evidence that proved conclusively that HBOS's focus on sales and marketing had got "markedly" out of balance with its risk management systems. I'd gone as far as to say: "I strongly recommend that the Board reconsiders its strategy for sales growth if it wishes to avoid risks to customers and colleagues."

It was a direct and head-on challenge to the bank's "stack 'em high, sell 'em cheap", "growth-at-all–costs" strategy but Chairman Stevenson had stood up and thanked me for my frankness in bringing the situation to the Board's attention.

In October I'd also addressed another meeting on the same subject, this time to the influential Group Audit Committee. Its Chairman Tony Hobson had personally thanked me and said in front of committee members: "I now understand just how serious things are at the bank." So confident was I that the message was finally getting through, that afterwards I emailed my two deputies James Davies and Tony Brian saying, "All's well that ends well". How wrong could I have been?

However, on that Guy Fawkes Day following the call from Crosby's secretary, I was now looking forward with some excitement to Monday's meeting at HBOS's head offices in the old woollens town of Halifax, West Yorkshire. I was sure I was going to find out who my new boss would be. I was curious and over the weekend my wife Maureen and I speculated about who might get the job.

Maureen is South American and I met and instantly fell in love with her on top of a mountain in Chile on Christmas Day 1988. She's always been my chief adviser. That's not to say I always acted on her words of wisdom but so often during our, at times, tempestuous married life she said things I didn't understand which later turned out to be true. Maureen knew most of my work colleagues but on the whole disliked their values and priorities which she saw as motivated by wealth and power. She was and still is an astute judge of character.

Crosby's decision to appoint a new Group Risk Director to sit on the Group Management Board and main Board of HBOS had been sudden and unexpected. Even though Crosby had spoken to me about it, I'd made it clear to him that I wasn't ready to apply for the post myself. That hadn't prevented me from suggesting to him the type of candidate who might best accommodate it. The way I saw it was that at last those of us working in the trenches on risk management would have someone to speak up for us at the highest level.

HBOS had burst onto the financial marketplace in 2001, the day before the devastating 11 September terror attacks on New York's twin-towered World Trade Center and the Pentagon in Washington DC. The stuffy but highly respected Bank of Scotland, founded in 1695 and Britain's oldest commercial bank, had merged with the swashbuckling former building society Halifax to form a group with an estimated market value of £28 billion and a workforce of 61,000.

Its top five executives hadn't a banking qualification between them but HBOS, the cocky new kid on the block, was out to challenge its main competitors – Royal Bank of Scotland/NatWest, Lloyds TSB, HSBC and Barclays – in established business sectors and also by expanding the Halifax's already market-leading share of UK mortgage lending. My job was to referee a safe and fair contest.

Crosby, who was the driving force, had trained as an actuary with life assurance company Scottish Amicable, before moving into fund management with Rothschild Assurance. At HBOS, he and Stevenson were like Siamese twins. Crosby was the dominant one, Stevenson playing second fiddle to his leader of the orchestra.

The saying goes that pride comes before a fall. Crosby wasn't short of that. In fact, many people would say that he suffered from its extreme form called hubris that only years and years of great success – with no failures in sight – breeds. He had been a truly great achiever for most of his career, and this is probably the greatest risk that any leader and the organisations they run can face. It makes them feel invincible. It makes them think invincible thoughts. Academic evidence now proves that it even changes the chemical balance in their brain so they can only see things one way – their own.

Mainly Crosby was a person who had been taken over by his own brilliance similar to so many other powerful figures in the banking world, such as Fred "the Shred"

Goodwin of Royal Bank of Scotland, Dick "the Gorilla" Fuld of Lehman Brothers, Matthew Greenburgh at Merrill Lynch whose epithet was "ELF" which stood for "Evil Little Fucker" and the infamous John Mack, aka "Mack the Knife" of Morgan Stanley.

Monday 8 November came. I arrived early for the 2pm meeting and drew my blue-green BMW 525i SE into the executive car park underneath the huge Trinity Road office complex feeling relaxed and looking forward to seeing Crosby. The bank's diamond-shaped HQ dominated the centre of Halifax and housed a workforce of 6,000, providing the main source of employment for the old Pennine mill town.

Halifax, like many of the other towns along the "backbone of England", was one of the homes of the industrial revolution. The Halifax Building Society had grown out of that incredible community spirit fostered by the textile industry boom, into one of the finest member-owned mutuals in the world. The Halifax was there to help its members manage their finances and buy a home. It was a noble and well-managed pursuit. It had made millions of lives better and happier.

That had all changed since the Halifax had been "demutualised" in 1997 to become a bank and Crosby had been given the top job. The Halifax was no longer a place of prudence. It was a place where sales came first, sales came second and sales came last. Crosby had recruited fresh-faced Hornby from Asda to turn the Halifax into a retailing giant by pursuing a "sales growth at all costs" strategy. The ex-Oxford and Harvard graduate was aged just 34 when he joined Crosby's management team in 2001. It always struck me as a strange idea to appoint a retailer to run a bank.

My sentiments were reinforced by a young, smartly-suited female cashier in the Scunthorpe branch of the Halifax. While I was on a fact-finding mission there as part of the sales culture review, she'd beckoned me over, and after checking the coast was clear she moved her head close to me and said quietly: "Paul, you won't tell anyone will you? But we'll never hit our sales targets and sell ethically." It's interesting how the frontline staff often know so much more about what's going on than the top executives or maybe they just have more finely tuned consciences.

After leaving my car in the basement parking bay, I made my way upstairs through the familiar corridors and vast open-plan offices of the Trinity Road building. I always aim to arrive early for meetings. I like to think that dedication, commitment and reliability are part of my make-up, along with truth-seeking and fairness. I can be annoying like that.

Dressed in chinos, open-neck shirt and jacket – smart casual had replaced the sober pin-striped banking attire of old – I arrived at the reception desk of Crosby's secretary. She recognised me immediately, smiled and said brightly: "Good afternoon, Mr Moore. James is expecting you and will be along shortly. If you'd like to follow me I'll show you to your meeting room."

I was ushered into a corner office that was occupied by Hornby whenever he was working in Halifax. The rest of the time it was used for visiting bigwigs. At one end was a ceiling-to-floor window that looked out over rows of slate-roofed terraced houses, while at the other end of the office near to where I had been shown in, was a rectangular light-pine meeting table with seating around it for eight people. The room had a cold, soulless edge to it as though not used for a while. I sat in the chair nearest to the door that the secretary had just exited and waited for Crosby in the quiet.

I was still excited but now the closer the news got the more nervous I became. Who was my new boss going to be? My mind went round and round in circles doing the scenario planning that only the risk management telemetrist can do.

I kept waiting – and waiting. Crosby was going to be late and I knew it.

When I joined HBOS in 2002, naturally he was one of the people I wanted to meet and get to know first. He was the Group CEO. I wanted to know who he was; what he thought; what he cared about; what he wanted from his new Head of Risk for insurance and investment, the bank's second-largest division. On my second day after starting, I phoned his office to arrange a meeting with him. I got one. He cancelled it. So I set up another and was really looking forward to meeting him and building our relationship. He cancelled it. Undeterred, I organised another rendezvous, at the bank's Old Broad Street premises in London and sat outside his office at the appointed time. Crosby's door was open and I could hear him chatting to a couple of senior colleagues in what I came to recognise as his usual excited and arrogant tone. There were laughs between the words. It was clearly not an important conversation. It was just the normal chit-chat between colleagues at an impromptu meeting. He never thought to think that I was waiting outside.

After I'd been waiting 25 minutes he came out in a rush. "Oh, I'm really sorry for doing this again Paul but I just have to catch my train to York and the taxi is waiting downstairs." But I had another idea. I was upset by his disregard for me and I wasn't going to let him get away with another cancellation. I just said, "Right, I'm coming with you to King's Cross in the taxi and we can meet there." So, the first meeting I had with Crosby took place in a black London cab being jostled and jolted as we made our way through the Capital's busy afternoon traffic – hardly ideal.

That was what he was like. He really had no regard for people like me in risk management. He thought he knew better. He thought he knew better than everyone.

And here I was again, waiting for Crosby. He finally arrived for our meeting in Halifax that day at 2.15pm. He was on his own. He sat down directly across the table from me. There were no initial pleasantries. No handshake, no eye contact either. Nothing. He just came straight out with it.

"Paul, I am doing a reorganisation and your job is being made redundant. I can't tell you who the new Group Risk Director will be now. That will be announced on Friday and these changes, including your redundancy, must be kept confidential until then."

Crash! Bang! Wallop!

Adrenaline shot. Heart thump. Massive shock. Long pause. Gather thoughts.

Hold on, I thought. My job couldn't be made redundant because the regulatory system required a bank to appoint a person to do my job.

"James, my job can't be made redundant," I said. "The FSA requires the bank to have someone in my job."

My confidence was returning. He could not make me redundant. Not just like that. It was illegal.

"No, James, my job cannot be made redundant. You can only dismiss me for performance management reasons and I have had excellent feedback from the chairman of the Audit Committee and others. And in any case, if you were going to attempt to make my job redundant, what process have you gone through – as you are required by law and by your own HR policies – to make a fair selection for redundancy?"

"I don't have to explain that to you," he replied.

"Yes, you do."

"No, I don't and anyway it doesn't matter."

With his next words he just swatted me dead like a fly.

"You've lost the confidence of key executives and non-executives," Crosby said calmly.

I was not giving up. Of course, he was firing me because I had challenged him and other members of the Board. I knew my rights.

I am a barrister by original profession and had been working as a specialist in financial sector regulation, risk management and corporate governance since 1984.

Before joining HBOS I'd been a top-performing partner at KPMG in London, one of the "Big Four" firms of accountants and professional advisers.

My first year at HBOS as Head of Risk for its Insurance and Investment Division (IID) had gone very well judging by the all-round positive feedback I'd received.

However in mid-2003, about one year into my time at the bank, the FSA came in and did a formal "risk assessment" inspection of HBOS. It expressed serious concerns about the risks of HBOS's sales culture and rapid growth strategy. As a direct result, I was asked to accept a promotion and take over as Head of Group Regulatory Risk (GRR).

In a nutshell, that meant that I would be accountable for ensuring that the bank had what is referred to in the jargon as the right "systems and controls" and was acting with "integrity" and "due skill, care and diligence". In layman's terms, I was responsible for making sure that the bank had the right checks and balances in place to avoid breaching the regulatory requirements and taking excessive risk.

When I got the call from Mike Ellis – who was HBOS's Chief Financial Officer and Head of Group Finance and Risk – offering me the GRR job, I felt proud. I think it is fair to say that I knew what I was doing in this space. I'd been there, done it and got the T-shirt. It was yet further recognition for the all the good work I had done over so many years and especially over the previous 18 months in IID. It was more financial security for my family – Maureen and our three children – or so I thought. I was never really a materialist but financial security was very important to me to be able to have a decent home for the family, pay the school fees, go on nice holidays and achieve financial independence as soon as possible so that I could get back to the freedom and adventure that I had enjoyed so much in my early life.

It would also give me a bigger canvas on which to paint my picture of what truly great risk management looked like.

Risk management is not about not taking risks. Risk and opportunity are two sides to the same coin.

To me the best example of risk management in the world is Formula 1 racing. Cars have better brakes, so they can go faster. Somebody once said, "Formula 1 racing has less residual risk than angling." Since the tragic death of Ayrton Senna on 1 May 1994 at the San Marino Grand Prix, not a single F1 racing driver had died until, sadly, Jules Bianchi, in 2015. One driver hit a tyre wall at Silverstone head-on at 180mph and only broke his tibia.

That's the way to do risk management. It's not about going slow; it's about going as fast as possible with the least negative consequence. It's about an amazing relationship between the driver, who is the risk-taker, and the engineers and telemetrists, who are the risk management advisers like me. Both have different perspectives of the risks involved; the driver sees the braking and the clipping points and maybe a little bit in the tiny wing mirrors. He sees a few indicators such as revs on or behind his steering wheel. He knows what gear he is in. But the telemetrists and engineers see all the data and can warn the driver of all sorts of possible problems relating to the engine, the gearbox, fuel, brakes, tyres etc. They are all in it together: to get that car around the track as fast as possible with as little risk.

This is the way risk management should work in business. It's absolutely not about the attitude, "The answer's 'no', now what's the question?" We only grow by taking risks. We only create by taking risks. We only profit by taking risks.

Yet the biggest risk in risk management is not being honest with ourselves and others because we're frightened of the driver.

At that summer meeting in London, I'd been completely honest with Crosby and the HBOS Board about the conclusions from the sales culture review. I thought I was being helpful. And, now, Crosby had shot the messenger and bearer of bad tidings.

Back in the fateful meeting room in Halifax that Monday 8 November, I challenged Crosby again.

"James, which executives and non-executives are you referring to and what was the reason they gave you for losing confidence in me? I told Mike Ellis before I accepted the job as head of GRR that, however polite my team and I were in carrying out our oversight activity, we were bound to upset some people."

Crosby shot back: "I don't have to explain that to you."

"Yes, you do," I said.

"No, I don't and anyway I have other meetings, so I am going to leave now but just remember this matter is confidential until Friday morning and it wouldn't be a good idea for you to breach that. I will make this announcement and others on Friday."

And, he just got up and left the room.

I was in shock – a fuzzy, sickly feeling – and my heart was still thumping. My mind was racing. What would I tell Maureen and the children? What should I do next? How could he be so unfair after all the hard work we had done to turn things round with the FSA?

He didn't even have the normal human empathy or conscience to bring someone from the human resources (HR) department with him to look after me as is normal in dismissals, in case I was upset. It seemed to me that he must never even have considered that the news might upset me.

Then, as I sat in the silence of the office reflecting on what had just taken place, I realised that Crosby, far from being sorry for what he was doing, actually appeared to be enjoying himself. His tone of voice and body language almost suggested that he was taking a kind of sinister pleasure in what he was doing. He was going to show me who was boss and that he could just eliminate me in an instant – and that he, seemingly, just didn't care.

Little did he know when he brushed me aside that day in Halifax what the future would hold for him and how, many years later, his hubris would meet its nemesis as the ineluctability of fate got to work on wrongdoing?

That day, as he satisfied his need to remove any obstacle in the path, he could never have dreamt, in his worst nightmare, that, one day, he would be forced to resign as the Deputy Chairman of the FSA. Nor could he have envisaged that after the whole truth about his disastrous strategy at HBOS was exposed by the Parliamentary Commission on Banking Standards in 2013, he would feel obliged to give up his knighthood and the sop of 30% of his £580,000 a year pension.

He was awarded his knighthood by Prime Minister Gordon Brown for his fine contribution to financial services, a contribution which had cost the taxpayer well over £20 billion, Lloyds shareholders more than £10 billion, caused 40,000 people to lose their jobs and untold misery to HBOS customers who have been mis-sold financial products.

Nor could he have imagined that, on that very day when he gave up his knighthood and a bit of his pension, he would be referred to publicly by Jeremy Paxman on BBC *Newsnight* in those most extreme defamatory terms, "the prominent incompetent". Of course, because this description was fair comment, there was no risk of a libel action against the BBC.

And, there I was on that very day sitting next to Jeremy Paxman in the BBC New Broadcasting House with the cameras rolling reading the words on the autocue before Jeremy even spoke them. I had my mouth metaphorically wide open hardly believing that, after all those years of trouble and strife, the truth had finally prevailed.

In the end, we do get transformed by trouble. But, for now, he'd fired me and I was on my own; all on my own.

I got up to leave. I felt detached from my body. I walked out into the hustle and bustle of the Halifax open-plan office. It was the same as it always was.

I was not.

No one even noticed me and I walked slowly in a daze past the desks of computer terminals towards the lift. I went to the ground floor. I went outside. I stood on the street. I rolled a cigarette and started smoking it. I started thinking. I needed a lawyer. I decided to ring Peter Hamilton.

Peter, a senior barrister at 4 Pump Court chambers near Fleet Street, in London, was not only a professional colleague with whom I had worked on a vast array of legal and regulatory matters (including the Equitable disaster) but also a close friend and confidant.

I'd first met him in autumn 1984 when he interviewed me for a job in the product development group of the legal department of Allied Hambro, which later became Allied Dunbar, and then was bought by Zurich Financial Services. He was the head of the legal department and the company secretary. I liked him from the word go. He had an aura of "goodness" about him. Over the years I developed the highest regard for him as a lawyer, a businessman of judgement and a man of complete integrity.

So there I was, standing all alone in a state of shock on the pavement outside the huge Halifax offices smoking a roll-up and I rang Hamilton. I nearly always call him "Hamilton" because at the Bar that's what we do, we call each other by our surnames. It's a sign of affection rather than formality.

I was in such a haze, I cannot remember that call at all except that I had it and that Hamilton was totally supportive of my position, that he said he would act for me and that I needed to find a really good solicitor.

I immediately rang another friend of mine, Michael Wainwright, a partner at Eversheds, one of the prestige London firms of solicitors. I had also worked with Michael over the years and I trusted him. He, or someone in his office, recommended Peter Frost at global law firm Herbert Smith but I decided to ring him the next day. I was suddenly shattered and couldn't face it then and there.

I just stood there under a grey November sky and thought about my family – Maureen, who was only 36 at the time, our daughter Emily Jane, 13, and our sons Daniel Thomas, 12 and Oliver Clive, 10.

It was then that the full impact of everything just hit me. I'd just been fired from one of the highest-paid jobs in banking. What would it mean for my family? What would it mean for me?

Crash! Bang! Wallop!

The shock was overwhelming and the tears just started rolling down my face. I knew I had to ring Maureen before my deputy James Davies arrived to be picked up. I unlocked my trusty old Nokia key pad again and dialled the number.

"Hello?"

"Hello, darling, it's me."

"Hi, how's it going?"

I hesitated. I thought about how proud she had been

when I got the job in the first place and how happy she was that we were back together again after a traumatic period of separation.

"He's fired me."

Maureen didn't hesitate: "Oh, don't worry Paul, it's all part of God's plan for you."

I hardly heard what she had said. I certainly didn't understand what she had said. I know I did not believe it....then, at least. But it has turned out to be true.

In autumn 2009, almost five years after Crosby sacked me, I was interviewed by journalist Michael Buerk for the iconic BBC Radio 4 programme *The Choice*. When he asked me how I felt about what had happened, I replied: "At the start it seemed like a disaster but, in the end, it's been Amazing Grace."

If you ask mental health professionals who work with whistleblowers, they will tell you that the psychological trauma suffered by people who speak truth to power, and then experience "shoot the messenger", can be just like post-traumatic stress disorder.

A mixture of dishonesty, injustice and no mercy, as a direct response to a person who speaks up because they care, is a potent cocktail in the armoury of non-violent personal attack. Unfairness at this level wounds the soul.

I now know that the story of genuine whistleblowers is often much the same. Most importantly, they speak up not because they are disgruntled but because they care deeply about the organisations for which they work. In return, and usually as a massive surprise to their child-like naive sense that they are trying to help, they are first ignored, then demonised, bullied and finally dismissed.

If they battle on and take it public, they find the massed ranks of the top London legal firms lined up against them, being paid by the unlimited financial resources of the organisations they have challenged, but with no financial resources of their own to fight back. The standard line of attack is to rubbish the whistleblower as a troublemaker and misfit whose personality disorders mean that the best place for him or her is in a secure hospital like Broadmoor.

Often senior executives have statistically more than three times the national average level of psychopathic attribute which, in fact, is about the same as the level found in Broadmoor.

If all of that wasn't enough for one person with limited resources to deal with, those who speak truth to power are then abandoned and treated as untouchable outcasts, even by all those friends and colleagues (often the large majority) who knew they were right. Once *persona non grata* with those in power, supporters turn turtle and scatter like the four winds to avoid any risk of contagion to their own reputations or careers by being associated in any way with the man or woman from the leper colony or contaminated with toxic waste.

In the end, no one protected me: not board directors, senior executives or non-executives; not committee chairmen or the supposedly independent investigators; not even the FSA.

Since then, with one exception, I have never been offered any work either as an employee or an adviser to any large private or public-sector organisation (e.g. a regulator) which operates in the financial sector. I haven't been approached by a single headhunter – and yet despite my differences and weaknesses, I was described in appraisal after appraisal throughout my career as having an almost uncanny competence in regulatory affairs, risk management and corporate governance.

That day Crosby fired me was the last time I ever went to Halifax.

It was my last tango in Halifax.

CHAPTER 2

"She's up on the Roof Watching the Bombers!"

I lost my parents when I was eight years old.

Mum and dad didn't actually die. They packed me off to Catholic boarding school, but it felt like a bereavement.

It was September 1966 and from living a life I loved in Brussels, I suddenly found myself residing in a dormitory hundreds of miles away in rural northern England, with Benedictine monks as my new adoptive family.

It was a very traumatic experience and that trauma has been a key part of my make-up ever since.

By all accounts Paul Russell Moore (my full name) had been a very good little boy, unlike my older brother Chris who was always getting into scrapes. My mother Jean always called me her "little angel" but my main nickname as a child was "starry bags" because I had a lovely pair of shorts in dark navy blue with white stars printed on them. Apparently I didn't like having dirty hands and used to hold them out with a grimace on my face to be cleaned by my mother while saying, "'ands, 'ands".

Being moved to Gilling Castle, the prep school to the well-known Ampleforth College, also seemed at the time a bit like a punishment and I couldn't get my little head around it. If I was so good, why had my parents sent me away from them? I suffered from bad homesickness for some considerable time. I used to lie in my dormitory bed, sending imaginary kisses through the airwaves to mum.

Of course I got over it, by building a force field around my feelings. Just as many young boarders do.

I was born on 30 October 1958, in a hospital in Bristol. My late father was Bernard Clive Moore from Stoke-on-Trent and my mother Jean Penelope Moore, who is now 89, came from Bristol. I am the second-oldest of four children, Christopher, 58, Louise, 53 and Nicola, 46 (ages in 2015).

My father was born on 7 May 1925 during the first general strike in British history. He came from a Catholic pottery family in Stoke-on-Trent. My great-grandfather, also called Bernard Clive Moore, born in 1850, was the famous potter who recreated ancient Chinese glazes, including what was called "true flambé". The chemistry of this glaze was complicated and, after he perfected it, he sold it to Royal Doulton which still makes pottery of this colour today.

Dad was a genius. And slightly mad. He got distinctions in every examination he ever sat until he went to university. He went to Ampleforth College, the same Catholic private school on the edge of the North York Moors that I stepped up to from Gilling Castle. He had two uncles who were monks there.

In 1942, when he was 17, my dad won an open scholarship to New College Oxford in physics and chemistry. When he got to Oxford, he discovered things other than just academic work, including how to smoke tea through a "hubble-bubble" whilst in the cinema. A hubble-bubble is another name for a shisha pipe, which is used to draw smoke through water, to cool it down before it enters the mouth. He was also the President of the Oxford Catholic Society, and one of his great heroes was the Blessed Cardinal Newman who wrote the well-known hymn Praise to the Holiest in the Height. Dad got a third-class degree. I suppose it was about time for him to live life and forget the academics for a while.

After university, he took a one-year specialist course in ceramics in Stoke-on-Trent where, once again, he was top of the class and gained medals for his performance. The essence of ceramics is a mixture of organic chemistry and engineering. After this course, he immediately went to work for a renowned pottery company in Bristol called Pountney's, also sometimes referred to as The Bristol Pottery. That's where he met my mother, while playing in a mixed hockey match. He was a keen sportsman and played rugby and hockey. Caving was another of his hobbies. He always told us that he married mum because she could drink beer faster than him.

While in Bristol, he clearly had a huge amount of fun playing rugby and getting up to all sorts of nonsense. He won a bet with his friends for being able to reverse the fastest along a beach in a car. He told me he got up to more than 40mph.

After Pountney's, he went to work at the Aldermaston

weapons research base in Berkshire, building the hydrogen bomb as a result of his exceptional capability in ceramics, physics and chemistry. The design of the bombs included ceramic parts and it was his job to work on this aspect of the project. But he didn't really like it, and he left shortly after when he was headhunted by Royal Worcester to go to Jamaica and set up a china manufacturing facility there. At the last minute, he decided against it and went to work for a specialist ceramic consultancy based in Stoke-on-Trent. He provided technical advice for the sanitary ware industry in the UK and all over the world.

Dad spent three years helping the Romanians to build a sanitary ware manufacturing facility in Bucharest, which meant lengthy periods away from home. In fact, he left the same week that my sister Louise was born, and mum tells me he only spent three months at home in three years. We went as a family to join him and live in Bucharest for six months and he decided to drive us there in our old Ford Classic car. He had it specially flown by "air ferry" from Southend to Switzerland and, loaded with provisions, we then drove more than 1,200 miles along mostly deserted roads through snowy Austria and Hungary to our temporary new home in a block of flats. Within days of arriving Chris and I developed mumps and the whole family came out in lumps after our apartment was found to be infested with lice.

After the consultancy, he was headhunted to go to work as the technical director for the largest sanitary ware manufacturer in the world, Ideal Standard. This job was based in the company's executive headquarters in Paris. Ideal Standard had factories in Germany, France, Italy and Belgium as well as two in the UK and he had a roving advisory role to all the plants' management teams.

After a couple of years in Paris we were forced to move up the road to Brussels when French General Charles de Gaulle kicked out all the American companies.

My dad worked for Ideal Standard for the rest of his full-time working life, and made a good living which provided a wonderful lifestyle for all of us.

He was a great inventor and he introduced major innovations into all the plants where he worked. He was always the favourite of the shop-floor workers because he made their jobs easier through the innovations he introduced. He wasn't much good at getting on with his bosses though, whom he thought were more interested in politics, power and money than working for the good of the business.

After my dad "retired", he did some consulting work, including going to China for six weeks to help them build a manufacturing facility right out in the boonies. I'll never forget what he said before he left. He rubbed his hands together with glee, and announced: "Paul, there's nothing that gives me greater excitement than the idea of a billion bottoms looking for a receptacle."

After that, he did what he always wanted to do, which was to set up a company to reinvent a key part of the technology for manufacturing sanitary ware. I worked with him in both 1989 and 1990 to help him enter into a joint venture with a public company called Porvair Ceramics, in order to set up a new firm to develop what is called pressure casting. My brother Chris joined that business in 1991 and is now the technical director of that relatively small but highly successful UK engineering business, exporting machinery and know-how all around the world. It's now called PCL and Chris is a part-owner after joining a management buyout some years ago. My dad would be proud of what he accomplished professionally. The new technology that he was a very key part of inventing is now used globally and has reduced the overall costs of producing sanitary ware by more than 10%.

Bernard was a good and kind man. He had a total dedication to the truth and was highly ethical. He loved his family and worked his socks off for us but, as is often the case with genii, he was odd. When he was good, he was very good, but when he was bad, he was horrid. People often use the expression, "Thinking out of the box". Well, my dad never had to do it because he was never in the box.

Creative minds don't think in a linear way. They dart around like the lightning in the little glass globe. Sometimes, in order to discharge their built-up energy, they have no choice but to strike the nearest lightning conductor, whoever that happens to be. As a family, we experienced the lightning strikes on many occasions. To further mix my metaphors, dad could erupt like a volcano.

He also had a drinking problem. To be honest, he

was an alcoholic. Eventually, aged 69, after driving 39,000 business miles due to his excitement about the new business, the grog really got dad. He began to lose that great mind of his. He couldn't live with it, and the vicious circle of low self-esteem, alcohol and rapidly increasing dementia became almost unbearable for us all to watch. It was a huge blessing for him, my mother and all of us when he suffered a major cardiomyopathy, brought about by his alcoholism, and then passed away at 73.

Looking back on it, I think his mind worked at such a pace that the only way for him to slow it down was to depress it with alcohol. He carried a Dictaphone with him everywhere, so that any time he had a new idea he could record it. Even when he was in church, every Sunday (an event he simply would not allow us to miss) during the sermon we would see him pulling a handkerchief out of his pocket and tying a knot in it, to remind him of whatever thought he had just had at the time.

He might very well have been slightly bipolar, using alcohol as his version of lithium, which is the depressant often prescribed to people of a bipolar nature. I was diagnosed as bipolar in June 2015: like father like son, it would appear.

Dad could be extremely funny and he had a number of stock phrases which he used. When we were little and I asked where mum was, he would either answer, "She's up on the roof watching the bombers", or "She went mad so we shot her". We got so used to these expressions that I don't think it was until I was 14 or 15 that I became conscious of them. He also used to say on random occasions and for no apparent reason, "Give me a bucket of sand and I'll sing you the Desert Song!" However, he hated organisational politics, and I would hear him ranting about it on numerous occasions. All he was interested in was doing the best job possible and the truth.

My dad was definitely a huge influence on me, and on all of us in the family.

Mum is a very different person altogether. She was born in 1927 to Eric and Grace Russell in Victoria Square, Bristol. Her father, who was born in 1898, had faked his age and flown Sopwith Camel biplanes in the Royal Flying Corps during the First World War. Once, the engine cut out as he was coming in to land at RAF Weston-on-the-Green, in Oxfordshire, and he crash-landed into the top of a thick coppice of pines.

Eric qualified as an engineer in Glasgow, where his father ran a well-known jewellery shop. Somehow, he met his future wife in Bristol and he used to ride his motorcycle down from Glasgow overnight to Bristol, on the non-tarmacadam roads. He became the assistant chief docks engineer in Bristol which, in those days, was a civil service job. He retired at 58 due to ill-health, on an index-linked pension, and died at the ripe old age of 95. He was a remarkable man, and I remember sitting next to his bed as he got older, when he would tell me all the things he used to do when he was a lad in Glasgow. These included walking 20 miles most

Sundays, collecting bird eggs (I still have the collection now) and playing ice hockey on the lochs under the light of oxyacetylene motorbike headlights.

My mum was one of two daughters who were treated by Eric like a couple of sons. She went to Clifton High School, an excellent private school in Bristol, then on to Bristol University to study botany and microbiology before working in the blood transfusion service. I'm sure that if she had carried on working, she would've got to the very top.

Grandma Jean, known affectionately as "GJ" by our children, is remarkably bright, has clear views, strong leadership skills and gets on very well with people. She can be a bit cranky and sometimes even bigoted, but she is one of the best people I know in the world. She never stops helping others. She was our rock and air-raid shelter when dad's cumulonimbus thunder clouds shot out bolts of lightning at us. She was a great cook, and provided us with the most amazing food whenever we were at home during the school holidays.

Mum was also quite a disciplinarian, a trait she'd picked up from her father, who would punish his daughters severely for any misdemeanours. She told me that if they misbehaved on one day, he would tell them that they were going to get a dose of corporal punishment but only the next morning: to give them plenty of time to reflect on what they had done wrong. Likewise, if we lied or were very naughty, she would beat us with the back of a hairbrush and send us to our bedrooms, to be "on bread and water" for the day.

Yet she nearly always relented and brought us boiled eggs and pieces of toast, cut into "soldiers". What she doesn't know is that after she beat Chris and me with a hairbrush, we used to pretend to cry and as soon as she left the room we'd start laughing, because it never really hurt.

She was, and still is, fiercely independent, and she expected us to be as well. She allowed Chris and me, from the very youngest of ages, to roam and adventure in ways that, today, would be thought of as completely irresponsible. At the ages of five or six, we would get on our tricycles, from our lovely house in Cheshire and ride more than a mile along a very busy road to a water feature where we could build dams.

The best way to sum up my mother is to tell a little story about something she did when she was just seven years old. Her father had promised to take Jean and her sister Alison, to Weston-super-Mare for a day out on the beach. They lived in Redland in the middle of Bristol, in a house in which my grandfather lived for 53 years. It's nearly 30 miles from where they lived to Weston-super-Mare. For some reason or other, my grandfather had to let them down but my mother was having none of it. She said to her sister, who was five, and her sister's four-year-old friend who was with them, in a pram, "Well, if dad won't take us to Weston-super-Mare, let's go there ourselves anyway."

So, off they went, over the Clifton Suspension Bridge that spans the 300ft-deep Avon Gorge and down the steep hill on the other side to the Weston-super-Mare road. Getting hungry, they tried eating raw beetroot from a field, but that didn't taste very good, so they sold the beetroot to passers-by and used the money to buy food in a local café. Naturally, my grandparents became very worried when they couldn't find their daughters, and they called the police. It wasn't until after 4pm that officers found them. Jean was still leading the troops towards Weston-super-Mare but now, as the little ones were very tired, she was pushing the pram with the youngest in the main seat and her sister, Alison, perched on the front. They were nearly 14 miles from Bristol.

That says it all, doesn't it?

Mum's still fit as a flea. She lives in her own house outside Bristol, gardens like mad and insists on driving the 250 miles to where we live in North-East Yorkshire. She sure is very independent and, with God's grace, she's got another 15 years or so in her. She is a truly remarkable person. I love you, mum, and don't you forget it!

There's no doubt my parents shaped my personality, psychology and general way of being.

When it came to family time, we always ate meals together and there was a completely "no-holds-barred" approach to communication. We were all fairly extrovert and no subject was off limits. The truth was everything to us – truth and fairness. The discussions would get very heated sometimes but we never really held grudges if anyone upset us. We got accustomed to conflict and resolving it.

We always had great summer holidays. When we

were very young we would go on holiday every year with family friends, the Hughes, first to Cornwall near Padstow and then Wales near St David's Head. As both families became better off, we started to go further afield. First, we went to Normandy in France and later we had a couple of holidays together in the South of France near St Tropez. My father bought an inflatable boat with a 25-horsepower engine on the back of it, and we took up water-skiing.

After France, we started going on holiday to a little island off the west coast of Italy called Giglio, which is where the cruise ship Costa Concordia ran aground and sank in January 2012. It was a lovely place, and we used the inflatable to go out to the beaches and the rocks surrounding the port where we could swim, dive and water-ski.

I met and fell in love with one of my first girlfriends, Michaela Orefice, on that island. She was beautiful, with blonde hair and came from Milan. Of course dad couldn't resist putting in his two pennyworth when he heard her name, saying to me, "Why are you going out with a girl called Michael Orifice?"

On one trip to Giglio in the mid-Seventies, when everybody was wearing Indian-style loose clothing, dad said: "I'll make a bet with you all that I could go down to the harbour in my Marks & Spencer's pyjamas and order drinks in two different bars and no one will bat an eyelid." And, he did. Us children kept an eye on him from a safe distance to avoid embarrassment but, sure enough, he went and ordered a Grappa (his favourite tipple in Italy) in two bars and we certainly didn't see anyone bat an eyelid. That was what he was like – odd.

I was eight when we moved to Brussels, where we lived in a new four-bedroomed house rented from some very nice Norwegians who always gave us a bottle of Aquavit at Christmas. The house was in Avenue Reine Elizabeth or Queen Elizabeth Avenue.

Brussels was a great place to live and, although it didn't have the sights of Paris it was a much easier location for foreigners. The Belgians liked the English. The Parisians didn't. There was also a great crowd of expats working for the European Economic Community or large corporates, often American firms, which were headquartered there.

I had taken up pony riding when I was about five years old, and the Belgians are mad-keen on horse-riding. There was a stable about 30 minutes bicycle ride from where we lived and Chris and I spent a huge amount of our time in the holidays messing about there and riding our own Welsh mountain pony, Darius. I became quite a proficient rider and was asked by the owner of the stables to exercise some of the most difficult horses, including the Arab stallion called Sheriff. He was an absolutely beautiful grey (white to non-horse-riding people), who held his neck high and pranced around like a Spanish dancer. The other great advantage of spending time at the stables was that there were a lot more girls than boys and it was there that I met my first girlfriend, Diane Stendhal. Later Chris stole her off me.

Being wrenched away from all that to go to boarding

school in Yorkshire was a huge shock to the system.

Gilling Castle was built by the prominent landowning Fairfax family on the other side of the valley from Ampleforth College. I had done my Common Entrance exam while at the American School of Paris, which got me into the "B stream" to begin with. However, I tried my hardest in all my schoolwork with a view to being promoted into the "A stream". Every Saturday morning we would have a spelling test with 10 words like soporific, lackadaisical, accommodation and parallel. By the end of that first year, I had not got a single answer wrong and I was awarded a box of chocolates for my efforts, plus promotion to the "A stream".

I always got good reports while my brother Chris, who was also at the school, got the opposite even though he was far brighter. Chris was given the nickname "Batty Moore" at Gilling Castle, which stuck with him throughout his time at Ampleforth. He was a lovable rogue and always up to mischief. On the other hand, I was determined and I wanted to make up for the trouble Chris caused by being good. I understand this is not an abnormal social dynamic in a family.

I wasn't really that bright at school but I was particularly good at sport, especially cross-country running. In my last year at Gilling Castle, I was awarded colours for all the main sports of rugby, football, swimming and cricket. I became a very accomplished wicket-keeper and opening batsman.

At 12 years old, I crossed the valley to "Junior House" Ampleforth College for two years, and then onwards to the main upper school for a further five years. When I was at Junior House, I went on a school skiing trip to Engelberg in Switzerland. I fell in love with the mountains and skiing. I took to it like a duck to water and was soon racing down the slopes on my wooden skis. I persuaded my parents to have a go too and before long we started taking winter skiing holidays, first at Flaine and then in another French Alps resort called La Plagne when dad bought a three-week timeshare there. The whole family became very adept. Dad, being the sort of person he was, decided to try out the new *"ski evolutif"* method using much shorter skis. Once again he was way ahead of the game.

On one occasion in Flaine, during a private lesson, the instructor said to me as we got to the top of the cable car: "Right, we will set off as soon as the cable car departs and meet it at the bottom before it gets there." We raced off and, sure enough, travelling at an average of more than 40mph, arrived at the bottom just as the cable car pulled in. I loved speed and I liked taking a risk, so long as I had the competence and it was all properly managed.

At school, I became good at Latin and Greek as well as English, French and history, but anyone at Ampleforth who was any good at the Classics was put into the work stream of the same name. In the end, I took A-levels in English, Latin, Greek and ancient history. I took English A-level in one year, which was the first time anybody had done that at Ampleforth. I loved it. The teachers at Ampleforth were a mixture of monks and lay staff and they were nearly all outstanding. The Classics teaching in particular was amazing. Everyone who did Classics was expected to apply to Oxford and I was no exception. I continued throughout my career at Ampleforth as a B+ candidate but never keeping up with the Classics 'A Team' students. I would probably have done better if I had done English, French and history.

I was a late grower and although I had always been in the 1st XV rugby teams throughout my time at Ampleforth, once I got to 16 I was just too small to cope with the young men against whom we were playing. So I started to play for the under-16s 2nd XV. In the final two years at Ampleforth I played for the 3rd XV, and was captain in my last year. We won every match. I played hooker by that stage.

My greatest sporting achievements though were as a cross-country runner and in my final year at Ampleforth we beat the famous Sedbergh School, on its course in the middle of the Cumbrian fells. Sedbergh was probably the best cross-country school in the UK. I still have a photograph on my office wall showing the first four runners from Ampleforth including myself at the front, with one Sedbergh runner at the top of that excruciating mile-and-a-half-long hill.

I got on well with a great group of friends at Ampleforth, as well as the monks and the lay teachers. I became part of the hierarchy when I was made a school monitor and ultimately head of my house, St John's. One of the heads of school was called Edward Stourton and he has become a well-known journalist and broadcaster with the BBC. Rupert Everett, the famous actor, was in my year at Ampleforth and I will never forget him playing Queen Titania in Shakespeare's play *A Midsummer Night's Dream*, as all the girls' parts had to be played by boys. I think we all knew he was gay even then. He was certainly pretty.

Julian Fellowes, the writer of hit TV drama *Downton Abbey*, also attended Ampleforth.

I learned to smoke and drink at Ampleforth, as both these activities were permitted after the age of 16. We also engaged in numerous extracurricular activities including target shooting, the Combined Cadet Force, camping, scouting, night hikes across the North York Moors and debating.

I had a great time and I loved being at Ampleforth. Along with my family upbringing, I suppose you could say it was the making of the man.

I toyed with my Catholicism in some depth until I was about 16 but never took it any further. The Abbot of the Benedictine monastery, where there were well over 100 monks, was Father Basil Hume. He later became the Cardinal of Westminster. Basil Hume had been in the same house as my father when he was at school, and he had joined the monastery immediately after he left Ampleforth. He was an inspirational man, and a great sportsman.

I suppose, as far as Ampleforth is concerned, you could say I did the Victor Kiam story on it. American entrepreneur Kiam said he liked Remington razors so much that he bought the company. I loved Ampleforth so much that I came back to live by it. We are now an integral part of that community.

Three generations of Moores have been to that school, with our youngest son, Oliver, having left in 2012. We are still friendly with many of the monks and we live in the area where all the schoolteachers live. Father Matthew Burns is one of our most favourite monks from Ampleforth Abbey. His brother was the famous actor George Burns, who took a lead role in the film *The Charge of the Light Brigade.*

I took my Oxford entrance exams in November and December 1977, applying to Exeter College. I was interviewed but didn't get in. My second choice university was Bristol, mum's alma mater. I was offered a place there starting in October 1978.

As a teenager, my mum always encouraged us to work to make money for the things we wanted. I became her friends' favoured gardener and hedge cutter, and made a lot of money in the holidays. I also worked in a Ford garage, preparing new cars for their excited owners.

With the cash I made from my toils, I saved enough by the age of 14 to buy a moped. On the Continent, you were allowed to ride mopeds (50cc motorcycles with peddles) at 14. Having a moped as well as a bicycle would give me freedom, excitement and adventure. Prior to the moped, Chris and I used to go off on long bicycle rides all over the place, taking picnics with us and generally getting up to no good.

Once engine-powered, I was the envy of Chris. He also wanted a moped but wasn't motivated to do the work to make the money needed. However, many years later I discovered that he would wake himself up in the middle of the night, sneak down to the garage, push it silently up the ramp and out onto the road and go for long illicit rides. I always wondered why I kept running out of fuel.

Most of Chris' time was spent mucking about and reading. He was the most incredibly avid reader you can imagine. He was able to read before he was four years old and he could consume vast numbers of books and magazines in almost no time at all. His head was full to the brim of knowledge and, since the internet revolution, even more so. I don't think I know anyone who knows quite as much as Chris does. He is a remarkable person.

Chris kept failing at Ampleforth because he couldn't be bothered to work and he didn't fit in with the standard education system.

After school and some attempts at retaking A-levels, Chris became very happy as a motorcycle messenger in London for quite a few years, making a good wage and indulging his passion for motorbikes. He then became a supervisor in an apple-packing factory in Canada where his wife, Anne, came from. Finally, at the age of 30, he suddenly decided to go back to school to take an engineering degree at the City of London Polytechnic. I think he realised that if he didn't do something about it, he would be doing repetitive jobs for the rest of his life.

He got the top first-class degree of all entrants of all the polytechnics in the Greater London region, and he won a prize for building the lightest structure over 12 inches high able to carry a kilogram bag of sugar. He was always a genius, like my dad.

Although very different personalities, Chris and I had a great time together as young teenagers, getting into adventurous situations and following my mum's example of being fiercely independent. When we travelled back from Ampleforth together to go to Brussels, we would take the train from York to King's Cross and have to get on a flight to Brussels. We would throw away our unaccompanied minors badges and do everything for ourselves, even from the age of about 11 or 12.

A year or so after I got my moped, Chris managed to scrape together enough money to buy a little Honda motorbike. Once he had that, we could stretch our wings (or wheels) even further and when we were 15 or 16 we would go off for trips of about 60 miles to camp in places like the Ardennes forest region of Belgium.

Chris is now an outstanding engineer working for the business that my father and I set up all those years ago. His creativity and determination to "make it all work" is remarkable. He is kind, honest, interesting and great fun. He is the font of all useless information.

After having our own children, when we were both riding the largest motorcycles available, we went on further trips together, one of the most memorable in South Wales. I was riding my Honda Pan European and Chris his Kawasaki Z1100. We've always loved motorbikes and the sense of freedom and power they give you. Life is only worth living if you take risks.

Chris is a truly lovely bloke. Everyone loves him. And

I am so much looking forward to his retirement, so that we can go out and ride our motorbikes together again around the North York Moors.

My two sisters, Lulu and Nicola, are very different types of people.

Lulu and I were about three years apart and she was very helpful in introducing me to all her good-looking friends. She worked in the events management industry for many years, organising huge conferences. She's a lovely person and we get on well. She's married to Toby and now lives in Stockholm, in Sweden, working as a professional dog walker, which is the best therapy she can have after so many years of stress and strain.

Nicola was born when I was 10 years old. When she was a small child, I was very close to her and took great pleasure in looking after her as a baby, changing her nappies and so on. She also, like my father, was very bright and got three As at A-level and a place to study engineering at Oxford University in New College which is where my father went. Sadly, as a result of spending too much time rowing etc, she failed her first-year exams and decided to switch to law immediately. She then went to Bristol University, as I had, and qualified as a barrister.

After a stint working in the Royal Air Force, she developed a reasonably good practice in the criminal law, but it's so badly paid that she took a job working in the Cayman Islands as a senior prosecuting counsel. She prosecuted murders, drug dealing and all the nasty stuff. In November 2014, she became the Attorney General for St Helena, the small British overseas territory in the middle of the South Atlantic, and has been involved in dealing with the island's much-publicised child abuse scandal. It has been a very difficult job.

When I left Ampleforth, before I went to Bristol University, I needed to get a job to earn some money.

Luckily, I was asked to go back and teach French and English at Junior House for two terms. This had become a bit of a tradition, and I followed on from others who had done the same job. It was great because it meant I would be paid in the holidays, including the whole summer holiday. I had thought about going and working in the Alps as a chef because I had become a fairly competent cook, having been taught by mum.

I also coached all sports but especially cross-country running. It was an extraordinary experience being on the "other side of the fence" immediately after having been at the school itself. Writing reports was highly amusing. I modelled my approach to teaching on the best teacher I ever had, who was called Ronald Rohan. He taught Latin, English and history. Anyone who was taught by Ronald remembers him as their best teacher. He had this ability to be highly disciplinarian at the same time as being kind. This is quite a trick.

After a wonderful holiday in Giglio that summer during which I won the cross-country race at the local fiesta (much to the annoyance of the local Italians), I prepared to go off for the next adventure in life – Bristol University.

Living It Up

I started at Bristol expecting to study Classics and then go on to qualify as a barrister, which is what a specialist career adviser had recommended I did. Within a month of starting I decided to switch to law immediately and reduce the number of years taken to qualify. Luckily, I was accepted to do the law course at Bristol starting the following October, so I left the university and started working for a market research company called Documentary Research Limited. This made me enough money to live and go on a few holidays, including a great skiing trip to Arabba in the Italian Dolomites where I fell in love with a wonderful girl called Julia Thompson.

By the time I left school and went to university, I had rejected the "smells and bells", ritual and dogma, of the Catholic Church, to engage in the Seventies culture of sex, drugs and rock 'n' roll. I was 13 in 1971. All the hard work of pushing the envelope out after the Second World War had been completed by the end of the Sixties. Those of us fortunate enough to enter our teenage years in the Seventies were lucky devils, if you see what I mean. We embraced the material and the secular world with every part of our body, mind and soul.

Later, many of us came to realise that materialism, secularism, consumerism and moral relativism were false roads to wellbeing, but we were young at the time and it definitely seemed like fun. Much of it, of course, we can't remember. The music of the Seventies was also amazing and this added a further spark to the alcohol and drug-fuelled activities in which we engaged. My favoured artists are Pink Floyd, Van Morrison, The Doors and Elton John and I still have most of my vinyl collection.

I had discovered the real delights of the opposite sex at the age of 17 with a lovely girl from Birmingham, on a surfing beach at Polzeath in Cornwall, when I was camping there during the hot summer of 1976 with my great friend Tim Hughes from the Hughes family we'd always holidayed with. June Hughes, his mother, was at school with my mum and they both had their first two children within a few months of each other. Tim was born five months or so after me and, believe it or not, my mum went into labour with me when she was having a dinner party with June and David Hughes. Once I'd found sex, it was going to be a problem putting the genie back in the box.

That first false start at Bristol University, and the years that followed studying law, truly set me off on the adventure that is life. I worked hard and played hard. I made good friends and we had the hugest fun that you could possibly imagine, even if there was a good deal of sinning involved.

I took up surfing as soon as I went to university and I was an active member of the Surf Club where I met another pal, Jo Parkinson. The group was a great bunch and we often used to go down to Barnstaple in Devon to surf in the winter months at nearby Croyde or Woolacombe. We did even more surfing in the summer months and I must admit that we smoked quite a lot of "wacky baccy" too.

In my first year at Bristol University, as was the way of things in those days, I had a lot of casual girlfriends. However, in my second year I met a girl from the first year also doing law called Mandy Cranny. I fell in love with her and we had a steady, if somewhat volatile, relationship. Her parents lived in the South Wales seaside town of Porthcawl, and this allowed me to indulge my new passion of surfing. I surfed there at Rest Bay two Christmas days in a row, wrapped up in a thick wetsuit, booties, gloves and wetsuit hat. It was freezing.

I completed my finals at Bristol in the summer of 1982. I worked hard and knew an awful lot about law by the time I had finished my course but, for some reason, I just couldn't seem to translate this into results in exams. I nearly always got firsts in my term-time written work but only ended up with a 2:2 in my degree. Mind you it didn't seem to matter much in those days.

In September 1982, I went up to London to study for my bar exams and I was a member of Lincoln's Inn, an historic society of lawyers based in a tranquil enclave of 11 acres in central London. I had a very happy time there sharing a flat in Hammersmith with another friend, Rupert Dorey, to whom I had been introduced by Jo Parkinson. Rupert, like Jo and my other friend Glynn Thompson, lived on the English Channel island of Guernsey and I spent quite a bit of time there enjoying myself and learning how to sail. I must have got some work done though, as I managed to finish in the top 100 candidates for bar exams that year, out of about 1,000.

My girlfriend Mandy's father, Pat, was a successful

builder and in the summer of 1983, after my bar exams, I had a superb practical learning experience working in his builder's yard as a fitter's mate repairing the Land Rover, digger and cement mixers. Pat and I got on very well and regularly played golf together. He'd taken up the sport after the sad death of his wife in January of that year and turned out to be a natural golfer. One day on the ninth hole at Royal Porthcawl Golf Club I witnessed him make an albatross: a hole in two shots.

During that summer, I met a chap in Porthcawl called Stuart Price, also from Guernsey, who introduced me to hang-gliding. I was immediately hooked. As an adventure, it was even better than surfing and was now my passion. As a result, I forgot about the whole idea of getting a pupillage to continue with my training as a barrister, and just focused on this new hobby. Little did I know then that it would be hang-gliding that got me into financial services?

All my colleagues who had taken their bar exams at the same time as me had already set up pupillages but I only started looking in about mid-September. I was very lucky and landed one which started in mid-October, working for a fantastic barrister called Robert Rhodes. He is now a QC, in a top chambers called 2 Crown Office Row, in the Temple area of central London. It was the same chambers in which former Labour Prime Minister Tony Blair and his wife Cherie worked and met. In my interview Robert asked whether I liked opera and, because my dad listened to it, I said, "Yes". That might have been the only reason he accepted my application. He played it all day long and we were working together in the same room. He was a mad keen fan of Richard Wagner and taught me a huge amount about the German genius' music. When I left him, Robert gave me a copy of a great recording of Wagner's Götterdämmerung (Twilight of the Gods), which is the final part of his famous cycle of four operas called The Ring. It is a truly extraordinary piece of music and I still play that record today.

On my very first day as a pupil of Robert's, I met him in North London and we went to St Alban's Crown Court, where he was sitting as a part-time judge (called an assistant recorder) of criminal cases.

Robert was an outstanding barrister, who did an awful lot of tax work, especially where there were criminal or quasi-criminal aspects to the case. He taught me a great deal and was a fantastic cross-examiner. He had prosecuted many major frauds and was a senior Inland Revenue prosecuting counsel. He was also instructed by one of the top firms of solicitors operating in this area, called Berwin Leighton. It dealt with all the old tax avoidance schemes and, in particular, the controversial Rossminster ones devised and marketed by accountant Roy Tucker. We were instructed by a chap called Tony Bunker, who had worked for the Inland Revenue's special investigations division. Before I'd ended my first six months pupillage, Tony offered me a job as his assistant. Robert advised me to take it and I did. That was my first paid job and it was a relief to be off my dad's profit and loss account at last.

I only worked at Berwin Leighton for about 10 months. The trouble was that I was completely obsessed by hang-gliding and didn't really want to be living in London. I yearned for the Welsh mountains where I'd learned to fly.

My escape route came to me one Tuesday while travelling by train into work. I was reading *The Times* newspaper's legal appointments section and spotted a vacancy for an in-house lawyer in the product development department of Allied Hambro, a large retail financial services company based in Swindon, Wiltshire. My very first thought was, "Swindon, ah, that's much closer to the Welsh mountains than London". On that basis I applied for the job.

One of the questions on the application form asked, "What do you look for in a job?" It was the first time I'd given that very much thought and it took me several hours to work out the answer: "Satisfaction through a sense of achievement." I got the post but more importantly edged 80 miles closer to my hang-gliding "home" in Wales.

I absolutely loved working at Allied Hambro which, shortly after I joined in December 1984, was taken over by British American Tobacco and renamed Allied Dunbar. It had a great culture of openness, excellence and ethics in which fear, blame and excessive pride had no part. It welcomed diversity of personality style and even mavericks. It created an organisation where everybody spoke up. Speaking up doesn't just save organisations from downside risks but it also encourages creativity and new ideas. This feeds directly into financial performance. It also makes an organisation a great place to work and fun at the same time.

Allied Dunbar also had a very strong sales culture and was often nicknamed, "Allied Crowbar". Its name also, amusingly, was an anagram of, "Dial A Blunder". Notwithstanding its reputation for having strong-arm sales tactics, it was never subject to disciplinary action by the regulators.

The legal department in which I worked was right at the heart of the company and highly regarded. It also had a compliance department (even before 1986 when the regulatory regime commenced) called "Special Services", run by ex-Merchant Navy officer Trevor Ward. He shortened the name of the department to the "SS" and he was ruthless on bad behaviour by sales staff.

The head of the legal department was a wonderful man called Peter Hamilton, who was years later to represent me in my dispute against HBOS. At Allied Dunbar, I also met product development actuary Phil Hodkinson, who became my first boss at HBOS.

Swindon was a great location for hang-gliding, being close to the Wiltshire Downs and not too far from Wales. On a good thermal day, Peter Hamilton would see me looking longingly out of the office window, and would say: "Paul, if you haven't got anything urgent on at the moment, why don't you just clear off and go flying and finish your work on the weekend?" What a great boss.

I was happy in my work, gained rapid promotion and by early 1988 had a share in my first house, a three-bedroom detached in Wootton Bassett, with Jason Prior, a close hang-gliding buddy and landscape architect. Jason is now one of the most senior executives at AECOM, which is a global provider of architecture, design and construction services for public and private clients. He is the chief executive of AECOM's planning, design and development practices and was the principle-in-charge of its planning work around the 2012 London Olympics. He is now working on the Rio 2016 Summer Olympics in Brazil.

Together we soon hatched a plan to take an extended hang-gliding holiday overseas for six weeks, starting in December 1988. At first we considered Australia but then our friend Stuart Prosser persuaded us to go to Chile where he had worked in the nuclear research centre, studying the effects of radiation on the bloodstream. He told us that the flying in Chile, over the Andes, was spectacular and at Christmas that year there was an international hang-gliding competition. We could therefore get lifts up the mountains and be retrieved after flying cross-country, which would make life a great deal easier. So we decided to go and I negotiated an extra two weeks unpaid leave with Peter Hamilton for the end of 1988.

When I joined Allied Dunbar, the Gower Report (named after its author Professor Laurence Gower) into investor protection had been published and it recommended an entirely new regulatory regime for the financial services sector. This was implemented by the passing of the Financial Services Act (1986).

This meant that, from the word "go", I was involved in designing Allied Dunbar's response to the new system: in effect, I was involved in regulation in the UK before it even began. I also helped in drafting some of the early rules of the self-regulatory scheme, as it then was. I had a particular interest in everything to do with selling practices including advertising, marketing, product disclosure and sales process. I had become convinced in the good of financial services but had seen some very bad behaviour. In a way, from the early days, I became something of a customer champion.

My final project at Allied Dunbar was in its entry to the residential mortgage business.

The firm had a direct, commission-only sales force of more than 5,000 people which very successfully introduced mortgage clients to a whole range of different providers. This meant the sales advisers could also sell endowment life assurance policies to repay those mortgages. In those days, endowment mortgages were definitely the best way to repay a loan to buy a house because they came with a 17% tax break, as well as a rapidly increasing stock market partly caused by higher levels of inflation than we are used to today.

We concluded that the sales team generated more mortgage business than pretty much any other provider in the UK. As a result, we decided that we should provide the mortgage funding for our sales force ourselves rather than handing it over to other credit providers. We didn't want to raise the funding ourselves or hold the mortgages on our balance sheet. So we got into bed with Kleinwort Benson, an investment bank that set up a company called Mortgage Funding Corporation Ltd. MFC would borrow the money on the wholesale markets, and our sales force would then sell the mortgages which were fulfilled with this wholesale funding. Allied Dunbar would administer the mortgages, and take an interest rate cut between the cost of the wholesale funds and the interest rate charged to customers. After we had originated sufficient mortgages, we would then securitise them and sell them on to institutions as high-yielding, low-risk assets.

Setting it up required many bleary-eyed nights spent in the offices of top London firm of solicitors Freshfields, eating takeaways and drinking strong coffee as we waded through piles of documentation. The hard work paid off though. After launching the business the company rapidly became the top mortgage provider in the UK. It was fascinating being involved from a legal perspective in what was without doubt one of the very first "originate and distribute" mortgage models, particularly working on the first securitisation of that business structure.

Before long I was approached by Kleinwort Benson to become its in-house lawyer. After much soul-searching (because I didn't really want to be in London and was, by then, living in a lovely house in Bristol where I had moved after selling up in Wootton Bassett), for the sake of my career, I took the job.

So, when I left Allied Dunbar on 10 December 1988 to go on my six-week hang-gliding adventure to Chile,

I knew I'd be coming back to start work at Kleinwort Benson on 23 January 1989.

Chile and Wife

On our way to Chile, Jason, Stuart and I decided to stop off for a few days in Rio de Janeiro, Brazil. We had a fantastic time sampling the local dishes and drinking plenty of Caipirinha cocktail (mostly rum mixed with lime juice and sugar). The highlight was hang-gliding from a take-off ramp perched above the long, sandy Ipanema beach where thousands of sun-worshippers work their tans amidst soccer and volleyball games and surfers ride the South Atlantic breakers. Rio was a fantastic experience but there was a life-changing one awaiting me over the Andes in Chile.

Our flight from Rio to Santiago took four-and-a-half hours and we touched down in the Chilean city full of excitement and expectation for the Santiago International Hang-gliding Competition that lay ahead.

The two great constants all the way down this long country are the Andes and the Pacific Ocean. The highest mountain in the Andes, Aconcagua, is about 60 miles north of Santiago and rises to 6,962m (22,841ft) but the peaks that surround Santiago itself are nearly 10,000ft. They are spectacular.

I spent a lot of time thermaling above some of these mountains. Such is the strength of the thermal convection that on one occasion I made a 6,000ft height gain in under eight minutes. It was all a bit too frightening for my risk appetite and so I preferred to fly later on in the day when the thermals were not quite so strong.

Right on the edge of Santiago is a beautiful 908m (2,979ft) mountain called Manquehue, which I have fond memories of hang-gliding over. We had to walk up about half-a-mile to the take-off point and we used to pay Chilean teenagers to carry our gliders and kit which weighed about 90lb – a luxury we never had elsewhere. On one outing I flew over the fortified residence of the Chilean President Augusto Pinochet. It was built on the side of the mountain and had watch towers and gun turrets sticking up from the corners. I managed to sneak a photo as I glided overhead, even though I knew I would be in serious trouble if I got caught with it and would probably be put in prison as a spy.

On Christmas Day, at the height of the southern hemisphere summer, the local Chilean hang-gliding club organised a barbecue for an orphanage under a beautiful tree at the bottom of their "training slope". Called Batucco, it was more than 1,000ft top to bottom, which put the UK's training slopes into perspective. Batucco was within a few miles of the flight path into Santiago Airport, and flying there I could look down on jumbo jets.

Not only were all the local flyers going to be at the event but also international pilots including people from Germany, Switzerland and ourselves. The club set up the barbecue and then drove to the top of the hill to rig up their gliders. Before taking off, they stuffed their harnesses with sweets, which they then dropped on the children from the air. The idea is to fly as low as possible but without losing enough lift to get back up to the top, and drop the sweets on the children from as low an altitude as possible. One chap was dressed up as Father Christmas while he was flying. Jason, Stuart and I thought this was a great way to spend Christmas Day and we went along for the ride.

I was busily rigging my hang-glider about 50ft from the front of the hill, when I looked up and saw a young woman sitting on a rock. I thought, "I'd like to get to know that girl!" So, being the front-footed person I am, I just went straight up to her and pretended to speak a bit of Spanish. It turned out she spoke fluent English and had been brought along to the event by her friend Danny (a girl). Her name was Maureen Oats Villaquiran and, up close, she was even more beautiful than from 50ft away. This made me even more determined. I was immediately smitten.

I went flying for a few hours with Jason and Stuart, dropping sweets to the children and then landed by the big tree where we started to de-rig our gliders to put on top of our four-wheel-drive car. I told my two chums about my intentions towards Maureen and we invited her and Danny out to dinner. They agreed.

Somehow or other, I managed to persuade Jason and Stuart to sit in the back of the car and I got Maureen to sit in the front, with me driving. As we pulled away, I pushed the cassette into the machine to play some music. It was a compilation tape made by my sister

Louise's then boyfriend. It was playing *She Drives Me Crazy* by The Fine Young Cannibals. Maureen turned to me and said, "That's my favourite track."

Crash! Bang! Wallop!

That instant, I decided I wanted to marry her.

I had never thought about marriage before. In fact, as an adventurous, freedom-loving guy, I didn't really like the idea of it. However love conquers all, and the trouble was that it was love at first sight.

It's yet another lesson in risk management. I thought I was managing the risk of personal injury associated with flying hang-gliders, and not the risk of changing my life of freedom and adventure through marriage and children. Then, suddenly, out of nowhere comes that Exocet missile you least expect – love. And it transforms your life.

Thank God I did decide that evening to marry Maureen and that she agreed. Every good man needs a great woman behind him and without her I could never have coped with everything that has happened.

Maureen's father, Peter (may he rest in peace) came from a famous Cornish tin-mining family, called the Oats. Maureen's grandfather had owned and run the huge Levant tin mine near St Just in Cornwall. Sadly, there had been a huge disaster and his wealth disappeared down the collapsed mine in compensation. More misfortune struck the family as he died of tetanus poisoning when Maureen's father was only 12 years old and, with most of the money gone, Peter and his mother had to move out of their large house in St Just with numerous domestic servants, to Brighton.

Peter went on to carve out a highly successful career with the famous Bank of London and South America and met Maureen's mother Leonor while working in Colombia. They quickly married and moved around South America as Peter rose through the ranks of the bank, eventually settling in Santiago. They had five children, Maureen being the youngest and to date the only one of a large family to have moved abroad, when she married me.

When I got back to the UK after that amazing trip to Chile, my heart was all a flutter. The problem was, I still had a girlfriend, Julie Pidgeon, living in my house in Bristol. There was only one answer. I got off the plane on the Sunday morning drove to Bristol, gave her the news and turned round to drive back to London and to Wandsworth, where I had arranged to live with my best friend from Bristol University, Charlie Martin.

On the return journey I was so tired I stopped for a rest at Membury service station on the M4. It was about 6.30pm and dark. I parked the car but left the engine running and laid my head back on the headrest with the intention of having a quick nap. I woke up four hours later at 10.30pm, shook myself awake and headed off to Charlie's house in London. Charlie is a senior partner at one of the most successful firms of solicitors in London.

I only worked for Kleinwort Benson for three months. Not long after getting back to the UK, I was headhunted to work for a start-up which was supported by top names in the private equity world. When I went to discuss the matter with my director at Kleinwort Benson, he told me I would be a fool not to take the opportunity as it looked like a great business move.

So, in April, 1989 I moved to work for a company called Ellastone that had a great business proposition in the retail financial services market. The senior management were all former Allied Dunbar sales managers and staff, and it looked like it couldn't fail. However, it did, but not without me learning a big lesson in the process: never let top sales people take accountability for anything operational. It also showed me a great deal about how not to do things – which is equally as important as the opposite.

I'd hardly got my feet under the desk at Ellastone before Maureen was on the Easter flight out of Chile to join me in the UK for a two-week holiday. The morning after she arrived, at about 6.30am on a beautiful spring day, I took her for a motorbike tour around London on the back of my BMW. There was no traffic and I gave her a real fright as I lent the bike over steeply to go round the roundabout in front of Buckingham Palace.

Maureen decided not to return to Chile and she gave in her notice over the telephone. She had taken a course in tourism and was working for a Chilean airline at the time.

Shortly after, I proposed to Maureen and we decided to get engaged formally on her 21st birthday, which was 4 June 1989. We went to Hatton Garden, near Holborn, London's famous jewellery quarter, to look for engagement rings. We'd only walked 50 yards up the road before we saw a three-diamond ring in a shop window and bought it within 35 minutes. We were clearly supposed to get married.

Maureen got a job working as a receptionist in a Mexican bank because of her fluent Spanish, and we rented a flat in Bayswater with her cousin Fernanda Villaquiran. Maureen's mother is one of nine children from Cali in Colombia and she has well over 30 cousins.

That spring, I had bought a flat in Brackenbury Village, Hammersmith, right next to Ravenscourt Park, with a friend of mine called Marcus Evans. It was a three-bedroom, ground-floor maisonette in Dorville Crescent. I'd met Marcus on the first day I joined Allied Dunbar where he was a manager in the training department and he ended up working at Ellastone as head of training. Ellastone's offices were based in Brentford, West London, only a short drive from Hammersmith, so living together made a lot of sense. I asked Marcus to be our best man.

Maureen and I had a wonderful time that summer in the UK, as all people in love do, but we didn't really know each other.

We set the date to get married in Chile as close to Christmas Day as we could: 22 December 1989.

Maureen, being a canny girl, bought her wedding dress in Debenhams for about £300 and when she went back to Chile in November had it smartened up by a local seamstress so that it looked like a very expensive dress in the end.

In the meantime I had the important matter of a stag

weekend to consider and a riotous assembly of 11 of us duly descended on Amsterdam. The party included my brother Chris, Jo Parkinson, Rupert Dorey, Glynn Thompson and Stephen Joyce. Marcus Evans was the *maître d'* and I'll never forget him leading us into bars, going up to the counter and saying, "55 beers please". These were the smaller beer glasses that you got on the Continent in those days and he ordered five beers for each person. What an efficient process. I can't reveal the other stuff we got up to but I can say that I was well-behaved. On the Sunday morning, Marcus made one of the most amusing remarks I ever heard him make.

We were sitting in a bar at about midday medicating ourselves with the "hair of the dog", when he turned to me and nonchalantly said: "I don't know why these Dutch bother to speak Dutch, when they speak perfectly good English."

Maureen had returned to Chile in November to prepare for the wedding, and I arrived a week or so before the due date. Sitting next to my dad having a beer in the warm Santiago sunshine, he turned to me and said he could not believe how good-looking the Chilean women were. I'd never heard him make a comment like that before.

Maureen and I got married on 22 December – the same day that Berlin's Brandenburg Gate reopened after nearly 30 years. The wedding was a great affair in a lovely Catholic church and, after Christmas celebrations with her family, we went off on a honeymoon first to the south of Chile, then to the Lake District region and then over the mountains to Bariloche, a ski resort in Argentina. It was a lovely Alpine kind of place with Swiss-style architecture all around.

The evening before we left, we ate shellfish and the next morning Maureen said she wasn't feeling too good. By the time we had taken the long bumpy bus ride back across the Andes to Osorno, where we had parked our car, she had a temperature and a nasty pain in her midriff. I was worried that she was developing appendicitis, but we had several hundred kilometres to drive northwards toward Santiago before nightfall. We were going to stay in a small town called Temuco about 680km south of Santiago. By the time we got there, I was becoming seriously concerned.

We went to the train station and, by the grace of God, it turned out we could put the car on the train and arrive in Santiago the next morning. We had our own private sleeping compartment and I still happen to have a photograph of Maureen looking terribly ill that evening. I'd rung Maureen's parents and told them to have an ambulance ready for when we got there. Maureen was stretchered off the train, put into the ambulance and had her appendix out within an hour of arriving at hospital. She was close to peritonitis.

That put the kibosh on the second part of our honeymoon, which was to have been a trip to the Atacama Desert in the north of Chile. I suggested she stayed in Chile for a while when I went back to the UK but she insisted on coming. With Maureen about to leave Chile for good there was a great deal of "wailing and gnashing of teeth" by her large South American family at the airport. As we were going through emigration, it turned out that she had failed to get some document she needed to leave the country and the officials refused to allow her to leave. So I got on the plane on my own with my bags and Maureen's in the hold and jetted off back to England to start 1990 minus my new wife. She had to return home with her family. Not the best start to a marriage.

I arrived home to a stack of post, including a letter from a headhunter which I ignored. Maureen, meanwhile, got the paperwork sorted and finally made it over a week or so later on 20 January.

To The Brink And Back

On the 29th, I went into work at Ellastone and the administrators were there. They gave us immediate notice, a cheque for one month's salary and other benefits, and took the keys to my company car, a BMW 320i with beautiful grey sports leather seats.

Interest rates were running at about 15% at the time. I'd had to buy Marcus out of his share of the flat in Hammersmith to prepare for married life, and needed £1,350 a month just to pay the mortgage. I calculated that we would be insolvent within six weeks.

Then I remembered the letter I'd tossed to one side from the headhunter, so when I got home I revisited it. He wanted to put me forward for an outstanding job as General Counsel and Head of Compliance at a new subsidiary of American Express, to be called Acuma. It was slap bang in the bull's-eye of my experience.

It was a revelation being interviewed by an American company with an approach to human resources management that was in a completely different league to anything that I had experienced. As part of the interview process, I had to spend a whole half-day with a highly qualified occupational psychologist to assess my personality and psychological make-up. The chap who worked with me was called Gurnek Bains and he went on to become my personal coach.

My boss at Acuma was Frank Skillern Jr who, like many CEOs in American companies, started his life as a lawyer. We were similar characters and got on like a house on fire. He was a complete Anglophile and an expert on Shakespeare. Frank had watched *Hamlet* being performed more than 50 times.

I would also have an even more heavily weighted reporting line to what American Express called, The General Counsel's Office, as well as to one of the senior General Counsels called Jan Breyer. Jan turned out to be one of the best, if not the very best, bosses I ever had. As well as being strategically brilliant from a business perspective, he was massively bright, great fun and he understood the English sense of humour.

The General Counsel's Office gave the local General Counsel real protection, and this meant that no local CEO could remove a General Counsel without the formal involvement and approval of his or her professional boss.

So, within a few weeks of losing my job at Ellastone,

I was offered what for me felt like the best job in the country. Not only that, Acuma had a brilliant strategy to introduce fee-based retail financial planning into the UK which American Express offered throughout the whole of the United States of America through its subsidiary IDS Financial Services, based in Minneapolis-Saint Paul. IDS was run by one of the most amazing people I ever met, Harvey Golub, who went on to become the President of American Express. Harvey was a chain-smoker who had a 40,000 ft^2 house on one of the most beautiful lakes near Minneapolis, which included his own automated car wash. In his office, behind his head he had two signs. One read, "It's the leader's role to define the current reality", and the other, "If you want someone to do A, pay them to do A".

IDS had proved that fee-based financial planning led to more sales of financial products, bigger case size, better retention of their customers' investments and far more repeat business. Those dynamics are, without a doubt, the right recipe for a successful retail financial services business and, with the American Express brand behind it, I thought I was onto a winner. To add the icing to the cake, the pay package was worth more than £100,000 per year.

I loved my time at Acuma, which lasted from February 1990 to February 1994. I learnt a lot, both about how to provide outstanding legal services to all the departments I looked after, as well as how to design the right strategy, structure, people and culture to lead a compliance function most effectively. As Head of

Compliance, I was also responsible for regulatory affairs and liaison with all the UK regulators, and so I gained even more experience of how they thought and what was required to maintain good relationships with them.

As I discovered more about my own psychology by working with Gurnek Bains, I was able to better manage people. I did need to make some important adjustments to my style, and it wasn't going to be easy. My upfront and no-holds-barred approach upset some people in the organisation, but I was always protected by Frank Skillern who told me that I had "the 007 licence". He said it was my job to find out what was going on around the company and to tell him anything that I was concerned about. So I did just that.

I spent quite a bit of time in Minneapolis-Saint Paul at IDS Financial Services, as well as some time in New York at the head office of American Express, right next to the Twin Towers. It was damaged in the 9/11 terrorist attacks.

While at Acuma, Maureen and I had two children and had another "bun in the oven" by the time I left. Emily Jane was born just before the Iraq War on 10 January 1991. Daniel Thomas came along on 10 June 1992 and Oliver Clive arrived on the scene a few months after I left Acuma on 3 June 1994. We'd had three children who were now under three-and-a-half years old. Some people might say that was bad risk management but looking back it's the best development that could have happened. As a joke, I often say that when it comes to children, the first 40 years are the worst but, at least, we are now on the downhill stretch.

In the summer of 1992, just after Daniel was born, we moved out of our maisonette in Hammersmith and into a three-bedroom house which was converted from part of Barkham Manor near Wokingham, Royal Berkshire.

After three years at Acuma, we had just about got the business performing to the right standard and demonstrated that the recipe that IDS Financial Services had made work in the US (with a sales force of about 8,000 financial planners) would also work equally well in the UK. Acuma had also proved that if you charge people for the initial advice – the financial Plan – they take the process much more seriously and then tend to implement their plan using your own financial products. When we compared our sales performance to the premier sales organisation in the UK, my old employer Allied Dunbar, we were beating them hands down. We had twice the number of product sales per customer; twice the case size; twice the persistency and twice the repeat business.

But now American Express had the Shearson Lehman debacle to deal with, and this was to put an end to what was looking like a very successful new retail financial services organisation in the UK.

Ten years or so before, American Express had decided that strategically it should not only be on the spending side of the economic equation (i.e. the American Express charge cards and travellers' cheques) but also the saving and investment side. That is why it had bought, on the advice of Harvey Golub, a McKinsey consultant, IDS Financial Services. As a result, it had also made an investment in Shearson Lehman and owned 49% of that company. The trouble was it failed to control its investment adequately and, following the junk bond crisis in which Shearson Lehman had been heavily involved, it only had one way to protect its investment, acquire the remaining 51%. It was the Victor Kiam story in reverse – American Express didn't like the company very much anymore but it had no choice but to buy it.

This meant that there was no capital left at American Express for any other businesses, particularly start-ups like Acuma. In my view this was short-sighted, and a great shame. However, in 1993 it was decided to sell Acuma. I was deeply involved in this project as the senior lawyer at Acuma. I knew that my departure date was going to be in February 1994, and I was incentivised to stay by being paid double my normal salary from 1 October, as well as by being offered a very generous redundancy package when I left.

My payoff was about £75,000 and, after a wonderful family holiday in the Turks and Caicos Islands with a heavily pregnant Maureen, and our young children Emily and Daniel, I flew off via Quito in Ecuador to the Galapagos Islands to meet and sail for six weeks with my pal Stephen Joyce, his wife Fiona and their two small children, journeying across the Pacific to Tahiti on their Swan 43 yacht. Adventure had always been part of my life, both in work and play, and the opportunity was not to be missed.

It was an unforgettable experience. I spent a week

waiting for the Joyce's in Galapagos, giving me time to explore the main island and go horse-riding, looking for giant tortoises. I walked powder-like, white-sand beaches, went swimming with sea lions in Tortuga Bay and sat next to blue-footed booby birds.

We set off sailing at night from Ayora, on the Galapagos island of Santa Cruz, with a full moon projecting into the big Pacific swell. The first stretch to the Marquesas Islands in French Polynesia was about 3,600 miles. The Marquesas Islands are 600 miles or so north-east of Tahiti, right in the middle of the South Pacific. They are the islands where the famous French Impressionist painter Paul Gauguin ended up living.

There is almost nothing to compare with being on the helm of a fast-sailing boat, right in the middle of the night with no one around, looking up at the stars of the southern hemisphere, watching the Southern Cross rotate in front of your eyes and with pilot whales swimming beside the boat, causing phosphorescence in the sea. Spiritual, or what?

Probably the most exciting moment on that stretch was catching a 45lb yellowfin tuna off the back of the boat. It was larger than Stephen and Fiona's daughter Katie, who was almost three.

After the Marquesas Islands, we sailed south-east towards the Tuamotu Islands, which form the largest chain of atolls in the world. They are the perfect desert islands. We went scuba-diving in Manihi with whitetip and blacktip reef sharks, and all manner of other marine life. I flew from there back to Tahiti and then, after a day or so, returned to the UK via Los Angeles.

It was early May and I'd left pregnant Maureen with two toddlers for six weeks. Understandably, the sailing trip caused a lot of upset with her and later I realised that what I did was completely wrong and selfish. It took her a long time to sort me out – well, at least to some extent.

Not only was I in my wife's bad books, I had no job and the day before Maureen's birthday on 3 June, Oliver was born. This was the cue to start looking for work. I didn't expect it to take very long but the economic climate was unsettled and, in the end, it took me a whole year.

After very nearly getting the job as General Counsel at J Rothschild Assurance (now the very successful St James's Place Wealth Management), Maureen suggested that I should consider consulting. This was yet another example of how she has exactly the right instinct about things.

I also wondered whether I might find work in one of Santiago's big banks. So we adopted a twin-pronged strategy. Firstly, we decided that, to reduce operating expense and to help with the children, we would rent our beautiful home in Barkham Manor. Maureen would go with the children to Chile for six months and I'd follow for three months from the end of October, to give me enough time to search for a job.

At the same time, I approached accountants

Deloitte and KPMG, where I had contacts. I also looked carefully into the idea of setting up my own consulting business with the name LawTech International. It would offer a mix of legal and operational technical advice relating to financial sector regulation which, by now, I knew inside out and was causing the financial sector a real challenge.

KPMG took the most interest in me and my ideas, and I was introduced to a partner called Marcus Sephton who was running a department in its financial sector practice. It had the dreadful name of "STARS", which stood for Special Technical and Regulatory Services. He seemed keen for me to join and work with him, to build an advisory business serving the retail financial services sector.

After Marcus had interviewed me, he asked me to prepare a presentation to give to him and his co-partners, Jonathan Jesty and Victoria Raffe, setting out how I would go about building the business and why I should lead it. I went to their offices about a week or two before I was due to leave for Chile and gave the presentation.

The whole presentation is here:

www.crashbankwallop.co.uk/library/2-1

Marcus called me on my mobile a couple of days before I went to Chile, to tell me that KPMG was going to offer me a job.

The initial offer letter arrived before I got on the plane on 29 October 1994, the day before my 36th birthday. It was a huge relief because it meant I could go to Chile safe in the knowledge that I had secured a good job and income for our growing family. I could relax and enjoy myself in the beautiful Chilean summer climate while still looking out for work over there. In fact I did come close to getting a job in a bank as head of quality.

However, I spent some considerable time while in Chile negotiating my KPMG deal in writing and over the telephone with Marcus. The original offer represented a massive pay cut of around £35,000 from what I'd been earning at Acuma.

To be fair, I had never operated in the consulting or professional services world before, let alone built a business in it, and so KPMG was taking a bigger risk with me. Although I realised I didn't have much room for negotiation, I was determined to understand exactly what I had to do to move onwards and upwards fast, and to make sure that this was documented in the offer letter.

The answer was simply: "Points mean prizes", or in KPMG speak, "Pounds mean prizes". If I brought the right level of fees into the KPMG coffers I could expect rapid promotion and increase in pay. I made sure that this was clearly stated in the offer letter, and I was now content to proceed. I believed in the strength of the market for regulatory advice and in my own ability to serve it.

As I had put it on the last page of my interview presentation to KPMG:

WHY PAUL MOORE?

Career to date

=

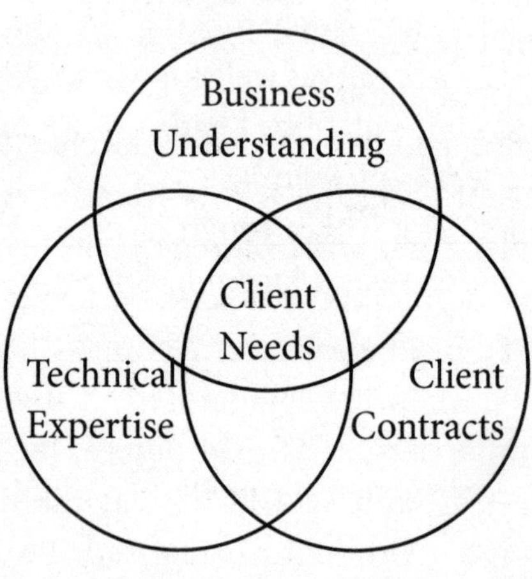

+

KPMG

=

Credibility with clients

I accepted KPMG's final offer a couple of weeks before Maureen, me and the children returned to a freezing, rainy UK in late January 1995. Yet another incredible new chapter was about to begin in our lives.

CHAPTER 3

Tom Fraser wasn't just ranting: he was, to use his vernacular, going absolutely fucking ballistic.

Although the Aussie was well-known for his colourful language and high-volatility, I hadn't quite anticipated a full-scale nuclear explosion.

Short and stocky with a tough face and the big fists of a boxer, Fraser was Managing Director of the UK financial services arm of Australian Mutual Provident (AMP) which owned insurers Pearl and Churchill – the latter more recently associated with its TV adverts featuring a talking, nodding dog with the catchphrase "oh yes!"

AMP was in serious trouble with the FSA for allegedly "churning" clients from one policy or investment product to another purely to generate more commission, and KPMG had been drafted in to independently validate the firm's internal checks on hundreds of its sales contracts.

As the KPMG partner heading the review team, I had some very bad news to deliver to Fraser: we'd overturned the majority of case studies, meaning AMP would have to redo the whole costly process. He wasn't going to be happy.

It was New Year 2002 and with some trepidation I turned up at AMP's head offices in Peterborough, Cambridgeshire to confront Fraser with our findings. The KPMG team often joked as to whether a meeting with him had been "fuck squared" or "fuck cubed", depending on the number of times he'd used that expletive. This one was about to go off the profanity scale.

Among three or four other members of the steering group attending the meeting was AMP's compliance officer Andy Bomphrey – who I'd first met years ago when working at Allied Dunbar. He had liaised closely with us throughout the lengthy and complex case-checking exercise and fully concurred with our conclusions – which we had a contractual obligation to share with the FSA and the Board of AMP.

Fraser, whose muscular frame gave him the build of a rugby hooker, was late arriving and an atmosphere of electric nervousness built up in the room as Andy and I read through again the wording of the report I was about to present. When Fraser arrived and sat at the table we got straight to business. Well, it was a classic case of lighting the blue touchpaper and standing back. Before I'd even managed to deliver the full message he went off like an atom bomb, "effing and blinding" and raging like a wild man.

And then he roared at me: "Get out of this fucking room, now!"

This wasn't a man you'd choose to pick a fight with, especially not in this mood, and so I quickly gathered together my papers and scuttled out of the door. In the melee behind me I heard him shout to someone, "Get our fucking lawyers on the phone". There was no doubt in my mind that he wanted me fired from the job.

At that time the stress of work combined with marriage problems had led to me drinking huge amounts of alcohol, and on Boxing Day 2001 I'd left the family home to go and live in Fulham, London, at the temporarily vacated house of Maureen's aunt Gloria.

For a couple of weeks after the rumpus with Fraser, I continued working on the project in Peterborough. One evening at Gloria's, while I was slouched in a chair slugging from a bottle of whiskey and getting seriously drunk, the phone rang. It was a partner from Lovell White Durrant, the City law firm representing AMP. Quite brazenly, the partner asked me whether KPMG would be prepared to enter into an agreement not to write the report – as agreed with the FSA – setting out our issues. I simply replied: "You can do a cover-up if you like, but I won't be any part of it."

A few days later I was removed as the engagement partner on the job and replaced by a KPMG colleague called Fiona Fry. I'm since led to believe by others who worked on the project from then on that Fraser and AMP got their wish, one way or the other (although I don't have direct evidence to prove this).

So, this was the dark side of KPMG, the company I started working for on 13 February 1995, as a happy, suntanned man with a bunch of little kiddies to feed.

Initially, I was based in Dorset Rise, near Blackfriars Bridge and not far south of London's famous Fleet Street. They were fairly gloomy offices: rather shabby and run-down inside, except for the meeting rooms where we would put on a show for the clients who paid our huge fees.

It was in sharp contrast to the large, luxurious personal office I'd had at Acuma, kitted out in the rich American Express style with leather sofas, swanky furnishings and even my own executive assistant. At KPMG I started work in an open-plan office on a tiny desk, squashed next to a rather annoying company "lifer" who looked down his nose at this rather strange newcomer.

Motto's abounded at the accountancy firm. "KPMG – Turning Knowledge into Value" was one. "KPMG – Audits not Plaudits" and, my favourite, "KPMG – It's Time for Clarity". These mini manifestos were plastered on brochures, signs and all over the place. After I came to know KPMG better, I used to joke with lead partner in regulatory services Marcus Sephton that they should change one of them to "KPMG – It's Time for Claret". A good deal of that variety of wine was quaffed by the partners and managers at KPMG, and even more by Marcus and I, who were strong on the lunchtime client sales pitches. Everyone worked hard and played even harder, particularly in the wine bars and posh restaurants of central London.

The focus of my work was on the retail financial services market, mainly helping clients to organise their regulatory, risk management and corporate governance systems, and despite the slight air of dinginess around the place, I took to the world of professional services like a duck to water.

At that time the economic climate wasn't terribly good but demand for the services of KPMG and its ilk was very healthy, mainly due to the fact that the retail market was getting itself into all kinds of messes. Regulatory rules were being broken left, right and centre, and we were employed on some huge projects helping financial organisations to reorganise their compliance arrangements and cleaning up after various mis-selling and adviser training crises.

My colleagues at KPMG were among the brightest and most creative I had ever worked with and it was no wonder big businesses were queueing up for their advice. They really did turn knowledge into value. But the best thing about KPMG was working with Marcus, my boss.

Marcus D'Arcy Sephton was quintessentially English. Six-foot tall, slim, graceful and with prominent features, he always looked dapper in navy blue suits with the waist band set at the Simon Cowell level, which is the old English way of dressing. Marcus was also a true master of the English cultural humour which we call "the importance of NOT being earnest". The more serious matters became, the more Marcus and I would indulge in that style of sardonic humour that only the British know how to do so well – and which sends the Americans crazy. He really is one of the good guys out there.

Business was booming and I was soon bringing in some large fees. However, despite loving my new job it quickly became clear that I just didn't fit the standard KPMG mould. My approach was to be completely upfront with clients, even if it meant causing some upset and future loss of fees. In most instances it had the opposite effect and they welcomed the truth. Nonetheless my unorthodox style only served to arouse suspicion and irritation in certain quarters of KPMG.

It's true that, as a result of a no-holds-barred communication culture in my family upbringing, my interpersonal skills definitely needed some honing. My *bête noire* was an inbuilt emotional response to four tendencies I didn't like: incompetence, disingenuousness, dishonesty and unfairness. If I saw any of this stuff happening, I could get quite nasty, even though my intentions were always honourable. I suppose I'd describe my behaviour in situations like this as righteous indignation gone awry.

After one particular KPMG office *contretemps*, Marcus took me aside for a chat and persuaded me to take on a personal coach. He pointed me in the direction of an American called Steve Kaplan and it turned out to be an inspired recommendation.

Steve had studied politics and philosophy at Harvard. He was a very bright guy, short and stocky with a slightly hooked nose. He had darkish skin, a full head of hair and quite a round face. After doing sales at IBM he set up his own consulting business that quickly morphed into personal coaching.

I developed the highest regard for Steve who had a great business brain and extraordinary insight into the people and politics of organisations. He also had an extremely strong ethical streak and held me to account about my ethics and behaviours on many occasions. He became a friend, a true confidant and my closest "trusted adviser" when it came to the detail of work matters.

The work matter that caused me the most upset at KPMG – and was ultimately the reason behind me leaving – was the fact that the promise made by Marcus that "pounds meant prizes" never materialised in a way that seemed fair to me, or even to Marcus. In 1996 my pay was increased to £70,000 a year but I felt deserving of more considering the amount of work I was generating for the company. However, I didn't rock the boat and in the September pay round of 1997 it rose to £90,000 with a £20,000 bonus. Shortly after, I was made a director in the STARS business. This came with an annual salary of £110,000 plus a £100,000 bonus and it was beginning to look as though the KPMG rewards system was finally catching up with me.

It should have been too. We were making millions of pounds of profit working with big-name clients such as Clerical Medical, Britannic Assurance and Royal London. A notable example was in early 1997 when I was influential in winning KPMG's first work at Prudential, and what a story that turned out to be.

"The Man from the Pru" had become the trusted financial adviser for almost one-in-three UK households but the insurance giant wasn't quite so popular with the regulator. Its entire sales operation was coming under severe scrutiny, so KPMG was hired to help. Our subsequent review revealed that the entire sales force needed retraining and we were invited to give a presentation to the main Pru Board.

Prudential's Chief Executive Sir Peter Davis wanted us to present on three fronts: how did the Pru get into such a mess; was it doing the right things to get itself out of it; and how could it make sure the same crisis wasn't repeated again?

Marcus, as the KPMG partner on this particular job, asked me to prepare a first draft of the presentation to the Board. It was a daunting prospect. Potentially millions of pounds in future contracts hinged on this boardroom performance. For a while I just sat in my office staring at the computer screen desperately wondering where to start. So I asked myself a simple question: "How did they get in such a mess?"

The only word I could think of was "arrogance". The Prudential thought it was the biggest and the best and was incapable of doing anything wrong. So I typed ARROGANCE in the middle of my main presentation slide.

To limit the inevitable shock, I decided to add a question mark after the word and qualified it with two powerful bits of evidence. Prudential had been running an advertisement campaign showing a picture of a man snuffing out a candle with his fingers, under the slogan: "There's a certain confidence that comes with experience." This slide was to be the body blow. The knock-out punch was to be delivered with a comment made by Prudential Chairman Sir Martin Jacomb that I'd found in the previous year's annual report and accounts. He'd said: "We're particularly proud of our well-trained UK direct sales force."

The question was, would Marcus sanction the use of such provocative material? As the partner it would be him delivering the message: another Tom Fraser moment in the making. But, after studying my draft, Marcus turned to me and said: "Yes, let's do it." That's what I admired about Marcus, he always wanted to try and tell the truth.

On the day of the presentation, Marcus and I felt like a couple of naughty schoolboys sat outside the headmaster's office waiting to be called in. The meeting was being held at Prudential's imposing terracotta-built Holborn building in London, the insurer's traditional home since 1879. As Marcus went through the slides I could see the Board members shuffling uncomfortably in their chairs: Sir Martin Jacomb didn't know where to look when his statement was quoted and neither did anyone else in the room.

The deathly hush around the table at the end of the presentation said it all.

Sir Peter Davis rose to his feet and after a pause that seemed to last for minutes, said: "You are the very first consultants that I have ever met who are prepared to tell us the truth, as it is, notwithstanding the risk to you and your commercial interests." Phew!

As it happened the message suited Sir Peter. It came at just the right time to allow him to make the changes to his organisation that he wanted.

On the back of the presentation a multi-million-pound set of engagements with the Pru was to follow and Marcus and I became the company's trusted advisers.

Marcus actively encouraged my open, honest and unstuffy approach although he regularly had to provide air cover for me from continuing disapproving voices. True to his word, he set me on course to become a partner with KPMG, a position only achievable with the support of friends in high places, the ability to make large amounts of money for the firm and passing through the dreaded partner assessment centre.

By 1999 I had become a partner for regulatory services and was delighted to be rated as "outstanding" in my company performance appraisal. Yet when it came to remuneration something still wasn't quite right. My partner profit share was well below the average even though my performance was close to the very top. Simply put, compared to the other KPMG partners, I wasn't getting my fair share of the profits. The question was, why?

Marcus had the devastating answer: it was all down to "The Paul Moore Factor". I was taken aback. It felt as though I'd been branded with some sort of strange disease. Marcus explained that "the KPMG system" just didn't work for someone like me. My distinct "factor" created such an atmosphere among those making the reward decisions that it overrode my performance. While Marcus didn't agree with them, other partners described it as a "values failure": my style and pace wasn't the "norm" and therefore went against the principles of the company charter.

It all finally came to a head at the end of the summer of 2001. On the advice of Marcus, I wrote a detailed paper to head of assurance Ted Awty, spelling out my case. Awty was a KPMG bigwig. A short, rather funny looking chap, he looked and acted a bit like Del Boy from the hit British TV comedy *Only Fools and Horses*: unusual for an auditor. Awty was accountable for all the different assurance services that KPMG provided. This is an extract from the paper I sent to him on 17 September 2001.

"The problem

I am not exaggerating when I say how frustrated, sometimes angry and sometimes just demotivated, I have become since I joined KPMG In 1995 with how unfairly I feel the "KPMG System" of reward and recognition has militated against my skills, abilities and performance. I feel even more aggrieved when all the messages which seem to have been coming down from the top (and particularly in FS) are saying that it is precisely those skills, abilities and performances that the firm needs to grow at this time.

Although this is about the money (school fees for three, good holidays and a desire for ultimate freedom from work demand that), to me it is equally about values, fairness and the successful future of this firm. If, having read this memo which sets out my case in detail, you genuinely think my assessment of what fairness is, is wrong I promise to listen carefully to what you say and am prepared to be persuaded. However, if I make my case, I trust that you will sponsor a proper discussion around the issues I am raising or tell me that there is nothing you can do about it, so that at least I can understand that the expectations I have always had and been given should be changed.

I am convinced that the future growth of the firm is critically related to the recruitment, development, motivation and reward of people with my sort of skills, even though people like me will cause a high degree of discomfort to some establishmentarianists.

So why is it, then, that notwithstanding extraordinary business performance, I only feel I have been fairly rewarded in one of the years since I arrived at KPMG? And why is it that I feel marginalized because of my difference in approach?

In fact, can you imagine how I must have felt last year, when Marcus told me that I had had a sizeable portion of my bonus cut because of the 'The Paul Moore Factor'. Those were his very words. He might just as well have said.... "Paul, you are obviously not wanted here, I suggest you go and work somewhere else".

"The Paul Moore Factor" sounds like some strange disease, doesn't it? It certainly feels like that — but what it actually means is someone who is very different in style and pace from other KPMG partners, who 'sticks out' but who does everything that it takes to build businesses and generate significant profit.

Other partners, in their attempts to justify the position, describe the Paul Moore Factor as a "values failure".... but it's a factor which causes discomfort because it is "ab — norm — al".

Change is about taking on different norms. Does the leadership of the firm have the courage to implement

Darwin and recognize people like me, even though this will cause discomfort?

So, if the Paul Moore Factor is actually what is inherently required to build profitable businesses, I cannot for the life of me understand how it can really be fair to penalise that 'factor'. I certainly cannot understand how that can make business sense. However, if this factor is going to militate forever against me and people like me at KPMG, I really need to know.

I have discussed how I feel with Marcus and although he understands and supports the real substance of my position (minus values failures), he has told me that that whatever he believes is right, "the KPMG system" is such that it simply does not work for someone like me because my distinct "factor" creates such an atmosphere with those who make reward decisions that it over-rides my actual business performance.

In these unfortunate circumstances, we agreed that I would write an expose of my history and achievements since I joined KPMG so that you can understand my position in the round and we can discuss the whole situation and agree a way forward.

Let me say before going any further that I want to solve this situation at KPMG but I really do need a final hearing and explanation of what the future looks like, so that I can put the whole "thing" to bed once and for all."

In the document, I set out my performance over the

years. You can read the entire document here:

www.crashbankwallop.co.uk/library/3-1

I met Awty on Friday 28 September, two days before the beginning of KPMG's new financial year, to discuss the issue and I thought the meeting went well. After the weekend, on Monday 1 October I sent Awty an email confirming what we had agreed. You can read the entire email here: www.crashbankwallop.co.uk/library/3-2

The last line read:

> *"You said that if the FS [Financial Sector] process did not satisfy me, I should appeal through the normal process to you."*

How prophetic would that turn out to be?

Awty wrote back one hour later:

> *"I agree. I will send a note which I have dictated, but obviously I am not as efficient as you in getting it processed!!!"*

However, I now knew from my experience of KPMG that whatever Awty might have said may never come to pass, so I developed a plan B. I would start looking around for other jobs.

In that year, 2001, the Halifax and Bank of Scotland (BoS) merged and become HBOS. James Crosby was appointed Group CEO in preference to Peter Burt, who had been the CEO of Bank of Scotland. Lord Dennis Stevenson, formerly Chairman of the Halifax became Chairman of HBOS. Andy Hornby of the Halifax became CEO of the Retail Division, the largest division. George

Mitchell of BoS, became the CEO of the Corporate Division, which was the third-largest division. As the Halifax did no corporate banking but was just a giant retail financial service operation, the HBOS Corporate Division was effectively what had been the incredibly successful BoS Corporate Division.

HBOS was massive. In its annual accounts for the year ending 2001, it reported profits of £2.5 billion and had a balance sheet of assets worth £355 billion. Retail accounted for £1.2m of the profits, the Insurance and Investment Division (IID) £472m and Corporate £306m. The bank employed more than 60,000 staff in 2001.

HBOS needed a new Board director to lead IID and in September 2001 it recruited from Zurich UK my old friend and colleague from Allied Dunbar, Phil Hodkinson. He was the only newly appointed director of HBOS; the rest of the executive directors and divisional CEOs came from within the Halifax or BoS.

I pinged him an email and asked him point blank whether he was looking for a Head of Risk. He was and, as it happened, KPMG was the auditor and first-choice professional adviser to both the Halifax and Bank of Scotland. In fact, I'd already done a big product development job at pre-merger BoS's new bank assurance operation which helped towards KPMG winning the audit work.

As well as contacting Hodkinson, I also put in a phone call to another contact of mine, Richard Sowerbutts. He was a senior partner at one of the other big accountancy firms Deloitte, where he ran its London financial sector regulatory services department. Amusingly, when I first met him in the early Nineties, he had a manager called Jerry Neudegg (pronounced Nude Egg). A right pair, they were, Sowerbutts and Neudegg. Richard was immediately interested in me potentially joining Deloitte. So I now had two irons in the fire.

There was no way, however, that I was going to give up on KPMG. From day one of the new financial year, on 1 October, in the run-up to the final partner profit-share decision which took place just before Christmas, I gave it everything.

I'd already secured the substantial engagement with Tom Fraser's AMP outfit in Peterborough and had also started carrying out work for HBOS in relation to its earlier acquisition of the assets and operations of the world's oldest life assurer the Equitable. Following its highly publicised collapse in 2001, we were called in to check if its risk management systems complied with FSA requirements.

I was actually on my way to a meeting with the Equitable in Aylesbury, Buckinghamshire on 11 September, when the Twin Towers in New York were attacked and as soon as I got there we watched the horror unfold on the TV in the CEO's office. The dust clouds from the buildings and the spreading panic jumped out at us from the television. It was dreadful.

These reviews were great fun to do and always led to further engagements because we never found any client who we thought conducted matters perfectly.

I partnered these complex and high-fee generating

engagements with an incredible team of regulatory specialists that I had recruited to KPMG over the years. I also used the experience of an "Associate Academy", which I'd set up, of more than 100 outstanding self-employed consultants who could work with our internal employees. The *K* Learning Associate Academy, as we called it, was a secret weapon that allowed my team to staff much larger engagements than we previously could have done using only KPMG people: and without incurring fixed employee-related expenses too. In 2000, just one job at mutual insurer Royal London generated more than £13.5m in fees in 10 months. This had been done with only 10 KPMG employees and more than 120 members of the K Learning Associate Academy.

Business was rolling in but then, out of the blue, the big one suddenly arrived on the doorstep. Like one of the biggest Christmas presents of all time for KPMG.

Just before the end of October I got a call from Steven Anderson, the interim Chief Operating Officer of the Equitable. "Paul," he said, "I've got a problem; can you help me?"

Resolving the predicament was simple in one way but complex in others. The simplicity was that all we had to do was to gather key data from about 75,000 hard-copy policy documents and enter it into a computer database. The complexity was that we had to do it in just three months and we would need more than 100 people working on the job at any given time. Furthermore, the work could only be done in the Equitable offices in Aylesbury (about 50 miles north of London), between

4pm and 11pm each day. The accuracy of the work had to be perfect because it was in preparation for a formal legal vote on what was called "The Compromise Agreement", and our work would be formally audited and signed off.

Somehow we did it. We put more than 220 people through the project in 14 weeks. We billed The Equitable for in excess of £2.2m in fees and made a fair net profit of about £850,000.

With that in the bag, I now felt quite ready for my formal appraisal and hopefully the fair profit share that Ted Awty had promised me.

I met with Marcus in early November to discuss my general performance and results as they were panning out for the current financial year. He already had a copy of my paper to Awty and I also had some written feedback from Anderson on the Equitable job. Here is an extract:

> *"Paul has been exceptionally helpful, objective and constructive, beyond that normally seen, even at partner level. He has broad 'political' feel and is able to temper the keenness of his young team from time to time. He has been an effective 'bridge' between ELAS and HBOS. It is his impartiality and total objectivity that has resulted in one specific assignment for KPMG from ELAS and the prospect of further general work which is the subject of discussion between us at the moment.*
>
> *I hope he can 'stick around'!"*

Anderson also said great things about the rest of the team as well. You can read the entire email here:

www.crashbankwallop.co.uk/library/3-3

After our appraisal meeting, Marcus wrote it all up in an email, which he sent on 7 November to Awty, Richard Coates, the newly appointed head of the financial sector practice at KPMG, and his deputy Jeff Tasker.

You can read the entire email here:

www.crashbankwallop.co.uk/library/3-4

Here are some key extracts:

"Before addressing the year under appraisal, I want to record that you are one of the firm's truly outstanding performers and I can understand how you might feel that, in the past, we have not truly recognised and rewarded your contribution. I agree with Ted Awty that we need to have proper regard to your past performance when looking to the recommendations on bonus for this year and base pay for next year.

You have drive, energy and enthusiasm; your level of commerciality and 'nous' is rare, along with your innovative capacities; you have an unrivalled knowledge of the retail financial services industry; you are without doubt one of our very best relationship and business developers and you are fun to work with, as your team attests."

After listing some of my achievements at KPMG, Marcus continued:

"However, you have had difficulty in being recognised by the firm as such a high performer because you are

so different from most of our people and, in particular, people who have been around for some time with a pure audit background. This recognition needs to be given as we move into darwinian times: your performance, and the energy and atmosphere of creative dissonance that you create, deserves to be rewarded. If the firm wants to Darwinian behavior then it should pay people to act in a darwinian way - and it should make an example of those people who represent the future of the firm. Of course this recognition requirement applies to the other STARS partners too, as well as to other Young Turks across the firm particularly in high performing areas.

Strangely, although many people know you as a real values champion, there have been instances over the years of non-values behaviour which cannot be tolerated and this has taken place recently this year (see section on Norms and Values below). I have to say, though, that they have generally been caused by the upset which our failure to recognise you has caused and in this sense, and this sense, they are understandable."

Here's the "*norms and values*" section:

"Along with the extraordinary performance you behave in ways that are not the norm for KPMG. That is why your performance is extraordinary. We do have to guard - and it is my job in particular to guard - against the natural reaction of many people to confuse such behavior outside the norms with "non-values" behaviour. It is not, and indeed in a period of change many of your behaviours need to become the new norms. You have suffered over the years from this and that has not been fair."

Then he got down to the matter of rewards.

"In the absence of values issues which have occurred in the summer, I would have recommended a bonus level of '3' which I understood you and Ted discussed as equating to total pay for this year of some £325,000. I think it appropriate, and you agreed, that I should recommend a deduction of, say, £15,000 to reflect the values issues. I also want to ensure a full discussion around your base pay to reflect the historical performance for which I do not believe you have been appropriately rewarded, as discussed with Ted Awty and others, and to reflect that you, your skills and performances are exactly those which the Darwin project needs to reward.

Marcus - 11/01"

The fact is, the "values issue" to which Marcus was referring in his email happened because a couple of other partners acted without integrity – one tried to take credit for *K* Learning after I did the work to set it up, and another refused to give me credit for a huge project that I had sold and handed to her on a plate.

The big problem with KPMG was that each person and department and office would fight against others to "get the credit" for work and "the numbers" instead of working together as one team for the benefit of our clients. There were numerous occasions when, instead of KPMG putting the best person on the job for the client, it ended up being the person who found out about the job first and who was at a loose end. However, the one person who distanced himself from this behaviour was Marcus.

In the face of such a powerful and positive appraisal from Marcus, I was feeling confident. The average profit per partner was about £410,000 per annum, and I was asking for £350,000 pa.

Six weeks later and just a few days before Christmas I got a phone call from Marcus. I was still in Peterborough working my socks off on the AMP job but I knew immediately, just by the tone of Marcus' voice and the communication lag, that bad news was coming my way. There was an awkward silence before Marcus dropped the bombshell.

It was clear that he was just as upset as I was.

They had failed to come up with the goods that Awty had effectively promised.

Crash! Bang! Wallop! Adrenaline shot. Heart thump. Massive shock. Long pause. Gather thoughts.

They hadn't even had the decency to explain to me in advance as to why they'd gone back on their word. But then it dawned on me. KPMG wanted me to "fit in or fuck off" – the real motto that clients never saw. For now, they had effectively fired me. They'd put me in a position where either I had to accept the KPMG status quo, fight them or leave.

It was late in the day when Marcus had phoned and the normally hectic AMP offices were quiet. I found myself standing alone in a corridor and I just headed for the exit. Outside in the carpark, I rolled a cigarette, got into my car and just sat there, smoking. I realised that now I really needed one of those jobs at Deloitte or HBOS.

The bad news from Marcus coupled with all the other stresses at work and major marital problems, led to a very unhappy Christmas. I was drinking heavily to cover up the cracks in our marriage and everything came to a head on Boxing Day when Maureen and I had a huge row in front of our young children. It ended with me getting into the car and driving to the house in Fulham that belonged to Maureen's aunt Gloria – one of her mother's eight siblings. Gloria and her husband Peter had gone to Colombia for several months and were not due back until April, so I planned to stay there until I sorted out a more permanent place to live. At that point, Maureen and the children seemed, very sadly, to be glad to see the back of me.

I was totally crestfallen. I desperately missed Maureen and the children. I was in the middle of two huge and complex engagements with AMP and the Equitable and I felt like KPMG had just stabbed a dagger in my heart. I turned first to the only medication I knew, alcohol – and then sometimes, other substances – to drown the upsets that were swilling around my heart and soul. I drank and drank between Boxing Day and New Year – Chardonnay wine and whiskey were my poisons of choice but, actually, I would drink anything in times of crisis.

Messed up as I was, as 2002 got underway I began to pull myself together. I forced myself to clear my mind and decided on a two-pronged approach – continue with the interviews at HBOS and Deloitte and, at the same time, look into the rules of appealing my profit share at KPMG. After all, that was what Awty had suggested back in October.

For the "profit share appeal process" I gathered all the evidence I needed, including the formal partnership deeds that governed the way KPMG worked. There were four key documents which can be read in full here:

www.crashbankwallop.co.uk/library/3-5

www.crashbankwallop.co.uk/library/3-6

www.crashbankwallop.co.uk/library/3-7

www.crashbankwallop.co.uk/library/3-8

I was granted an extension of one month to the 14-day time limit for appeal. There was nothing to say how the profit share should be calculated but standard partnership law addresses that issue. Partners owe a duty to each other which is called "Uberrima Fides" or "Uberrimae Fidei". It means a duty of "utmost good faith". This was the principle that governed the way that the KPMG Remuneration Committee was supposed to act, when sharing out the spoils of each year. It seemed to me that KPMG was in clear breach of this principle.

I prepared an appeal submission based on my paper to Awty and Marcus' appraisal report. See:

www.crashbankwallop.co.uk/library/3-9

To support my case I also printed out the financial performance figures from the KPMG client system, both for 2000-2001, as well as for the new financial year from 1 October to February. That year I made a profit of £2,811,000 with the next closest partner, Fiona Fry, making £1,322,000.

The whole spreadsheet with the numbers for all the

partners in the financial sector practice is here:
www.crashbankwallop.co.uk/library/3-10

I also splashed out several thousand pounds on hiring a Queen's Counsel or QC – a top barrister – who specialised in UK partnership law. After reading the papers I'd prepared he said: "If the facts are as you have instructed me, I have never, in my entire professional career, seen a clearer case of unfair profit share and breach of "Uberrima Fides". If you decide to litigate, you will win."

Barristers never say that, it's too risky. I should know, I am one.

Towards the middle of February I scheduled a meeting with Jeff Tasker, who was now interim head of the KPMG financial sector, to discuss my appeal against the profit share. Marcus agreed to accompany me.

By this stage, I was getting to the end of the interview processes with Deloitte and HBOS. My final interview at Deloitte's was with the senior partner John Connolly. People called him JC for short and joked that the initials also worked for Jesus Christ. He definitely thought of himself as God-like, running the most profitable firm of accountants in the UK. I'd also finished my interviews at HBOS where I liked everyone I met and I began to think that I might very well end up there.

Marcus and I went to the meeting with Jeff Tasker feeling fairly upbeat. Tasker was standing in for Richard Coates who'd had a sudden heart attack. It was a shame because Coates, a partner with KPMG in Leeds, was a straight-talking northerner with whom I could have done business. Tasker, although a nice guy, was a bit of a "wet blanket" auditor type. He was stereotypical KPMG and would have found me threatening from 5,000 paces, let alone in the same room.

I opened proceedings: "Jeff, you know the background to this meeting but, in a nutshell, I need to tell you that I am seriously considering formally appealing my profit share under the provisions of the partnership deed."

There was a long pause before Tasker responded.

"Well, Paul," he began. "There aren't any partners... still...at KPMG who have appealed their profit share."

Silence.

Crash! Bang! Wallop!

I can't remember what happened next in the meeting but I know it ended shortly after. There was just no point trying to argue the toss after that thinly veiled threat.

I went home and got drunk.

The next day I rang Marcus and he finally put it on the line. "Paul, it's time to move on from KPMG."

Within a couple of weeks I'd received offers of a partnership with Deloitte and the role of Head of Risk for HBOS's Insurance and Investment Division. I was safe. Thank God.

However, there was still one major hurdle to get over: I had to pass medicals for both jobs but I was in a mess physically and emotionally. I noticed that I'd begun to suffer with terrible perspiration problems especially under my armpits – most embarrassing. So I decided to take a break from the grog and the other stuff for a couple of weeks while waiting for the medicals.

These medical check-ups by BUPA were "The Full Monty". There would be electrocardiograms while I rode a static bike, numerous blood tests and tests for breathing capacity and strength. The final joy for the over 40s was the digit "where the sun doesn't shine" to check for prostate cancer. Lovely!

Failure could result in the offer of employment being withdrawn and frankly I was a little bit concerned. So it was a huge surprise when I came through with more or less top marks. Even my liver tests seemed really good and my cholesterol was top of the pile. Which was splendid news because I could get back to the booze – and I did. It was time for a celebration and, as my work at KPMG had now come to an abrupt halt thanks to the Tom Fraser eruption, I was free to do what I liked.

My only concerns now were which job to accept and negotiating my way out of KPMG with the best pay-off. I just wasn't up for a legal battle.

Marcus swiftly helped me to agree a deal with KPMG. I would be paid up to the end of March and allocated a substantial profit share for that year.

As for HBOS or Deloitte, the choice was made easy. Deloitte wanted me to report to a guy called Mark Davies but after spending an evening out with him I knew that it would never work. I wanted to join HBOS, for several good reasons.

The merger between the Halifax and BoS was a brilliant strategic move by Peter Burt and James Crosby. Halifax had the largest retail franchise in England (and maybe the world) and BoS had one of the very best corporate banks, which had navigated itself through the credit cycles very skilfully. It was a marriage made in Heaven. It would bring the expertise of The Halifax to the retail market north and the prowess of BoS in the corporate lending market south. From the outside at least, their leadership team looked truly unbeatable.

Also, it was sometimes frustrating doing consulting work because I'd get to the point where I thought I could do some real good and then had to move on. Often the client regressed and I had to return later to sort out another fine mess, because they hadn't implemented my recommendations properly. HBOS was the perfect place to put everything into practice.

Most of all I was looking forward to working with Phil Hodkinson again but before I said yes to the job I had some important issues to discuss with him. This conversation took place at Hodkinson's impressive home in Holyport, just outside west London. I had visited his house before because we had stayed friends ever since our Allied Dunbar days.

I sat in his smart living room in an armchair and said: "Phil, I've decided I want to join HBOS and work with you in IID but I have three non-negotiables."

"Oh, what are they?" he said hesitantly.

"Firstly," I started, "this job is going to require a great deal of travelling and I'm not prepared to put myself to any travel pain. That means that if I want to hire a chauffeur to drive me in a comfortable car to and from my home in Berkshire to Old Broad Street or to Bristol, Aylesbury, Leeds or Halifax, I will. And it's always first class on trains and business class on planes."

"Oh Paul, that's no problem," he said, sounding relieved.

"Good. Secondly, I am not prepared to join unless I can change the pay scales in my department and use the same ones that exist in the professional services firms. This way I can recruit the best people and have fewer of them. In fact, I'll save you money doing this. But it may need some of your political capital to get through the HR department."

"Paul, that's no problem at all. I agree with you."

"I knew you would. Finally..."

I paused as I knew this one was going to be the most difficult to sell.

"I'm not going to start at HBOS until Monday 1 July."

He looked shocked. "Paul that's not good; I thought you were available and could start immediately."

"I'm sorry Phil, I'm completely stressed out and in a little bit of a mess personally. I need to sort myself out with an extended break of three-and-a-half months. It's far less time than you would normally have to wait for someone of my seniority and no one at HBOS is going to criticise you for having to wait that long for a new grade eight Head of Risk. Are they?"

He leant forward in his chair: "Paul, you're right. That's fine and it's better you get a good rest because there is going to be a lot to do."

"Good," I said and I got up and shook his hand.

We then relaxed and celebrated our deal with top-quality red wine, his favourite tipple – a bit like Marcus.

For the first time in months I felt truly happy. I'd got a great job to look forward to and as I would be based in Leeds, I hoped to persuade Maureen and the children to move north with me. It would be a fresh start for all of us. I could not bear another minute away from them and I now had three months of absolutely no work to put my life back in order. It was time to dry out, take some exercise and have fun.

CHAPTER 4

My First Year at HBOS and a New Force in Risk Management

I had been medicating my misery with copious amounts of alcohol. I wasn't a pretty sight. Living apart from Maureen and the children made me miserable and the huge stress of work and job interviews over the last six months had only fuelled my levels of drinking. Now, instead of just glugging vast quantities of my favourite tipple of Chardonnay, I'd speeded up the process of liquor-induced anaesthesia with whiskey and, sometimes, vodka. It was faster and more effective.

It was mid-March 2002 and in just over three months I'd be joining HBOS, the UK's fastest-growing bank: I had to sort myself out, quickly. First on the list of priorities was getting back together with Maureen. I still loved her and separation wasn't working. Although I didn't realise it then, most of the problems in our marriage were caused by me. I'd become detached and dictatorial but I knew we had to resolve our differences, if only for the children.

During the period we'd been apart our only contact had been shuffling Emily, Daniel and Oliver from one car to another so that I could spend some not-so-quality time with them. It had to stop.

I plucked up the courage to phone Maureen who had

stayed with the children at our modern six-bedroom, four-bathroom house in the leafy Surrey village of Windlesham, near to the famous Wentworth and Sunningdale golf courses. Windlesham was prime commuter and stockbroker belt. The house had a huge double garage where I not only kept my Magic 3 hang-glider but also the 1100cc Honda Pan European motorbike which I used to commute the fun, but risky, 37 miles to KPMG's offices at Canary Wharf. I loved avoiding the horrors of the crowds on the trains and Tube, and weaving my bike through the London traffic was a real and physical way to practise risk management.

It was a huge relief when Maureen agreed to meet me. I told her I would do anything to make it work and she agreed to give our marriage a second chance.

Just after we got back together I remember lying in bed with Maureen while she read to me a passage from St Paul's letter to the Ephesians, about the way husbands and wives and parents and children are supposed to behave towards one another. She then went on to quote from Selwyn Hughes' book *Marriage As God Intended* which stresses a husband's role in providing "loving leadership". It says: "Some husbands I know view leadership in the home in the same way that a drill sergeant surveys his men on the parade ground. He struts up and down in front of his family, barking orders and shouting, 'I'm head of this home'. That's not leadership – that's dictatorship."

This had an immediate effect on me. I realised that I may have been the leader but I hadn't been the "loving leader". I had wanted everything doing my way.

Maureen had always been a person of very strong Catholic faith ever since I had met and instantly fallen in love with her that Christmas Day in 1988. Almost the very first question her matriarchal mother, Leonor, asked me when I met her was whether I was a Catholic. I remember hesitating and answering, "Well, I suppose so."

I had been brought up a Catholic and educated at Ampleforth, the most famous private RC school in the UK. However by the time I was 17 in 1975, I had packed in what I saw as all that doctrinal 'nonsense'.

When I answered Leonor's question, I remembered the old adage, "Once a Catholic, always a Catholic". It served my interests well because I had decided to marry Maureen the evening of the day I had met her and there might have been an argument if I had said I wasn't.

After we were married and had become parents, Maureen and the children had always gone to Sunday Mass without me. I had no truck with any of that anymore. In my mind, it was for fools and all about fear and guilt. I didn't like the hypocrisy of it all. Jesus was about looking after the poor but I just looked at the wealth and power of the Vatican and it made no sense.

Maureen had booked to go to Chile in the Easter holidays, which were just about to start. She would be taking the children, who at that time went to Eagle House in Crowthorne, the preparatory school attached to the prestigious Wellington College in Berkshire. However Emily Jane (Mimi for short) had made us extremely proud by securing a September place at St

Mary's Ascot, considered to be the best Roman Catholic all-girls school in the country.

Because we had been separated, I'd not been included in the family holiday plans. So I asked my therapist, Bill Casey, to travel with me to Marbella in southern Spain for a week or so in early April to do some intensive person-centred therapy sessions. I really needed to sort myself out.

Steve Kaplan had introduced me to Bill in 1998. He thought I would find it useful to explore myself in a deeper way than he was able to, and try to understand how my psychological make-up affected my behaviours. I had never thought of "doing therapy" but once I got into it, I found it truly fascinating. In my very first session in Bill's comfortable sunlit flat in West Hampstead, London, he asked me two questions: "What do you want to achieve?" and "What do you think is wrong with you?" I answered: "I want to become a better husband and father," and to the second question, "I'm abnormal!" He said, "What do you mean by that?" and I answered, "I just feel different. I just don't feel like I fit in."

I spent more than four years having regular therapy sessions with Bill. He represented, without doubt, a cornerstone in my journey of personal and spiritual development and making sense of life and my part in the world. Sadly, he passed on only a few weeks before I started writing this book but his life force lives on in me.

In Spain, Bill really helped to sort me out. We stayed in a two-bedroom townhouse in La Heredia, a hillside development just up the road from the resort of Puerto

Banus. It hardly stopped raining and was the wettest April ever recorded on the Costa del Sol, but it was good for therapy and meditation, and I could feel the poisonous cortisol draining from my body.

After Bill left, I spent time with some Swedish friends, Lena and Joachim Zetterlund, who lived nearby. One morning during a howling gale and downpour, Joachim said that he was keen to go up a mountain behind Marbella to look at a new development, where building had just started, called The Sierra Blanca Country Club. So I went along with him. Standing on that mountainside under La Concha, a 4,000ft pinnacle of rock, with a splendid view of Marbella, the Mediterranean and Africa, I felt a sudden urge to have one of the new luxury villas.

I went to the sales office there and then, and met Asiz Farman, the Iranian sales guy. I asked him which site I should go for and he said that Plot 25 was the best. The total cost, including taxes would be 1.07m euros – about £625,000 at that time. He needed a 10,000 euro deposit to reserve it. I told him to hold it for me until I had spoken to my wife. I rang Maureen in Chile and pretty much browbeat her into saying "yes". I went back to Asiz, signed the reservation contract and transferred the money. It was a foolish, whirlwind decision based on emotion with absolutely no reflection and one that would later come to haunt me.

Maureen and the children returned from their "wonderful" almost month-long Chilean break to discover that I'd decided to go sailing for a couple of weeks with my great friends Stephen Joyce and Glynn Thompson. On reflection, perhaps not the best of moves when attempting to patch up a fragile marriage.

Stephen is a larger than life Irish character with five brothers and a sister. He could have drunk grog for Ireland. I'd sailed with him in 1994, when we journeyed across the Pacific from the Galapagos Islands to Tahiti in his Swan 42 sailing boat.

Glynn had been a pal of mine for even longer, since about 1980. I had shared a flat with him and Jo Parkinson – the son of Cyril Northcote Parkinson, the former Mensa Chairman. Glynn had introduced me to Stephen and we embarked on numerous raucous drinking evenings together over the years.

We all flew direct to Antigua where Antigua Race Week was going on. It brought huge numbers of interesting and wealthy people together to pit their racing yachts against each other. They would follow up a day's racing with party after party. We spent a few days in Antigua having fun in the sun before sailing to St Barts, one of the swankiest of the Caribbean islands, with wonderful white-sand beaches. We stayed there for a couple of days and then sailed the very short stretch to St Martin, where we were leaving the boat.

I was back home, suntanned and relaxed, by the third week of May just in time for Oliver's first Communion. He was very nearly eight. Given my feelings about Catholicism, I didn't really want to attend the ceremony being held at the very simple Church of St Francis of Assisi, next to St Mary's Ascot. In the end it all went quite well and I actually enjoyed the occasion.

The following weekend we travelled North for Ampleforth College's Exhibition Weekend. It's a lavish affair and the main parents' weekend of the year with speeches, exhibitions, tea parties, concerts and plays. We went because Maureen and I were seriously considering sending Daniel, 10, and Oliver to the prep school there, Gilling Castle. They would then go on to the main school, Ampleforth College, when they were 13. My father had gone there, as well as my brother and me. It was a family tradition but it was also a great school. We wanted to show the boys the school and Exhibition Weekend when it was the best time to see it, as well as offering a chance for me to meet up with some old chums.

It was a fine affair and I felt a warm, inner glow being back at my alma mater. We all went to the High Mass in the huge Abbey Church on the Sunday and I began to feel some kind of spiritual stirring in my soul. I loved singing the hymns, accompanied by the 700 or so older boys and parents. I like to think I have a decent voice and I sang loudly. I felt revitalised and happy to be coming back up North to work for HBOS.

But just before I started my new job at the bank on Monday 1 July, something extraordinary happened, which catalysed the biggest change in my life as well as the lives of those around me. It was a revelation, my "Road to Damascus" moment.

It was about 2.30am on Saturday 29 June. In the Catholic calendar, this was the feast of St Peter and Paul, my very own feast day.

One moment I was asleep in bed next to Maureen, the next I was suddenly wide awake. Crash! Bang! Wallop! Good God! What's happened? I elbowed Maureen with my right arm.

"Maureen, something incredible has just happened," I said.

Maureen, struggling to wake up, said, "What on earth are you talking about?"

"I just woke up and suddenly remembered all the words of the prayer of St Francis of Assisi. I've not heard or said it since I was 18. It was like being hit over the head by something."

"Well, tell them to me then," said Maureen.

I spoke the words of the complex prayer slowly and clearly and with a real sense of truth and love in my heart. I felt exhilarated, peaceful and joyful at the same time. This is how the prayer reads:

"Lord, make me an instrument of Your peace.

Where there is hatred, let me sow love; where there is injury, pardon; where there is discord, unity; where there is doubt, faith; where there is despair, hope; where there is darkness, light; where there is sadness, joy.

O, Divine Master, grant that I may not so much seek to be consoled as to console; to be understood as to understand; to be loved as to love;

For it is in giving that we receive; it is in pardoning that we are pardoned; it is in dying that we are born again to eternal life."

Less than two days later, I was picked up from our Windlesham home in a chauffeur-driven silver Mercedes S320, and taken to Heathrow Airport to catch a flight to Leeds Bradford Airport for my first day at HBOS. I would be Head of Risk for the Insurance and Investment Division, reporting to my old friend and professional colleague for so many years, Phil Hodkinson. I felt excited and ready.

During the short flight I found myself sat next to football manager Terry "El Tel" Venables. He had just taken over the helm at ailing Leeds United and I watched as he drew squad positions with a Biro on his breakfast napkin. It was 1 July 2002 and unknowingly we were both flying into heavy turbulence.

Banking On Success

My first year at HBOS was one of the best of my career.

I loved working with Phil Hodkinson – who understood my vision and strategy – and with almost everyone in the IID leadership team.

As well as Phil and various committees, I also reported to the current Head of Group Regulatory Risk, a good man called Arthur Selman. Arthur had been through the mill for many years at the Halifax and he was somewhat sceptical of the executives' competence, or desire, to act ethically in relation to regulatory requirements. Especially when ethics got in the way of sales. Of course, he turned out to be right.

IID was the life assurance, pensions, general insurance

and investment management arm of HBOS. It ran Halifax Life and Pensions, Halifax General Insurance, Clerical Medical and the Equitable Operations, which provided third-party administration to the defunct Equitable Society, and Insight Investment Management. IID also had majority shareholdings in the direct-only general insurer called "esure" (which also provided insurance products for Sainsbury's Bank), as well as the specialist wealth management business St. James's Place Capital – I sat on its Board as a non-executive director.

At that time, IID ran the third-largest life, pensions and investment group in the UK. Almost one-in-10 households were covered by its General Insurance arm. Insight Investment Management, by early 2003, managed assets of nearly £70bn. IID was a huge and complex business. In 2003 it made £887m pre-tax profit out of a total of £3.8bn. In 2004 that figure had risen to £1,067m out of £4.6bn.

The legal entity that owned all the businesses in IID was called HBOS Insurance and Investment Group Limited. I was a board director of this holding company and others in the group. My role made me a key member of the IID Executive Management Team.

Because of IID's sheer size good risk management, for which I was accountable, was critical to its success and this allowed me to put into practice in one huge business everything that I had learned over many years. Ironically, as an eager 43-year-old executive, I remember saying confidently to Maureen before I started at HBOS, "Well, Darling, this will be the last job we'll ever have to do. I should be able to retire completely by the time I'm about 53, or maybe even earlier."

My senior role within HBOS, one of the largest companies in the world, also brought perks of the job. As one of the top 30 or so executives in the bank, I was entitled to a new car and was looking at a Mercedes 320 S Class but in the end I kept the old one from my KPMG days. With my pay package we could have had almost any consumer luxury we wanted, but for Maureen and me it wasn't about buying "stuff" and beating the "Joneses". Money was for school fees, decent holidays and the earliest route to financial freedom possible. I have never really been a materialist even though, like everyone, I have succumbed to the temptations of greed and consumerism at times.

Having the chance to work with Phil Hodkinson made my job easier. I'd known him since 1984 at Allied Dunbar and we had got to know each other very well both professionally and socially. His wife Julia was and is an outstanding athlete.

Phil was about 5ft 9in with blond wavy hair and clean features. It would be fair to describe him as rather non-descript and, in a sense, that was what he wanted to be. He was the exact opposite of a trendsetter. He was the archetypal "ordinary man on the Clapham omnibus" – in a good way.

Phil was an actuary by profession – those are the people who deal in mathematical statistics in the insurance world. He was ultra-analytical and circumspect. His mind worked like a Rubik's Cube and you could almost see it "click, click, clicking" away.

He was also highly attuned politically, something I was not. I was primarily searching for truth and fairness. Phil was interested in the truth but also in playing a mental game of chess. He was a utilitarian – a pragmatist. He sought the greatest good for the greatest number of people and he was nicknamed "the Teflon Man". Nothing stuck on him – not even me.

He was essentially an ethical and moral person and always knew the difference between right and wrong. He was also very kind. But when power, position and his political reputation were in play, he would work out an argument that justified him doing what he did even when, in his heart and soul, he probably knew it was wrong. Yet I believe he would have made a much better CEO of HBOS than James Crosby.

We were a strange pair really but our differences in style and thought process complemented one another very well. We made a great team. We thought very similarly about all things business and, in particular, we agreed about how best to manage risk and regulatory affairs. So the relationship in that regard was a marriage made in Heaven.

Of course, in the end, when the chips were finally down for me, he must have decided that his own position at HBOS was the priority. Even though he described Crosby's decision to dismiss me as "unconscionable", he must have rationalised that by not resigning and by staying on the Board at HBOS, he would have been doing "the greatest good for the greatest number of people". But, even on that measure, he turned out to be wrong in the end. Had he supported me, who knows what might have happened? Maybe, HBOS would never have gone down?

I was based in the huge, austere-looking Halifax office complex in Lovell Park, Leeds. It was a lifeless building that had originally been the headquarters of the Leeds Permanent Building Society before it had been acquired by the Halifax. I occupied a large, dull office close to Phil's.

I inherited a team of 20 people who reported directly to me and more than 100 others from risk and compliance operations scattered throughout IID. Pretty much all of them seemed demoralised. I made it my first job to meet as many people as possible from IID and the rest of the HBOS Group to get a true feel for how the business worked.

The HBOS Group was split into operating divisions each with its own CEO and Executive Management Team and in 2004 employed about 70,000 staff.

IID was one division but there was also Retail, primarily comprised of the Halifax and the very much smaller retail arm of Bank of Scotland. Retail served all individual customers, as well as small and medium-sized businesses with their deposit and borrowing requirements. This also included the vast array of other financial products which the HBOS Group manufactured and sold, including life assurance, general insurance, pensions and investments. Its pre-tax profit in 2004 was £2,059m.

The Corporate and Treasury division made loans to

big business (and quite often took equity stakes) and organised the wholesale funding for the HBOS Group. Its 2004 reported pre-tax profit was £1,376m (of which Corporate made £1,114m and Treasury made £262m). The International division included HBOS's Australian bank, Bank West and Bank of Scotland (Ireland). Its pre-tax profit was £312m.

The total reported HBOS Group profit before tax and exceptional items for 2004 was £4.6 billion, up from £2.3 billion in 2001 – the year HBOS was formed from the merger of the flamboyant former building society Halifax and the stuffy but highly respected Bank of Scotland. Over the same period the HBOS share price out-performed every other major bank. As it transpired, much of that profit turned out to be illusory and was really a sleight of hand by the accountants.

Sitting above the divisions in the organisational hierarchy were so-called Group Functions such as Finance and Risk, and Internal Audit which, through various committees, were required to set Group-wide standards and policies (subject to formal approval by the Board) that the operating divisions followed. Then came the Group Management Board (GMB) run by Group CEO, James Crosby, and made up of the Divisional CEOs, plus most of the Heads of Group Functions. The Group Functions were also required to carry out oversight and make sure that each of the divisions had implemented and were complying with the Group-wide standards and policies. Above the GMB sat the formal HBOS Board ("the Board"), which approved the overall HBOS business strategy, signed off Group standards and policies and was accountable as the ultimate overseer of risk and regulatory compliance.

When it came to governance, the buck stopped with the Board. Making absolutely sure that the executive managed the business in a controlled way was probably its most important accountability.

The formal Board Control Manual reflected all this, by requiring there to be a majority of non-executive directors on the Board and its key governance sub-committees. This was supposed to mean that there was a proper separation and balance of power in the boardroom and that the non-executive directors could always outvote the executive directors, if necessary, to keep the business in line.

Board Chairman, Lord Dennis Stevenson, later described it as "the best board I ever sat on". Enough said.

Various policy-setting committees, which I regularly attended, met monthly and agreed what group-wide standards and policies were required. They then drafted them, approved them, and sent them via the Group Audit Committee for formal approval by the Board.

This overall risk management framework (invented by a partner at accountants KPMG) was called the "three lines of defence model" and continues to be adopted by most large corporates. In my view, it doesn't work but it is designed to protect businesses from potentially catastrophic decisions slipping through the net undetected.

The first line of defence lies with the operating division executives and risk management functions, the second with group risk functions and the third with Group Internal Audit.

The basic problem with this is that the staffing of Group Internal Audit does not generally include specialists in the various areas of risk management and compliance, but primarily people who are qualified in financial reporting and statutory audit. This is a fundamental Achilles' heel of the model along with the touchy subject of trying to ensure, where necessary, that specialist risk management professionals can challenge over-exuberant or delusional executives without fear of losing their jobs.

In addition to HBOS's internal systems were the very important roles that the statutory auditors and regulators performed in relation to governance and risk.

HBOS's auditor was KPMG. Its accountability was to make sure that the financial reports and accounts represented a "true and fair view" of the financial health of the company. To be able to do this KPMG needed to have a very close understanding of all of the affairs of HBOS, particularly the bank's financial and risk management systems and controls. The KPMG audit partner was called Guy Bainbridge who always attended the meetings of the Group Audit Committee and who had a large team of KPMG specialist accountants carrying out work throughout the entire organisation during most of the year. Whatever the very specific role of the statutory auditor is relating to signing off the accounts, having been a partner at KPMG myself and worked on statutory audits, it's fair to say that the audit team between them is party to all the knowledge and information that they need to have a much more general view of how well controlled a company is. KPMG knew what was going on at HBOS even if it was not its formal legal role to report on it.

HBOS's key regulator was the Financial Services Authority (FSA). The FSA (now split to become the Financial Conduct Authority and the Prudential Regulation Authority) had been created by Tony Blair's New Labour after his party's landslide general election victory in 1997, and it came into force after the passing of The Financial Services and Markets Act in 2000. The introduction of the FSA consolidated all of the regulation and the conduct of all financial services companies into one organisation, including banks, insurance companies, fund and investment managers and building societies.

Prudential regulation relates to the financial soundness and capital requirements of these authorised firms. Conduct regulation (as the name suggests) relates to the way they carry out their business on a day-to-day basis and how risk-taking is monitored. It also focuses very much on financial products and their development, marketing and sales, servicing and operations (especially IT systems).

It was the FSA's job to set the rules of the "game", assess the regulatory risks in HBOS and supervise its activities. Where necessary, it could instigate investigation, enforcement and disciplinary action for serious breaches of regulatory requirements.

The key Principles For Business which formed the generic backbone of what the FSA required, included integrity, due skill, care and diligence, adequate systems and control of risk management, acceptable financial resources, proper market conduct, treating customers fairly, clear and fair communications with customers, and acting openly and cooperatively with the FSA. All good common sense.

From the perspective of HBOS's shareholders and other stakeholders (basically customers, employees, suppliers and society as a whole), KPMG and the FSA were supposed to provide truly independent oversight and assurance to ensure that the business remained under control, so protecting its stakeholders.

A copy of the full Board Control Manual is available here: www.crashbankwallop.co.uk/library/4-1

On reading its contents one is left asking why and how the whole HBOS Board managed to avoid its accountability for what happened to HBOS and why no one, other than Peter Cummings, the former head of the bank's Corporate Division, was held to account either by the FSA, the Civil Courts or maybe even the Criminal Courts.

There was a lot to absorb, so I started organising my "meet and greet" schedule immediately after my first day in the job. I rang James Crosby's secretary and organised a meeting with my most important new "client". He cancelled me twice and sometime later, after

I'd finally managed to speak with Crosby during that cab ride across London, I asked Phil Hodkinson to get some feedback from him. He wrote this email to Phil in response:

> *I had a very good chat with Paul while you were away. My very first impressions are that he's just right for the job. He really seems to have a passion about our strategy and has a good understanding of how it works and how it has to work. In a way it made me realise how important that is for the regulatory risk professionals and how much it has been missing in the past....but it was just one meeting.*
>
> *James*

Within a week of arriving at HBOS, I also went down to see my new internal clients and Clerical Medical, based in my home city of Bristol. I remember it well because it set the tone for what I was trying to do when it came to my vision and strategy.

I was meeting one of the top executives at Clerical Medical, a very pleasant guy called John Spellman. As we talked I asked him a question that I often put to new executives with whom I worked: "What do you thing of the way risk is managed around here, and what's your biggest risk?" He replied without hesitation: "The biggest risk around here is drowning under the risk management process."

Spellman was right. His statement summed up the problem with how risk management was and often still is done. Instead of being a way to achieve real business excellence, it becomes an irritating, bureaucratic and expensive nightmare: a perfect example of, "the answer's 'no', now what's the question?" To make the point I often say, "Health and safety will shortly be the death of us all."

It was my goal to change all this but key to my success would be one or two vital new recruits. James Davies, from my team at KPMG, was my main target. I was determined to persuade him to join me for the ride.

I called him within a week and said, "How about it, James?" It was lucky I did, as he was already into the interview process for the job of Head of Risk and Compliance at Bradford & Bingley, a bank that had been a building society and which was now trying to compete with Halifax in mortgages and giving independent financial advice to retail clients.

I had secured with Phil a non-negotiable agreement on salaries for new recruits before I started at HBOS. James would be expensive and I guessed that he would need at least another £40,000 a year above the next highest-paid member of my staff.

Phil and I were both working in HBOS's Old Broad Street offices the day James came in for his interview. The building was as luxurious and grand as you would expect of a huge bank. It was right next to Tower 42, which had been the tallest building in the City of London under its original and still best-remembered name of the NatWest Tower.

The window out of the back of my office overlooked the newly constructed Gherkin building and I could see the workmen hanging over the side fixing the windows in place. Scary but not nearly as much fun, I thought, as being at 8,000ft thermalling on a hang-glider.

James was tallish, clean-cut, with brown tidy hair and was always dressed smartly. He was a devoted Chelsea football fan and loved all sports. A great guy.

I had recruited James into my team at KPMG from the Personal Investment Authority – a precursor regulator to the FSA. Jim Evans, also one of my team at KPMG (and more recently the interim remediation risk and compliance director at payday loans firm Wonga), had introduced us. When I had worked at KPMG with Jim, he had been appointed our team's Director of Fun! James, on the other hand, was somewhat more serious than Jim and outstanding from the word go. I remember training him up on a review of compliance arrangements we had carried out at William Mercer – an actuarial consultancy and wealth manager, which subsequently became part of the global professional services firm Marsh & McLennan. It only ever took one go to show James how to do something; after that he always did the job brilliantly. He had everything you needed in a risk management and compliance adviser. He understood the business; he built outstanding relationships with people of all types and style and, most important of all, he gave confident and understandable advice and assurance to his clients, which demonstrated creativity, technical excellence, judgement and integrity.

He is now the Global Head of Risk at private healthcare company BUPA, having spent several years after his time at HBOS as Head of Risk of HSBC bank's

Insurance and Investment Division. He told me that he loved working at BUPA because the culture was so much better than working in banks, and I can believe it.

I always liked to recruit people who had a different style to me but who shared the same values and, as I'd anticipated, Phil instantly connected with James. As soon as James had left the building Phil phoned me and said we should make him an offer immediately to avoid losing him to Bradford & Bingley. James was earning about £90,000 a year at KPMG and I reckoned that between £105,000 and £110,000 should secure his services. Phil replied: "Offer him £115,000."

I picked up the phone to ring James and caught him as he was still just outside the building. "James," I said, "The man from Del Monte says 'yes'. Phil has asked me to tell you straight away that he is very keen for you to join our team in IID. He told me to offer you £115,000. How does that sound?"

James said: "Yes, that's fine I'll join but subject to one condition. Only if I can recruit Mike Gardener." Mike was another key member of my team at KPMG, and was the safest pair of hands.

"Great idea," I said, "now when can you start?"

James joined just a few months later and what a relief it was to have him on board.

The first few months at HBOS passed in a whirlwind of getting to know people and learning how the organisation worked. My blueprint for risk management was not going to change, it was just a question of how best to implement it.

I did most of my best work sat in the back of a luxury Mercedes, driving me in an out of Old Broad Street from Surrey. It sometimes took two hours to get there but it was a quiet time when I could think, catch up with emails, make phone calls or draft important documents. I completed the first version of my communication document on vision and strategy for risk management in the back of one of these chauffeur-driven cars. I remember one day saying to the driver that risk management wasn't rocket science. It was all about "thinking things through thoroughly" and he replied, "Well, it all just sounds like the application of common sense to me." That really does sum it up. The more gobbledygook that you hear spoken around the subject, the less likely it is to be effective. The driver was spot on.

At the same time as all this was going on, HBOS's HR department appointed a relocation agent to look for a house for my family to rent for the year. She found one in less than a week: Beacon Banks on the top of a ridge in an ancient village called Husthwaite on the western edge of the North York Moors. It was a big, six-bedroom house with a large garden and its own tennis court. Set in the stunning Hambleton Hills, it had spectacular views on one side to York Minster. From it you could also see the famous Kilburn White Horse – a huge symbol cut into the limestone hillside of Sutton Bank – and the ruins of the Cistercian Monastery at Byland, next to the village of Wass where we were to end up living later.

Husthwaite was only a 15-minute drive from

Ampleforth Abbey and College. I knew my way around the area and where all the best pubs were. It was the perfect house to make a fresh start with the family and the ideal place to begin a new way of life.

Maureen flew the 250 miles North to see it. Like me, she loved the place, and we signed the lease for a year. We agreed that if she or the children didn't gel with country life, she could move back into the house in Surrey and I would commute. The family would move in after the end of the winter term, in mid-December.

Before then, in the third week of November 2002, I had a major event to organise.

As part of my "change management plan" I had invited Chairman Lord Dennis Stevenson to come and meet the IID team in Leeds, where we would outline to him our new approach. Bouncing off Crosby's clever strapline for HBOS, "A New Force in Banking", I had decided to call our presentation The HBOS Insurance and Investment Division – A New Force in Risk Management.

Stevenson, a respected City grandee, accepted my invitation along with a number of other senior HBOS figures. He was a wily-looking chap, wiry and bony with a long, hooked nose. As I got to know him more, I always found him to be unctuous, weasely and a bit slimy. I never really trusted him. He played the fiddle (violin) and, when it came to his role as Chairman of the bank, as will be seen, it turned out that he fiddled while HBOS burnt. He more recently gave a very good interview on Radio 4 about the effects of clinical depression from which he had suffered. Interestingly, the name of his main trading company is "Cloaca Maxima" which is Latin for the main sewage system in ancient Rome. Why he would use a name like this for a company is up for grabs but anyone who knows might like to tell me?

On his arrival in Leeds, I announced him to the team and then let them do their personal introductions.

The PowerPoint presentation that followed (www.crashbankwallop.co.uk/library/4-2) explained our objective to increase the value of the business to shareholders while remaining faithful to the needs of customers, colleagues, regulators, communities and families.

Through a series of colourful slides I stressed the vital importance of having the right mix of people and skills, the need for simplicity linked to clear accountability, and critically, a culture of openness and excellence where high standards of business conduct and ethics flourished. I emphasised that what couldn't be tolerated was an environment that engendered fear, blame and pride.

It turned out that hubris led to HBOS's Nemesis, its downfall.

Afterwards Stevenson came over to me, shook my hand and was very complimentary about the team and the presentation.

My team was now becoming re-moralised and the Chairman's praise further boosted motivation. It was developing a purpose, an *esprit de corps*, and we were beginning to have some real fun and to trust one another.

The response of Stevenson to our event only served to reinforce our confidence in the new ideology for risk management. We were happy and ready for lift-off. New Year, 2003, would soon be with us and results would be expected.

I also got "buy-in" from all my other key stakeholders around IID and in Group Regulatory Risk. In particular, I presented a detailed draft version of the action plan to the IID Executive Management Team, in late November 2002. The key players in that team, who all reported to Phil Hodkinson, were John Edwards who ran Clerical Medical, Howard Posner in charge of Halifax General Insurance, Dougie Ferrans the Insight Investment Management leader and Keith Abercrombie who was responsible for Halifax Financial Services.

The full version of the presentation and my notes can be found here:

www.crashbankwallop.co.uk/library/4-3

www.crashbankwallop.co.uk/library/4-4

It's an updated version from the one presented to Lord Dennis Stevenson.

The members of the IID team were all right behind the new manifesto and even expressed their excitement at the business-focused approach that I was proposing. I remember Howard Posner being particularly eager and saying that it, finally, looked like we were going to refocus risk management from being a bureaucratic nightmare into something of real business value.

Although in 2003 it was crucial that we should identify, assess and manage all existing material risks in IID, the most important consideration for that year in the division was to focus attention on our people and culture.

We just had to start with ourselves and make sure that the people in our own risk management and compliance department were, indeed, "*The right people with the right mixture of skills*". We needed to be sure that they knew what they had to do and how to do it. At the same time, we needed to make an informal start ourselves on "*Leading a culture of openness and excellence in which fear and blame and pride have no part*". We could only achieve this by becoming exemplars of the behaviours required to normalise such a culture ourselves.

Over many years of hands-on coal-face experience in numerous FTSE 100 and other large financial services companies which had suffered major risk management and regulatory failures (as well as in my research on other financial sector catastrophes), I had come to the firm conclusion that the root cause of most risk management failures often lay in the dangerous combination of the wrong culture and the wrong people. Both in the risk management function, as well as the executive.

Often the risk managers are "geeky", and in banks they are usually mathematicians or the like. Yes, maths is important but it's probably the easiest part of the risk management equation. The more difficult bits are anthropology (culture) and psychology (human behaviour) and, quite frankly, plain old common sense.

As for the executive, my practical experience was proving that the greatest risk to any organisation was senior executives with psychopathic/sociopathic attributes. Sadly, there seemed to be a lot of this sort about. When it comes to big business it's not the cream that rises to the surface but the exact opposite. There's no bigger risk than this in any organisation. The book *Snakes in Suits* explains the research in detail.

Of course, I couldn't do anything directly about the executive at this stage but I could do something about the 120 or so risk and compliance advisers around IID. So, with the help of my trusted external advisers, Dr Brian Metters and Gary Storer (both experts in organisational development who I engaged to work with me at KPMG to build ***K*** Learning), we set about transforming the entire competence framework, performance development and performance management systems for my team. Most importantly, we established the right training to embed the new structure and called it, The New Horizons Skills Development Programme.

At the heart of everything was the new leadership and competence framework aimed at enabling well-informed decision making. It explained what to do and how to do it around HBOS's core "DNA" which includes the requirement for employees to act with courage. The competence framework is detailed here:

www.crashbankwallop.co.uk/library/4-5
www.crashbankwallop.co.uk/library/4-6

The New Horizons programme lasted the entire year and a one-page description of it is here:

www.crashbankwallop.co.uk/library/4-7

It started with each delegate obtaining detailed

feedback from their colleagues on how well they put into practice the new behaviours required. This would give them a benchmark of their performance from which to start. We then convened a Springboard Skills Course, a three-day residential during which we taught everybody exactly what the framework meant, and we practised the relevant behaviours and activities in role-plays. We taught our risk professionals to understand their own personality style, and how to assess the personality styles of the executives who they would be advising on risk management. We did this by training them in the Myers Briggs psychometric model.

The programme also included an Action Based Learning Project, which enabled each team member to practise on the real projects on which they were working. Finally, each delegate was required to make a formal presentation to senior members of the IID executive management explaining what they had learned and how they had put it to use.

On a personal note, of all my endeavours in the professional field of risk management, I consider the development of the new competence framework and the New Horizons programme to be my finest hour.

Managing risk (which is what business is all about) is the output of the combined effort of the executive risk-taker and the professional risk-management adviser, working together. It is about excellence and thinking matters through thoroughly.

My boss Phil described New Horizons as "transformational". It significantly improved the morale and the performance of the team and, over a six-month period we started to become trusted advisers to the executive and to receive positive feedback. We really began to achieve that year and it was an exhilarating ride.

Along with this, I also set up a group called The Risk Management Development Forum to bring together all key stakeholders to enable the change management required to get the job done.

For the detail see:

www.crashbankwallop.co.uk/library/4-8

www.crashbankwallop.co.uk/library/4-9

www.crashbankwallop.co.uk/library/4-10

Another positive impact that Phil and I made was ditching the bank's cumbersome and bureaucratic Risk Register which often ran to tens of pages and replacing it with a one-page, at-a-glance Risk Map. It used directional arrows and green, amber and red colours to track all the division's risks and show whether they were getting better or worse. The simplicity of it became a hit at Executive Management meetings and the IID Risk Control Committee. Risk management has been made too complex, too bureaucratic and too "box-ticky" in the past. This one-pager was a highly symbolic move in our efforts to make it simpler and much more effective and alive.

See www.crashbankwallop.co.uk/library/4-11

A Risky Business

However, not everyone was convinced of the benefits of change.

In my job as Head of Risk for IID, I not only had accountability in relation to IID but also the HBOS Retail Division (i.e. the Halifax) that sold IID products such as life assurance, pensions, investment funds and general insurance including the infamous payment protection insurance (PPI). This cross-divisional accountability caused trouble from the word go, because the main areas of risk at the outset connected me directly to an executive called Jo Dawson, who was a real handful. She ran a part of Andy Hornby's Retail banking empire called Retail Regulated Sales, selling life assurance, pensions and investment funds to Halifax and Bank of Scotland Investment Services customers.

Dawson was recruited to HBOS by Crosby from roadside assistance and vehicle recovery provider Green Flag, and she had been a relatively junior manager in the NatWest bank prior to that. She had little experience of banking and financial services but was good at sales. The profitability of the types of products she sold was normally much higher than for standard banking products. For example, the money made from a Halifax customer investing in a Halifax Corporate Bond Fund (CBF) was probably twice that of leaving it on deposit with the bank and, as the bank now told itself that it had unlimited access to wholesale funds and did not need the deposits, it wanted to switch customers into corporate bonds. The problem was that this created a natural conduct risk of mis-selling CBFs.

Dawson was in her mid-30s, with a blonde bob of hair and "well-built", as the euphemism goes. She was clearly very bright, in a Machiavellian sort of way. She was manically ambitious too and would tread on, and destroy, anyone who got in her way. She very much represented the cultural dysfunctionality which I called the "not invented here syndrome". You wouldn't want to meet her in a dark, narrow alley at night. She lived in an emotional tone which can only be summed up as "spoiling for a fight".

If Dawson didn't come up with the idea, or if you suggested that she might be wrong, you would be in for a very rough ride. She had a particular habit of "blowing hot and cold" to make you feel off-balance, so that you were never quite sure where you stood or how she would respond on any particular day. Sometimes she was all sweetness and light, and other days she was nasty and aggressive. You always felt like you had to "tip-toe around the tulips" with her. Yes, she probably had a pretty healthy dose of psychopathic attribute for which, in the final analysis, one should feel a level of compassion. She could be charming and manipulative but she lacked in empathy and conscience. She could be cruel.

In a carefully worded report commissioned by HBOS the following year, when a decision on the appointment of Group Risk Director was being made, Egon Zehnder International (EZI), one of the world's top firms of headhunters, highlighted aspects of Dawson's character, saying:

> *"Jo's absolute drive to succeed can make her demanding to work for and her tendency to be somewhat inflexible and a bit abrasive at times can inhibit her ability to build deep relationships across businesses. She has something of a track record of confrontations within HBOS and is not a natural diplomat."*

Given that Dawson was obviously Crosby's preferred candidate, it is likely that they would have been careful to choose the softest words and manner to criticise her, so one can only imagine what they really thought of her.

One day in the middle of my first year at HBOS, I had a conversation with Phil about how difficult my team and I were finding it to build a meaningful working relationship with Dawson. I asked him for some advice and he replied by saying that she was one of the only people he had ever met with whom he'd not been able to get on. That was telling, because Phil got on with pretty much everyone.

One person that did see eye-to-eye with Dawson was James Crosby. She was his protégé; his little favourite and that made my department's job of dealing with her all the more delicate.

Dawson believed in and led exactly the opposite sort of culture to the one I espoused for effective risk management. Fear, blame and pride were at its heart but it did drive short-term sales, and that was what Crosby wanted. Not surprisingly, he thought she was brilliant.

So, despite all the positives of my first half-year at HBOS, there were still a lot of big risks flying around the place, especially in Retail which was growing like billy-o and outperforming its competitors by a substantial margin. The focus on sales, marketing and growth was relentless and I was instinctively concerned about the risks of mis-selling. In simple terms, the strategy appeared to be "stack 'em high, sell 'em cheap" or "growth at all costs" but, at that stage, I did not have all the evidence to prove this.

The sales approach dovetailed perfectly with the career background of Retail's CEO Andy Hornby. He had been one of "Archie's Babes" at Asda, where he had run the George brand of value clothing. During the 1990s and early 2000s the supermarket chain was led by businessman Archie Norman and became a kind of finishing school for young executives in the retailing industry, hence the babes tag.

I wasn't unduly concerned about the sale of general insurance products at that time, because they were not directly regulated by the FSA until 2005. However, I had noticed that in 2001 the sale of PPI (which has now turned into a huge scandal and cost Lloyds Banking Group more than £12bn in compensation) accounted for nearly 12% of HBOS Group-wide profits. This did worry me, especially after I was witness to Howard Posner – who ran the HBOS department that "manufactured" PPI – being browbeaten on the telephone by Crosby for failing to hit PPI sales targets on personal loans. If Crosby himself was that interested in PPI sales there must be a risk there, I thought. I determined that after I'd handled the other priorities on my list, I would have to look into this.

Dawson's Regulated Sales Force troubled me from the word go, as there had been plenty of mis-selling scandals in the past. My colleagues and I tried our best to work with her in a non-threatening way but she remained defensive and aggressive. I had every right to "kick her tyres" though. It was my job to check that she was managing risks adequately – and although I found that she wasn't, I was still there to help and advise. I wasn't the enemy but she couldn't see that.

Irrespective of the problems with Dawson and the Retail Division, we were making good progress on all fronts. I had a great relationship with Phil and most members of the IID Executive Management Team. The new approach had created a feel-good factor and we were gaining credibility with the IID Divisional Risk Control Committee, chaired by Tony Hobson, the former Group Finance Director of investment and insurance services firm Legal & General.

The biggest risk faced by IID at that time related to Clerical Medical's insurance funds which were being put under pressure by a rapidly fluctuating stock market. Basically, as the stock market went down it began to look as though the financial obligations that Clerical Medical had made to its policyholders might not be covered by the value of the stocks and shares held by the company. In simple terms, there was a risk that Clerical Medical might become insolvent.

The FTSE 100 Index of leading UK companies had declined from very nearly 7,000 points in 1999 to 5,217 at the end of 2001. It dipped to a low of 3,287 in March of 2003, a drop of more than 50% in value in less than three-and-a-half years. When I arrived at HBOS at the end of June 2002, the FTSE 100 was at 4,656. So between then and March 2003 it dropped by more than 1,350 points or nearly 30%.

This presented a major threat to profitability because then most insurance companies running so-called With Profits funds invested heavily in equities such as the shares of FTSE 100 companies. As the market went down so did individual investor bonuses and there was a real danger that the value of the fund might not be able to meet basic contractual guarantees. With Profits insurance companies, including Clerical Medical, were in a Catch 22 situation.

They could play safe and switch from equities into bonds and fixed interest investments, but the more they did, the more their sales of equities drove down share prices further which just exacerbated the dilemma. The FSA was for a large part to blame, after "crying wolf" about the potential solvency problems, thereby destabilising the markets. It was the FSA's primary statutory objective to "maintain market confidence", so this was a serious failure on its behalf.

The whole saga led to one of the most bizarre situations I had ever found myself in from a risk management perspective.

In early March 2003, a Board meeting had been scheduled for IID's holding company of which I was a director. Phil was now rotating meetings around IID's various business locations so that we could meet local management, and this gathering would be in Surrey at the Reigate offices of esure, the direct general insurer in which IID held a majority shareholding. esure was the brainchild of English entrepreneur Peter Wood, founder of insurer Direct Line which he'd sold to Royal Bank of Scotland. When Wood's non-competition agreement with RBS expired, he decided to do it all again and went to RBS's arch rival HBOS for the money to do it. Film director Michael Winner coined his controversial "Calm down, dear!" catchphrase in the subsequent esure TV advertising campaign, an off-the-cuff remark later quoted in Parliament by Prime Minister David Cameron, much to the anger of ministers. Personally, I found the ads nauseous but they were extremely effective for the market which esure served.

Inevitably top of the Reigate meeting agenda was the Clerical Medical situation. The basic proposal was to authorise HBOS's Insight Investment Management to sell £2 billion worth of equities in the Clerical Medical With Profits Fund, and reinvest the proceeds in lower-risk bonds and fixed-interest investments.

This is where, for me, it got personal. Over the previous few months, I'd been watching the stock market plunge and was considering the best strategy for the fund held in my own self-invested personal pension plan. I had exited equities and reinvested in fixed-interest assets when the FTSE 100 was at about 5,700, quite a number of years before the 7,000 apex. The FTSE 100 was now at 3,380, so before that day's meeting began – being a faithful HBOS employee – I issued instructions to transfer my entire fund into an equity high-income fund managed by Insight Investment Management.

At the meeting there was a long discussion on the equities sale proposal but it was clear that the general consensus would be to go with it. However, when it came round to my input, I challenged the other directors strongly as to whether, given the basic fundamentals of equity markets at the time, it was indeed the best risk management decision to sell the equities in the Clerical Medical Fund. I didn't mention my personal decision of that day but I was definitely putting my money where my mouth was.

In the normal course of business, it is almost always the case that the head of risk management is urging caution in the face of the over-exuberance and optimism of the executive. In this case, unusually and perversely, I was advising against following the rest of the market.

Risk management is not about avoiding risk but weighing up the balance between the risk and the opportunity. In my view, based on the analytics of the situation, there was a greater risk in selling equities than finding another way to mitigate the threat of continued falls in the market. A Board decision to sell equities would never be criticised later because everyone else was doing it: even if the markets rapidly turned around and policyholders lost out. This "group think", or more like "group agree", is the bane of truly effective risk management. It's the age-old story of the lemmings and the cliff and was at the heart of the root cause of the whole banking crisis. "Everyone's doing it, so it can't be that risky."

In the end, the Board decision was taken to sell the equities.

A few weeks later the FTSE 100 hit its low of 3,287, and from there rose 18% by the end of 2003. Maureen and I were laughing all the way to the bank, unlike the Clerical Medical With Profits policyholders.

Another significant event of my first year at HBOS relates to the development of a Group-wide ethics policy, something very close to my heart.

Phil, as a main Board director of HBOS and a member of the Group Management Board, took the lead on everything to do with corporate social responsibility, which included running the HBOS charitable foundation. He cared about this stuff deeply and did the job very well but I think it sometimes created a good bit of "push me, pull you", given his pragmatic nature.

Phil works on the Board of Business In The Community. Its President is Prince Charles and the charity is part of The Prince's Responsible Business Network. Its website proclaims the charity's members "*work together to tackle a wide range of issues that are essential to building a fairer society and a more sustainable future*". The Chairman of the Board is (at the time of writing) Antony Jenkins, the CEO of Barclays until he was sacked in July 2015. Although Jenkins is no doubt a good chap, given Barclays' past history of having a total lack of corporate social responsibility, he is hardly likely to inspire confidence in the general public on these matters.

In any event, Phil was asked by Crosby in mid-2003

to develop the ethics policy and he asked me to help him write a first draft. We decided to call the document, *"HBOS: our commitment to the way we do business"*. It would be short and easy to understand, devoid of the legalistic jargon that often makes this kind of corporate policy so difficult to implement.

We came up with a final draft towards the end of 2003 but the drawn-out committee process of gaining formal approval meant it missed the cut-off time to appear in the 2003 HBOS report and accounts. It made the 2004 edition, which came out after I had been fired.

In hindsight, from my point of view the most ironic paragraph came under the heading "Colleagues": *"We will create a safe working environment which encourages openness, honesty and mutual respect, and where colleagues can constructively challenge and ask questions."*

The statement covered HBOS's commitment to honest, fair and open dealings with its 2.5 million shareholders, 22 million customers, 64,000 staff, thousands of suppliers and society as a whole. In what clearly turned out to be a failed attempt to ensure HBOS practised what it preached, we added an important final paragraph: *"We will measure our progress against this commitment and report this regularly to shareholders, customers, colleagues and suppliers. Wherever possible, we will independently benchmark or verify that it continues to meet their expectations."*

Another act Phil and I undertook in IID, which was highly symbolic, related to the development of a new policy to manage the risks around fraudulent expense claims.

The standard system in almost all big companies then was more or less the same. The claimant completed and signed their expenses form, passed it to their boss for checking and then usually after a cursory glance, accounts authorised payment.

This approach was designed to manage the risk of fraudulent claims but in practice it didn't work. It operates on the basis that the claimant cannot be trusted but studies show that less than 1% of submissions are actually dishonest. As a result managers either waste valuable time wading through piles of applications or they push them through to accounts without hardly looking at them. The whole process simply plays into the hands of the deceitful few.

At HBOS my expenses were pretty large and complicated, so each week I would hand my receipts, categorised and in date order, to my secretary who used them to complete my monthly claim, which I'd quickly check and sign. Phil, who was probably busier than me, would take it as read that all was honest and accurate and, if he didn't see any glaring errors, would sign it off.

So at one of our regular one-to-one meetings, Phil and I decided to send out a loud cultural message that we trusted people. This fitted with our strategy of achieving "simplicity with clear accountability not bureaucratic complexity".

In future each employee would sign off their own expense claims, without having to go through their boss. Based on their job and anticipated expenses tab, individuals were placed in a standard "monetary band". If, in any month, they exceeded the upper limit of this band, an accounts clerk would go through their claim with a fine toothcomb. There were two further controls. Firstly, everyone was told that at least one of their expense claims, every year, would be checked thoroughly by accounts. Secondly, there would be random, detailed inspections over and above the minimum annual requirement.

This way staff were treated as competent and trustworthy rather than the opposite, and expensive managers were relieved of time-consuming clerical duties which could be carried out by experienced and competent clerks in the correct department, at a much lower cost. The tiny minority still intent on trying to fiddle the system would now probably think twice.

When the new policy was unveiled to IID, the effect was instant. Everybody understood it immediately. It was truly symbolic of what we were trying to achieve.

By using the simplest and most common of all the risk management systems, the one that applied to expense authorisation, we had put into practice everything that we told our division we cared about when it came to risk management.

It's often some of the commonest workplace practices that contribute to the biggest and most costly of disasters for organisations, while also putting workers at all levels under excessive stress. Expenses are one example but emails and social media are other classics and a clampdown on the proliferation and reliance on emailing was another area of "risk" I looked into while in IID. On one occasion I admonished Phil for sending out responses to emails before 5am, telling him that it gave off the wrong cultural signal. It suggested that his recipients were also expected to be working at this time in the morning. After that, he agreed to hold his emails in his outbox and press the send button at a more civilised hour of the day.

What this all boils down to is the crucial importance of having the right life-work balance, of which I'm a huge supporter, if not having always been a faithful practitioner. This isn't just because it's what makes life worth living but also because I believe that it improves the health (and, in particular, stress levels) of staff, as well as the culture of an organisation. It not only improves staff productivity but risk management. People who are physically and mentally healthy think matters through more carefully and exercise better judgement. Too much cortisol (the chemical produced by stress) does the opposite and is a symptom of what's referred to in business parlance as "management stretch".

The issue of management stretch even found its way onto our one-page risk chart. We assessed it was almost certainly occurring at HBOS and estimated it could be costing the bank up to £50 million a year. Personally, I rated the risk more highly than this but, just by having it on the graph, we began to raise the awareness to the executive and non-executive alike.

As an initial way of tackling the matter, I suggested conducting a formal life-work balance review of my own risk management staff. To do this, I brought in a firm of consultants called Let's Do Life that specialised in this unusual area of study, and it came up with some interesting results.

It was clear, given the stresses and strains of people's jobs, that the single most important change they said would help was the right to work flexibly and, within reason, from home with the relevant technology support, saving significant amounts of time wasted in commuting. Many people felt that if they could do their quiet written work at home, free of interruptions, it would be of better quality.

The whole report of the study is here:

www.crashbankwallop.co.uk/library/4-12

The "Smileometer" was another hare-brained idea I brought in as part of the initiative, which involved a very simple quarterly staff survey intended to check how happy everyone was in the department i.e. how much they were smiling. A copy of this survey is here:

www.crashbankwallop.co.uk/library/4-13

My first year at HBOS in IID was certainly a rollercoaster ride. It had been fulfilling and successful despite my being as busy as the proverbial one-legged man in a bottom-kicking competition. Yet, the workload was about to get even heavier. So much for my life-work balance.

In mid-2003 the FSA came in to carry out its formal regulatory risk assessments of the main HBOS operating divisions of Retail, IID, Corporate and Treasury along with other key areas, in particular, Group Finance and Risk. The regulator wanted to be sure that HBOS was managing its numerous risks effectively.

These inspections were called Arrow visits, which stood for Advance Risk Operating Framework, and were conducted to assess the risks that HBOS might pose to the FSA's four statutory objectives. Effectively these were maintaining market confidence, consumer protection, fighting financial crime and consumer education.

The visits follow a simple format. The FSA dispatches a small senior supervisory team into HBOS to review documentation, interview main staff, attend meetings and generally observe goings on around the bank. On conclusion, it issues a formal rating of the firm or the relevant part of it, on both a Likelihood and Impact scale of risk. Likelihood relates to the probability that the risk will "crystallise" i.e. actually happen, while Impact grades the potential consequences. Both scales are rated as High, Medium High, Medium Low or Low.

The FSA then drafts a letter to the Board with an accompanying Risk Mitigation Plan (RMP) which sets out what it expects the bank to do to reduce the risks as it sees them. This letter is signed off at the FSA by one of the senior executives.

This correspondence starts in draft form, including the RMP letter. Then discussions take place with the firm where disagreements can be aired, and after a number of months, a final version is agreed which forms the basis of the ongoing supervisory activity of the FSA in relation to the bank for the coming period – which can be a year or more depending on how extensive the RMP is.

It was clear from the beginning that the FSA wasn't at all happy and had considerable concerns about the increasing risk profile of HBOS. This was hardly surprising, as the bank was out-growing and out-performing its competitors by a hefty margin. Quite rightly, rapid growth over and above the normal market place pace always raised suspicion. The FSA was on the right track.

When the Arrow visits were finally completed the FSA's findings made for uncomfortable reading. It rated HBOS as a High Impact risk across the board, and a High or Medium High Likelihood risk in relation to all of its statutory objectives, bar Consumer Education (many commentators questioned why this last objective was in the Financial Services and Markets Act 2000 at all).

In the main letter which accompanied the risk ratings and the RMP, the FSA wrote:

> *"There has been evidence that development of the control function...has not kept pace with the increasingly sales driven operation......there is a risk that the balance of experience amongst senior management could lead to a culture which is overly sales focused and gives inadequate priority to risk issues."*

And, with a final attack, the FSA concluded that, in the assessment,

> *"...the risk posed by HBOS Group to the FSA's four regulatory objectives is higher than it was perceived..."*

This was a major blow and embarrassment to Crosby and his "New Force in Banking" strategy, which was being studiously implemented by Andy Hornby. It seriously threatened to stymie the rapid expansion game plan he had promised to investment analysts.

What I did not know (and didn't find out about until at least the middle of 2004) was that at the time the FSA had written to the Board, it had also orally required HBOS to increase by 1% what is termed its Individual Capital Requirement. This meant that HBOS had to set aside more money than the standard amount required, in case the FSA's fears became a reality. This matter was kept secret because had it been disclosed to the markets, it would definitely have had a significant impact on HBOS's share price and reputation for risk management. I should have been informed of this as it was a very important part of the context in which I needed to carry out my accountabilities.

In spite of the storm clouds gathering around HBOS, my contribution to IID appeared to have been well-received by all except Jo Dawson. Later, in my year-end appraisal, Phil's summary of my performance made the hard work all the more worthwhile. Phil wrote:

> *"Your vision for risk management within IID was clearly articulated 18 months ago and now through execution is producing solid results, leading to extremely good feedback from the IID Risk Control Committee and the IID Exec."*

He added:

> *"You have demonstrated your ability to turn strategy vision into tangible, measurable results in the past 12*

months within IID and Retail, and you have addressed all of the priorities set out in last year's assessment. Well done. In addition, you and your team have delivered a number of very substantive risk assessments within each of the IID businesses, in Retail and in SJPC [St. James's Place Capital].

"You have also adopted a more flexible personal approach ... listening more, talking less, reducing self-promotion, relaxing more and being less assertive ... and others have responded well.

"The investment you are making in your people and the wider IID risk management population is really paying off ... not only in their skills but also their motivation and energy levels."

(See www.crashbankwallop.co.uk/library/4-15)

I was particularly proud of the feedback we received at the end of the New Horizons programme, when each delegate presented to a panel of four senior executives from each of the IID main businesses. They discussed what they had learnt from the programme and how they had put it into practice in their action learning assignments.

Keith Lovett, Chief Operating Officer of Insight Investment Management, observed:

"What I have seen today has been evidence of a change of attitude and mind-set, the result of the gift of investment in me as a person. The learning is almost secondary to that and here the distance travelled is huge, everyone now has energy, drive and motivation.

> *You are now developing a risk-based approach to risk, focusing on the big things that will make a difference for the business, focusing on what will score goals. You have immersed yourselves in the business to gain that understanding so that you know your audience. The 360 was the key to all this and feedback is very powerful."*

(The rest of the feedback is here:
www.crashbankwallop.co.uk/library/4-14)

This internal feedback came in the wake of my final appraisal at KPMG which had read:

> *"You are truly one of KPMG's most outstanding performers. You have drive, energy and enthusiasm; your level of commerciality and 'nous' is rare, along with your innovative capacities; you have an unrivalled knowledge of the retail financial services industry; you are without doubt one of our very best relationship and business developers and you are fun to work with, as your team attests".*

So I felt that life was coming together nicely for me, at home and at work. It seemed from here on in it could only be onwards and upwards. There was no reason to think otherwise.

CHAPTER 5

The Final Countdown at HBOS – Speaking Truth to Power

In mid-September 2003, I received a phone call from Mike Ellis, HBOS's Chief Finance Officer. I knew him already from my work in IID and recognised his broad Yorkshire accent the moment he spoke. He was a cuddly looking, jolly-faced chap with a mop of white hair: privately I often thought he'd make a great Father Christmas, and it's fair to say that on this occasion he was indeed bearing gifts. Much later a very senior colleague of mine told me that he always thought of Ellis as, "a malevolent version of Giuseppe, the toymaker, in the Pinocchio story!"

HBOS was by then one of the fastest-growing large banks in the world and certainly outstripping its competitors in the UK. It was no secret that the bank was coming under serious scrutiny from the FSA for its gung-ho activities, and the young guns on the HBOS Board were keen to bring a swift end to the regulator's unwelcome attentions. It appeared I'd been selected to head off the FSA at the pass, so as to speak, and Ellis was ringing to offer me promotion to the high-profile job of Head of Group Regulatory Risk.

In any climate this role would have presented a huge challenge but HBOS was currently heading into the eye of a storm. It would be a big step up for me and the prospect produced an instant tingle of nerves and excitement at the same time. It was obvious that HBOS's trajectory was rather pacey and the culture in parts of the bank dysfunctional to say the least. There was little respect for the rules of play, including risk management and treating customers fairly – and the FSA clearly found it all very unsettling.

I didn't say yes to Ellis' offer, not then on the phone. I asked first for a meeting with him to set out my plan of action and get his approval for it. I needed to do some risk management before accepting the job.

Ellis agreed and suggested we meet for a chat and drink as soon as convenient at The Feathers pub in Helmsley, a tourist honeypot and the main market town for the North York Moors National Park. He had a house not far away in well-to-do Hovingham, an attractive village complete with stately home, Saxon church and ancient ford. We now lived in nearby Wass, an equally beautiful spot located next to the ruins of the Cistercian Monastery, Byland Abbey. Our young family loved it and we were soon nicknaming ourselves The North York Moores.

We still live in Wass, in a former gamekeeper's cottage surrounded by wooded hillsides and lush, rolling countryside. It always provided a haven from the cut-throat world of high finance.

The North York Moors National Park itself is truly stunning with deep glacial valleys, forests and rugged coastline. The actual Moors are the largest area of heather-clad moorland in the world. There's no better feeling than walking our Hungarian vizsla dog called Laszlo there especially in August, when the heather finally flowers, and the entire expanse is lit up with a rich deep-pink hue. Walking through the heather, pollen explodes in front of you like puffs of smoke and the grouse take fright and show off their high-speed, low-level flying skills.

I arrived at The Feathers for my meeting with Ellis filled with hope and enthusiasm as well as an appropriate degree of circumspection. It was late September 2003, a few weeks after our initial telephone conversation, but I remember the occasion as if it was yesterday. I knew the pub from the mid-1960s when I was at Gilling Castle. My parents often stayed at The Feathers when they came to visit my brother and me.

It was like stepping back in time as I walked inside and I half expected to see mum and dad standing at the old, wood-panelled bar. Instead I was met by the gentle hum of customer chatter and laughter and the homely whiff of roast dinner wafting through from the adjacent oak-beamed restaurant. I felt confident and relaxed.

Ellis greeted me with a firm handshake. He was the son of a miner-turned-steelworker and left school at 16 to go into local government, spending 20 years in finance roles in Sheffield, Wales and London. He joined Halifax Building Society in 1987 as Group Treasurer and for the next two decades held senior positions at key moments in the life of that venerable Yorkshire institution: the 1995 merger with the Leeds Permanent

Building Society, the 1997 conversion to Halifax plc and the 2001 merger with Bank of Scotland when he became CFO.

Bizarrely, having retired as CFO of HBOS at the end of 2004 just as I was fired, he returned to the job in the summer of 2007, the same year he was awarded an OBE for his contribution to financial services. Ellis was back in post when the proverbial hit the fan leading to the forced acquisition of HBOS in October 2008 by Lloyds Banking Group.

He's now the non-executive Chairman of the Skipton Building Society which has assets of £16 billion. However, unlike Crosby who surrendered his knighthood, Ellis appears to have hung on to his gong and his position as a person formally approved by the regulators to act as a chairman of an important financial institution. Why?

We ordered two frothy pints of John Smith's beer and exchanged the typical niceties about the weather etc before moving away from the bar to sit at a small table out of general earshot. I then told Ellis that sorting matters out at HBOS was going to be very difficult. What was urgently needed, I said, was more rigorous checking to ensure all areas of the bank were complying with FSA requirements. Improved communications with the regulator were vital, as well as gaining the full co-operation of the HBOS operating divisions in Group Risk's work.

This last point reflected what I already knew, that there was what I call "a cultural indisposition to challenge" in key parts of the bank. By that, I meant that people were not prepared to speak up when things were going wrong and in breach of the regulatory requirements for fear of upsetting people and, maybe, even losing their jobs. This was especially so in Retail which at the time was the largest and fastest-growing division, run by Andy Hornby and his Chief Operating Officer David Walkden, who had the marvellous and publicly celebrated nickname of "Whacker".

Bank executives such as Hornby and Whacker were supposed to follow the word of the FSA's rulebook – an extremely weighty tome – but they often strayed. Buried in all the jargon, there was one section that always stood out for me, The Principles for Business. This consisted of a simple list of common-sense statements relating to a firm's behaviour in such areas as business integrity, taking due skill, care and diligence, risk management systems, financial prudence, market conduct, relations with regulators and perhaps most importantly the fair treatment of customers. If the banks had followed them and the FSA had supervised and enforced them properly, the banking crisis would have been avoided.

They are easy to understand, even for those not involved directly in financial services.

We ordered another round of beers and then I explained to Ellis that however polite my new department and I were in carrying out our work, we were definitely going to piss off some senior people – so top-level backing was crucial. I'm a qualified UK barrister and an experienced forensic investigator –

someone once called me "a born-again Perry Mason" after TV's fictional criminal defence lawyer – and I knew we'd run into resistance once we got going.

As the ale continued to flow, I became increasingly confident that Ellis was taking on board my wishes and concerns. From a distance he had always seemed like a decent bloke but as I got to know and work with him more closely I realised how traditional and staid he was. He avoided conflict like the plague and was astute to bank politics. A control freak, Ellis bit his nails very short and often popped pills – I think they were to deal with indigestion.

Mostly, he was Crosby's man and CEOs get the numbers they want by appointing CFOs who do what they are told and keep the auditors under control. I suppose I never really stood a chance.

Towards the end of our meeting in Helmsley, I remember saying to Ellis that it was critical that at all times he provided his visible and vocal support to GRR's work and that he promised not to permit disgruntled executives to lobby him against us behind our backs. "Mike," I said, "if there is ever so much as a cigarette paper between you and me, we will fail."

In his thick Yorkshire twang, he replied: "Am reet be-ind ya."

I paused, smiled and replied, "In that case I'll take the job," and we shook hands on it.

It transpired that my trust was to be totally misplaced. I accepted a self-serving statement from Ellis, in a pub, without corroborating it. I hadn't managed the risk to my own personal circumstances, a common trait of those who speak truth to power. As one psychologist put it, whistleblowers have a kind of pathological desire for the truth.

In early October, not long after our session at The Feathers, Ellis formally announced me as the new Head of Group Regulatory Risk saying he was "delighted" to welcome me and my team on board. He went on to say something that was very important but did not happen:

> *"As part of the organisation review James Crosby has made it clear that he is keen to strengthen our hand in delivering against our responsibilities and we will be taking steps to clarify and reinforce the role of Group Finance and Risk over the coming months. Indeed, I'm confident that Group Finance and Risk will play an increasingly important role in the development of HBOS."*

The full announcement is here:
www.crashbankwallop.co.uk/library/5-1

As the new head of GRR, I was replacing Arthur Selman who had been the most senior regulatory risk and compliance executive at the Halifax and subsequently HBOS for many years. As well as reporting to him in IID, I'd worked with him on a major project when I was a partner at KPMG, after Halifax had purchased the operations of life assurer Equitable following its much-publicised insolvency, and I had a very high regard for him.

Selman knew what he was doing and did his very best to get the bank to do the same. The fact was that, during those early days of HBOS and The New Force

In Banking, however hard he tried, he was doomed to failure. Selman was approaching retirement, and as I took over he opted for a role in the Public Policy Unit, an area in which he had specialised.

I inherited in the region of 130 staff and had a budget of more than £8m but despite Selman's efforts my team was somewhat demoralised by its inability to get the executive to listen.

HBOS's Group Risk department was split into GRR, which I was now leading, and Group Financial and Operational Risk (GFOR) run by the highly intellectual and very "geeky" Dr Andrew Smith. Andrew was a big chap, 6'3", large hands and feet and a rather academic looking face with neat brown hair. He was always smartly dressed. Because he was such an intellectual, he might have come across to some people as somewhat aloof. I liked and respected him.

He had more qualifications than you could swing a cat at: a first-class MA from Cambridge in theoretical physics; a Cambridge doctorate in theoretical astrophysics; an MBA from The University of Warwick. Andrew had also tutored at Oxford in applied mathematics; he was a visiting research fellow at the Warwick Business School in financial derivatives, a qualified actuary and a fellow of the Institute of Actuaries. He had one of the biggest brains of anyone I ever met and truly was a "rocket scientist".

By coincidence, he had also been a partner at KPMG and I had known him vaguely there. He joined the Halifax in 1999 as the Chief Credit Officer and took up the role of Head of GFOR when Halifax and Bank of Scotland merged.

It was Andrew's job at HBOS to concentrate on the financial, mathematical and prudential side of the risk management equation and I needed to work closely with him for technical support.

Like myself, Andrew also expressed concerns to the HBOS executive and was ultimately turfed out of the organisation a little more than six months after I was, once again with a rigorous gagging clause. Andrew is now Angela, having undergone gender transformation after leaving HBOS. Perhaps one day she'll tell her own story. I admire the courage of someone who in their 50s finally accepts that they are actually a woman in a man's body and does something about it. It can't be easy.

As an FSA-appointed Approved Person, mine and GRR's accountabilities were complex and wide-ranging, covering eight operating divisions. I not only reported to Ellis but also the FSA, the operating divisions' CEOs and Risk Control Committees, the Group Audit Committee and the HBOS Board.

The Approved Persons Regime was at the heart of the new regulatory system and was implemented by the FSA in its rulebook.

Prior to this, although individual authorised firms could be subject to disciplinary and enforcement action, no individuals within the management of those firms could be directly held to account except under the criminal law.

Under the new set up, key executives, with specific

accountabilities deemed important for the proper working of the regulatory system, needed to be formally approved by the FSA before taking up their roles and were subject to strict rules. Each individual was personally bound by these rules in a contract entered into directly with the FSA. The most senior executives took on the most accountability. I was the approved person for control function (CF) 10 covering compliance oversight and CF11 which dealt with the reporting of money laundering. I also had a very important role in working with Dr Andrew Smith who was the approved person for CF14 risk assessment. In fact, I should also have been an approved person in this category. I had to bear in mind at all times that it didn't put me and my family at personal risk for failing in my duties. If it did, I could be banned from the industry and incur unlimited fines.

In spite of breaching most if not all of the principals stated in the rulebook, almost no one in a senior approved person role in any of the banks leading up to the financial crisis of 2008 has ever been held to account.

About 45 of my GRR people were dedicated to processing "suspicious reports" relating to potential money laundering and other financial crimes but the rest of the staff were dispersed throughout the UK. The largest group was in Edinburgh – Bank of Scotland's traditional home – but there were teams in Halifax and Leeds (primarily my staff from IID) plus a few 'roving' individuals including my right-hand man James Davies who worked from his home in Beaconsfield,

Buckinghamshire, and travelled around the country.

I also had management responsibility for hundreds of other bank regulatory people but the existing internal system for managing and communicating with them was dysfunctional, meaning most never knew exactly where overall authority lay. That could put them in a very awkward position in terms of whether to report to their local executive or GRR, and it had created an institutional conflict of interest that was pervasive in risk management throughout HBOS. This flawed organisational structure was very much at the heart of the control problems at HBOS and other major banks that adopted exactly the same structure. It needs to change. It must change.

Before I took any specific actions in my new job, I needed to get a high-level view of the lie of the land. So, I spent the first few weeks in my new role going around meeting everybody and seeking to understand the status quo. I had a good idea of what action was required but didn't want to pre-empt the opportunity for staff to give their input and to persuade me that my hypothesis was wrong.

On 5 November 2003 I wrote and formally introduced myself to the whole GRR team. While offering reassurance about the transitional period, I implored staff "to always think of change as an opportunity to move things forward in a positive way" and I explained that the leadership team would be meeting the next day to discuss the game plan. I also outlined my professional background and added some personal notes about family, hobbies and so on. I finished by inviting them all to join me in becoming A New Force In Regulatory Risk Management.

The whole announcement is here:

www.crashbankwallop.co.uk/library/5-2

The next month-and-a-half was a veritable tornado of activities and work. We had to get on top of all of the major regulatory risks that HBOS now faced following the FSA's Arrow visits, including an immediate investigation into mortgage endowment complaints and the number of cases the Halifax was rejecting for compensation. We also had to develop a draft business plan for GRR to present to the executive and the Group Audit Committee meeting that was scheduled for 9 December.

While keeping our heads just above water with the FSA, a detailed organisational review of the whole department was also urgently needed. With this in mind I wrote to the GRR team again, on 21 November, promoting an open-door environment for discussion of any issues.

I called my draft business plan for 2004-2005 "The regulatory environment – a key strategic challenge". I wrote:

> *"With our regulatory risk profile arguably as high as it has ever been, it is clear that managing our regulatory risks over the coming year (and maybe more) will be a major challenge.*
>
> *As Dennis Stevenson will say in his statement in the Annual Report and Accounts 2003: 'Regulation*

> *represents both society's consent to our activities and an opportunity to create advantage over our competitors'."*

I went on to warn about the significant financial impact on the Group's business plans of failure to meet the challenge.

Being new to the GRR job, I had to mind my "Ps and Qs" but what worried me most was the final subject matter on our list:

> *"The Plan recognises that the Group continues to drive through ambitious business growth targets with .... a determination to fulfil its promise to the market of hitting its target of 20% ROE [return on equity] by the end of 2004."*

If I had been writing purely in the vernacular, I might very well have written, "Our growth-at-all-costs business strategy and how we can achieve that without over-revving the engine". I would also have made it bullet point number one.

The full business plan can be read here:

www.crashbankwallop.co.uk/library/5-3

On 9 December, I attended my first Group Audit Committee meeting. I'd not yet taken over formally from Arthur Selman so he spoke first. He told the committee about the FSA's increased concerns over HBOS Group's activities generally, its approach to Corporate lending and the behaviours of key individuals in senior management. An additional committee meeting had been arranged for January to finalise a response to the FSA's concerns.

Selman then handed over to me and I presented the summary risk management plan for 2004-2005. The committee minutes recorded my warning, "that regulation is likely to become more difficult and increasingly onerous in terms of management focus". I also highlighted our drive for quality training and development of GRR staff, and the reorganisation review that was now underway. It all appeared to be well-received.

Here is what I reported to the committee:

www.crashbankwallop.co.uk/library/5-4

Just before Christmas I wrote a third communication to GRR, outlining the progress of the plan, summarising its priorities and announcing a major conference on 11 February 2004 for the whole department. This would involve an overnight stay with dinner and drinks at a hotel in the elegant spa town of Harrogate, North Yorkshire.

My communication can be read in full here:

www.crashbankwallop.co.uk/library/5-5

Thankfully, on 18 December, the day before I jetted off for my family Christmas holiday, we completed GRR's own detailed review of the mortgage endowment complaints handling project in the Retail Division that the FSA had expressed such deep misgivings about. The regulator was due to come in and do a more detailed probe in early January but we'd decided to pre-empt this by carrying out our own investigation. We did find problems but didn't believe that these had materially impacted on customers.

Here is a copy of the "talk book" we put together as our report on this review:

www.crashbankwallop.co.uk/library/5-6

It had been a hectic few months and I really needed a break from work, so it was with great relief that I boarded a plane at London Gatwick for two weeks in the sunshine of Dubai, in the United Arab Emirates. Maureen and I had developed a set schedule for holidays to ensure sufficient time off to manage the stress of my job and be together as a family. About a year in advance, we would book 2 ½ weeks off at Christmas, 2 ½ weeks at Easter and three weeks in the summer. In between, Maureen and I tried to take a long weekend together on our own without the children.

That year we were spending Christmas and New Year in the Middle East's playground of the rich, with a great friend of mine Glynn Thompson and his two children, Alice (I'm her Godfather) and Ben who are the same age as ours. I was familiar with Dubai having carried out some consultancy work there while at KPMG.

Our hotel was fantastic. It had a huge swimming pool complex and a 200m running track through beautifully landscaped gardens which I used every day to run 20 laps. It had three or four different restaurants and a great sauna complex. On New Year's Eve the hotel set out 2,000 candles throughout the communal areas and threw a lavish party.

One evening we took the children to dinner at the top of the Burj Al Arab, the iconic hotel designed to look like the sail of a yacht on the Persian Gulf. Colin

Montgomery, the famous golfer, was also dining there. Our eldest son Daniel, who was then 12, insisted on trying a dish that included caviar. He didn't like it but it made for much hilarity.

We had a couple of trips to the famous Wild Wadi waterpark at the Jumeirah Beach Hotel, making particular use of the steepest and fastest slide called the Jumeirah Scarer. On that particular slide, it was very important to keep your legs tightly crossed to avoid the involuntary enema that might occur if you didn't. We also went into the desert in four-wheel-drive cars, which was great fun and followed that up with an outdoor dinner at a Bedouin camp where we tried the shisha pipes and watched a display by a supposedly Arab belly dancer who actually turned out to be a rather good-looking Russian girl.

On Sunday 4 January, we flew back into Gatwick on a typically unpleasant British winter's day and drove the five hours back up North to our home in Yorkshire.

An Accident Waiting To Happen

Returning to a frenetic HBOS was a shock to the system. My promotion had become final on 1 January 2004 and on top of all my other duties, I now had to fill in my section of the Bluebook Report, a monthly information pack circulated to the main Board members and the bank's 40 top executives one rank below them. I worded it carefully.

The FSA's Arrow visits and resulting risk mitigation

plans along with its specific concerns regarding Corporate's credit handling of its commercial property lending were the main topics of discussion. I highlighted the bank's aggressive expansion plans, Retail's sales culture and *"different style of management"*, the size of the With Profits life businesses, pressures on management dealing with regulatory matters, and the continued need to convince the FSA that HBOS was effectively controlling its growth risks.

I wrote:

> *"Although we can agree with many of the detailed points the FSA makes, we do not agree that the points they make support a conclusion that HBOS' control environment has deteriorated or that the risk to the FSA's objectives have increased. In any event, as Mike Ellis commented in his paper to the Audit Committee: 'We will tackle the risk mitigation programme with gusto and determination to satisfy the Audit Committee, Board and FSA that risk management is firmly under control in HBOS'."*

I hoped that this short and clear summary for the top executives around HBOS would be enough to make sure they were under no illusion of how difficult the regulatory challenge to HBOS would be. Obviously, at that stage, although I had my serious suspicions as to what I was going to find, I did not have the full evidence, so I had to take my lead from Ellis when I said that we did not agree with the regulator's conclusions.

You can see my full report here
www.crashbankwallop.co.uk/library/5-7

It was around this time that Ellis wrote his now

infamous "accident waiting to happen" report to the Board of HBOS on 27 January 2004. In it he spelled out the bank's position in relation to the FSA's observation that *"the Group's strong growth had outpaced the ability to control risks"*.

See: www.crashbankwallop.co.uk/library/5-8

Years later Ellis would rue the day he used such strong expressions, as one ended up in the highly publicised title of a damning report by The Parliamentary Commission on Banking Standards into the near-collapse of HBOS. Published on 5 April 2013 it was called, "'An accident waiting to happen': The failure of HBOS."

It's also interesting to note Ellis' comments in his report to the same January Board meeting about the FSA's worries in relation to HBOS's "atypical" approach to credit risk management in the Corporate Division, which was run by "banker to the stars" Peter Cummings. The Parliamentary Commission on Banking Standards estimated that the "*... aggregate customer loan impairments on Corporate's division loans in the period 2008 to 2011 totalled some £25 billion, equivalent to 20% of the end of 2008 loan book, not counting further impairment and write-downs on equity and joint-venture investment.*"

In this regard, I think it is fair to say that this is probably the worst credit risk performance of any major bank in the world, ever. Someone told me later that if this situation had occurred in a Chinese bank in the 19th or early 20th century, the senior management would have been put to death by burning them on a funeral pyre.

The red flag being raised over Corporate's lending policies was disturbing enough but there was another potentially damaging issue bubbling away under the surface of Hornby's Retail division: the burgeoning sales of Halifax Corporate Bond Funds (CBFs).

CBFs became one of the "*causes celebres*" of my time at HBOS.

To put it simply, a bond is a loan or an "I owe you" (IOU). Investors who buy corporate bonds are lending money to the company issuing the bond, in this case the Halifax. In return the company makes a legal commitment to pay the investor back in full, with regular interest payments.

There were big financial incentives for HBOS in encouraging existing customers to switch from deposit accounts into CBFs, and as interest rates had gone down in the early noughties following the ".com, .gone" crash, it was even easier for providers of CBFs to sell them to yield-hungry investors.

I'd already identified this as a serious risk while in IID, and to be on the safe side had been trying to persuade Jo Dawson to let my team conduct our own review. Since the launch of the Halifax CBF in 2000, extremely high volumes of sales had been made by her specialist sales force. At its peak in early 2003, CBF sales accounted for around 70% of all new money being invested into the various HBOS funds. Approximately 116,000 CBF contracts were sold between January 2002 and October 2003. Precise management information was not available but the total number of CBF sales since 2000 exceeded 165,000 and the overall size of the fund by late 2003 was well in excess of £2 billion.

I wasn't the only one worried. In mid-2003 I'd been sent an ominous email on the subject from Dougie Ferrans. His Insight Investment Management was the part of IID responsible for managing Halifax's CBFs. He said he was very concerned on two fronts; firstly, the flood of investments into the funds was such that it was becoming impossible to find sufficient quality corporate bonds to match the risk profile of the fund; secondly, at a regular meeting with Dawson's sales team, he'd warned them that the yield on the fund was going down and that they should amend their marketing materials accordingly – but they had refused to do so.

Dawson repeatedly maintained that she and her regulatory specialists had the matter under control but she was finally backed into a corner by a timely and fortuitous FSA intervention. As well as flagging up concerns in its Arrow visits, the regulator announced a separate industry wide "themed review" of CBF sales generally, and as Halifax easily topped the league for selling this type of product, the FSA decided to put HBOS under its spotlight first. Much to her chagrin, Dawson now had no choice but to submit to a GRR review.

We kicked off this detailed process in late November 2003 and in no time it was causing serious argy-bargy with Dawson and her minions. Exactly what I'd warned Ellis about in The Feathers started to happen. Executives, subjected to scrutiny, bypassed me and my team and approached Ellis directly trying to get him to change my approach. It was going to be a hard slog.

As my Dubai holiday quickly became a distant memory, all attentions at work turned to the reorganisation along with preparations for the 11 February conference in Harrogate.

We finally got agreement to the necessary GRR restructuring at the end of January. What had been most satisfying for me was the broad range of senior management involved in the review's decision-making process including Ellis, who had spent many hours listening to input from people. I could now get on with sending out a GRR-wide communication detailing the new organisational structure and how it would fit in with our responsibilities.

It can be seen in its entirety here:

www.crashbankwallop.co.uk/library/5-9

The following week we all gathered on the Tuesday night at the hotel in Harrogate for dinner and an opportunity to get to know one another. About 100 of the Department came to the event. I can't recall the name of the hotel but it was a rather dingy place close to the town's conference centre, looking a bit tired and worn out after all those conference delegates had stayed there. The food was ordinary but we all stayed up late drinking and chatting.

The next morning we got down to business with Ellis kicking off the conference followed by me, delivering a broad-ranging presentation on vision, strategy, structure, people and culture as well as key priorities and plans. I followed almost exactly the same approach as I had in IID. There was one particularly powerful quote I used, which had been penned by the legendary marketing man Joseph Sugarman:

> *"Each problem has hidden within it an opportunity so powerful that it literally dwarfs the problem. The greatest success stories were created by people who recognised a problem and turned it into an opportunity."*

Never in my entire professional life had I been involved in such a complex, demanding and high-risk remedial project but once the conference was over and the message delivered, at least we could get moving on all fronts.

My slide presentation can be seen here:

www.crashbankwallop.co.uk/library/5-10

My stress levels were by now running high and there was the added pressure of having to prepare a major progress report for the next Group Audit Committee meeting on 9 March. The report had to be with the company secretary for distribution by 1 March, so I had very little time to do all the work required to make my first report effective. Pumped full of adrenaline, cortisol and, in the evenings, a plentiful dose of good-quality wine and sometimes whiskey (Jameson was my preferred brand, the version I was introduced to by my drinking mate, Stephen Joyce), I managed to meet the deadline. My report didn't make for comfortable reading although it repeated many of the things that I had already said.

The entire report is here:

www.crashbankwallop.co.uk/library/5-11

All the extra work generated for GRR as a result of the Arrow visits meant I was finding it difficult to switch off even at home. Most evenings I'd just flop onto the settee, drink alcohol and fall asleep. It was all work and no play and I was neglecting Maureen and the children, not because I wanted to but because I didn't have any time. I wasn't the best of company. Someone said to me once that you spell love, T I M E. On that basis, all my love was focused on work.

By the time the Group Audit Committee meeting came around we had completed most of our evidence-gathering fieldwork on the CBFs review, with some alarming results.

Part of the survey had involved ringing customers to ask them how they'd ended up putting money into CBFs and to establish whether or not they understood the risks and differences between investing in a deposit account and a CBF. The initial feedback was so worrying (23% of those questioned were not aware there were any capital risks attached to CBFs), that I decided to test the water myself by attending a sales advisory meeting in one of the local Halifax branches. It was a real eye-opener.

The customers at the advice session I sat in on were an elderly married couple and although the financial adviser did an excellent job trying to explain CBFs, I was completely convinced that the husband and wife never really grasped the potential to make losses on their quite substantial investment.

Meanwhile, due to difficulties getting agreement with Dawson and her team, I wasn't able to finalise my report on CBF sales in time for the Group Audit meeting, but James Davies and I had met with Hornby to give him a brief "heads up" on our preliminary findings. The whole situation posed potentially serious repercussions for the bank. The regulatory rules insisted that all sales of financial products must be "suitable" (and documented as such) for the individual needs of each customer.

When I came to addressing the meeting, I warned committee members that failure to give appropriate advice about CBFs could leave HBOS wide open to big compensation claims if investors lost money. In addition, I explained that if Retail's risk controls were found to be flawed, the bank could be forced to go through the extremely expensive exercise of checking all of its 165,000-plus CBF sales for suitability.

In my oral update, I said that in conducting our review, we had identified potential issues relating to the overall design of the systems and controls for ensuring compliance with the regulatory "suitability" requirements for the sale of CBFs.

Understandably, the committee expressed some concern at my comments. However I said that more detailed corroboration was required and I'd report back at the next meeting, once the final report had been completed.

The formal minute relating to my oral update read as follows:

> *"Paul Moore advised that GRR was close to completing a review of Corporate Bond Funds (CBF) sales within Retail. This was an important piece of work, given the substantial sales volumes of CBF in 2003 and the focus that the FSA was currently giving to products of this type. Of particular importance was the degree to which customers understand the risk of the product. There is evidence to suggest that some customers may not fully understand the risks and this could expose HBOS should there be unfavourable market conditions."*

Ellis had gone on holiday straight after the GRR Harrogate conference, so to fill him in on developments I sent him an email on Sunday 21 March, the day before he returned to work. There was a real hullabaloo building up in Retail that Ellis needed to be updated on. From the very start of the Arrow visits, the golden boys and girls of HBOS had taken the FSA's criticisms personally and Hornby and his Head of Risk Whacker Walkden had already been giving Ellis and the FSA a hard time. They argued that the FSA's risk assessment was all based on unsubstantiated perceptions and bore no resemblance to the reality on the ground, where as far as they were concerned everything was hunky-dory.

However, it was becoming clear to my team that this was not the case and that the FSA had been accurate in its appraisal.

The deadlock with Retail was reaching the point where Ellis was going to have to start playing hard ball but he went back a long way with many of his colleagues in the division. Pre-merger, most of them had worked together at the Halifax and Ellis had been inclined to side with their position. Ellis was also particularly friendly with Whacker, so I needed to put him on notice, as quickly as possible, that he may soon have to deliver some bad news to his mates. This was going to be a challenge and was the main reason for my emailing him.

In it I wrote:

> *"The facts are pretty clear that the FSA did have some reason to have the concerns they expressed in the Arrow Letter about growth potentially outrunning controls. We are working cheek by jowl with Andy [Hornby] and David Walkden but the fact that they went in so hard against the FSA at the beginning is now making their position more difficult."*

The hot topic of CBFs was already making headlines in the Press and I reminded Ellis of the FSA's imminent themed visit. I said it was very important to get his input on CBFs and other issues in Retail.

> *"Eg, on the day of the launch of the Fund [Halifax CBF] the extra income provided by a £10,000 investment into CBF in comparison to the Guaranteed Reserve Account [deposit account] in return for the extra risk was 50p per week....do you consider that recommending someone to switch – irrespective of the strength of the disclosure – would be suitable / fair for that marginal benefit....this same scenario happened at other times throughout the sales history....and with interest rates on the way up there are increased risks that customers won't get their capital back?*

Also Retail Reg Risk Management set no limits on how much of a person's savings could be switched so customers were recommended to switch very substantial percentages of their savings."

I explained to Ellis that we needed to talk urgently as we were due to brief Dawson later that week on GRR's findings.

Read the whole email here:

www.crashbankwallop.co.uk/library/5-12

On Thursday 25 March, from GRR's point of view, something very serendipitous happened. Dawson received a telephone call from Julie McFaul, one of the senior supervisors of HBOS at the FSA, to say a supervisory team would be coming in between 13 and 15 April to carry out its themed review of CBF sales. Naturally, this heightened the tension even further and increased the fightback from Dawson's camp just as we were trying to finalise the report of our own review into her department's selling tactics.

A first draft of the CBFs report was discussed in detail with members of Dawson's team at a heated get-together during the week of 22 March and some of the behaviour at that meeting was reportedly not good.

The same week James Davies (who was now one of two deputy heads of GRR alongside Tony Brian), Andy Sheppard (the specialist regulatory adviser carrying out the detailed work) and I had a difficult conference call with Ellis to discuss the issues associated with switching customers from deposit accounts into CBFs. I remember saying to James and Andy afterwards:

"Gosh, he just doesn't get it, does he?"

At least in a few days I'd be able to leave behind the pressure-cooker environment of HBOS and jet off on a family holiday to Chile. The reprieve would do me good but there would be much to do on my return in two-and-a-half weeks.

In response to the Arrow visits each division was working hard to agree Risk Mitigation Plans with the FSA, and the HBOS Board had agreed to carry out some key pieces of work.

As well as the review of selling practices relating to CBFs, there would also be a probe into the balance between sales and controls within Retail. At first the FSA had considered bringing in an independent expert (for what is technically termed a section 166 "Skilled Persons Review") to deal with this but after discussions with my team and I it was agreed GRR could do the work under my leadership. This project, which was huge, was run under the banner of the Sales Culture and Controls Review.

Dr Andrew Smith's GFOR department would review not only the approach to handling the problems of solvency and fairness in Clerical Medical's With Profits funds, but also the degree of independent challenge in Corporate banking's credit approvals.

Finally there would be an independent inquiry into risk management effectiveness throughout the HBOS Group as a whole, to be carried out by "Big Four" auditor PricewaterhouseCoopers (PwC) as a section 166.

With any projects like this, detailed terms of reference

– in other words the scope and limitations of the work to be carried out – had to be agreed before proceedings could start, so these were drawn up over the first few months of 2004 in numerous discussions with the FSA.

Immediately after the Lent term finished on 25 March at Gilling Castle, where Daniel and Oliver went to school, we left to go on holiday to Santiago, Chile, where we would be staying with Maureen's family. We drove with the excited boys to pick up their sister Emily from school at St Mary's Ascot and the next day flew via São Paulo in Brazil to Santiago, a flight which takes in total about 17 hours.

All of Maureen's family lived in Chile, so visits there were numerous. As of today, the total family complement over there of mother-in-law, brothers and sisters-in-law, nephews and nieces and great nephews and nieces, is 31. Maureen is one of five siblings (in order of age in 2015); Philip 59 (a banker), Catherine 57 (an ex-British Embassy consul), Graham 55 (an experienced finance director) and Anna Claudia 50 (working at the British Embassy and ex- British Council). Maureen who is 47 is the youngest. Her mother, Leonor, who is in her 80s met her husband, Peter Oats when he was running the branch of Bank of London and South America in Cali, Colombia in the mid-Fifties.

Peter, who passed on a few years ago, was the grandson of the famous tin miner, Francis Oats from Cornwall, who became the President of the De Beers mining company. Peter joined the Indian Army after going to school at Clifton College in Bristol and saw plenty of action in the Second World War, particularly in Greece which had been invaded by Nazi Germany. When he was demobbed, he joined the famous Bank of London and South America where he spent the rest of his working life.

Maureen was born in São Paulo when her father was the personnel director (then called "staff manager") for the whole of the bank in South America. After Brazil, he ran the big branch of the bank in Nassau in the Bahamas at the time that Bank of London and South America was taken over by Lloyds Bank. His last job was in Santiago where he had organised the first $100 million syndicated loan to the copper mining industry. The family loved Chile and so he retired there.

So far as his banking experience was concerned, he told me one day that when it came to credit risk management, he always spent a great deal more time focusing on the reputation and honesty of his clients than he ever did on the mathematical models and business plans. What a shame that HBOS didn't do that.

Peter was one of the most charming and wonderful people I've ever met. He personified honesty, kindness, impeccable manners and hard work. After he retired, he ran the British Legion in Chile, where there were many old soldiers, and was awarded an MBE for his services. He always said that MBE's were awarded for "My Bloody Efforts" and OBE's for "Other people's Bloody Efforts"!

Leonor, his wife and my mother-in-law, likewise, is a wonderful person. Similar to most families in South America, she was the matriarch and I called her, "Leo the lion". Her values and sense of what was right shone through everything she did and everything she expected of her family and those around her. And she didn't take prisoners in this regard. She made a perfect banker's wife and a great role model for her family.

Chile may not be one of the most popular holiday destinations with the British but is a truly beautiful country. It is 4,300km long excluding its claim to Antarctica and only 350km wide at its widest point. In the North it has the driest desert in the world called the Atacama. In the far South it stretches to Cape Horn through glaciers and fjords and towering pinnacle mountains. Towards the South, about 1,000km below Santiago, there are numerous active volcanoes and a stunning "lake district" with some of the best trout and salmon fishing in the world. In the middle of the country around Santiago vast quantities of fruit and wine are produced while the long coastline and Humboldt Current yield a rich fish harvest. It has great forests to produce lumber and the largest copper mines in the world.

The weather in Santiago, which is on almost exactly the same latitude as Sydney in Australia, is absolutely incredible. In high summer it's a dry, blue heat averaging about 29C (84F) in the day and cooling off nicely in the evening. In the autumn, from the end of March, it's a soft mellow temperature but almost always sunny. In the winter there's skiing at Farellones, about a 90-minute drive from the centre of Santiago.

Chile has also been very successful economically and is held out as an exemplar in South America. The Chilean peso has appreciated in value against the US dollar by more than 20% in the last few years. Santiago has a highly developed and well-designed financial district with some great architecture. It has numerous five-star hotels, top-class retailing, quality built residential apartments and houses and its city landscaping is as good as anywhere in the world.

When anyone thinks of Chile, the dictator Pinochet and the "disappeared" often spring to mind. The former President Augusto Pinochet's military government was accused of killing and torturing thousands of political opponents during his time in power. His term in office ended after the 1988 referendum as to whether the country wanted a return to democracy (Chile had been the oldest democratic country in South America). The result was a close-run 52% to 48% in favour and Pinochet duly stepped down. He later ended up spending a longer holiday in the UK than expected when he was placed under house arrest for alleged war crimes.

Our trips to Chile are always big family affairs. Sometimes, for a Brit (or a gringo as we are known there), it can all be a bit too much and, even for an extrovert such as myself, I would retreat to my bedroom alone for some peace and quiet. This also allowed me to catch up on any urgent work matters that came my way, although I did my best not to let business interfere with our family holidays.

That particular year, 2004, I did get disturbed quite often on HBOS issues. Still, we had a fantastic time going to the house on the lake owned by one of our niece's (Connie) future parents-in-law at a place a few hours' drive from Santiago. We also went sea fishing near the seaside resort of Viña del Mar. The Pacific swell was big and rolling and several of us on the small fishing boat got terrible seasickness but thankfully not Daniel or me. I think I must have gained my sea legs on that memorable Pacific voyage in 1994 with the Joyce family.

We flew back from our Chilean break on the evening of Easter Sunday 11 April arriving in Heathrow the following morning and driving up to North Yorkshire to throw myself back into the cauldron that was HBOS.

While I was away, the proverbial had been hitting the fan in a serious way in relation to the CBF's review. On 2 April, after Andy Sheppard had presented the revised draft of the report to all the relevant people, the lobbying of Ellis had begun in earnest. Ray Milne, a senior executive in IID who was responsible for CBFs and had been integrally involved in the survey, sent an email to Ellis complaining about the findings. He hadn't copied me in on the email, which he should have done, but he sent it to James Davies, who Sheppard was reporting to on a day-to-day basis.

For Milne, anything that might slow down CBF sales would seriously affect the profit and loss of Halifax Financial Services (part of IID) and he wanted to do everything to avoid that. He wrote to Ellis saying,

> *"...this second draft is worse as regards our key concern – which is the strong suggestion that due to treating customers fairly we need to include non-regulated products in the 'best advice' process for regulated products.*

> *"Potentially this means having to train PFAs in all HBOS products ... and taken to extremes could mean that in other non-regulated scenarios we must always put the customer in the best product. This issue is beyond the scope of the review."*

Milne's full email is here:

www.crashbankwallop.co.uk/library/5-13

In Milne's email trail there was Sheppard's email attaching the second draft of the report and a separate detailed paper setting out precisely why we were so concerned. Sheppard had done his very best to be polite and analytical in his email and to change the language in the report so that it was more digestible to Dawson's team but he clearly hadn't succeeded.

At one point in Sheppard's email he questions what the likely outcome would be if a customer complained to the Financial Ombudsman Service.

> *"If you believe, as I do, that the Ombudsman would rule in favour of the customer, then I submit that we have a genuine risk issue here and, therefore, a legitimate finding."*

Here is the second draft and Sheppard's detailed paper about the suitability of deposits versus CBFs:

www.crashbankwallop.co.uk/library/5-14

www.crashbankwallop.co.uk/library/5-15

The problem was that the FSA was due to start its supervisory visit to HBOS on 13 April and its officials would need time to digest our CBF report before they arrived. If it didn't get to them it might give the impression we had something to hide.

I'd had numerous telephone calls with Davies and Sheppard, while in Chile, on this topic but because of the pressure being applied by Ellis, Milne and Dawson's team, it was decided to put everything on hold until my return and just tell the FSA that due to unforeseen circumstances the report had been delayed. In the circumstances, this was probably the best option.

On the Tuesday of the week I got back from Chile, the FSA came in to start its review.

While all this CBF bickering was going on the even bigger and more potentially antagonistic Sales Culture and Controls Review was also now underway. Such was the scale of the initiative, my GRR team was being assisted by seconded specialists from accountancy giant Ernst & Young and we were all racing to meet a self-imposed deadline of 27 July to report to the HBOS Board.

In spite of the continued wrangling over CBFs, we gained a bit of breathing space by finally getting our report on the matter delivered to the FSA on 21 April. In a nutshell our findings, in order of importance, were:

- *At least 6.56% of the 167,000 CBF contracts sold may not have met the regulatory requirements for suitability, meaning nearly 11,000 customers may have been victims of mis-selling.*
- *Concerns about "concentration risk". This occurs when an adviser recommends a customer to invest more than a certain percentage of their total portfolio in one type of product. We found that typical concentration levels were between 20% and 50% but in exceptional cases much higher.*

- *We discovered that some investors were being sold CBFs when they had no apparent need for income, and without this being documented.*
- *We were 100% sure that "churning" – switching a customer from a guaranteed deposit account into CBFs where the additional yield was marginal but there was a risk to capital – breached the FSA's principle of treating customers fairly.*

The entire report is here:

www.crashbankwallop.co.uk/library/5-16

While we waited for the FSA to complete its report we took it upon ourselves to write to all 167,000 CBF investors carefully explaining again the risks and offering them an opportunity for further discussion or a free switch back to a deposit account.

On 26 May, unusually, I decided to attend the Retail Risk Control Committee and report on the CBF review. Dawson was at that meeting. Her face was like a picture from a horror story, rather ghoulish, and she shook her head vigorously throughout my address. It didn't go unnoticed by James Davies either.

When the meeting minutes finally came out they did not accurately reflect what I'd said, so I had them revised even though they'd been signed off by Charles Dunstone as a true and complete record. He was the committee Chairman as well as a non-executive director on the HBOS Board. Away from the bank he was Chief Executive of the highly successful mobile phone company Carphone Warehouse.

The FSA's report on CBFs came out on 28 May and almost entirely supported everything we had said and written. It vindicated our work and we celebrated privately without gloating, but Dawson was on the back foot again. The same day she emailed her team, Hornby and Whacker and transferred all the blame to GRR, six times making direct criticisms of us in her missive. I wrote to James and Andy Sheppard saying:

> *"I suggest that on the points made by Jo [Dawson] against GRR, we simply ignore them as sour grapes unless she takes them further. Dignified silence."*

James Davies emailed me back saying:

> *"Wholeheartedly agree. Confidence restored that we do in fact know what we are talking about."*

The full email trail is here:
www.crashbankwallop.co.uk/library/5-17
I forwarded the whole email trail to Ellis on 4 June, including Dawson's response, with some further important messages. It was time to start calling in his commitment to me made in The Feathers. I wrote:

> *"We [GRR] are absolutely up to our eyeballs on everything...and it is a bit nerve racking in case we miss something in the heat of the chase...we need your support to get through this difficult time...it feels like we are trying to land 6 F1 11s on an aircraft carrier within five minutes...crashes feel almost inevitable."*

I told Ellis we'd also give him an update on the Sales Culture and Controls Review.

"Mike some really big change is going to be needed to re-balance things and we are all going to need to work together to move into the new world."

As is normal with all FSA formal reports, there is always a requirement to respond. This meant that for the next three weeks or so people were racing around trying to sweep things under the carpet. Basically anything to avoid the truth, personal responsibility or having to make proper amends to customers.

Dawson was trying to corner us by appealing to the very top of the organisation to get her way. The lobbying was now not just to Ellis but Crosby too.

While we were completing the formal response to the FSA, Dawson dropped casually into an email:

"I am sending it (at his request) to James Crosby for review on Monday (28 June) so it must be in a form that everyone at HBOS agrees to at this stage... and will be sent to the FSA the following day."

I replied immediately asking why Crosby had asked to see a copy and to tell Dawson that Davies was finalising his input at that very time. She replied:

"Don't know but he has always taken an active interest in CBF .... he has a copy of the FSA letter – presume you gave it him or Mike? – which he has been through. Can only assume he sees our response as fundamental to overall relationship with FSA and potential implications for perceptions of bank assurance operation and indeed structure of industry.

Think he is also aware of the debates that have been

ongoing and wants to ensure a HBOS group response is appropriate. Guess as Chief Exec, he can see anything he likes! Certainly I always find his interventions very helpful & value-adding as he knows this industry inside out and is of course an FSA Board member.

Great that James D is on with review but at this late stage ***we need the final words rather than additional comments*** *and given James strong reputation / relationship with FSA, we are relying on him to come up with form of words which will constructively put their minds at rest!"*

She was trying to corral me and my team by appealing to a higher authority. I wrote back saying we hadn't sent a copy to Crosby. I suspected either she or Ellis must have done so. She finished off the interplay with what she must have thought was her *coup de grâce*:

"On CBF, I thought he might have mentioned it at dinner on Monday? I know he has spoken of it with both Mike E and Andy H – probably because of the considerable heat the GRR report caused internally ...I know Ray [Milne] spoke with John Edwards too re the process."

She knew that earlier that week Crosby had had dinner with GRR's senior management team and me in Edinburgh and she continued trying to put the frighteners on by making it clear that background conversations had been going on with Ellis, Hornby, Milne and his boss John Edwards who ran Halifax Financial Services. The entire email trail is here:
www.crashbankwallop.co.uk/library/5-18

I was well aware that the work that we had done had truly pissed off Dawson and her team but I wanted to attempt to mend broken fences.

I let the dust settle for a few weeks while we completed the reporting on the Sales Culture and Controls Review and then phoned Dawson suggesting we had a private get-together to resolve our differences. She agreed. We booked the meeting for 30 July, just before my family's long summer holidays and after the full HBOS Board meeting on 27 July.

To make her feel at ease, I agreed to meet in her office on her territory. The meeting was at lunchtime. It was a soulless office in the huge Lovell Park building in Leeds. I knew my way around from my days there in IID, and as I walked into her office, I saw the trolley with the sandwiches, drinks and coffee prepared for us. We opened the dialogue with the normal trivial comments, no doubt about the weather or the like, while selecting our food and beverages. I then sat down preparing myself mentally and emotionally to build bridges.

But Dawson didn't sit. She put her plate and drink down on the round table I was seated at and looked me straight in the eyes with the level of aggression of a streetfighter. She leaned forward towards me and pointed her index finger straight between my eyes less than six inches from my face and said, in the most threatening way anyone had ever spoken to me: "I'm warning you, don't you make a fucking enemy out of me."

Crash! Bang! Wallop! Adrenaline surge. Immediate increase in heartbeat. It took my breath away.

I simply couldn't believe what she had done and said. On any analysis, personal or professional, it was gross misconduct. It was a virtual assault. How could she possibly think that she could do something like that and get away with it? She must have thought or known that she was immune from any punishment. I simply couldn't believe it.

I said nothing. I couldn't think of anything to say. There wasn't anything to say. Responding in an aggressive way myself would have been a huge mistake. Perhaps that's what she wanted me to do. So there was a deathly silence for a moment or two. But, after the short pause, Dawson simply returned to normal as if nothing had happened.

In a somewhat surreal atmosphere, our working lunch resumed and as we nibbled sandwiches we calmly discussed all the pressing issues, including the Sales Culture and Controls Review that, by that stage, was proceeding through the report drafting stage.

By the end of the meeting, notwithstanding the appalling way in which it had begun, I felt as though we had actually made some progress.

I never spoke directly to Dawson about that incident again.

The next day, she sent me a long email. It was manipulative in the extreme. I think the realisation had dawned that her outburst might put her at risk and so she had decided to try to "re-professionalise" our communications. It's a long email with my comments inserted into her own text. This is how she started:

"Good to catch up yesterday and I do hope your troubles with the house you are building in Spain are soon behind you!"

And this is how she finished the email, with my own comments in bold where applicable:

"Paul – as I stressed many times, both me & my team are passionate about ensuring our business is managed in a way that is both safe for the customer and indeed for the Group. ***We know you are and have never doubted that.*** *We really are on the same page here!* **Agreed.**

We now need to get into the details / specifics and nail down recommendations for change so we can get on with implementing and improve the overall risk management process & capability. ***James will agree a precise agenda and measures of success with you and your team. I will ask for specific feedback at appropriate times.***

I look forward to hearing from you on the specifics detailed above. ***Jo, as I said, I am 100% confident that whatever has happened so far, our intentions have always been right…I can only apologise that, as yet, we have not managed to inspire the confidence and trust that we would have wished. We will try even harder over the coming period."***

The full email is here:

www.crashbankwallop.co.uk/library/5-19

Within a day or so of Dawson's verbal assault, and before the subsequent email correspondence, I spoke directly to Phil Hodkinson, my mentor, to ask his advice about what I should do. I could have reported Dawson to the group HR director and required an investigation and disciplinary action to be taken. Alternatively, I could ignore what she had done and continue to try to build a proper professional working relationship with her.

Hodkinson and I agreed that the consequences of making a big song and dance about it would be counter-productive. We discussed the relationship between Crosby and Dawson and felt the personal and professional risks of making a formal complaint would be very high. As a result, I decided not to raise the matter formally with HR.

So that was effectively the end of the CBF's saga. If only I could have said the same for the Sales Culture and Controls Review.

They're Animals Around Here!

Ultimately the main objective of the review was to assess the risks to customers and HBOS itself associated with the marketing, sales and distribution of the bank's financial products, to recommend changes where necessary and identify areas of regulatory concern.

GRR would be probing into every aspect of the sales process from product design and staff training to sales commissions and the way selling took place at branch level.

Part of our work would involve a confidential staff "culture" survey carried out through the bank's internal intranet.

A major assessment would be undertaken to examine the effectiveness of Board, committee members and approved persons in dealing with complex risk, regulation and internal control issues, plus the quality of their training and development.

A detailed analysis of the structure, resources and operating procedures of the whole risk management framework and its relationships with regulators was also required.

It was a massive project, being directed by James Davies who in turn was reporting to me. When drawing up the complex terms of reference we had deliberately put Ellis into the fray as the project sponsor because we were going to need his firepower when it came to the final report.

The main part of the review involved interviews with senior management, executive and non-executive directors, regional, area and branch managers and staff, call-centre workers, support groups and the risk management teams. About 15 staff worked permanently on the initiative until the fieldwork had been completed, alongside five or so seconded Ernst & Young staff. We had a mass of evidence gathering to do, let alone analysis and report writing.

Because of the resistance we had already encountered from Retail and Whacker over CBFs, we concurred that this time we'd have to overwhelm any detractors with data to the extent that they couldn't possibly argue the toss over our findings.

This approach was later confirmed as justified

in an email I received from a vexed Ernst & Young contractor, complaining that while trying to finalise his report, he'd spent over two hours arguing about the exact drafting of just two sentences. He went on to say that with this sort of culture in operation in the Halifax, there were serious regulatory risks. I couldn't have agreed more.

By the end of May 2004 we had completed one of the broadest, deepest, most intense and forensic evidence-gathering exercises I had ever been involved in.

We had spoken to more than 30 senior managers including Hornby, Whacker and his Retail Head of Risk Jack Cullen. We also held formal talks with Charles Dunstone, and each interview was conducted against a structured agenda and list of questions, so that we could compare and contrast the answers.

In addition, the review team had visited 23 geographically selected Halifax and Bank of Scotland branches around the country to establish whether the evidence was systemic across the board or if there were "hot spots".

We conducted seven focus groups after taking advice from a culture assessment expert on getting the right mix of people to produce a balanced and fair view. A total of 125 counter staff nationwide, who dealt directly with bank users, were questioned too and we visited two telephone call centres where we listened in on agents talking directly to customers.

Members of my team waded through a 1.5m-high pile of documentation on policies, standards, procedures, management information and meeting minutes and they went into two Bank of Scotland Investment Services (BOSIS) branches. BOSIS was the specialist investment advisory sales force – made up of staff from failed insurance firm Equitable – that serviced the higher net-worth customers of the Halifax and Bank of Scotland. These days, this would be called wealth management.

It was an immense achievement. I was extremely proud of the GRR team members and told them so.

My role in the whole review was primarily to stay in the background and keep my powder dry for the final communications to Hornby, his executive team, the Group Audit Committee and the HBOS Board. However, I remained integrally involved at all stages, leading, challenging hard, motivating and helping the team to analyse the evidence accurately and fairly. I was also involved directly in the reporting stage as the senior editor. So far as the actual work of evidence gathering was concerned, I took part in the interviews of Hornby, Dunstone and Cullen. These were fascinating to say the least and I'll return to them shortly.

At the very outset we trawled through any documents that might help us understand the culture within Retail: one of those was the results of the annual MORI staff survey. It has a dedicated section dealing with culture. It asks respondents if they agree, disagree or neither agree nor disagree to the following six questions:

- *People are open and honest with each other.*
- *Managers here accept that the occasional mistake will happen.*
- *I work for a progressive business.*
- *Good performance is fairly rewarded.*
- *I am encouraged to make decisions in relation to my job, where appropriate.*
- *It is safe to speak up and challenge the way things are done.*

When we reviewed the 2003 survey results (and later on in May the 2004 results), the retail division scored better than most other parts of the organisation on the cultural indicators. At first sight, given what we had been experiencing, we found this surprising and built in our own culture survey into our interviews, focus groups etc. Before long we discovered that the messages coming from the frontline staff were completely at odds with the results of the MORI survey. When we questioned people on this discrepancy their answers were always the same: "Oh, we never tell the truth in the staff survey because we don't trust that it's anonymous."

To corroborate the statements I came up with a cunning "Baldrick-like" plan – after the character from BBC TV comedy *Blackadder*.

In my early days in IID, I had recruited an outstanding individual to my risk team called Karina McTeague. She was a lawyer and had worked directly for Bank of Scotland CEO Peter Burt when his bank made its hostile bid for NatWest and lost out to its rival the Royal Bank of Scotland.

After the merger of the Halifax and Bank of Scotland, she decided to get some experience of sales management, joining Retail as an area sales manager responsible for a large number of Halifax branches. This was the job she was doing just before I recruited her. This meant that she would have had direct experience of what the culture was like out there in the field.

Karina had since been headhunted by Lloyds TSB Scotland as General Counsel and Head of Risk but my plan was to phone her anyway. This was not strictly permitted but I knew I could trust her and that she would maintain confidentiality.

So, I met her for lunch in a chic restaurant in Edinburgh one day and we got talking about the culture in the Halifax sales management. When I asked her what she thought about the difference in staff survey results her response was instant. "Oh," she said, "that's easy to explain. Just before the launch of the annual staff survey, when we had our sales management meetings with area directors, it was made quite clear to us that we were to make it known implicitly that people who answered the key questions in the staff survey in the 'wrong way' would be found out."

Karina told me this was one of the reasons why she had decided to leave sales management: she just didn't like the culture.

She is now Director of Supervision of Retail Banking at the new Financial Conduct Authority, one of the most important jobs in the regulatory system today. Perhaps there is hope for the future yet.

As this kind of evidence started to roll in we felt that it was a reasonable assumption that everything else would go downhill from now on. As I later stated in my evidence to the Treasury Select Committee in February, 2009: "You can have the best governance processes in the world, but if they are carried out in a culture of greed, unethical behaviour and indisposition to challenge, they will fail."

Now back to those interviews. The sessions with Hornby, Dunstone and Cullen – in that order – were, for tactical reasons, left until last. Davies and I hoped that Cullen, as the person primarily responsible within Retail for assessing and mitigating risks, might effectively "spill the beans" and corroborate our findings.

We always conduct these senior management interviews with two people. This is for two good reasons, firstly so that one person can lead the questioning and the other can take detailed notes and, secondly, so that everything that is said at the meeting can be corroborated. As these were the most important interviews, I decided that James Davies should accompany me as the leader of the review.

Prior to the interviews, I organised a *tête-à-tête* with one of the non-executive directors, a Scotsman called John Maclean who I knew could be relied upon for an honest opinion on the lie of the land. I asked him what he thought of the Retail Risk Control Committee. He paused, tilted his head to one side and said: "Well, they got that appointment wrong, didn't they?" He was referring to Charles Dunstone's committee chairmanship.

When I asked what he thought of Hornby his answer was very telling. All Maclean said was: "The cleverest way to be arrogant is to pretend that you're not!"

The first of our meetings took place with Hornby in his sparsely furnished corner office on the second floor of the Halifax main office building in Trinity Road.

Hornby was a baby-faced looking chap with brown eyes and a smiley face. He always looked relaxed and confident. He didn't have a very distinct look about him: no fancy clothes or bow ties. He fitted in and was very much a "man of the people". He didn't look arrogant. To me, at any rate, he didn't even look like he was pretending not to be arrogant but, of course, I didn't know him as well as John Maclean.

I once asked Maureen what she made of him just from photographs and what she had heard about him from me or read in the newspapers. I often consulted Maureen because I had found her instinctive, non-evidential, advice almost always on the button. For someone like me, this was "countercultural" but the instincts of women and, particularly, one's wife are not to be underestimated. She said that Hornby seemed very like Tony Blair and was probably Machiavellian. I think she was spot on. I wonder whether he has ever read Machiavelli's famous book, *The Prince* which turned out to be Mervyn King's (the Governor of the Bank of England prior to and during the 2008 banking crisis) chosen book on the famous BBC Radio 4 programme called, *A Good Read?*

Hornby's career had started with the Boston Consulting Group where he shot through the ranks before moving to Blue Circle Cement and then on to Asda as Retail Managing Director. Personally, I liked him and thought he was trustworthy. He was affable, charming, relaxed and seemingly very open to input, even if it was difficult. He certainly wasn't like Dawson. He made you feel at ease and like you were his friend. Hornby was also a great motivator, speaker and an inspirational leader to the Retail Division. Having managed one of the largest banks in the world, he now runs the bookmaker Gala Coral – a company clearly better at risk management than HBOS was.

I was keen to understand more about Hornby's relationship with Dunstone. So, in his office before the formal interview got started, as we were getting cups of coffee and talking about the weather and Bristol City Football Club's (Hornby's team) latest results, I nonchalantly asked: "Oh, Andy, how well do you know Charles Dunstone?"

Hornby told me that "Charles" was a good friend of his, he often had dinner with him and they spent time together outside of HBOS. This was a bit of a red flag to me because of the potential conflict of interest that could build up through a close relationship with the committee chairman who was supposed to be holding him to account.

As Hornby, Davies and I sat down with our drinks to begin the interview, I asked Hornby a favourite "warm up" question of mine: "So, Andy, what keeps you awake at night around here?" Without hesitation, Hornby told me that what worried him most was sales of payment protection insurance (PPI).

PPI covered customers who borrowed money from HBOS, for the repayment of their loans in the event of redundancy, disability or death. It could be attached to credit cards, personal loans or even mortgages. It was one of the most profitable products at HBOS and accounted for more than 10% of group-wide profits when I joined the company. In fact, selling the actual credit, i.e. the loan to the customer, was never as profitable as selling the PPI. This being so, in the business planning round and before the start of each financial year, Hornby's Retail Division was set specific "conversion ratio targets" for the number of PPI contracts to be sold as a percentage of the number of loans sold. It was around 75%, if my memory serves me correctly.

Hornby revealed that in a recent analysis done by Retail, it was discovered that as many as 17% of customers sold PPI would not have been covered because they were self-employed and automatically excluded. He also told me and Davies that when customers repaid their loans early they were never given a refund of the premium on the PPI policy which was always taken up front and added to the loan. This meant that customers were paying premiums for the insurance cover from which they could never benefit. This is a bit like paying an annual premium for a car insurance policy, selling the car in the middle of the year and never getting a refund.

Given the volumes of PPI being sold, if Hornby was correct, this was no longer just a risk (something that might happen). It had now become a real issue (something that had happened). Risk professionals, to distinguish the two, often say that a risk is the "cowpat" in the middle of the field towards which you are walking, but that an issue is the "cowpat" that you have already stepped in.

This information, volunteered by Hornby, only served to heighten my fears about the risk to HBOS from PPI sales and the need for an urgent review of the whole situation. I'd been fired before I had time to get round to it.

Now, in 2015, the total compensation paid by Lloyds Banking Group for PPI mis-selling has exceeded £12 billion. I often wondered after the interview, if Hornby had talked about PPI to try and put us off the scent in relation to the much more serious problems of the overall culture in his division.

The awful thing about this is that it is a criminal offence, under section 397 of the Financial Services and Markets Act 2000, recklessly to mis-sell PPI. We now know that HBOS and all the other companies in the market place continued to mis-sell PPI aggressively and knowingly for many years after this. As a barrister, I would say that this provides very strong evidence of criminality by the Board of HBOS and should be investigated by the relevant authorities.

After the initial shock revelations, the rest of the interview with Hornby went according to plan. He downplayed the potential risks that we had identified as well as telling us that there were already actions in place to solve things. It was what I expected him to say, but I'm convinced Hornby never really knew the full story of what was going on right under his nose, for the simple reason that staff were too scared to tell him.

The following week, Davies and I headed off to see Dunstone at his Carphone Warehouse offices near Wembley, in London. It was another extraordinary meeting.

On the way there in the taxi, I remember seeing a massive billboard poster advertising the airline easyJet. It showed a good-looking woman in an orange bikini with a rather ample bosom and the strapline, "Weapons of Mass Distraction!" It made us smile.

Dunstone was rather like Hornby himself. He was a cheeky looking chap with a soft and kind face. He was amiable in the extreme. He obviously knew an awful lot about retailing but very little about financial services or banking, although it turns out that Carphone Warehouse has been fined for mis-selling insurance attached to its mobile phones.

He certainly knew absolutely nothing about regulation and risk management from a technical perspective. John Maclean was right, but the problem with all these non-executive appointments is that they are essentially controlled by the executive, so, from Crosby and Hornby's perspective, they almost certainly thought that having Dunstone as Chairman of the Retail Risk Control Committee was the right appointment. Personally, I think that could be a breach of their fiduciary duties as directors.

Well, just as Davies and I stepped into Dunstone's office, he strode up to us in a very cheerful manner and with a grin on his face said the most amazing thing: "I'm glad you two are here because, to be honest, I'm not entirely sure I know how to be the Chairman of the Risk Control Committee."

Straight from the horse's mouth: unbelievable.

Prior to the interview I'd pre-warned Davies that I'd be asking Dunstone about PPI in the wake of Hornby's comments. In the middle of another line of questioning, I said: "Charles, just out of interest what do you make of PPI?"

He arched forward in his chair with a confident air and said: "I'm glad you asked me about that Paul, because, by coincidence I was only just talking to Andy Hornby about PPI last week and he assured me that we had no ethical or mis-selling issues in that area."

Davies and I looked at each other. We were flabbergasted.

It was time to give Dunstone some advice. I said: "Charles, at this stage, I am going to stop the main meeting and explain something to you about risk management which is extremely important." I allowed a bit of a pause. "Believe it or not, only last week, when James and I were interviewing Andy, he actually told us that one of the main things that kept him awake at night was potential mis-selling of PPI which is exactly the opposite of what he told you.

"This is a good lesson that, in your role as Chairman of the Risk Control Committee, you need to be aware that self-serving statements by the executive, that no problems exist in areas of material risk, should not be relied upon without independent corroboration of what they're saying. The lawyers say, 'self-serving statements without corroboration bear no weight in the laws of evidence.'"

I think it's fair to say that Dunstone was also flabbergasted when I told him this.

Within a short time of our meeting, Dunstone must have spoken to Hornby about this, in breach of his interview confidentiality agreement. I know because it was used as a criticism of me in the KPMG report that supposedly independently investigated my allegations after I was fired. KPMG strongly suggested that I had acted unethically by asking people to maintain confidentiality. It was wrong. I told no one else at the time but feel now it needs to be in the public domain.

The final senior management interview I conducted was with Jack Cullen. Once again Davies accompanied me. We met in another standard issue room in the Halifax head offices.

Cullen was a good chap. Unusually for senior executives in Retail, he had come from Bank of Scotland and very much fitted with its more prudent and respectful pre-merger culture.

Just as we had hoped, he "blew the whistle" on what was going on in Retail, and evidentially provided us with the "icing on the cake". It was endorsement from the most senior risk management professional in the division of the evidence that we had gathered elsewhere in our review work.

At the start of the meeting he looked stressed and nervous. By nature, as we had found in our earlier dealings with him, he was a typically dour and introverted Scotsman. He was highly analytical and balanced and knew what he was doing but his experience of living in the Retail Division had clearly been very unpleasant. Cullen reported directly to Whacker Walkden, which made matters even worse for him. Whacker was Hornby's bully boy and this reporting line should never have been allowed as there was bound to be a conflict of interest. No wonder Cullen had asked for a transfer back home to Bank of Scotland.

Here are some direct extracts from the original notes of the meeting made by Davies and I. Cullen showed us an action plan he had constructed which contained statements such as: *"Leadership and focus on risk matters has had no priority"*; *"Sales regarded as more important than anything else"*; *"Risk not seen as a core business imperative or competency"*. When we later asked for a copy of the plan we were sent a new version with some of these points deleted.

Cullen was the only executive left from four who had moved down from Scotland after the merger and he told us that at the time it *"was all about growth and making the business succeed"*; *"The culture was of 'don't tell me the bad news'"*; *"You always had to prove things beyond reasonable doubt"*.

He went on:

"And you know they are animals around here and unless you can prove it…it's always good news reporting."

I asked him if he thought his position might be affected if he spoke up, and after a pause for thought he said: "*Well there is that…but…not just that…*" and he continued to describe management as gung-ho.

He said the business was going hell-for-leather to be number one in the marketplace and he worried that risks had been underestimated.

"I'm having to prove all this [strong emphasis] with HUGE personalities, with HUGE intellects…all jockeying for position."

Cullen was clearly a fish out of water in the Halifax pool. He described how the cautious culture of Bank of Scotland had been eradicated by Retail.

"I mean, if you just get your head kicked in irrespective of service, you are going to get a sore head, aren't you?"

He was in full flow now and referred to a slide used in a branch presentation which stated:

"What should we do more of…SALES, SALES, SALES… what should we do less of…RMS [Risk Management System] / SERVICE."

Risk management in Retail needed a full overhaul but Cullen said everyone blamed Risk for the situation.

"I was working from 6.30am to 7.30pm and all day Sunday."

The interview was almost turning into something of

a therapy session and what Cullen was revealing about the bank's culture was shocking to say the least.

He admitted:

"My problem is that I'm too honest…my levels of integrity are too high."

Sales quality, he said, was never as important as sales volumes and there was a 70 / 30 imbalance between focus on sales and management of risk.

Cullen explained that the development of financial products was neglected because top managers in Retail were mainly consultants and marketing specialists, not bankers.

"So long as they hit both the top line and the bottom line, how that is achieved does not really matter."

At this point Cullen said, *"I feel a bit like I'm cheating here"*, implying that he shouldn't be telling us the things he was. It was true to say his revelations had literally taken our breath away.

A full copy of my notes of the meeting with Cullen is here: www.crashbankwallop.co.uk/library/5-20

Davies and I had worked together since 1997 on many complex regulatory assignments but we had never experienced anything like that meeting. It told us absolutely everything we needed to know.

The Retail Division was in serious breach of the key regulatory requirements. It wasn't acting with due skill, care and diligence. It didn't have adequate systems and controls and, in particular, risk management systems. It wasn't paying due regard to the interests of customers and treating them fairly. Most seriously, if we had continued with an adversarial investigation, it looked as though we would almost certainly have found that Retail was failing to act with integrity.

Davies and I felt like men in a rowing boat trying to slow down an oil tanker.

It was all very well having the evidence but getting it across to the key people in a way that led to the changes required was going to be a very tough call, probably the toughest in my professional life. Nevertheless, we were still confident of success, although we realised that it was likely, given the Group's growth strategy, the same culture problems probably existed in the other divisions.

With this in mind it gave me some comfort at least, in relation to the Corporate Division, that a review was already underway of its atypical credit risk management led by Dr Andrew Smith with the assistance of KPMG as an independent third party. PwC was also carrying out a detailed analysis of the overall risk management effectiveness at HBOS. Any serious skeletons found in other divisional cupboards would be reported at the highest level.

After we'd written up our notes, Davies and I discussed the risks to Cullen from what he'd divulged. We had the highest regard for what he had done and wanted to protect him. So we made the unorthodox but ethical decision not to put his notes on the formal record in case they were leaked to Whacker. If they had been, Cullen's career would probably have come to a swift and nasty end.

Meanwhile, separate to the review work, GRR had received some good and bad news.

The good news was the results of our own departmental 2004 MORI staff survey. We had a 99% response rate, the highest in HBOS, and in just about every area the feedback represented a huge "tick in the box" for the reorganisation. A presentation of the results produced by GRR's HR director, Irene Grant, is here: www.crashbankwallop.co.uk/library/5-21

Here is an extract from the communication I sent out to the GRR department:

Colleague Opinion Survey Results

You will have already seen Mike Ellis's message about the big improvements in the Group Finance & Risk Colleague Opinion Survey results. I am truly delighted to be able to tell you that the response rate and general pattern of responses from colleagues in Group Regulatory Risk was even more positive.

See: www.crashbankwallop.co.uk/library/5-21-1

As can be seen from my photograph, by this time I was feeling pretty knackered.

When it came to the cultural indicators from the survey, I was particularly pleased to see that 72% of the department felt that it was safe to speak up and challenge and that 91% considered their work to be interesting.

My entire communication is here:

www.crashbankwallop.co.uk/library/5-22

The bad news was related to the build up to (and my reporting at) the Group Audit Committee meeting scheduled for 8 June. After the CBF's fallout from the committee's last meeting in March, this one was going to be crucial. My preparations had to be right and there was a great deal to report on.

A final report was required on the CBFs review, a progress briefing on endowment complaints handling in Retail, an update on the Sales Culture and Controls Review, the latest on PwC's probe into HBOS's risk management effectiveness, plus a host of other issues.

Critically, it was now time to start briefing the committee on what I wholeheartedly believed was the most serious risk to the success of the organisation: the cultural indisposition to challenge pervasive throughout the bank. Not only had I witnessed it, my staff working on the CBFs and sales culture reviews had complained of the awful behaviours that they had encountered. They genuinely felt like they were going behind enemy lines even though their intention was always to help HBOS as a whole and the individuals on the other side of the table too.

Naturally, I wanted to discuss in advance with Ellis both my written report and what I proposed to say at the 8 June meeting, yet despite badgering him several times he kept saying he was too busy to meet.

However a few days before the committee sat, the final eruption of the CBFs volcano blew tons of debris into the stratosphere and caused a pyroclastic flow.

On 6 June, Ellis wrote to me asking for a detailed chronology of everything that had happened on the CBFs review, the individuals involved and what opportunities Retail were given to comment on the report. Although he denied it, the tone of his email felt like it was the beginning of a witch-hunt.

Emails flew back and forth and I sent a final one the day before the Group Audit Committee meeting. This contained my first formal and deeply heartfelt appeal to Ellis to support the cultural change that was clearly required. I prayed that it might work.

> *"Mike, we have spoken at some length this morning on this and more generally about the current issues in dealing with Retail. We really do have to do something... and you may wish to lead this...to change the whole tone of engagement. This is not a battle of wits but a joint attempt to do what is right for the organisation.*
>
> *Some behaviours are going to need to change, particularly the sentiment that constantly questions the competence and intentions of GRR... We need you and Andy [Hornby] to intervene here to create a watershed so we can move on from the issues of the past (from which we can learn but not blame) to the brave new world of the future... We must all be as one and communicate as such. We will get there but there will also be some pain in the process of change. Paul."*

The entire email chain is here:

www.crashbankwallop.co.uk/library/5-23

Ellis finally agreed to meet me half-an-hour before the committee meeting in the offices at Old Broad Street, where it was being held. This was hardly satisfactory considering the sensitivity of the matter I would be broaching. When I got to Ellis' office, the door was closed and he was in a meeting. I tried to interrupt but with no luck.

So I followed the principle that had stuck with me all my life when the chips were down. I would go by the advice given by Polonius to Laertes in Shakespeare's Hamlet:

> *"This above all: to thine own self be true, and it must follow, as the night the day, thou canst not then be false to any man."*

The meeting was being held in the main boardroom around a huge 20-seat oval table. I was on the side facing the window that looked out over the City of London. My written report to members had been carefully crafted to explain the progress of the oversight programme in the most positive of terms without underestimating the challenges that lay ahead.

My report is available in full here:

www.crashbankwallop.co.uk/library/5-24

When it came to my turn to speak, I announced to members that I had something very important to say. I could see I had their full attention.

"I would not want the committee to be under any illusion as to just how strong the tensions were as my GRR team and I carried out our legitimate and required oversight work and that my team and I had encountered behaviours in certain parts of the organisation which I consider to be unacceptable. In my view, these behaviours demonstrate a cultural indisposition to challenge which is one of the biggest risks that any organisation can face."

I went on to say that this was an early warning and,

at this stage, I wanted to try to resolve these matters myself without any assistance from them. However, I said that if I needed help, I would let them know. There was a deathly hush. I guess it was the first time that anyone had made such a comment.

After a number of inquiring responses from members, I thought we were about to move on when, out of the blue, committee Chairman Tony Hobson asked me a question. The tension in the room was palpable and I could sense the irritation in Ellis who was sat next to me on the right.

The soft-featured, mousy haired Hobson lent forward so that he could see me around the portly figure of Ellis, who was seated next to him, and said: "Paul, do you have a direct reporting line to me?"

I thought, 'That's a poisoned chalice of a question'. I didn't, and I knew if I said that I should I'd be in even more trouble with Ellis. So I answered: "Tony, I think you should ask the chief financial officer that question." And he did.

Ellis looked flustered: "No, under the three lines of defence model of corporate governance only the Head of Internal Audit has a direct reporting line to you."

I didn't agree but at least for now I had avoided smart-suited Hobson's tripwire question. However, he hadn't finished.

Hobson lent around Ellis again, looked at me intently in the eyes and said: "And what do you say to that Paul?"

Depersonalise it, I thought.

"Well, Tony, in my view, I think if you put 10 experienced regulatory risk professionals, with no conflicts of interest to manage, in a room and asked them that question, I believe that, at least seven or eight of them would tell you that, anyone, like me, who has a direct accountability to oversee the activities of the executive in matters relating to regulation or risk management, should have at least an equal weighted reporting line to the non-executive. This is for the obvious reason that if such a person needs to raise challenges with which the executive may not be comfortable, he or she will be protected by the non-executive in so doing."

I could sense Ellis erupting beside me like Mount Vesuvius.

"Thank you, Paul," said Hobson, "you can now continue with your update to the committee."

After that, the only matter that I referred to was the final report relating to the CBFs review that I re-emphasised raised "very important issues" for HBOS in relation to "treating customers fairly".

I also drew the committee's attention to some important passages from the FSA's Financial Risk Outlook 2004:

- *"The sizeable sums which firms continue to pay to customers by way of redress and the steady flow of disciplinary cases arising from mis-selling demonstrate that many firms have still not given sufficient priority to the regulatory requirement to treat their customers fairly."*

- *"It is a core part of senior management responsibility that they embed this principle throughout the firm's culture and implement it in its strategy."*
- *"We will strengthen our focus on this aspect of firms' management controls, so that it becomes a key part of our regular monitoring, risk assessment and risk mitigation programmes."*
- *"We continue to have concerns about the extent and scale of mis-selling of financial products to retail customers. The problem arises from a combination of factors: financial products are often inherently more complex (and sometimes made to appear more so than is necessary); the customers for those products often do not have the skill set needed to understand and assess them properly: and those selling the products have not always acted responsibly."*

As soon as the meeting ended and before we had even left the boardroom, Ellis came up to me and said, "Come to my office immediately". I knew I was in for a rollicking. In the quiet of his room Ellis was clearly still fuming and told me that he wanted to have a formal meeting with me the next morning in Edinburgh to discuss what had just happened.

Having returned to North Yorkshire from London that afternoon, I got up at 5.45 the next morning to drive to Darlington to take the train to Edinburgh. I went straight to Ellis' office. I knew what was coming. He was going to have a performance management discussion with me. He was apoplectic about what had taken place the previous day, but I was also furious with him for failing to meet with me before the meeting, not taking my email seriously and for his angry response to me raising legitimate points.

There is nothing that gets to me more than a mixture of lack of caring, incompetence and unfairness. Over the last few months, far from sticking to the bargain that we had agreed at the pub in Helmsley the previous September, he had done the exact opposite.

At our meeting that morning in Edinburgh, he gave me a right "bollocking". He told me that my behaviour in the boardroom was completely outrageous.

By the time he'd finished, I had lost my patience. Without shouting but in more than an assertive way, I said: "Well, Mike, your actions in this matter simply prove the point that I was making to the committee. You have a cultural indisposition to challenge, yourself. And, so far as the reporting lines are concerned, I have been in more FTSE 100 boardrooms advising directors on regulatory and risk management matters than you have had hot dinners. I know what I'm talking about. If you don't believe me, let's get those 10 experienced professionals and ask them."

My response took Ellis by surprise. He didn't seem to know what to say. I think he was expecting me to leave the room with my tail between my legs and, henceforth, be a good little minion. He didn't counter attack but just mumbled something that I couldn't properly hear. So I left the room.

That was the only occasion at HBOS when I lost my

patience with anyone, including Dawson, but for two or three weeks afterwards I was so angry and upset about what was going on that I went about my job without sufficient compassion in my heart. I never let this anger show in public or with the people over whom we were carrying out our oversight work. However, on one or two occasions I let off a good deal of steam in private meetings with my own team from GRR. It was a natural response but it set a bad example and was against the culture we wished to create.

To be completely fair, all the people we were dealing with, including Dawson and her team, had been caught up in a system and culture at Halifax for many years that led them to behave in the way they did. It was bound to be difficult for them to change but I, perhaps naively, was sure that the vast majority of people would buy into a new culture, over time, if given the right leadership and opportunity.

Our problem was that, given the exceptionally high level of regulatory scrutiny under which we were operating in 2004, we had no choice but to get on with the job in the rigorous way I had warned.

There was one final astonishing twist to emerge from that Group Audit Committee meeting.

As normal, that meeting was attended by a representative of HBOS's statutory auditors, which was KPMG. Having been a partner at KPMG I knew the people there very well. The partner in charge of the audit was called Guy Bainbridge and he attended all the Group Audit Committee meetings. He was there on 8 June and witnessed the entire scene although he made no comments at the meeting about what I'd said, supportive or otherwise.

The following day, after my unpleasant meeting with Ellis in Edinburgh, I got a telephone call from one of the most senior partners at KPMG who was a good friend of mine (and still is). I won't name him, for obvious reasons, as he still works there. He told me that the previous day (i.e. the day of the meeting) Bainbridge had called him to relay what had taken place and told my friend that he thought that I must have had a "death wish".

Once again, this is incredibly telling of the current system of corporate governance in large companies. Here was the statutory audit partner expressing his view that to raise a highly important challenge in an Audit Committee meeting was tantamount to signing one's own death warrant. If that's what the auditors thought, it's no wonder that the banking crisis took place.

Auditors are an absolutely fundamental part of the governance system. They are supposed to be the "gatekeepers" of the "true and fair view" of the formal financial statements of large companies. If the Head of Regulatory Risk says that he has found a cultural indisposition to challenge, this should put them on serious notice in terms of both the profit and loss, and the balance sheet and they should take it seriously. But no, raising a challenge would be too likely to lead them to losing the audit and all the audit and non-audit fees that go with it.

As I wrote later in a formal letter to the Financial Reporting Council, the most senior regulator dealing with the accounting profession, following my dismissal from HBOS and the resulting KPMG investigation:

> *"It seems to me that, in any civilised and developed society, if we cannot be satisfied* ***so that we are sure*** *that we can trust and rely on the competence, integrity and independence of our professionals – the very people who are supposed to be the best educated, brightest and most honest people in society – we are in real trouble.*
>
> *I have developed a very strong concern, over a considerable period of time, about whether fees come before independence, objectivity (or, sometimes, even competence) in important parts of the accounting profession. I also think that the evidence, from a range of sources, seems more and more to support this conclusion."*

Far from expressing his concern for my future career at HBOS, Guy Bainbridge, a highly experienced auditor should have been proactively and vocally supporting my concerns. He should be ashamed of himself.

Behold The Mad Monk

Before completing the story of the Sales Culture and Controls Review, I'd like to talk about myself, my style and my dedication to personal development. After all, there are always two sides to any story.

Ellis and the others were beginning to find me a cultural "round peg" trying to fit into "a square hole". They wanted me to comply with their way of doing things. The question is, why wouldn't I? What was it about me that, notwithstanding the obvious risks to my personal position at HBOS, kept me keeping on in the face of clear signals to shut up? Was I an arrogant, cross-grained troublemaker and misfit? Did I deserve what I got coming to me? It certainly makes for an interesting psychological analysis.

I come from a family background that had taught a "no-holds-barred" approach to communications. For us as a family, truth was far more important than feelings or anything else. It didn't take me long once I got into the world of work to realise that I was a little different from the norm and that this could cause difficulties.

In my first real job at Allied Dunbar between 1984 and 1988, things were rather different there to elsewhere. Diversity of personality and style was encouraged and was culturally of the norm. Speaking up or being eccentric was promoted because it added to the creative mix. I loved this about Allied Dunbar and while there I chose to go on an effective communications course that was a bit of an eye-opener because it showed me how important it was to adjust one's preferred style to the audience to whom you were communicating. This did not come naturally to me.

Before I joined American Express in 1989 as General Counsel for its subsidiary Acuma, I had to be interviewed by a professional occupational psychologist to find out what I was like. I had never experienced anything like this before and it was enlightening when I read the report written by Gurnik Baines. As a result, I became so interested in my psychological make-up and how it affected my work that I asked him to be my personal coach. This was quite normal in American companies and has now become much more common in the UK.

During my work with Gurnik, I came to realise that I was a very different kind of person and, in many respects, didn't fit in with the normal "organisational politics" of things. It seemed that whenever it came to the crunch, irrespective of what it might mean for me personally, truth and fairness came first. Also some of my behaviours had to change: I needed to be more sensitive to the feelings of others and office politics if I wished to progress. The problem at Acuma was somewhat exacerbated because my original boss who recruited me, Frank Skillern Jr, was, himself, a lawyer and he told me I had a "007 licence" and it was my job to keep the company safe in the face of increasing regulatory scrutiny.

When I got to KPMG, in 1995, although I enjoyed success very quickly, I had an early "run-in" on a project we were doing with Clerical Medical International with a very successful consultant called Louis Jordan. Louis is now one of the most senior partners at Deloitte and, despite our *contretemps* 20 years ago, he is still a good friend.

As a direct result of this run-in, my sponsoring partner at KPMG, Marcus Sephton, introduced me to Steve Kaplan who became my personal coach there in 1996. Steve continued to work with me when I joined HBOS.

The coach's objective is to help the "coachee" to develop personally and professionally and to achieve his maximum potential. This is normally done by gathering what is often referred to as "360-degree feedback" whereby work colleagues provide confidential and anonymous observations on a person's performance and then the findings are used to design a personal development plan. This information should never be used as a weapon to performance manage someone or apportion blame. Indeed, it demonstrates the good faith of the person concerned because it shows they want to improve.

The best way to carry out this exercise is to allow the coach to speak directly to those giving feedback as this makes it a much richer experience. This had always been my approach.

Steve had worked closely with me in IID and got on well with Phil Hodkinson. In 2004, he conducted face-to-face interviews for me with Ellis and three more senior executives than me, along with 13 of my peers or direct reports. Steve's formal report was then shared with Ellis and the HR professionals who supported my development.

Of course, like everyone, I had plenty of things to work on. No one is perfect and I have never denied that I have an unusual and strong personality that does not always fit with the politics of the organisation or the preferences of some individuals. Not only that, in my role advising on risk management and regulatory affairs, playing politics for personal advantage was an absolute no-no and it was in this area that Steve and I never really saw eye to eye. The fact is that sometimes it was my job to deliver the messages that others would avoid like the plague: messages that could well be described as political faux pas.

Steve completed his interviews during May and June and his report provided very strong evidence that, in most respects, people at HBOS thought that I was doing a very good job. The first paragraph of the Executive Summary read:

> *"Well done! A strong effort under some very difficult circumstances... Perhaps the most noticeable and lasting impression of the interviews was the overall amount of good will that you have generated and / or has been extended to you. The magnitude and genuineness of this widespread sentiment among the interviewees was quite impressive, almost overwhelming. It speaks volumes about both yourself and the value you are perceived to offer to the organisation, as well as the calibre of the leadership itself."*

However, it wasn't all positive. Steve pointed out that I needed to develop my skills, *"in the area of building relationships, delivering change and managing people"* and that *"certain behaviours"* needed to be addressed. He said I must gain the trust and confidence of top executives as someone *"with whom they not only <u>can</u> but ideally will <u>want</u> to do business"*.

In the final section of the report, Steve summarised my key developmental areas for the following year as follows:

- *Focus more on others – "Instead of being interesting, you need to be interested..."*
- *Learn to listen!*
- *Learn to adapt your style to suit the audience and the circumstances.*
- *Clarify your role / responsibilities vis-à-vis the senior management team.*
- *Become a better manager.*
- *Give* <u>*all*</u> *staff a fair chance to earn your respect, trust and confidence. Do not form quick judgements.*
- *Adopt "one size fits all" behaviour.*

Steve concluded:

"You are blessed with enormous talents and strengths that make you the envy of many others. You also have a huge appetite for a challenge and for personal growth. You need to make some fundamental changes to the way you operate to bring about the results you need and the success you want. You can have a key role and a future at HBOS – if you want it. It's up to you. You can do it!"

Ellis gave me the worst feedback of anyone by some margin, irrespective of the fact that he had written me a positive performance assessment for GRR for the first half of the year.

The full report is here:

www.crashbankwallop.co.uk/library/5-24

I think it's fair to say that Steve always had mixed feelings about me. What he had really wanted to achieve over all the years of working with me was to teach me how to "fit in" and manage the organisational politics properly. In the end, he failed at that but it wasn't his fault. I worked very hard on my personal development and made significant improvements over the years but I could not change my real essence: who I really was.

On a final amusing note, I always used to set a great deal of "cultural store" in people's nicknames. Anthropologists will tell you that nicknames (epithets e.g. the swift-footed Achilles), often tell you a great deal about the person they describe. In banking there are some good ones and I've already mentioned a few. My nickname at HBOS was "the Mad Monk"!

Cash or Cabbage?

Returning to 9 June and the vicious dressing down from Ellis: I didn't have any time to immediately dwell on it. Davies and I had agreed to brief Hornby on 11 June on our culture review findings, so we had a document to prepare for the meeting.

As our line manager, we thought it best to update Ellis first about what we were going to say to Hornby. We saw Ellis on 10 June and he asked us to add a few more details to our "talk book" briefing pack that gave it more substance.

As planned, on 11 June we met Hornby in his office in Halifax and gave him a copy of our document, stressing the importance of not making any copies. We didn't want this stuff leaked before we had completed our work and written our formal report. In the preliminary remarks, we gave as much credit as we possibly could. We said that it had been an enormous business achievement to change the culture in Retail to focus on marketing and sales but that there were some important lessons to learn. We went on to stress that the way the findings of the work were communicated and agreed was going to be very important indeed.

The entire document is here:

www.crashbankwallop.co.uk/library/5-25

On our slides covering preliminary findings, we had chosen our words carefully but we wanted Hornby to be under no illusion as to the seriousness of what we had found. Therefore, when we gave our oral update, we concentrated on expanding our views on the culture issues. We told Hornby that notwithstanding the fact that he spent an awful lot of time talking to frontline staff in the branches, they were not giving him their honest views of how things were. We explained what we found in relation to the staff survey, and the fact that they told us in their droves that they never gave honest answers because of their fear of retribution.

We added that we'd compiled a document setting out detailed evidence from our fieldwork and this did not make pretty reading. We explained that the management culture created an atmosphere of fear and blame. We revealed to him that there were examples of management bullying people to hit sales targets as well as a number of totally inappropriate incentive schemes run by branch managers including "The Saturday Slayer", and an extraordinary one called the "Cash or Cabbage" competition. This allegedly operated as follows: hit your sales targets and get cash; miss your sales targets and get awarded a cabbage. It is difficult to think of anything more humiliating than that.

We alerted Hornby to the fact that given both our responsibilities and his own under the FSA's Approved Persons Regime, we would have no choice but to share our findings with the regulator in detail as they were at the heart of its statutory duties to protect consumers.

Hornby listened carefully and was fully engaged. He seemed upset about the staff survey findings. He never spoke a cross word and seemed completely understanding. After the meeting, James and I genuinely believed that he was well and truly on board.

Over the next few weeks we completed our fieldwork and then convened a meeting of the entire review team to analyse the detailed evidence and finalise our findings, conclusions and recommendations.

By late June a preliminary draft of our report went to Hornby and Whacker Walkden. On 4 July having worked closely with James, Hornby and Walkden, I was able to give a formal report in writing on the matter to Ellis and send him copies of the draft report and the detailed findings of selected branch visits. At this stage, everything looked like it was going according to plan.

In my accompanying email to Ellis, as well as setting out the timetable leading up to the formal report to the HBOS Board on 27 July, I highlighted the dilemma of how to deal with the findings from the branch visits and the likelihood that the dysfunctional behaviour we had found could lead to customer detriment. The report would be going to the FSA and needed to be completely transparent, so a consensus on an appropriate approach was essential.

The entire email is here:

www.crashbankwallop.co.uk/library/5-26

It's worth noting here that it is a tortuously difficult task when writing reports like these to strike the right balance between "telling it how it is" and "giving credit where credit is due", but at the same time making things clear for anyone who is able to read between the lines. This is made even more difficult when taking into account the following statement in the FSA's Principles for Business:

> *"A firm must deal with its regulators in an open and cooperative way, and must disclose to the appropriate regulator appropriately anything relating to the firm of which that regulator would reasonably expect notice."*

The problem of striking the right balance is increased exponentially when operating in an environment like the one we found at HBOS. It's a never-ending exercise in arguing the toss about everything.

Further skulduggery and jiggery-pokery ensued before we finally got into the boardroom on 27 July. The primary driver of this, in Davies' and my opinion, was not Hornby but his henchmen Whacker and long-term colleague and friend Ellis. In the run-up to that main Board meeting, relationships between GRR and key executives within Retail, as well as ours with Ellis, reached an all-time low as we were pressurised ever more to water down the drafting of our report. In the end, we simply refused to dilute it any further.

Entering the fray around this time, without any apparent consultation with anyone including the Group Audit Committee or the current heads of Group Risk, Crosby unexpectedly announced his intention to create a new General Management Board and main Board-level role with the title Group Risk Director (GRD). Instead of the Group Risk functions reporting to the CFO, after the appointment they would report to the new GRD. This meant that Dr Andrew Smith and I would have a new boss.

What motivated the move by Crosby is open to speculation but he promised a rigorous selection and assessment process for both internal and external candidates, to be led by headhunting firm Egon Zender.

The news was encouraging because it looked like Crosby and the Board were beginning to implement their commitment to strengthen the role of Group Risk. It also meant that we'd have someone at the top table every day speaking up for us.

Personally it wasn't a job I considered myself ready for and, despite the difficulties, I was enjoying the challenge of my current role. Nevertheless Crosby separately asked Dr Smith and me to meet him privately to discuss who we thought the new post should go to. I knew Smith would say that he should have the job but I had different ideas.

I met Crosby in his office in The Mound in Edinburgh one early summer's afternoon. He was his usual charismatic and extrovert self. I told him immediately that I didn't want the job and he looked surprised.

Then I said: "James, would you mind if I gave you some risk management advice about the new GRD appointment?" He laughed. Here was the head of GRR about to give him some risk management tips. He clearly found that funny.

"James, I strongly advise you against appointing any internal candidate to this role," I said. "The previous history of relationships may cause problems." I meant the political relationships. "Also, any internal candidate will have built up a world view of HBOS and a set of assumptions about the way things should be around here that may not be helpful."

I advised him that the appointee should come from the outside, be at the very end of their executive career and so would have no fear or conflict of interest in speaking up.

"And James, I hope you won't mind me saying this" – and I paused for effect – "You are a rather larger-than-life character and so, the person that you appoint, needs to have the courage to – how can I put it – grab you by the ears, shake you and say 'James, slow down, you're moving too fast, you've got to make the morning last!'".

Crosby laughed again, thanked me and I left his office hoping my advice would do the trick.

We completed the final draft of our formal report

in time for a timetabled meeting in Edinburgh on Monday 19 July with Whacker, Cullen and other members of their team. By that stage I think Whacker had realised that we were not going to make any further amendments. Although the meeting was intended to build bridges, it didn't.

At our get-together with Hornby back on 11 June, he had suggested that before the main Board met we present to his executive team. So on 22 July Davies and I joined the regular management meeting, on this occasion being held at the offices of Birmingham Midshires, the specialist "buy to let" mortgage provider within the Halifax group. Hornby opened the meeting and made it clear that we had his full support. However, watching the body language of Walkden and Dawson, who were among the gathering, it was quite clear that they, and others, were not on board. That meant trouble.

Later on that week I bumped into Dawson and to my surprise she smiled at me. That put me immediately on my guard.

"Hi Paul," she said. "How do you feel about the fact that Mike Ellis and James Crosby have been writing your report on the Sales Culture Review over last weekend?"

She was referring to the previous weekend, before the acrimonious meeting in Edinburgh on the 19th at which we were supposedly agreeing a final draft of the report.

I was shocked by Dawson's comment but I suddenly

realised what was going on. Ellis had decided that the only way to put me back in my box was to write his own version of the report to send to the Board directors.

I rang Ellis and he confirmed that this was the case. I asked him, why? He told me that he thought my report was too long and that, although it would be distributed along with the other papers for the Board meeting, he had decided to write a shorter version. This was complete baloney. Notwithstanding the enormously detailed work that we had done, we had managed to confine our report to just 17 pages. Ellis knew that the Board directors were all very busy and if presented with a short report by him, that was all they were going to have to read. This meant he would have control over what the report said.

However, Ellis wouldn't be able to prevent me attending the Board meeting where I could make oral comments that would have to be minuted. Also, Hornby had agreed with Davies and me that he would give the formal update to the directors and then invite me to add any comments, which I'd promised I would keep short and to the point.

The weekend of 24-25 July was a nervous one. I sat and reflected carefully as to what I should say when Hornby handed over to me. I needed to make these words count. They were crucial.

This had become even clearer when I received a copy of Ellis' Board report. As suspected, it massively underplayed the seriousness of the situation:

"In summary, the control environment within Retail requires strengthening in some areas to meet the growing demands of the business and emerging regulatory requirements, a fact that has been recognised by Retail. Indeed, some progress has already been made but there remains more to be done as is outlined in this report. The key to success will be to adjust the balance without 'swinging the pendulum' so far that it destroys the business that Retail have successfully developed to the benefit of both HBOS and its customers."

Ellis went on:

"Generally, the Governance framework and high level systems and controls are fit for purpose but some improvement can always be made."

He concluded:

"Regulatory risk appetite in Retail is low, in keeping with a Customer Champion strategy, but the control environment needs enhancing to support the strategy. While it is not believed that there are systemic issues giving rise to customer detriment, tackling the issues set out....will ensure that the risk and control environment keeps pace with the business and emerging regulatory requirements. Controls do, however, have to be commensurate with the risks involved and customers reasonable expectations in order to avoid 'swinging the pendulum' so far in the direction of controls that it destroys what Retail have built and hinders the business from delivering customer friendly products and services."

The idea that the "... control environment requires strengthening in **some** areas...." was a misrepresentation of our findings. It needed a root and branch overhaul.

The statement that, "Generally, the Governance framework and high-level systems and controls **are fit for purpose but some improvement can always be made**", again totally understated the problems. The conclusion saying, "**The regulatory risk appetite in Retail is low**,..." was so absurd as to be unbelievable, even laughable.

This report by Ellis is perfect evidence of the fundamental problem at HBOS that led to its downfall. When senior executives, and especially the CFO, cannot tell the truth to the Board in situations of significant and material risk, there can be only one ending to the story – a catastrophe.

Ellis was not a safe pair of hands. He would not speak up to Crosby or the Board. He would not put accuracy, competence and truth in the way of meeting the numbers. What was worse, he was also in charge of risk management. Ellis was the fundamental part of the problem himself. He's now Chairman of the Skipton Building Society which has assets of £16 billion. Let us hope he has learned from his experiences at HBOS.

All's Well That Ends Well

It was quite clear that I was going to have to make sure that my oral comments to the Board made matters abundantly clear and that they were properly minuted.

However, I decided that this Board meeting, the first that I had attended, was not a time for ad-libbing. I took out my notebook and wrote down what I was going to say verbatim. I still have that notebook to this day.

The Board meeting started at 10am on Tuesday 27 July. I got an early train from York to King's Cross and then a taxi to Old Broad Street. I arrived there by about 9.45am and made my way upstairs to the C Suite.

It was the normal pandemonium that preceded big meetings of this nature when all the great and the good are gathered together in one place. As usual, the mood was upbeat. To the outside world, HBOS was flying away and outperforming all of its competitors. Regulation and risk management was the last thing on the directors' minds.

Fifteen minutes later, they had all disappeared into the boardroom and I was left in one of the offices nervously waiting to be called in to give my update.

All was quiet on the Western Front. I knew what I was going to say and I just hoped that Andy would stick to his agreement and report our critical review properly.

The Board would also be receiving an update from PwC on its extensive, soon-to-be-completed review of HBOS's overall risk management effectiveness. My deputies, Davies and Tony Brian, and me had been interviewed as part of the process and the final report stated:

> *"We were particularly impressed with the limited number of people we met in GRR."*

PwC would have received fees well in excess of £1m for this work.

In addition, Dr Andrew Smith and KPMG were due to report on their findings of the "atypical credit risk management" in the Corporate Division. It was going to be a big day in the boardroom in relation to risk management and regulatory affairs, whether the directors liked it or not.

I was distracted from my thoughts by a knock on the office door. "Paul, you're about to be called into the meeting. Could you come and sit outside so that when they're ready for you, you can go straight in," said one of the ushers.

I walked out of the office, turned left past the smart cherry wood reception area, opened a set of double doors and turned right. The boardroom was on the left a short way up the corridor. There were a few chairs outside and I sat in one. Although I was confident, I felt my heart beating slightly faster and harder than normal. The wait outside the boardroom that day seemed interminable. It was probably only a few minutes.

"Paul, you can come in now." I stood up and went in through the right-hand doors. There they all were. All the key players and some others. It's a strange feeling walking into a room full of people who have been conducting a meeting. It's like walking into the heat of the battle. You feel like a stranger. The gaze of every single person in the room is directed at you like 40 laser guns. The metaphysics are obvious.

There was an empty chair on the side of the

boardroom table closest to the corridor. It was the only one, so I knew where to go. Once again I looked out of the window towards the Gherkin building. It felt a bit like that famous chair in TV's *Mastermind*: black leather, deep and comfortable, probably too comfortable in some ways. Almost directly opposite me sat Lord Dennis Stevenson, the HBOS Chairman. He sat slightly off to the left at about 11 o'clock. Crosby sat next to him with Ellis to his left and then Hornby.

"Well, it's over to you, Paul," said Lord Stevenson. "Tell us about the Sales Culture Review."

"Thank you, Chairman," I said.

"I'm glad to say that, having discussed our work in detail with Andy [Hornby] and having presented to his executive management team only a few days ago, we have agreed that, rather than me giving a formal presentation, Andy will give you the formal update and when he's finished, I may just add a few key points of my own. So, Andy, it's over to you."

"Thank you, Paul," said Hornby. "Before I start, I want to thank Paul and his team and the staff from Ernst and Young who worked with him, for the excellent work they've done in difficult circumstances and with challenging timescales."

Our plan for communicating to the Board was working like clockwork.

Hornby then spent about 10 minutes giving the Board his update. He did an exceptional job and got the balance right. He demonstrated that he stood right behind us and that matters were serious and had to be changed. He accepted responsibility for the position his Retail Division was in and, never once, tried to pass the blame to us or anyone else. I was delighted.

Then, as agreed, just as he ended, Hornby said, "Paul, have you got anything to add to what I've said?"

"Thank you, Andy, and thank you for your clear and comprehensive update. And, yes, I do have four key and important points I want to make, Mr Chairman."

I opened my cheap ring-bound notebook at the page where I had written my verbatim comments.

"Firstly, the Board should be aware that, although not stated explicitly in the report, the review has shown that the FSA were justified in having concerns as to the balance between the sales culture and the controls in Retail. This has become markedly out of balance.

"Secondly, the key to correcting the balance is to set up a well-considered, robust and achievable action plan, led by the divisional executive management team, which does not destabilise the major consumer benefits which Retail have so successfully brought to market with their product strategy aimed at simplicity, transparency and price. GRR will support, advise and oversee Retail's plan on a close and continuous basis.

"Thirdly, in the context of that action plan, very careful consideration should be given to exactly what standards and policies we consider to be consistent with Customer Champion strategy, The Way We Do Business [the ethics policy], and the current, as well as anticipated, regulatory standards. It will be this thinking that will underpin process design, risk and control management systems and the management information needed to monitor current performance. This will require a review of Retail's risk management systems."

"And, finally,..." at which point I glanced around the boardroom. My final point, as is often the case, was going to be my most important and I wanted to gain maximum attention. "...From a strategic perspective, very careful consideration should be given in the development of Retail's operating and strategic plans as to exactly what level of sales growth is achievable, given current capacity, without putting customers and colleagues at risk."

I had taken less than a couple of minutes to sum up months of detailed work.

And that was it. That was all I was going to say. There it was, in a nutshell. Retail was out of control and needed to do something about it. Central to this was a fundamental review of the "stack 'em high, sell 'em cheap" strategy introduced and led by Crosby.

There was an uncomfortable silence while the Board took in what I had just said. I knew that I had done the trick and that whatever they had made of Ellis' short report, they would no longer be under any illusion as to where things stood. It was serious and they needed to do something about it as a matter of priority.

Lord Stevenson finally broke the ice and piped up: "Thank you, Paul. Good we now have a Head of Group Regulatory Risk who is prepared to tell us what we need to hear. You can leave now."

I got up, walked towards the door slowly and said under my breath, "Thanks be to God"!

I meant it.

By that stage, we had been living in Yorkshire for nearly two years and, during that time, my journey in faith had well and truly begun. The catalyst had been that extraordinary moment in the middle of the night and the prayer of St Francis of Assisi.

As soon as Maureen and the children came up to join me in Yorkshire in December 2002, I had been going to Mass either in the parish church in Ampleforth of Our Lady and St Benedict or at Ampleforth Abbey Church itself. I had also started to do some deep reading about the Christian faith and referred to the Catholic daily Mass readings almost every day. The messages of the Christian gospel were not only becoming clear but had begun to make a huge amount of sense to me. Praying was a revelation and the one thing that became absolutely clear to me was that faith was a mystery. What is more, you only experience that mystery of faith when you actually take a leap of faith. I had taken that leap and the more I leapt, the more faith I got. The more faith I got, the clearer my mission became and the more peace I felt.

I was still in a mess but my faith was making a real difference. My drinking was becoming a real problem. I found myself drinking secretly from Maureen and the children. I used alcohol to calm me down, stop me thinking and take me away from the strains and stresses of feeling like I didn't fit in. I hadn't quite realised it by then, but I was beginning to think that I might be suffering from alcoholism. I knew it ran in families and I knew that my father had died of a cardiomyopathy brought about by alcoholism. Years after I had been fired by HBOS, I started to go to Alcoholics Anonymous (AA) and that incredible fellowship saved my life.

As soon as I had walked out of the boardroom that day in July 2004 all the stress of so many weeks and months drained from my body. Suddenly, I felt completely and utterly exhausted. I slumped in a chair in one of the offices to gather my thoughts and relax for a few moments. The great thing was we were off for a long, family summer holiday at the end of the following week on 6 August. Hurray.

I rang Davies to tell him the good news of what happened in the boardroom. I told him that they had "got it" and what Stevenson had said at the very end of the meeting. I even said I now thought that we were safe from Ellis.

The full versions of our report, version 2 of the selected findings from the branch visits (somewhat softer than the first version) and Ellis' short report to the Board are here:

www.crashbankwallop.co.uk/library/5-27
GRR final report.
www.crashbankwallop.co.uk/library/5-28
Selected findings of branch visits.
www.crashbankwallop.co.uk/library/5-29
Ellis' short report.

After speaking to Davies I got in a taxi, went to King's

Cross, took the train to York and drove the 35 minutes home to Wass. When I walked in I collapsed on the sofa in our little snug and poured myself a stiff drink. I told Maureen what had happened at the Board meeting and we both celebrated believing that everything would now get easier.

Throughout the many difficult years of my professional career and, particularly, during those first 10 months after I was promoted at HBOS, Maureen was my closest confidante and trusted adviser. Even though she had no professional background or, for that matter, many academic qualifications, she just understood. It was amazing. She would let me waffle on at length about all the trials and tribulations and would soak it all in. And, when the going got really tough she would often be the one who made the best judgement call of what to do next. She had an extraordinary insight into pretty much everything and everyone and even at both a physical and metaphysical distance. She had faith in God and was my rock and, whatever happened, she knew in her very soul that He had a plan and, just like the Joseph and his amazing Technicolor Dreamcoat story from the Bible, "It was all meant for the good". Thank you so very much for everything you are and everything you do, my dearest Maureen, and thank God for your deep faith which has protected you and me from sinking in the mire of human trials and tribulations.

I can't remember what happened in that last week or so before we went on our summer holidays but I guess it would have been like it always was; clear the decks, handover as much as possible to others and pray that no crises would happen while I was away which would interrupt my much-needed holiday and family time. I knew that when we got back in late August, it would be back to the same old perpetual grindstone. We'd only just started at HBOS and there was still a huge amount more to do.

September would be the time for preparing for the next crucial Group Audit Committee meeting, as well as making a start on developing and writing operating plans and budgets for the following year. It was a never-ending cycle but I remember thinking that I probably only had another five years before we would be financially independent and could do what we liked.

We flew out to Malaga, in Spain, on 6 August and were due back on Sunday 29 August. We had rented an apartment near Marbella and Puerto Banus in a complex called Los Naranjos, which means The Oranges. It was cheap and cheerful but perfectly comfortable. We could look up the mountain from the apartment roof-terrace towards where our new luxury villa was being built. We had put the deposit down in April 2002 but there had been delays due to geological problems, so they hadn't even started building it yet. However, we went up with the children and took photos of where it would be and looked out over the amazing view.

One particular memory from that holiday was reading a book by a psychologist who had survived a Nazi concentration camp in the Second World War. It was called, *Man's Search for Meaning* by Viktor E

Frankl. From his experiences, he developed a whole new psychological methodology to deal with the post-traumatic stress caused by living in and surviving the concentration camps. Good always came from bad and he proved it. As it says in Job, "He giveth and taketh away"; something that I was about to experience myself.

I just love reading and read very widely on a whole range of topics. For me, it was at the heart of my continuous personal and professional development. One of my very favourite books which teaches us so much about life is called, *The Road Less Travelled* by M Scott Peck. This is a book about personal and spiritual development and the first three words of the book are "Life is difficult." Never a truer word was written. Another is by the well-known American philosopher, Ken Wilber, called *A Brief History of Everything*.

I'm not a fan of sunbathing and so I would spend much of my time on holidays in the shade reading, which took me away from the stresses and strains of work and built the cerebral filing cabinets of my knowledge and understanding.

Another highlight of that holiday was one day going to a fabulous beach called Bolonia on the Atlantic coast, just north of the Straits of Gibraltar, to meet up with friends, the Joyce's, who were staying somewhere nearby.

Bolonia has a long, fine-sand beach and lovely, clear cool ocean. It also had the best Chirringuitos (simple Spanish restaurants, often next to the sea) that we knew. My favourite lunch there comprised "chorizos, huevos y papas fritas" or, in English, sausage, egg and chips, but of course, the sausage was the highly spiced Spanish version and was delicious. They also made an amazing rice pudding with nutmeg for dessert.

That day, we were all lying on the beach after a good lunch and the children were playing in the water. Oliver, our youngest, was just 10 years old. Suddenly, he gave out an almighty scream and started clutching his foot. I picked him up and carried him to where we were all sitting under our umbrellas. He was screaming in pain. None of us knew what was causing it. There seemed to be a small mark on the bottom of his foot but it didn't look very serious. Fiona Joyce, who was a GP, suggested putting ice on it. That only appeared to make matters much worse and he screamed even louder. Oliver was in paroxysms and Maureen and I were getting very worried. We were miles away, as far as we knew, from any medical facilities so we decided to carry him back to the car in case we needed to rush him to a hospital. As we struggled across the beach, we caught sight of a red cross on the side of a small hut. This was the last thing we had expected but we made straight for it.

The main reason for the hut being there was to treat the many cases of people standing on weever fish. These tiny little creatures swim in the shallows and bury themselves in the sand but have a sharp dorsal spine with a very nasty venom in it. When someone stands on one, it is complete agony. Anyway, as soon as we got there, they knew what the problem was and stuck his foot into warm water with disinfectant in it. The pain subsided almost immediately, which was a great relief to Oliver and us. They told us that the very worst thing to do was to put ice on the wound as this increases the pain. After Oliver's pain had subsided and because he suffered major reactions to bee stings, he was given a powerful antihistamine injection to avoid any swelling on his foot. It was very convenient that Maureen's mother tongue was Spanish and she could communicate with the medics.

Since that time, I've always worn swimming shoes on that beach.

I often went running early in the morning when it was cool along the Golden Mile, a wonderful track on the seashore between Puerto Banus and Marbella. At school, I could run the standard cross-country course of about 5 miles in just under 28 minutes, including the 250ft hill in the middle. Since we now lived so close to Ampleforth, I had taken up running in the old boys' cross-country match that took place on the first or second Saturday of the Lent term. I always came last but I didn't care. One year, I decided to take our new puppy Laszlo on the run, much to the amusement of the other participants. At least he kept me company as the others ran off into the distance.

We flew back in to Leeds Bradford Airport on 29 August. The following day was a bank holiday. I went back to work on the Tuesday only to be met by the normal torrent of emails and other communications. It always took quite a few days to get back on top of things after a holiday and, by the time I'd done this, it was time to start preparing my formal report for the next Group Audit Committee meeting scheduled for 11 October.

Reports had to be with the company secretary by Monday 4 October at the latest, to allow time for them to be printed and sent out in hard copy to all the people attending the meeting, but in any event it had to be on Ellis' desk for 27 September. Committee papers could take a great deal of time to read, let alone understand or digest. Charles Dunstone one day said to me: "Well, Paul, even if I had time to read the papers for the Retail Risk Control Committee, which I don't, I wouldn't understand them anyway!" The amount of paper was ludicrous but it gave the illusion of governance. As The Parliamentary Commission on Banking Standards later observed:

> *"Governance at HBOS was a triumph of process over purpose."*

The fact of the matter is that the entire governance systems of major organisations, public or private, simply don't do "what they say on the tin". Nor does the statutory audit. The speed and complexity of business since the Internet and mobile communications revolution has just got too much for the current design of corporate governance. It needs a major overhaul, including a fundamental change to the fiduciary duties of company directors. I write a lot more about this in Part 2 of my memoirs.

Davies, Tony Brian and I were very concerned that the more detailed 17-page report on the Sales Culture

Review had not been printed and included in the Board papers for the meeting on 27 July.

It's true that Ellis had said that copies were available "on request" in his own shorter report but it was very unlikely that any of the directors, in those circumstances, would have asked for one. This meant that the full report had, as yet, never been formally tabled at a meeting.

As a result, the three of us decided to table the whole job lot at the Group Audit Committee meeting in October. This would mean that at least the four main Board non-executive directors who formed the committee would have read the more detailed report.

On 23 September, Davies and I attended and gave a formal update on the review to the Retail Risk Control Committee. For the second time, when the minutes came out, they were inaccurate and I had to have them amended. I was beginning to think that the Company Secretary's department thought that it was okay to write and sign off minutes of formal meetings which were not, in reality, a true and accurate record.

The final minutes of that meeting are here:

www.crashbankwallop.co.uk/library/5-30

The inaccuracy of the minutes of the Retail Risk Control Committee meeting made me realise that I had not been sent a copy of the extract of the Board minutes following our update at the meeting on 27 July. This was obviously wrong. The extract relating to the part of the meeting that I attended should have been sent to me, as a matter of course, for review before being signed off. I immediately emailed the Company Secretary's department and asked for a copy. When they finally arrived and I got to read them I was appalled. They didn't minute what I'd said at all. In fact, they seriously misrepresented what I had said.

> *"In summary, the GRR review confirmed that the Retail governance framework and high level systems and controls were fit for purpose; and Retail regulatory risk appetite was low; but improvements could undoubtedly be made – to meet the growing demands of the business, and emerging regulatory requirements. This was acknowledged by Retail to be the case: but it was essential to effect improvements without destroying the key strengths of the business."*

The minute writer, who was Harry Baines, HBOS's General Counsel and Company Secretary, had obviously written the minutes directly from Ellis' own report and ignored what I'd said. Baines had even certified them as a true record.

The entire extract is here in section 7 of this document www.crashbankwallop.co.uk/library/5-31

I was working at home that day. It was Friday 1 October and I drafted an email to the Company Secretary's department.

I was sitting at my desk in our little office at home next to "the snug" which is where we all hunker down on those cold winter nights to watch the TV or listen to music. It's a lovely little room, part of the original Keeper's Cottage with a low-beamed ceiling and a little fireplace. At the time, Maureen was in there. She knew what was going on and I called out to her about my email. I asked whether she thought that I should send it to Ellis first for his approval or whether I should send it directly to Pamella Connolly who was Baines' executive secretary. I read the draft of my email to Maureen.

"Pamella, Thanks for this. I just wanted to check that the minutes covered the points I made. I am still not sure as to the exact protocols associated with minute writing at HBOS but they don't quite follow my own notes of what I said." I'd gone on to repeat the four key points I'd read from my notebook, and finished my email by writing: "Not sure whether you want to do anything about this? Perhaps you should have a quick word with Mike Ellis. Regards, Paul."

Maureen told me that it would be much better to send it to Ellis first to see what he had to say. So I inserted a message to Mike, above the draft message, saying:

"I was a little surprised at the difference between what I had actually said and the minutes...see my note below which I have not yet sent to Pamella. Shall I send it? By the way James and I had a similar issue with the Retail RCC we attended and I have had the same issues in relation to the one I attended on 23 September.....It is obviously very important that minutes do accurately reflect the key points which were made."

Ellis responded on Sunday 3 October as follows:

"HBOS minutes are not a record of verbatim comments as this would be incredibly time consuming and repeat a lot of what is in the agenda papers and, therefore, a matter of record. We encourage open discussion at meetings

and wouldn't wish people to be speaking – just for the record. If there is something important that is said and not covered in documents of record – then it should be minuted – but I thought that the Board minute was OK. You should be under no doubt that we do and always will adopt proper procedure. I can't comment on the Retail RCC as I wasn't there."

He suggested I take up my concerns with Harry Baines.

"The Board minutes for July were approved at the September meeting," he wrote.

It was a cleverly written email suggesting he was committed to adopting "proper procedure" while giving me the option as to what I should do.

I discussed this correspondence with Davies on the Monday. We faced a serious dilemma. Here we had Baines and Ellis trying to shield my report from the Board. This was a serious matter on any analysis: legal, regulatory or ethical. The Board minutes were always made available to the FSA so this was a failure to act with integrity. We also had our own obligations under the Approved Persons Regime that put us at risk if it was to come out later that we had been involved in some kind of cover-up. What were we to do?

We decided that, as we'd now tabled the full version of our report for the upcoming Group Audit Committee meeting, caution was the better part of valour. So I wrote back to Ellis on 5 October and simply said: "Thanks… I think I'll leave it…"

The email trail is here:

www.crashbankwallop.co.uk/library/5-32

But, the matter still wasn't over.

I had completed the final draft of the Audit Committee report on 27 September and sent it to Ellis for review. He made only minor amendments at that stage.

The entire final report is here:

www.crashbankwallop.co.uk/library/5-33

The hard copies of all the papers for the Group Audit Committee meeting were distributed on 4 October. I didn't check them because I assumed that my report and the attached appendices would be included. Later that week on 8 October, which was the Friday before the meeting, I checked them. To my consternation, the full version of the Sales Culture Review was not there. At that point, I assumed that this was simply a clerical error and so I rang up my secretary and instructed her to forward the report again to the Company Secretary's department and ask her to send it out to the relevant distribution list for the Group Audit Committee meeting papers. This included the entire HBOS Board, even those who were not on the Audit Committee.

Alison Owen, who worked in the Company Secretary's department, immediately forwarded our email to the distribution list including Ellis. On Sunday 10 October (the day when Ellis often caught up with his emails) he sent me this missive:

"Paul, This really looks bad and just look at the circulation list! There was no need to attach the appendices to your report

in the first instance as they have already been seen / made available to all Board members. But if you were going to do so we ought to have got it right. People will be wondering why we are circulating separately a document they've already seen – it looks like we're making an issue of it when we're not."

By now I'd had enough of Ellis' games. I was seething. A few hours later after our normal family Sunday lunch and when I'd calmed down, I replied to Ellis:

"Mike, I am sorry you feel so strongly about this but, with all due respect, this document (i.e. the full GRR report) has not been seen or formally put on the record as you state. Your short paper presented to the Board has been seen but not the full report."

I said that the FSA would have expected to see a full copy of such an important document and as it was referred to anyway in the main text of our report, someone would have noticed it missing. I asked Ellis if I could meet with him for a few minutes before the Audit Committee meeting the next day. I needed to have another frank discussion with him, if only to warn of the potential personal regulatory risk he was placing himself in.

Ellis replied just before 8pm that Sunday evening in a somewhat more conciliatory tone. He said the full report should possibly have gone to the Retail Risk Control Committee but admitted,

"I didn't review your paper before it went as I didn't have time and it didn't go to GMB [Group Management Board]. If Group Secs misprinted – then this didn't help – but in reality it wasn't necessary to send the paper."

The entire email trail is here:

www.crashbankwallop.co.uk/library/5-34

The next morning, I got up early, went to York station and got the train to King's Cross. Once again, I made my way across the City in a taxi to Old Broad Street. The meeting started at 10am as usual in the same boardroom. I sat down next to Ellis and could almost feel the tension between us.

When it got to my point in the meeting to report to the committee, something unusual happened. Just as I was about to start, Tony Hobson, the committee chairman, said: "Paul, just before you start I want to say something." He'd never done this before. "I want to thank you very much indeed for having tabled the full version of your Sales Culture Review because now I realise just how serious things are."

"Thanks be to God", I said under my breath. I was truly delighted. We had the support of the chairman and there was nothing Ellis could do now. It was time I had a private meeting with Hobson to sort these matters out once and for all. I was going to suggest that the Group Risk departments, including Crosby's new Group Risk Director, should report to Hobson.

Normally, I'm dead against winning arguments against people by appealing to a higher power but things had gone too far. Ellis had become a major risk to HBOS.

The Group Audit Committee meeting minutes are here: www.crashbankwallop.co.uk/library/5-35

They recorded that I'd said relations with the FSA

were growing stronger but that it was important not to be complacent and that careful consideration needed to be given to realistic levels of sales growth in Retail. I'd also reported that Retail had established a so-called Category 1 project to resolve the issues arising out of the Sales Culture Review.

> *"Its scope included dealing with all aspects of the sales process, including the balanced approach to objection handling, as well as an investigation into specific areas of potential customer disadvantage / unacceptable sales behaviour identified during the review and referred to in the report."*

I left the committee meeting at 2pm in an exceptionally good mood and later that afternoon emailed Davies and Tony Brian who had been waiting with bated breath for news: *"All's well that ends well!"* How wrong could I have been?

Exactly one month to the day, and almost to the hour, later, when I met Crosby on that fateful 8 November in Halifax, he did the Alan Sugar on me, "You're fired!".

So, we are now almost back to where I started this sorry tale, this tragicomedy. But there's lots more to tell about what happened after I was fired by Crosby.

Meanwhile there were two other important pieces of work that HBOS had agreed with the FSA to carry out, as part of the Risk Mitigation Plans following the 2003 Arrow visits. They were the PwC section 166 Skilled Persons Review on the overall risk management effectiveness at HBOS and the review of the "atypical credit risk management" in the Corporate Division.

Updates on both these matters were given to the Board on 27 July at the same meeting at which I reported on the Sales Culture Review. I was not present, although I believe I should have been, for those parts of the meeting. However, I managed to obtain copies of the minutes relating to the items. I was still suspicious about whether or not these minutes were accurate, but nevertheless the contents were telling.

The entire minutes relating to these two items are here: www.crashbankwallop.co.uk/library/5-31

What Ellis had to say about PwC's review was another fudge of the facts. The minutes said PwC was *"clearly satisfied that Risk Management within HBOS was effective and satisfactory. In Mike's view the FSA (and the Board) should be satisfied with the outcome of this exercise."* A meeting would be held in August between HBOS, PwC and the FSA to discuss the report. The minutes added: *"Although this had been a costly and time consuming exercise, three years after the merger the Group had received external validation, following a very thorough review, that its Risk Management Infrastructure was sound."*

One paragraph stated: *"Whilst the Report contained a number of recommendations about improvements that could be made…"* When I looked at the actual PwC document, the recommendations ran to more than 10 pages.

The document is available in full here:
www.crashbankwallop.co.uk/library/5-36

It seemed to me that PwC had decided to soften the

high-level messages it was giving but to manage its risk by making sure that there was a comprehensive list of recommended changes to which HBOS had agreed. This is a standard way of professional services firms managing their client relationships and getting the job done. I am also quite sure (because its people told me), that PwC gained a significant amount of comfort about the future for the effectiveness of risk management at HBOS from the new vision, strategy and plan of GRR.

After Ellis had given his report, the partner from PwC gave his update, followed by the senior manager from PwC who had led the engagement. PwC's Chris Taylor was minuted as reporting,

> *"...based on their comprehensive review, PwC were satisfied that there was real and constructive challenge taking place within the group".*

On credit approvals in Corporate, PwC "were happy to support current arrangements. Although arguably atypical, they were effective and arose following conscious decision-making, for good business reasons. Whether the FSA would support or be convinced by this view remained to be seen."

I am quite sure that Taylor would not have written the last sentence of the first paragraph if it had not been for the much more rigorous oversight that GRR had begun to carry out over the past nine months or so.

I think PwC did do a good job but ultimately its recommendations didn't really get implemented. Perhaps PwC could have agreed an on-going role to audit the implementation of its plan but without doubt the FSA should have insisted upon this. As St Bernard of Clairvaux put it so eloquently: "The road to Hell is paved with good intentions."

So far as the review of credit risk management was concerned, the minutes made extremely interesting reading. The lack, in almost all cases, of any kind of independent challenge to corporate lending was among the key conclusions. They provided an excellent explanation of how and why HBOS Corporate Division ended up incurring an estimated £26 billion of loan losses on a total loan book of £116 billion, far worse than the appalling performance of Royal Bank of Scotland. And, what is more, this loss on loans does not include the losses that HBOS made when it also invested in the equity of companies, which happened frequently. No one has yet identified the level of losses on equities but I would be surprised if it was less than £10 billion. This would make the total losses £36 billion, more than 31% of the total loan book. This is an astronomical figure which could not merely be explained through incompetence and may very well include criminal dishonesty. This is yet to be investigated.

> *"The Division's processes were already subjected to continuous review and improvement; the KPMG/GFR review contained some positive suggestions that would be adopted; 'independence' was not the same as, or a substitute for, 'competence'. Nonetheless, pragmatically, changes would be made, and the details would be confirmed to the Board in due course."*

The FSA wanted a continuous independent review of credit approvals but HBOS was not going to have any of that. This would slow it down.

Rarely in my professional life have I read a more Machiavellian set of reasons for avoiding, or perhaps I should say evading, proper separation and balance of power in relation to the management of a material risk. KPMG obviously went along with this. That was both incompetent and unethical and it should be held to account by the relevant authorities, including the Financial Reporting Council. Sadly, that's not going to happen while so many of that regulator's senior executives are ex-KPMG alumni.

An example is John Griffiths-Jones, the former Senior Partner of KPMG and now Chairman of the Financial Conduct Authority. He later told his partners' conference that the reason KPMG had not "raised the red flag" in its statutory audits of big banks was because it would have been commercial suicide. In other words it would have lost its whopping fees.

This continuous "aiding and abetting" (if not conspiracy) by the Big Four firms of accountants – Deloitte, PwC, Ernst & Young and KPMG – and professional advisers in the wrongdoing of their large corporate clients is at the very festering moral and political heart of what is "rotten in the state of Denmark". If society doesn't do something about this, we are all in real trouble.

So, after what appeared to have been a watershed moment at the Group Audit Committee meeting, I was feeling a great deal more relaxed.

The next item on my busy agenda was to write the draft of my departmental operating plan for 2005 to 2006.

We had already carried out a good deal of work in preparation for this and I believed that everything was heading in the right direction.

I completed the document on the weekend of my birthday, 30 October, partly with the view of it providing the basis for an agenda at an off-site senior management team meeting I'd arranged for the next month. I'd booked a luxury hotel in the Lake District from the evening of 9 November until the morning of 11 November to discuss the business plan which was entitled More Of The Same – But Even Better.

It identified, in an extensive list, the key regulatory risks facing the organisation as we saw them. With hindsight the first three points made for prophetic reading:

- *Being able to demonstrate that our growth is under control and will be achieved without a substantially increased risk appetite.*
- *Continued focus and improvement in our approach to risk management generally.*
- *Treating customers fairly.*

The entire plan is here:

www.crashbankwallop.co.uk/library/5-37

Precisely the opposite of managing these risks happened at HBOS and for some reason the FSA failed to follow through on its proposed "*close and continuous*" supervision of the bank.

Surely it had nothing to do with James Crosby being appointed a non-executive director of the FSA in January 2004? This was an extraordinary decision and people might conclude that it was either gross incompetence or, worse, some kind of crony capitalism by the powers that be? Crosby was indeed close to the leaders of the ruling Labour Party.

On that Hallowe'en Sunday 31 October, with my blueprint for the future at HBOS completed, I turned off the computer and relaxed with Maureen and the children for what little remained of my birthday weekend. I don't recall any "trick-or-treat" callers at Keeper's Cottage that evening but a trap had already been set for me later that week.

CHAPTER 6

"The Decision was Mine and Mine Alone"

I was still in a state of total shock when James Davies found me, dragging hard on a cigarette outside the bank's head offices. Moments earlier I'd called Maureen to tell her Crosby had fired me: my head was in a spin. It was just another grey November afternoon in Halifax but, for me, it felt as though the world had ended.

"Is everything alright, Paul?" said James. I took a deep in-take of breath, another draw on my cigarette, composed myself and attempted a smile: "Yes, I'm fine, James. Come on, let's get the car."

James and I had pre-arranged to meet after I'd seen Crosby, so that he could come and stay at my home in Wass for the night, as the next morning we were both travelling to the Lake District for the three-day, off-site business planning meeting. My UK management team would be gathering at a small but exclusive hotel on the shores of Ullswater for what had become an eagerly anticipated annual "bonding" session. As James lived near London it made sense for him to stay up North with me.

The two of us walked the short distance to the underground executive parking bays to collect my car but we hadn't even driven up the steep hill leading out of Halifax to the M62 motorway before I cracked.

Although Crosby had instructed me to keep my dismissal confidential, I knew I could trust James to keep quiet.

"Crosby's fired me!" James had sensed something was wrong but nothing this bad. He was clearly knocked sideways but he said nothing. There was the deathly hush of a person witnessing an execution. It said it all.

It was ironic. Only a week or so ago we had both been musing in a private moment about the past year and agreed that, although it had been the toughest we'd experienced, we had done the best job since we started working together. That was saying something too, considering how many other complex and difficult regulatory projects we'd worked on over the years at KPMG. We knew we'd regained the confidence of the FSA because it had told us so. Our department had also emerged smelling of roses from the recent independent "Skilled Persons Review" of HBOS's risk management effectiveness, and since the Group Audit Committee meeting in October we now believed we had the confidence and, therefore, protection of committee Chairman Tony Hobson, the respected former Finance Director of life assurance company Legal & General. We both turned out to be wrong.

James knew that Crosby's decision to fire me was unfair and, after the moment of silence, said so in unusually emotional style and terms. Like me, he also knew why he'd done it and thought – although he didn't say it then – that being the tenacious character I was and doing the job the way I had, what happened was hardly that surprising. James offered me nothing but sympathy and support on that journey back to Wass.

As we drove we were debating why Crosby hadn't told me who the new Group Risk Director would be and why he was waiting until Friday to announce it, when James leaned back in the cream-leather passenger seat of my BMW, folded his arms and chuckled to himself. "I bet he'll appoint Jo Dawson," he said light-heartedly. It lifted the gloom in the car and we both laughed loudly. The mere idea that Crosby would appoint sales manager Dawson seemed so ridiculous as to be comical. The fact that she had threatened me and James knew made it even more hilarious. This was tragicomedy at its very best; only the British could do this.

I really don't remember much of what happened when James and I got to our home that night. It was a blur. A mix of adrenaline, alcohol and the myriad of thoughts in my head created a whirlwind of emotions and responses. It was a heady cocktail.

What I do remember is the astonishing way in which Maureen responded to the news of my dismissal which would have floored most people's partners. While I felt like the world was falling apart, she was a rock. Without her support, not just that day but in the years to come as the story of the banking crisis and my part in it unfolded, I would not have survived and could not have done what I did. It was not a soft, mushy sort of support. It was not sympathy or pity. Nor was it anger and hatred. It was a strong, bold and fearless type of support – but peaceful at the same time. It was a support full of faith in the future. It was a support born out of her deep Christian faith, trust in God and unshakeable belief that, in the end, the truth always sets you free. It was the same faith that believes that we get transformed by trouble and that good always emerges from bad. It was the faith that I had also just begun to explore again myself as I joined HBOS.

The Morning After The Night Before

The next morning, Tuesday 9 November, following a late and restless night, I woke with a surprisingly clear head considering the amount of red wine I'd downed and after a leisurely start James and I left Wass for the two-and-a-half-hour drive to Cumbria for the meeting which would bring together my top 14 managers.

My team descended on the lakeside hotel late afternoon in a buoyant and enthusiastic mood. Despite the queasy feeling in the pit of my stomach, I greeted everyone in the bar for drinks before we all freshened up prior to a gourmet dinner, sadly wasted on me. The real work would be done on the Wednesday and Thursday but the gathering was equally seen as a great opportunity to re-engage, "chew the cud" and develop the sort of *esprit de corp* that any team needs to perform to the highest standard. It was particularly important for GRR as we all worked in such geographically diverse locations so spent very little time physically together. The agenda essentially covered a review of the department's performance for 2004 and a full discussion and agreement of the operating plan for 2005 and 2006.

From a personal perspective, it all felt terribly surreal.

There I was, supposed to be providing the team with the strategic vision and inspiration to celebrate our performance in the incredibly difficult year that had almost passed, as well as to prepare and "gee" everyone up for another difficult year that was about to start – and yet I had only been dismissed the day before by the Group CEO and told that I had lost the confidence of key executives and non-executives. That was hardly a vote in favour of what we had been doing or what we might plan to do. Not only that, but Crosby had also forbidden me to tell anyone that I had been dismissed until he had made the formal announcements on the Friday of that week. James Davies knew but no-one else could and I had to behave as if nothing had happened, as if it was "business as usual".

My only confidant was James, so we would both have to behave as if nothing had happened. It was going to be a very difficult few days pretending all was hunky-dory but I was determined to act professionally and to the very best of my ability. Whatever Crosby and others might think, I was confident that GRR was carrying out its approved business plan efficiently and to the book. That's what my team members expected to hear and that's what I told them.

The simple fact was that Crosby hadn't kept his side of the bargain in "strengthening our hand in delivering against our responsibilities" and "taking steps to clarify and reinforce the role of Group Finance and Risk". He'd done the exact opposite.

I'd given the draft business plan we discussed in The Lakes the title "More of the same - but even better". The tragicomedy of this was not lost on James or me.

At the same time as leading the management meeting, I also needed to consult lawyers about my legal situation and protect my position with HBOS itself. Michael Wainwright, my close solicitor contact at Eversheds, a top London international law firm, had advised me to try to engage Peter Frost at commercial lawyers Herbert Smith (now Herbert Smith Freehills) also based in the Capital. During a break I rang him but he told me that he was conflicted from acting for me against HBOS, but recommended a solicitor called Clive Howard at another London legal services firm called Russell, Jones and Walker (now Slater & Gordon). It was well-known and respected for representing claimants in complex employment law disputes against large companies and, in particular, whistleblowing cases – although, at that stage, I had no idea that I had a whistleblowing claim against HBOS.

I phoned Clive immediately from the hotel and explained the position. He was only too delighted to take on my case. Clive is about 5ft 10in tall with brown hair and a friendly face. He's softly spoken and smiles a lot, which always made me feel at ease with him. He has also represented some of the highest-profile whistleblowers in the UK and only works for claimants, so has no conflicts of interest.

Clive told me that, as a first step, I needed to ask Crosby, without making reference to the fact that I had consulted lawyers, to provide me with a full explanation, in writing, as to why he considered my role at HBOS was redundant, the process he had adopted in making that decision and the precise reasons why I had lost the confidence of certain executives and non-executives.

To get the ball rolling I spoke by phone to David Fisher, the HBOS Group HR Director, at 4.30pm on 9 November. He sent me a file note of the call and the next day, so that there could be no disagreement about the matter, I wrote directly to Crosby confirming my position. This is part of what I wrote:

"In our meeting on Monday you started by telling me that due to a reorganisation there was no longer a role in HBOS for me. You did not explain the process that you adopted for arriving at this decision or who the person was who would be able to fulfil the accountabilities for which I am currently responsible. You then went on to add that you felt it would only also be fair to tell me that there had also been issues of confidence in me and my performance raised by key executives and non-executives.

In this regard, could you please let me know the process and the basis on which you arrived at the decision that there was no longer a role for me at HBOS? Could you also please elaborate on what the issues of confidence were, particularly having regard to the excellent progress we have been making in our approach to risk management across HBOS?

I accept that Group Regulatory Risk have 'raised the bar' in relation to its accountability for group-wide oversight of the effectiveness of regulatory risk management in the operating divisions. The fact that we were going to do this was explicitly stated in our 2004 Business Plan which was presented to, and accepted by, the Group Audit Committee in December 2003. In carrying out that oversight I accept that, on occasions, my team and I have been obliged under the Approved Person Regime to raise some very challenging issues for the organisation, particularly in Retail.

As the leader of Group Regulatory Risk some of the most difficult issues have been for me to communicate. The challenges that we have raised have not always been comfortable for those to whom they have been addressed – nor, for that matter, has it been comfortable for me and my team. But it has been my accountability to raise such challenges – and it has clearly delivered results. Tony Hobson only last week commented to me what a 'turn-around' he thought there had been in the confidence which the FSA had in HBOS. The positive comments explicitly made about the people PwC met in GRR when they carried out the S166 Review of Risk Management Effectiveness is another reason why I need to understand more about the confidence issues to which you referred in our meeting.

In these circumstances, I think it only fair that I should understand what the issues of confidence are that have led to this situation.

On the issue of there being no continuing role for me at HBOS, I believe that I am actually entitled to a full explanation of why that is the case and the process and thinking adopted to arrive at such a decision.

I look forward to hearing from you on my requests for further explanation of the circumstances leading to your decisions and rapidly moving to a fair and reasonable closure having regard to the three key matters I set out above."

On the 11th, the final day of the management meeting, I got a message relayed to me from Fisher saying Crosby would give me the explanations I was seeking the following Monday 15 November. We finished at Ullswater in the afternoon and, after dropping off James, I drove straight home to await the formal announcements the next day and find out who would be appointed the new Group Risk Director. Would it be Dr Andrew Smith? Unlikely. An outsider perhaps? Jo Dawson? Not even Crosby would be that foolish. The HBOS Board and especially the non-executive directors wouldn't allow it. Anyway, the FSA would never formally authorise a sales manager with no experience of advising on risk management, regulation or governance as an approved person for these crucial roles.

Of course, when I got home I hit the bottle again. I also continued what I'd been doing over the last few nights at the hotel, scanning the facts and wading through swathes of emails and reports from the past year. Maureen had long gone to bed when my batteries finally went flat but I retired that night with renewed confidence.

Crosby couldn't possibly get away with it. The evidence was overwhelming. HBOS was in trouble with the regulator. I had been asked to sort it out and the feedback from colleagues suggested I was doing a very good job of it.

Crosby must have essentially made the decision to fire me on his own, in clear contravention of FSA requirements, HBOS's own governance systems, the explicit group HR policies and any ordinary person's notion of fairness. And it was against HBOS's own ethics policy which stated:

> *"We will create a safe working environment which encourages openness, honesty and mutual respect, and where colleagues can constructively challenge and ask questions. We will offer equal opportunities for all. We will provide the opportunity for all colleagues to develop their skills and knowledge, and to enjoy fulfilling careers. We will offer competitive remuneration with total rewards linked to individual and collective performance, and the opportunity for colleagues to participate in the success of HBOS."*

Yes, once all the facts came out, the tide would turn and Crosby would have to do a volte-face – an about-turn.

On Friday morning 12 November my bedside alarm clock woke me as usual to the six o'clock headlines on my favourite BBC Radio 4 Today programme. I felt as though I'd been asleep for five minutes. The story of veteran Palestinian leader Yasser Arafat's death, the day before, was still dominating the airwaves but I had my own breaking news to look out for.

Formal announcements of major re-organisation

are highly organised affairs in large publicly quoted companies like HBOS. In this case, first Crosby would send a memo by email to his "Insider Group", then a few minutes later a general announcement would go out on *HBOS Today*, the company-wide intranet and employee communications platform.

Shortly after that the Group Finance and Risk department would get the message on its own internal news sheet, *The Standard*.

I'd not prepared a GRR communication because, apart from my dismissal, I knew nothing else. Once I knew something I would write to my staff. I didn't even know precisely what the Group Finance and Risk communication written by Mike Ellis would say, although I had requested to have final sign-off of anything it said about me.

However, the fact was that whatever spin anyone tried to put on it, no one would be under any illusion as to why I was going: I'd challenged Crosby's expansion plans.

I'd had a smoke, a coffee, a shower and got dressed and was sat poised impatiently in the office at home when *The Insider* announcement flashed up onto my company laptop, bang on 10am. I clicked to open the document and immediately started to read. One sentence in Crosby's memo leapt out at me:

> *"Jo Dawson moves from her current role as Retail's Head of Advisory Sales to Group Risk Director reporting directly to me".*

And then it happened again. Just like the Monday when Crosby fired me.

Crash! Bang! Wallop! Adrenaline shot. Heart thump. Long pause. Gather thoughts.

Crosby had appointed his protégé, the sales manager, Dawson; the "lady" who had threatened me over the Corporate Bond Funds review.

It turned out that James Davies' ridiculous joke was the best example of the expression, "Many a true word is spoken in jest".

Dawson had been able to action her warning, "Don't make a fucking enemy out of me", in the most extraordinary and ruthless way. Not only had she obviously been one of those "key executives" who had lost confidence in me but she had managed to implement her threat by actually taking my job.

Before I could gather my thoughts, five minutes later *The Standard* pinged through to my email inbox and I opened it to see what Ellis had to say.

He knew very well that I was running my management meeting that week. He must also have known that Crosby had fired me. Yet he never contacted me during those three-and-a-half days before the formal announcements. Why? Was he scared of me? Was he embarrassed? Did he just not care?

Ellis' announcement in *The Standard* was banal. They usually were. He wasn't much of a communicator. This is what he wrote about Jo Dawson:

(See www.crashbankwallop.co.uk/library/6-1)

Organisational Changes Announced

Mike Ellis

Following the announcement of senior management changes in HBOS Today, this edition of The Standard looks at what these changes mean for colleagues in Group Risk.

What's changing?

I'm delighted to announce that Jo Dawson (currently Head of Advisory Sales in Retail) has been appointed Group Risk Director with effect from 31 December 2004. Jo will report to James Crosby and will be a member of the HBOS Executive Committee.

Jo Dawson

Jo joined Halifax in June 2000 as General Manager Retail Sales with responsibility for developing sales through the branch network before moving on to her current role as Head of Advisory Sales.

Before joining HBOS, she was Business Development Director at Green Flag and prior to that held a number of senior management positions at NatWest in both Retail & Corporate as well as Central Strategy & Finance roles.

Commenting on her new role Jo said "Having truly world-class risk management across the whole of HBOS is a real source of sustainable competitive advantage in our business. We have a strong platform on which to build and excellent risk management professionals both in the centre and in the divisions. It's an exciting opportunity - and the prize for success is enormous".

This is what Ellis wrote about my dismissal:

Paul Moore (Head of Group Regulatory Risk) will be leaving HBOS. Until he leaves Paul will work with Jo to ensure a smooth handover of responsibilities. Over the last two and a half years Paul has led both IID Risk and GRR through major renewal programmes whilst delivering a significant 'business as usual' agenda. The 'New Horizons' Programme in particular will create a strong foundation upon which GRR will be able to build for many years to come. We wish Paul every success in the future.

It was obvious from his statement that I'd been sacked and I wasn't going to try to persuade people otherwise. I quickly typed out an email message to the whole of my department and sent it out at 10.13am.

"You will have just read James Crosby's communication in HBOS Today setting out his plans for wide-ranging organisational changes at the top of HBOS including the appointment of Jo Dawson as the new Group Risk Director.

In this regard, you will, no doubt, also have read Mike Ellis' communication in The Standard, which he sent out a short time ago and which tells you that I will be leaving HBOS.

For my part, although I am naturally very sad not to be able to play a longer term role in the development of GRR, I am also hugely proud to have been involved with you all in making such significant changes and progress over the last year.

In my view, our achievement as a team has been remarkable and has clearly had a major impact on the confidence with which the FSA is now treating HBOS as a whole. Thanks so much to you all for coming on this journey with me, you are a great bunch.

My and our job now is to work together with Jo to effect the most professional and smooth transition as possible to enable the department to continue the excellent progress it has been making.

No decision has yet been made on my leaving date but there is a good deal to do before then. As soon as we have decided the most appropriate date, I will let you all know.

We must take some time for a real celebration of our performance and hard work in 2004."

The very next thing I did was ring Phil Hodkinson. He answered as he always does, "Phil speaking." I didn't announce myself – he'd recognise my voice.

I just said: "Well, what do you think of that?" He replied without a hesitation: "The decision was unconscionable." Knowing how balanced and fair Phil always was, his comment had a particularly powerful impact that gave me considerable comfort.

At 10.27am, I received the following email from Howard Posner who ran HBOS General Insurance. It read:

> *"I am immensely sad you are leaving. You have done a great job, created a great team, and left a quality legacy. I hope we can have a beer to mark your going and I wish you luck in your next enterprise."*

Not much later I got a call on my mobile from Dougie Ferrans, Chief Executive Officer of HBOS's £75 billion asset management business Insight Investment Management.

Dougie had become a close professional colleague and, almost, a personal friend. He was a truly great business leader and I had a very high regard for him. He had known Crosby for many years and worked with him when they were both fund managers at Scottish Amicable.

I think it is fair to say that he was not only a professional colleague of Crosby but also a friend of his.

The first thing he said was, "That's the worst decision James Crosby's ever made in his life." A few days later Ferrans wrote this letter to me:

Douglas Ferrans
Chief Executive

Insight INVESTMENT

HBOS plc

Insight Investment

www.insightinvestment.com

Telephone calls may be recorded

PERSONAL

17 November 2004

Mr Paul Moore
Head of Group Regulatory Risk
HBOS plc
1 Lovell Park
Leeds
LS1 1NS

Dear Paul

I thought I would drop you a quick line to say how sorry I was to see you were departing HBOS. I fully understand why!

You have achieved so much in such a short space of time . . . often unrecognised by those around you. I have thoroughly enjoyed working with you and having you as a trusted colleague (and pal). The same can be said about you by all of the Insight team...

You have been a tremendous asset to the IID and Group businesses and I am sure you will go on to bigger and better things elsewhere.

Let's have a jar before you go (at the Forum?).

Regards,

Dougie

I knew exactly what he meant by, "I fully understand why!" It was because I'd challenged Crosby.

I received many other messages of support both in writing and orally from colleagues in HBOS at all levels. The idea that Dawson was right for the Group Risk Director's job appeared to be treated almost universally with disdain.

It is quite extraordinary that she would have had the hubris to accept the role. It carried very high personal risk and the mere fact that she accepted demonstrates quite clearly that she knew nothing about risk management!

A few days after the announcements, after having trawled back over meeting minutes, correspondence and reports and boosted by peoples' support, I began to believe I was on much stronger ground than Crosby might think.

I even said to my secretary one day: "Don't worry, he'll have to go. The evidence is unequivocal. He won't be able to resist it."

By now I was in full consultation with my lawyers, Clive Howard and Peter Hamilton, a barrister. Clive advised me that not only did I have a case for unfair dismissal and breach of contract but that I also had a whistleblowing claim against HBOS.

The law on whistleblowing in the UK is complex but, in essence, an employee is protected if he or she discloses information which in their reasonable belief tends to show that a person is failing or is likely to fail to comply with any legal obligation and, if so, that the reason (or principal reason) for the employee's dismissal was that he or she raised that information.

Information of this nature is called a Protected Disclosure and if an Employment Tribunal finds that an employee has raised a Protected Disclosure, then it is for the employer to prove that the reason or principal reason for the dismissal was not because they raised the disclosure, or disclosures, in question but for something else.

In this regard, raising information, as I had done, as to

the actual or potential breaches of the FSA's regulatory requirements was clearly sufficient to have amounted to Protected Disclosures and we didn't think it would take a tribunal long to agree.

UK whistleblowing legislation was never originally designed with heads of risk, compliance or internal audit directly in mind, as it was effectively their jobs to blow the whistle on foolish, unethical or illegal behaviour.

It also turned out that the FSA itself had very specific guidance on how it would treat an authorised firm and an approved person who acted to the detriment of a whistleblower.

The relevant section of its rulebook read:

> *"The FSA would regard as a serious matter any evidence that a firm had acted to the detriment of a worker because he had made a protected disclosure about matters which are relevant to the functions of the FSA.*
>
> *Such evidence could call into question the fitness and propriety of the firm or relevant members of its staff, and could therefore, if relevant, affect the firm's continuing satisfaction of threshold condition 5 (Suitability) or, for an approved person, his status as such."*

The ability of HBOS to continue with its fierce sales and growth strategy and, at the same time, comply with the key FSA Principles for Business was precisely why I had raised the challenges to the bank's Board in the first place.

My concerns related particularly to principles one, two, three and six:

1	Integrity	A *firm* must conduct its business with integrity.
2	Skill, care and diligence	A *firm* must conduct its business with due skill, care and diligence.
3	Management and control	A *firm* must take reasonable care to organise and control its affairs responsibly and effectively, with adequate risk management systems.
6	Customers' interests	A *firm* must pay due regard to the interests of its *customers* and treat them fairly.

In effect, the FSA guidance on whistleblowing meant that if the FSA found any evidence of HBOS acting to the detriment of a whistleblower, this could call into question the actual authorisation of the whole bank itself, as well as the individual authorisation of anyone involved who was an approved person, especially Crosby.

It felt to me like the metaphorical noose was tightening around Crosby's neck and my confidence and energy was returning.

To take the battle for truth and justice forward, I agreed with my lawyers that we would set about preparing an Outline of Case to present to HBOS and its advisers. This would contain easily sufficient evidence to make our case but without it containing all the evidence. We decided the first person to present it to should be Chairman of the Audit Committee, Tony Hobson, the most senior director at HBOS responsible for overseeing the actions of the executive. Our strategy was to demand a detailed independent investigation which would then force the HBOS Board to reconsider Crosby's decision.

Very importantly, I was formally advised by Peter Hamilton that I had no choice but to blow the whistle on this matter beyond the Board of HBOS directly to the FSA itself. This was not a voluntary matter because, as I was an Approved Person of Significant Influence under the FSA regime, which meant that that my function (my job) was *"one which is likely to result in the person responsible for its performance exercising a significant influence on the conduct of the firm's affairs, so far as relating to a regulated activity of the firm"*, I had a personal regulatory obligation to comply with The Principles for Approved Persons which stated: *"An approved person must deal with the FSA and other regulators in an open and cooperative way and must disclose appropriately any information of which the FSA would reasonably expect notice."*

If I did not comply with this statement I could be subjected to direct disciplinary and enforcement action myself. It was absolutely obvious that I should disclose what had happened, and my views on why, to the FSA. The regulator should have suspected it in any event. Not only that but, even if I had been the sort of person who thought that what had happened to me was just an opportunity to make money by forcing HBOS to pay the highest possible compensation to me, that was just out of the question. Indeed, the records will prove conclusively that we refused point blank to enter into any discussions about settlements until after I had fulfilled all my regulatory responsibilities.

A barrister myself, I'd practised law for 12 years of my career and as my children will attest, I am stickler for the evidence. As a result, I was and still am a meticulous record-keeper and so finding all the key evidence that supported my case wasn't at all difficult. I had kept every document, email and note I took and in a highly organised fashion. I still have every document I wrote on my first desktop PC which I got when I joined American Express in 1989.

I wrote the first draft of the Outline of Case and compiled all the documentary attachments but it would have to be Hamilton who produced the final version to avoid the danger of me writing any self-serving statements that could potentially destroy my defence.

Meanwhile, we finally got Crosby's response to my 10 November memo on 23 November and, to our great delight, it showed him up to be a person who thought he could do exactly what he wanted with impunity and without having to give any proper explanation to anyone. It also proved that he had no regard whatsoever for HBOS's own governance systems, its HR policies, its ethics policy called "The Way We Do Business", the regulatory requirements or employment law – let alone just basic fairness. It was clear that he had drafted the memo himself with no proper legal advice and without thinking very carefully about the risks. It was also contradictory. In one paragraph he wrote:

> *"The decision regarding your role ...was taken quite independently of the choice of individual to take on the role of Group Risk Director."*

Then in the next he put:

> *"The new Group Risk Director role has inevitably led to some delayering to avoid "compression", particularly in view of the mix of skills and experience in the new team."*

Crosby completely failed to recognise the foolishness of referring to the "mix of skills and experience in the new team" when the only person who had joined the team was Dawson and she had no skills and experience in risk management.

He was just plain wrong when he wrote:

> *"It is not appropriate for me to set out in writing the process through which the decision was reached."*

His response proved that, for a highly intelligent man, he was in the iron grip of hubris and that his level of confirmation bias was so high that he had no perception at all of the risks.

One phrase in the memo summed up his state of mind perfectly:

> *"The decision regarding your role was mine and mine alone."*

Yes, it is true, “Power corrupts and absolute power corrupts absolutely.”

It was a long journey in faith and many years before I finally found a way towards forgiveness and the real desire for reconciliation with Crosby. I wrote to him offering it but he has not responded, yet.

That mixture of wilful blindness, lack of integrity, unfairness and no mercy is a hard journey to travel for the victim – as is overcoming the sense of self-righteous indignation. But, it’s also a rocky road for the perpetrator, particularly after the Nemesis takes place. As former British government Cabinet Minister Jonathan Aitken has proved – when he faced his confessional moment in prison following his fall from grace for perjury and perverting the course of justice – forgiveness and peace race towards repentance and Godspeed.

Ultimately, if both sides come through their journeys, the respective experiences are both redemptive. The truth really does set you free and forgiveness releases you from the self-destructive force of anger and hatred.

CHAPTER 7

The Outline of Case –
"There is an Overwhelming Inference that Mr Moore has been dismissed... because he has done his job well..."

A short time after receiving Crosby's "the decision was mine and mine alone" memo, something quite surreal happened.

I had to go to Edinburgh for a formal handover meeting with Ellis and Dawson.

Due to major refurbishment work, we couldn't meet at Ellis' office in the splendour of The Mound – a grand domed Victorian edifice set in the shadow of Edinburgh Castle high above the city's famous Princes Street, and headquarters to Bank of Scotland for two centuries. Disappointingly the venue was moved to a bland room in a modern non-descript building nearby.

This was the very first time I would be communicating with Mike Ellis since Crosby had fired me on 8 November. I had received not a single telephone call or email or anything else from Mike since that day. He had expressed no empathy and given no explanation to me for what had happened.

The meeting was bizarre. Ellis, probably due to

embarrassment, was determined to transmit that it was all business as usual and that my dismissal was an unfortunate case of redundancy and had nothing to do with my performance.

Dawson, on the other hand, would have remembered her aggressive threat to me earlier that year and must have known that it could easily have amounted to gross misconduct if I had made a formal complaint. She may have wondered whether this might surface and get in the way of her promotion and her authorisation as an approved person by the FSA. Then again, as Crosby's rising star, she may have felt immune like he obviously did. However, Dawson had absolutely no experience of advising on or leading departments which advised on risk management, regulatory affairs or corporate governance.

Suffice to say, the body language of both of them was very "shifty" and the meeting was awkward. Neither Ellis nor Dawson expressed any sympathy, let alone compassion, for my dismissal. I think they were both fearful that if they did they might cause legal difficulties.

Ellis accepted my self-assessment of GRR performance for the year which would form the basis of my annual appraisal for bonus purposes. In essence, the evidence strongly supported the view that we'd had an outstanding year – just as James Davies and I had agreed only a few weeks before.

Here are two slides from the "talk book" document I took to the meeting:

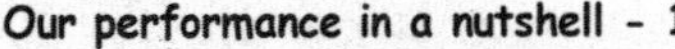

Our performance in a nutshell - 1

- HBOS regulatory risk profile reduced. FSA's confidence significantly increased. Additional ICR to be removed. No regulatory censure.
- Positive outcome of S166 - "We have been impressed with the limited number of senior personnel that we have interviewed in GRR"
- Positive feedback received from George Mitchell, Alistair MaCrae, Steven Cragg, Colin Matthew, Richard McDonald (BOSI), George McArthur (HBOSA)
- "Our relationships with GRR in particular have been good......We are quite comfortable to rely on GRR......and that is the real test" Kirstie Canneparo - 26th November 2004
- "I can't believe the turn-around in our relationships with the FSA" - Tony Hobson - November 2004
- Major organisational change in GRR effected highly successfully - MORI.

Our performance in a nutshell - 2

- "An excellent year all round building on a similar result in 2003. The New Horizons programme has been transformational. The work with HBOS FS in SJPC (life-saving support!) was excellent and both are emerging in much better shape as a result. You have recruited some excellent people and have inspired many of the old GRR folks to new heights." Phil Hodkinson 30 November 2004.
- "Phil, Thanks for the opportunity to contribute and to see the IID executive views [on GRR]. Very helpful. Its obviously very positive feedback for Paul and the team and I can only reiterate your positive views. Tony" Tony Hobson 30 Nov.
- Outstanding oversight and advice work carried out in Retail despite difficulties which has added significant value and protected Retail from **undoubted** FSA intervention. Courage in action.

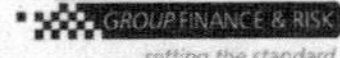

You can see the entire document here:
www.crashbankwallop.co.uk/library/7-1

The meeting ended. Ellis thanked me for the presentation and he and Dawson stood to stiffly shake my hand before I left the office in a bit of a haze. Dawson stayed behind, presumably to avoid any chance of bumping into me again on the way out.

As I walked down the corridor to leave the building, I passed the offices of all the other HBOS Board directors. One of them was occupied by Mark Tucker, the new CFO designate and, noteworthy, a professionally qualified football referee – I suppose you could say, another whistle blower! He was due to take over from Ellis on 1 January 2005 and had joined the company a few months earlier from the Prudential. I didn't know him well but had spent some time with him at a Group off-site meeting and I'd found him to be most personable.

As I passed his office, I glanced sideways to see Tucker beckoning me to come in with a gentle movement of his hand, as if he didn't want anyone else to know. I was slightly surprised at this but nonetheless went in. He closed the door and offered me a seat. When I'd settled he looked me directly in the eyes in a soft and empathetic way and said he was very sorry to hear that I would be leaving – something that Ellis hadn't done, and never did. Then he said: "Do you mind if I give you some advice?"

I wondered what was coming but replied: "Of course not, I would welcome it."

There was a pregnant pause as he gathered the "momentum" to say what he had to say. "Paul, if I was you I wouldn't make a big fuss about leaving HBOS.

I would go quietly. Otherwise, you might find that it could affect your future career prospects."

Here was a highly respected individual, about to take over the second most senior executive role at HBOS, warning me in a caring, non-threatening way, that if I sought justice by fighting my corner I might put my career at risk. Tucker was showing me kindness in the best way he could by trying to stop me making matters worse. I really appreciated it.

I can't remember exactly how the conversation continued but I'm sure that I took the opportunity to put my case to him and that, without expressly agreeing with me, it seemed clear that he did. I may be wrong and I might have simply interpreted what he did as support but I don't think so.

Tucker's advice turned out to be absolutely "on the button" but I never really gave it any serious consideration. I wanted truth and justice, and what was more, I still thought I had a good chance of turning things around.

Perhaps that was where, in a very different way to Crosby, I was also in my own iron grip of hubris. It was certainly a kind of blindness and naivety – blindness to the risks to one's own career in situations like this.

So I just threw myself into preparing a battle plan with my lawyers and by Thursday 9 December we had almost finished drafting the Outline of Case which set out a summary of our legal submissions and the evidence that supported them. My long-time friend and colleague Peter Hamilton was the architect of this legal masterpiece.

Hamilton, an insurance and regulatory specialist, was (and still is) outstanding. Born in 1941, he was nearly 64 at the time but he'd been the obvious choice to represent me. A very distinguished-looking man – tall, chiselled features, handsome and with snow-white hair – he looked like a Heavenly judge from one of the great Masters' paintings. In fact he's an atheist and I sometimes tease him by asking him to say, "Thank God, I'm an atheist!" He also took great pride in being in competition with the journalist Jon Snow for who could wear the most garish tie. Actually, Hamilton was rather Bohemian at one level and definitely liberal by inclination. Tragically he was born to a grieving mother after his father, a pilot in the South African Air Force, was shot down over Somaliland after Italian leader Benito Mussolini's invasion of Ethiopia.

Our strategy was to make a first approach to Group Audit Committee Chairman Tony Hobson. So I rang him on 9 December and asked him to meet me and my lawyers privately on Monday morning 13 December in London. I explained to him that the situation was very serious from a regulatory perspective and we would be bringing detailed documents setting out our position which we would leave with him. I also told him that it was vital we meet face-to-face as there were matters we had not put into the documents that we wanted to draw to his attention.

At the same time we were keen to "eye-ball" him. Lawyers use the expression, "The demeanour of the witness is also evidence", and it applied here. We wanted to see his body language. You can often tell more from that than all the emails in the world.

I'd always found Hobson to be measured, kind and intelligent. He chaired meetings fairly and wasn't at all gung-ho. He certainly took no persuading to agree to a meeting and seemed, on the phone at least, to be sympathetic.

I'd told Clive Howard that what I really hoped for was to be reinstated at HBOS in a way that Crosby would not lose face. Reinstatement is one potential remedy for unfair dismissal that an employment tribunal can order. However, it doesn't happen very often for the obvious reason that the relationship between the parties has normally broken down irretrievably. Personally, I did not feel that way. I naively believed we could resolve matters fairly with Crosby if only we could get the attention of people like Tony Hobson, HBOS Chairman Lord Dennis Stevenson and the FSA. Over the years I'd often had to manage situations in which people had made foolish mistakes in the name of protecting their own personal position and making money. This was just the nature of the beast. My approach was that if somebody, including me, did something wrong, admitted it, apologised properly and learned from it, then everyone should just move on and forget it.

Clive had listened to me like a good, client-focussed solicitor but clearly thought I was mad.

I just wasn't a political animal and found it very difficult to think in a Machiavellian way. I recently discovered that some people who seek to gain and maintain power, actually use the Italian writer Niccolò Machiavelli's book, *The Prince*, as a kind of training manual. It states, as bold as brass:

> *"It can be said of men that they are ungrateful, fickle liars and deceivers. They shun danger and are greedy for profit. Therefore it is necessary for a ruler who wishes to maintain his position to learn how to be able not to be good."*

My delight at Hobson's response lasted precisely one day. At 5.25pm on Friday 10 December the following carefully scripted email from Hobson dropped into my inbox:

> *"Paul*
>
> *I picked up your message and left a reply on your mobile, the gist of which I summarise below. Unfortunately, following our phone conversation on Thursday, I am now committed to another meeting on Monday morning.*
>
> *I am anxious to ensure that the Audit Committee investigates your concerns, but this investigation, of necessity, has to be measured and to the timetable that the Committee feels to be appropriate. My resources are limited and therefore, I do need to have a clear statement of your concerns and the evidence you wish us to consider. Thus, a two hour presentation from you and your lawyer would not fit the bill. Specifically, it would make it very difficult for me to ensure that I have presented your concerns and evidence appropriately to my Committee colleagues.*

Thus, the way forward is for you to let me have a written statement of your concerns as soon as possible. I will then consider them with my Committee colleagues and then arrange a meeting with you, one to one.

You are absolutely right to bring these matters to my attention. This has always been my open offer to you, David and Andrew, at all times since I assumed the role in 2001. Once received, I will ensure that your concerns are given the proper attention.

Tony"

You can find this email here:
www.crashbankwallop.co.uk/library/7-2

Lawyers can normally tell the difference between an email written by the lay person and one drawn up by a lawyer for the lay person to send. When I read Hobson's my immediate reaction was that it was of the latter. We can't be certain but the clear inference was that other people at HBOS had "got to him" and told him not have the private meeting with us. Given the clear importance of the meeting from a regulatory perspective, there was no good reason for him to prioritise another one. It was beginning to look like he was "turning turtle". The meeting was now off so we'd just have to send him the documents.

Clive and I read Hamilton's final draft that weekend and it was a work of art. It was clear, concise and powerfully understated. Less equalled more. It was Hamilton's drafting at its best and he had produced it almost exactly 20 years to the day since I had first started working with him professionally at Allied Dunbar on 10 December 1984. I had seen a lot of his drafting over the years and had always been in awe of it. The Outline of Case was as good as I had ever seen. He had not only put his technical skills to work but I could feel the strength of his emotional support in it. This is just one example:

> *"There is an overwhelming inference that Mr Moore has been dismissed from his job as Head of GRR because he has done his job well and for making one or more 'qualifying disclosures' as defined in s.43B of the Employments Rights Act 1996."*

It was advocacy at its best in writing. It was advocacy at its best in writing. Hamilton was a highly respected expert in financial services law and regulation, even having sat on the disciplinary committee of an earlier regulator to the FSA called The Personal Investment Authority. He had the perfect credentials to be taken seriously by the FSA in this matter. If this didn't do the trick then nothing would. It is well worth reading and sums up my case against HBOS perfectly.

The original document and its 19 supporting documents here:

www.crashbankwallop.co.uk/library/7-3 in a separate folder called, "Peter Hamilton's skeleton".

We dispatched the Outline of Case with the accompanying documents by courier to Hobson on Monday 13 December. The covering letter from Clive read as follows:

Private & Confidential
Mr Tony Hobson

Our Ref: CPH/dds/597504.1
Your Ref:

13 December 2004

BY COURIER

Dear Mr Hobson

RE: PAUL MOORE

I enclose Outline of Case together with supporting documents on behalf of Paul Moore.

Paul has taken advice both from this firm and from Counsel, Peter Hamilton. We thought it was appropriate for these documents to be presented to you at a meeting. We still believe the meeting is appropriate.

The Outline of Case was prepared by Counsel on the basis that it would be presented to you at a meeting with additional information provided by oral submissions. It should therefore be read in that light.

We still believe a meeting is appropriate and therefore should be grateful if you could let us have your dates of availability.

As the Outline of Case states, we ask that HBOS:

a) Initiate an independent investigation as set out in paragraph 59.

b) That Mr Moore be asked to co-operate (he will agree to do so) with the investigation.

c) That appropriate protection be provided to Mr Moore pending the conclusion of the investigation.

d) That Ms Dawson should not be permitted to take up her proposed role as a Group Risk Director until the conclusion of the investigation.

As you will see from the papers, Counsel has advised that Mr Moore needs to make full disclosure of the matters set out in the documents to the FSA. We need to discuss this aspect with you.

We would add that if we have not received appropriate assurances as required above, Mr Moore has been advised in any event to see the FSA prior to the end of this year. We need these assurances by close of business on Friday 17 December 2004. For your information Mr. Moore has a meeting provisionally fixed with the FSA on Tuesday 21 December.

Finally, you will see that the allegations relate, inter alia, to James Crosby. Whilst we consent for the details of this matter to be provided to the Chairman, we believe that the details should not be provided to James Crosby prior to the investigation.

Yours sincerely

Clive Howard

Enc Outline of Case and supporting documents.

C:\Documents and Settings\352194\Temporary Internet Files\OLK70\L1213THx.doc

THE LAWYER AWARDS 2000

Web Site: www.rjw.co.uk
Regulated by The Law Society.
A list of partners can be inspected at our offices in:
London Wakefield Birmingham Bristol Manchester Sheffield Newcastle Cardiff Associated Office: Edinburgh

Hobson confirmed receipt of the letter and Outline of Case and immediately referred us to Harry Baines, HBOS's General Counsel.

Clive wrote to Baines on 16 December repeating the fact that I had regulatory obligations to inform the FSA of the matters referred to in the Outline of Case. In the same letter I also asked Clive to make a formal request that I should be kept in post "actively carrying out" my duties while the investigation which we had demanded was undertaken. This was an attempt to avoid actual dismissal and to put into effect my desire to "wind back the clock".

Baines replied on the same day. Here is a copy of his letter:

Paul Moore

Dear Sirs

Thank you for your letter of 16th December. I confirm that I am the appropriate contact within HBOS. I also confirm, as you already know, that an independent investigation will take place in relation to the issues raised by your client. Mr Moore will be contacted, and asked to co-operate with that independent investigation, in due course. Your letter of 13th December indicates that he will do so.

In the discussions that have taken place with your client, and evidenced by the draft Compromise Agreement – to which we have not had a response – the Company has indicated its willingness to discuss the precise terms upon which Mr Moore would leave the HBOS Group. But that willingness to discuss terms does not extend to a reconsideration of the details or timing of the reorganisation that has been announced, which will go ahead as planned.

On assuming the role of Group Risk Director, Ms Dawson will take over responsibilities most recently carried out by Mike Ellis, **not** by your client. This is not simply a re-allocation of your client's responsibilities. The role of Group Risk Director is considerably broader, and more senior, than your client's role – which, under our reorganised approach to the management of Risk, will no longer exist.

As your client's role will no longer exist, it follows that he cannot be kept in post, "actively carrying out" his duties, whilst the investigation takes place.

I regret, therefore, that I cannot give you the confirmation that you seek.

Yours sincerely

H F Baines
Company Secretary

It was good news in that HBOS had now formally agreed to carry out an independent investigation but disappointing that I wouldn't be kept in post while it was conducted. My dismissal would therefore take effect from the end of play on 31 December 2004. Nonetheless, I remained confident in the knowledge that any proper independent investigation would see all the evidence and Crosby would then be in serious trouble: probably even more so with him being a non-executive director on the Board of the FSA.

We responded to Baines' letter on 20 December:

Private & Confidential
Harry Baines
HBOS plc
The Mound
Edinburgh
EG1 1UZ

Swinton House 324 Gray's Inn Road London WC1X 8DH
Tel 020 7837 2808 Fax 020 7837 2941 DX 202 Lon/Ch'ry Ln
Direct Tel 020 7837 2808

Our Ref: CPH.MRN.597504.1
Your Ref:

20 December 2004

By e-mail only:
harrybaines@HBOSplc.com

Dear Sir

RE: PAUL MOORE

Thank you for your letter of 16 December 2004. I think as we have already indicated by e-mail, the fax number used to send your letter was incorrect.

On behalf of our client, we confirm that he will be meeting with the FSA today. We note that you were not able to give us the confirmation that we sought.

We wish to make two points.

Yourefer to discussing precise terms on which Mr. Moore would be leaving the HBOS Group. We have set out in detail the concerns that our client has concerning regulation and compliance. It is inappropriate at this stage to discuss the terms on which he would be leaving and that is why you have not had a response from us in respect of the compromise agreement.

We note that you state that Ms. Dawson will take over responsibilities most recently carried out by Mike Ellis and not by our client. There seems to be a misunderstanding on your part as to the duties which were carried out by Mike Ellis.

Mike Ellis did not carry out the Control Function 10 Oversight Role. Our client carried out this role. He was in charge of oversight. Jo Dawson is having papers completed whereby she takes over the Control Function 10 Oversight Role.

Therefore Ms Dawson is taking over responsibilities most recently carried out by our client, not Mike Ellis.

Yours faithfully

Russell Jones & Walker

Baines, just like Crosby, had made a serious technical mistake which just supported our case both for unfair dismissal and on the whistleblowing claim; my job could not be made redundant and Ellis never did my job. If I went, Dawson had to take over my job and she didn't have the credentials. Even if she had, then I could only have been removed for not doing my job properly.

So the die was cast. We were off to see the FSA.

And so we did: that very day, 20 December. We met Kirstie Caneparo at 3pm at the FSA's Canary Wharf offices at 25 North Colonnade, just above the Pitcher & Piano bar that I used to frequent so often in the old days at KPMG.

Caneparo was the manager of the FSA's supervisory team responsible for HBOS. I'd met her many times and she was always the consummate professional. She had a big, complex and very difficult job and had led the Arrow visits to HBOS – that resulted in my promotion in 2003 – and all the follow-up supervisory work. She was highly intelligent, had great instinct and attention to detail and went about her business in a careful and quietly spoken manner. There were some from HBOS who didn't treat Caneparo with the respect she deserved but even so she always behaved impeccably with everyone.

I had a high regard for Caneparo and am pretty confident that nothing that followed in the HBOS saga, and my part in it, was really her responsibility. My guess has always been that, whatever happened and whatever part she played in the FSA's failure, was due to political pressure from above. I may be wrong and, of course, if she had been put under undue influence to do things that were wrong, she should also have blown the whistle.

As part of my day-to-day job at HBOS, my team and I would meet with Caneparo or other members of her team to discuss specific areas of supervision as and when required. On 26 November, less than a month before I was meeting her now, we'd held one of our quarterly "stock takes" in the HBOS boardroom in Old Broad Street. My deputies, James Davies and Tony Brian, along with members of her team were also there and everyone was in a very good mood. We were all beginning to feel that we were making progress in taming the beast that was HBOS. It was at that very meeting that Caneparo said:

> *"Our relationships with group regulatory risk in particular have been good. We are quite comfortable to rely on GRR and that is the real test."*

From my experience it was almost unheard of for a lead supervisor to make an open positive comment like that. It's rather risky in case something goes wrong shortly afterwards. So I remember very well how exuberant James, Tony and I were after that meeting.

Well, the saying goes that a week is a long time in politics. In this case, 24 days was a lifetime in the regulatory affairs of HBOS and Paul Moore.

We had sent Caneparo the Outline of Case that morning of 20 December but hadn't attached the documents. It would be better for her to make a demand for them from HBOS which she had the power and responsibility to do. By doing it this way, there could be no arguments about whether I had breached my confidentiality clause in my contract of employment.

You can see a copy of our letter to Kirstie here

www.crashbankwallop.co.uk/library/7-4

It had not only been hard work over the past month or so but it had been very emotionally draining getting to this point in the fight. I trusted my lawyers to put my case in the best possible way but, I suppose more importantly, I felt I could trust Caneparo to understand it and treat it with the seriousness that it deserved.

After some short correspondence between Caneparo and Baines, the documents were duly sent over from HBOS on Thursday 23 December giving her the key evidence to support our allegations.

Christmas 2004 was now upon us but it wasn't to be a very happy one for my family and me. Actually, I don't remember much about it. I suspect I spent most of it in an alcoholic stupor. What I do recall is the constant and unwavering support of Maureen and my friends.

It was definitely not a happy New Year. On 1 January 2005 HBOS enforced the dismissal date it had set. I was out of work.

Furthermore, we had refused to negotiate any financial settlement with HBOS, despite its attempts to force us. We did not want to be or be seen to be acting in conflict of interest, trying to drive the highest possible settlement by agreeing to cease and desist from pursuing our case against HBOS. For now all I could do was uncork another bottle of wine.

CHAPTER 8

The So-Called "Independent KPMG Report"

It's incredible the huge sense of foreboding an innocuous brown envelope can generate.

For three days one such A4 package lay menacingly on the mat underneath our front-door letter box: with my destiny neatly tucked away inside.

It had arrived at our cottage by special courier and I'd signed for it, but I just couldn't face reading its contents. So I just left it on the floor. I walked past it umpteen times, stared at it and once or twice nearly opened it. For two nights that anonymous brown envelope kept me awake.

It was 1 May. Four months of angst had culminated with KPMG delivering its verdict on my dismissal from HBOS. Now its final report was lying in my hallway and today I'd steel myself to peruse its findings.

Although it was good that the bank had agreed to an independent investigation into my allegations, I'd had mixed feelings all along about the appointment of its own auditor KPMG to run the enquiry. Initially though – after becoming officially unemployed on 1 January 2005 – I'd had a few important practicalities to deal with before concentrating my energies on the investigation.

I negotiated with HBOS to keep my life assurance and disability cover under its scheme, for the financial protection of Maureen and the children. The bank also agreed to continue paying me and to hold off talks on my dismissal settlement, until KPMG had carried out its probe. My contract of employment entitled me to 12 months' notice and the equivalent of a year's wage, so any continuing pay could be offset against the final financial settlement. HBOS agreed to all of this without argument. As well as my office printer, it also allowed me to keep my laptop with access to the bank's email and server system for ease of communication. This meant too that I was able to retain and copy all of the key emails and documents which supported my case against HBOS: a somewhat risky move from its perspective, I would say.

My legal team had received the news on 11 January about the appointment of KPMG to carry out the investigation, in an email from HBOS Company Secretary Harry Baines' office:

> *"We have now retained KPMG to carry out the independent investigation into the matters raised by the dossier that you submitted to Tony Hobson prior to Christmas. The partners concerned are Giles Williams and Adam Bates. Giles and Adam would appreciate an early conversation with you and I have given them your HBOS email address and mobile telephone number as the most convenient way of making contact. You should expect to hear from them in the very near future."*

See www.crashbankwallop.co.uk/library/8-1

My immediate concern was the obvious conflict of interest in HBOS's auditors doing the work. I wasn't even sure if KPMG was actually permitted under its own rules on conflict management to accept the engagement, let alone under the code of conduct of the Institute of Chartered Accountants in England and Wales (ICAEW), the self-regulatory body that supervises accountancy firms.

Much later, one of KPMG's most senior partners, and a good friend of mine, said to me on the phone: "What KPMG did in relation to your investigation was completely wrong."

What was more worrying was that Giles Williams would be one of the two KPMG partners leading the investigation: we had history.

Williams was a tall, good-looking, bespectacled guy, with golden hair, and was always smartly dressed. I'd worked closely with him when I was at KPMG. We were in the same Special Technical and Regulatory Services department – STARS for short – within the firm's financial sector practice and while I respected and quite liked him we had very different personalities and styles. This made Williams uncomfortable with me and on one occasion he completely lost his temper. It was something trivial but he shouted at me and there was a big scene. We were both being sponsored for promotion to become KPMG partners at the time (in 1998), but after that spat we never worked together directly on any specific job. It was with this in mind that I felt it wrong for Williams to have been involved in, let alone lead, the KPMG engagement to investigate my allegations against Crosby.

The other reason why KPMG should never have considered accepting the work was because I'd been a partner there myself. It was all just too incestuous to be truly independent, so I sent an email to my solicitor, Clive Howard, asking for an urgent meeting to discuss the matter.

See www.crashbankwallop.co.uk/library/8-2

Despite all the obvious signs of conflicts, it never entered into the equation that a professional firm such as KPMG would seek to cover up or act inappropriately in a situation like this. And even if it had been inclined to be biased or prejudiced, it wouldn't be able to resist the overwhelming evidence that I had in my possession.

However, my wife Maureen totally disagreed that KPMG could be trusted. She took the view that the firm would take the huge fee money and never find against HBOS. I argued strongly with her about that: nowadays I take her counsel more seriously.

In the end my lawyers and I decided not to make a fuss about KPMG's appointment, partly because the evidence was so clear in my favour but also due to a telephone conversation I had with James Davies in early January. During the call we agreed that it would be totally inappropriate for us to communicate with one another during the course of the KPMG investigation, which he described as a "heads I win, tails they lose" situation. Davies explained that if the investigators found in my favour, Crosby would have to go and I'd be back at HBOS. If they found against me, no one including the FSA would believe them because of the blatant conflicts. Accepting KPMG's appointment was a beautiful "finesse", he said. For the record, Davies wrote to me to confirm our agreement not to be in contact. See www.crashbankwallop.co.uk/library/8-3

My legal team replied to Baines' letter on Friday 14 January setting out three conditions:

> *For the attention of Tony Hobson [chairman of the Audit Committee]:*
>
> *We have read confirmation that KPMG will be carrying out the independent investigation.*
>
> *On behalf of Paul, I should be grateful if you would confirm that:*
>
> 1. *we will be provided with a copy of the Terms of Reference of the investigation.*
> 2. *the FSA were consulted and approved the selection of KPMG.*
> 3. *the investigation will be led by the Audit Committee as non-executives, and KPMG will be managed by and report to the Audit Committee.*

See www.crashbankwallop.co.uk/library/8-4

In the meantime I'd been asked to attend my first interview with KPMG scheduled for Wednesday 19 January. I wrote to Group Audit Committee Chairman Tony Hobson on 17 January requesting his formal confirmation for the discussions to begin.

See www.crashbankwallop.co.uk/library/8-5

To speed things up I later rang him and he confirmed his agreement over the phone.

As the "complainant" in the case, I would be the first witness and I believed that the chief reason for the meeting with KPMG was to gain some initial input from me before terms of reference for the investigation could be finalised. So I was fairly relaxed about not having as yet received a formal written response from Hobson to our three conditions. I felt 100% sure the case would be a "slam dunk".

The 19 January meeting took place at KPMG's modern offices in Farringdon Street, London. I knew them well from my partner days and it felt strangely like coming home when I walked into the airy reception area. The build-up over the preceding two months had been intense and if anything I was overexcited at the chance to get everything off my chest. The evidence would speak for itself, so I didn't feel I had anything to be worried about.

Adam Bates, the head of KPMG's forensic practice, led the meeting along with Roger Meads, a "regulatory expert" who it seemed had stepped in to replace my old sparring partner Giles Williams. The interview started at 1pm and lasted almost five hours. I felt both exhausted and relieved when it finished. The evidence just tumbled out of my head, through my mouth and out onto the table in a glutinous mixture of facts combined with a high degree of emotion. Bates, a sharp-looking chap of average height with short-cut hair and agreeably affable, recorded the meeting but there was no cross-examination to test what I was saying. They just let me talk.

After the meeting, I felt a huge sense of relief at having

got everything off my chest. It was like that feeling you get after you have felt seasick for a long time and finally you throw up. A couple of days later I sent an email to Bates which covered a number of issues vital to the running of an enquiry of this nature, and also to gain clarification on other matters agreed upon during the course of the interview. One of the key points was to secure a written understanding that anyone spoken to, however senior, would be made aware by the investigation team prior to interview that their evidence would remain anonymous and their positions be protected. I wrote:

> *"For example, if a board director was to corroborate allegations that the CEO had failed to act with integrity or with due skill, care and diligence, that board director would be protected."*

I agreed to provide notes indicating relevant areas for questioning of individuals that I had suggested for interview, along with my thoughts on the scope and limitations of the investigation and how the facts provided proof of a breach of specific FSA regulations.

I also asked for confirmation to be sent to me and my advisers Howard and Hamilton, that HBOS, through Hobson and Baines, gave its consent to us seeing the terms of reference and KPMG's final report. In this regard I referred to sections of the Employment Rights Act relating to individuals making protected disclosures and their right to be given such information, and I pointed to the whistleblowing charity website Public Concern At Work as a source of guidance. Legislation includes protection for whistleblowers who go to the media or Members of Parliament when their concerns have not been reasonably dealt with.

See www.crashbankwallop.co.uk/library/8-6

A week later on 28 January, Bates wrote back denying that he had agreed to consent for us to have the terms of reference and final report. I'd actually asked him to confirm it through Hobson and Baines, not him personally, but I was still shocked at his response. My 19 January interview had been suspended by Bates himself after only three minutes, specifically to address this issue. I'd insisted on getting the matter cleared up before carrying on. During the 22-minute adjournment, I spoke to Hobson and Baines and obtained verbal confirmation from both of them to us receiving copies of the documents. It was only on the back of this that the hearing with Bates resumed.

See also www.crashbankwallop.co.uk/library/8-6

After taking a short holiday in a failed bid to de-stress, I wrote back to Baines on 1 February. On the subject of terms of reference, I suggested that the KPMG investigation needed to consider all the matters set out in Hamilton's Outline of Case relating to the allegations of regulatory irregularity. This would solely be to establish whether there was sufficient evidence to trigger further steps through the FSA's own enforcement procedures. I pointed out that if the investigation team found either *prima facie* or conclusive evidence of regulatory wrongdoing, then not only should it say so, it should also make recommendations to HBOS to take appropriate action.

I gave examples of some questions the enquiry team might wish to consider. These included whether the evidence supported a case to answer that Crosby acted in contravention of a number of the Principles for Approved Persons in making my position redundant and appointing Dawson to take over key aspects of that role. In this respect, was he also in breach of his powers under the Board control manual and group HR policies, and should he have consulted senior management, Board colleagues and the Audit Committee before dismissing me?

There was the question of possible failure by Crosby to ensure compliance with the FSA's system for appointing fit and proper approved persons, and of Dawson and Ellis being in breach of their regulatory obligations too.

I also provided Bates with a long list of names of individuals the investigation team could interview, and why it was relevant to do so. These included: my deputies James Davies and Tony Brian; external consultants Andy Sheppard and Andy Gordon; GRR lead relationship manager Mike Gardener; Ernst & Young sales culture review secondee Richard Mais; Jack Cullen; Phil Hodkinson; Dougie Ferrans; Guy Bainbridge; Peter Hamilton; Steve Kaplan; my senior executive assistant Ian Thomson; HR manager Irene Grant; Dr Andrew Smith; members of the Audit Committee and Group Management Board; Crosby; Stevenson; Hornby; Ellis and Dawson.

See www.crashbankwallop.co.uk/library/8-7

Minutes after sending the email to Bates I sent a separate one to Baines requesting formal written confirmation on the issue relating to the terms of reference and final report.

See www.crashbankwallop.co.uk/library/8-8

We got no reply so I followed up Baines on 3 February.

See www.crashbankwallop.co.uk/library/8-9

Again no response. My next email to him on 7 February I marked "URGENT". I reminded him:

> *"No doubt you will be fully familiar with the Employment Rights Act and why it is so important for the person who has made qualifying disclosures in good faith to be kept fully appraised of the outcome of investigations, so that it is possible to determine whether the actions taken as a result are those which could reasonably be expected to have been taken. Please can you now confirm urgently that we can have copies of KPMG's terms of reference immediately and a copy of the report in due course?"*

See www.crashbankwallop.co.uk/library/8-10

I even put in a request for a "read receipt" on the email which later gave proof he'd read it at 8.31am on 8 February. I still have a copy of the receipt.

See www.crashbankwallop.co.uk/library/8-11

By now, I was beginning to smell a rat. Clive Howard also followed up with HBOS by email but received no formal agreement to us seeing the terms of reference.

See www.crashbankwallop.co.uk/library/8-/8-11-1

As a result, on 9 February, we sent a formal solicitor's letter dealing with our request for the terms of reference and telling them that, if we did not get them, we would no longer cooperate with the investigation.

See www.crashbankwallop.co.uk/library/8-12

I was due to have my second interview with Bates and the KPMG investigation team on Friday 18 February but by the afternoon of the 17th, we'd still not received the elusive terms of reference. So at 1.28pm I wrote a final email to Bates telling him:

"If we do not receive Harry's confirmation by close of play today, unfortunately, we will have to postpone my follow-up meeting with you until we do. I will let you know whether we can proceed by 9.30am tomorrow. If you do not hear from me by 9.30 tomorrow, you can assume that I have not heard from Harry and, therefore, our meeting will not be able to take place tomorrow as planned."

See:
www.crashbankwallop.co.uk/library/8-13
www.crashbankwallop.co.uk/library/8-14

At 3.13pm I emailed Baines yet again:

"Are you able to provide me with the confirmation which Clive Howard sought in his letter? If you cannot provide the confirmation, I shall have to cancel my meeting with KPMG tomorrow and I would like to know sooner rather than later so as to give them notice. Please phone me on my mobile [number provided]."

See ww.crashbankwallop.co.uk/library/8-14-1

Baines replied:

> *"I'm sorry if communications look a little disjointed, but I am out of the country at present. You should have received a copy of the terms of reference during the course of today. The written KPMG report will be made available to you in due course."*

Disjointed? More like, disingenuous, I thought.

See www.crashbankwallop.co.uk/library/8-14-2

At 3.31pm that day we received the terms of reference from Baines.

(See www.crashbankwallop.co.uk/library/8-15)

They were dated and had been agreed on 24 January 2005 – 25 days earlier. They had been "stringing us along" and acting in bad faith. By deliberately withholding a copy of the terms of reference they had no doubt hoped we would continue with proceedings without having seen them.

When I had sent my detailed email to Bates on 1 February, setting out precisely what the terms of reference should include, he already knew they'd been agreed by HBOS, KPMG and the FSA. He should have said so. Bates and Baines had done everything they could to put Hamilton, Howard and me off the scent when in fact they should have been arranging a meeting with us to discuss those terms of reference. HBOS, far from wanting to investigate a serious whistleblowing claim properly, seemed hell-bent from the very outset on stifling my allegations.

The letter said the review would focus on:

- *The GRR relationship with the Board, the executive, divisional management and relevant associated risk and audit committees;*
- *The appropriateness of the GRR structure and processes for fulfilling their oversight and monitoring responsibilities;*
- *The chronology, methodology, reporting and follow up / resolution of the mortgage endowment complaints, corporate bond fund and sales culture reviews performed in 2003 / 2004 and relevant recommendations set out in Appendix 1 of the PWC report on the risk management framework;*
- *The appropriateness of the group's processes for identification and assessment of candidates for the Group Risk Director and appointment of Jo Dawson;*
- *Whether the group followed its defined processes when making the position of Head of GRR redundant.*

The full version is here:
www.crashbankwallop.co.uk/library/8-16

It is abundantly clear that they were not detailed or precise enough. They certainly did not cover all the items that I said they should cover in my detailed email to Adam Bates on 1 February, following my first interview with them. I consulted with Hamilton that afternoon about whether the terms of reference were adequate. I didn't think they were but Hamilton thought them sufficient because they had specifically referred to the Outline of Case he'd drafted. Hamilton's document was so clear about all the allegations of regulatory breaches by Crosby and others at HBOS that, on any sensible interpretation, the investigation had to deal with them all if it was to be accepted by the FSA.

So, the next morning, 18 February, I went for my second interview with KPMG's Bates and Roger Meads. It was a lovely sunny day and I felt that this time, after the overly emotional and rather disorganised evidence that I gave in the first meeting, I could put matters right and get my testimony properly "marshalled". I still had faith in KMPG.

This time we met at KPMG's head office in Salisbury Square, down a narrow lane running south off the easterly end of Fleet Street, London. It was a sturdy, distinguished-looking building with a big atrium with marble floors. It was the sort of office that you would expect a firm like KPMG to have. I had been there many times before and was very familiar with the place.

As I sat in the reception area, waiting to be taken to the interview room, my mind cast back to a lunch I attended there just before I became a partner. It was standard protocol for prospective partners to be subjected to the "meet and greet" of the "great and the good" of KPMG. On this occasion the Senior Partner of the firm, Mike Rake (now a Sir) was there. Those of us who were delegates for partnership had to wear name badges so that the Senior Partners could put "names to faces". They would have heard about us in the discussions of who should be promoted to partner but they would not know what we looked like.

The previous financial year I'd managed to generate some huge fees for the partnership and had been rewarded with KPMG's highest-ever bonus for a non-partner of £100,000. It was a stand-up lunch and I was milling around when Rake came up to me. I watched his face as he looked at my name tab and then put two and two (or should I say one and £100,000) together. I could almost see him saying to himself: "Ah, so that's the chap to whom we paid that huge bonus."

Now, once again, I was relying on KPMG to do the right thing by me.

After a while sitting in reception, I was shown to one of the downstairs meeting rooms where Bates and Meads were waiting, along with a secretary to operate the recording device. I was calm, good-natured and confident.

I should not have been. From the minute the meeting began at 10.28am, they cross-examined me with a ferocity that I was just not expecting. It was like being the accused in a court of law, facing a barrage of questions from the prosecuting barrister. Hang on, I thought, this is supposed to be an investigation into whistleblowing allegations. It's not meant to be adversarial. I was not a defendant.

The meeting lasted one-and-a-half hours. It was awful and it frightened me. I cannot remember much of the detail but I do still have a hard copy of the transcript. However I do recall one very telling moment.

At the first meeting with KPMG on 19 January I'd very specifically asked Bates to interview Dougie Ferrans, one of the most senior people at HBOS to come out and say that Crosby was wrong to fire me. I'd already spoken to Ferrans to check that he was OK with this and assured him – as Bates had assured me – that any evidence he gave would be strictly confidential. Towards the end of this second interview, I was referring to Ferrans' comments and was asked by Bates to paraphrase the letter Ferrans had sent to me expressing how sorry he was to see me go. The nondescript Meads then asked: "What do you think he [Ferrans] means by, 'I fully understand why'?"

I replied: "I don't know; I thought you were going to ask him. I did put his name down as someone who you might like to ask. I don't know whether you have."

Bates chipped in: "We haven't seen him yet."

I couldn't believe it. In whistleblowing cases such as mine, investigators should always interview the most important supporting witnesses first before hearing from those speaking against the allegations. Nevertheless, I assumed they would get round to talking to Ferrans and others including Phil Hodkinson and James Davies. For me, I suppose that's what comes from living with a child-like sense of naive trust in truth and justice that sadly just does not exist.

It was 1pm exactly when the interview finished. Its tone and style had been akin to the Spanish Inquisition and I was in a state of turmoil. The whole line of questioning had been aimed at challenging my competence, professionalism, integrity and performance. It seemed the primary purpose of the investigation was now to undermine and discredit me while justifying Crosby, Ellis and Dawson's actions, rather than looking into whether they had acted fairly in response to my challenges concerning regulatory compliance.

As soon as I'd left the Salisbury Square offices I phoned Howard, and we decided I should write a paper setting out what had happened at the interview which we could then use as the basis for a formal response. Before doing this, I spoke at considerable length to Steve Kaplan, who was able to "read the tea leaves" better than anyone I knew. From his own thinking and having spoken to others, Steve had already come to the conclusion that I would never get a fair hearing from the investigation, particularly while the matter had not been made public. His advice was simple: "They are out to get you and cover up the whole affair. Hit back hard."

So that's what we did.

Firstly I wrote a detailed account of my second interview with KPMG, then I had a telephone conference call on Monday 21 February with my lawyers to discuss it. In a nutshell it proved that HBOS and KPMG had acted inappropriately in the way they were conducting the investigation. A full copy of what I wrote is here: www.crashbankwallop.co.uk/library/8-17

We sent out our response to Hobson just before the weekend, on 25 February, expressing my concerns. In the letter we said:

> *"Only last Thursday, 17 February, did Paul and I receive a copy of the terms of reference of the investigation. There is nothing in the terms of reference which would suggest*

that KPMG treat Paul Moore as the 'Defendant'. Indeed it is clear from the terms of reference that KPMG's task is an open-ended one where establishing the facts in an impartial and uncontentious manner forms the first stage.

"KPMG need to establish the facts of this case. Whistle-blowing issues have been raised in relation to the regulatory compliance of some of the most senior executives at HBOS. Having regard to the subject matter, and the nature of the investigation that is required, it is essential that the investigation is carried out in all times in a way that is totally beyond reproach. KPMG need to act with the intention of gathering facts. It is essential the investigator must maintain a neutral viewpoint and suspend judgement until all the facts are established. It follows that questions should always be asked in a non-judgmental and certainly non-accusatory manner. This is not what happened on 18 February. Paul was subjected to very hostile questioning throughout the meeting.

"It is therefore essential that I raise these concerns with you now. You should also be aware that once we have received the transcript of the meeting on 18 February, Paul will use that opportunity to clarify and provide full responses to the issues covered.

"Separately, in terms of timing, David Fisher has informed me that the KPMG report is being presented to the Group Audit Committee on 8 March 2005. It was confirmed expressly to Paul at his meeting on 18 February by Adam Bates that the investigation would not be completed until the end of March. Why is there this discrepancy? No report can be presented until the investigation has been completed.

"I am copying in David Fisher to this e-mail and would ask David to consider this issue on timing because for reasons set out in correspondence with him, he would be aware that the date when the report is completed is crucial."

See www.crashbankwallop.co.uk/library/8-18

Hobson replied on Monday 28 February. On the subject of the terms of reference, he said they had been developed *"carefully and thoroughly"* and the committee was *"very comfortable"* with them. *"You have seen them as, also, has the FSA."*

He went on:

"Since being instructed, KPMG have approached their task with great diligence and independence of mind. Interviews have been conducted with almost 30 very senior HBOS individuals. This includes the Chief Executive, the current and former Group Finance Directors and a number of other existing and former Group Board Directors. I know from my own experience that the KPMG approach has been extremely thorough and probing, which is entirely what both you and I would expect, if KPMG are to address the serious allegations made by Paul. I am sorry if Paul found the experience uncomfortable but, as far as I am aware, he has not been treated in any different way from all the other interviewees. Your implication of bias, or improper behaviour by KPMG, is without foundation and is totally rejected.

"The Audit Committee does not control the 'process' in relation to these interviews. All issues of process have been left to KPMG. Interviewees have been asked to review

the transcripts of their evidence and to clarify any issues which are unclear. Your note suggests that Paul intends to change and supplement the answers he provided to KPMG's questions. This is not my understanding of how the process is supposed to work, but I leave that as a matter to be discussed between Paul and your client.

"The Audit Committee has a regularly scheduled meeting on 8 March. At that meeting, KPMG are due to provide the Committee with an update on their investigation. Given the extent of the work that they have carried out to date, I have made it clear to KPMG that I expect their report to provide their current opinion in relation to the issues raised in the Terms of Reference. Their written report will follow in due course, but I have also made it clear that I do not expect matters to drag on.

"The issues raised by your client are serious. They have been taken very seriously by me and my colleagues on the Audit Committee and they are being investigated most thoroughly by KPMG. It is very important that these issues are resolved expeditiously so that there is clarity for the organisation and our regulator."

See www.crashbankwallop.co.uk/library/8-19

This letter was clearly not written solely by Hobson. It was carefully crafted by lawyers but it was no more than a sequence of the kind of self-serving statements which bear no weight in a court of law without evidence to corroborate them.

On 22 February Maureen and I flew to Malaga in southern Spain for a short holiday to recover from the stress of the HBOS affair and the KPMG investigation.

But we also had some business to do there. Building work was underway on our villa near to Marbella and we had to check things out before paying the next instalment of the purchase price to the developer – some 300,000 euros.

Buying the villa turned out to be the biggest risk management mistake I ever made in my life (mainly because I didn't listen to my wife) but, at the time we contracted to have it built, I was still well and truly singing my own version of the Madonna song, *Material Girl*. The fact was that, from a financial perspective, HBOS had been paying me an absolute fortune. My total remuneration package had been worth up to a maximum of about £850,000 per annum depending on the performance of the HBOS share price, which had been soaring. The very least that my total package was worth under the terms of my employment contract was about £575,000. So, the odd one-million euros for a villa in Spain didn't seem like an awful lot at that point in time. Of course, it was and it is. Looking back, I feel a real sense of having been caught up in a system which made it seem like this was right, when in fact it was wrong.

I quite readily accept that I was being paid far more than I actually deserved (as all top bankers were and still are). I also now know in the very depths of my soul, after everything my family, friends and I have been put through over the years, that the love of money and the material world is not what gives you peace and wellbeing. No, for me what ultimately counts are the four Fs: Faith, Family, Friends and Fun, in that order.

Having said that, I am absolutely not against abundance and don't believe that poverty is the only way to peace. It's not the money itself or the abundance or the joy it can provide to yourself and others that's the problem. It's the love of money – greed is the problem. Doing and being good is totally consistent with making money but the world hasn't quite worked that out yet. We really do all need to free ourselves from the slavery of greed and the damage it does to others, ourselves and our wonderful planet. There's also nothing wrong with working hard, creating and generating abundance for yourself, your family and others. Just so long as you don't become self-centred and addicted to the material world. We need a greater focus on being and relating and a lesser focus on doing and having.

After visiting the villa, we drove to Granada to stay with some Spanish friends called Miguel and Mercedes De Almanza. Then, the following day, we went with them to spend a night at a magnificent and vast olive farm in the rolling Andalusian countryside near Ojen (pronounced Oken). The farm was owned by Miguel's brother who was chief of staff for the King of Spain. Apparently, some of the olive trees were 2,000 years old and the *finca* – the farm – was typically Spanish with a cobbled courtyard in the middle and the buildings all around. It was a wonderful place and very relaxing.

While we were there, Andalucía had its biggest snow fall ever – more than one metre in places – and we got stuck on the motorway in huge queues while driving to and from the *finca*.

Another funny thing happened while we were there.

Driving back to Granada, we got a call from Gilling Castle, our youngest son Oliver's prep school, to tell us that although he'd been found safe and well, he had run away from school on the night of Saturday 26 February. Apparently, Oliver and a friend had an altercation with one of the teachers and had been disciplined. Feeling hard done by, the boys had decided to walk the few miles to our home in Wass and stay there until we got back from Spain. However, they got cold feet (metaphorically and literally) and instead holed up in the crypt of Ampleforth Abbey Church, somewhere they were familiar with because they both sang as trebles in the college choir. At about 9.30pm (before they'd even been identified as missing from Gilling Castle), they were spotted by some girls from the school who told one of the Abbey monks, who then went down to the crypt to investigate. Oliver and his pal were hiding behind a curtain where the Schola robes were hung. When the monk called out for them to show themselves, Oliver's friend immediately stepped from behind the curtain with his hands up and said loudly, "I surrender". Oliver was furious that his mate had given up without a fight as he felt that if they'd kept quiet, the monk might have gone away.

Unfair Tactics

Maureen and I flew back to Leeds Bradford Airport on Monday 7 March not only to face a showdown with

Oliver but far more ominously the next round of KPMG shenanigans.

On the Friday before we'd returned from Spain, I'd phoned Bates and asked him for two copies of the full transcript from my 18 February second interview with KPMG to be sent to Clive Howard as a matter of urgency. Even though the hearing had taken place more than two weeks earlier, this had still not been done, and we needed to see the transcript prior to KPMG giving an update on its investigation to the Tuesday 8 March Audit Committee meeting.

A hint as to what HBOS and KPMG were plotting had come in an email I'd received on 22 February from David Fisher, the bank's new Head of Group HR. It was the day Maureen and I had gone to Spain and although I'd scanned through the short message, I hadn't picked up on the significance of a brief comment that Fisher, no doubt in all innocence, had made. I say in all innocence, because Fisher had been a senior colleague of mine in IID in 2002 and from my experience of working with him I don't believe he would be knowingly underhand. There was nothing very unusual about Fisher, who was a typical career executive. He was a shortish, thin and healthy looking chap with a shiny bald head and a straight gaze. Fisher had a hard and uncompromising style and approach to things. He seemed to enjoy a challenge. I always like such people because they are similar to me in that way, and I think there was a mutual respect between the two of us. I may be wrong but on this occasion I suspect he wasn't relishing the task of dealing with my dismissal.

On the subject of which, if my legal team and I were to opt for an Industrial Tribunal hearing in relation to my whistleblowing claim against HBOS, there was a time limit of 90 days for issuing legal proceedings which was fast approaching on 30 March. As a result, Clive Howard was pushing HBOS for a non-compensation, contractual settlement and wrote a letter to Fisher on 16 February basically saying get real, cough up or we will issue proceedings. Howard's letter is here:

www.crashbankwallop.co.uk/library/8-19-1

It was Fisher's reply to this that arrived on 22 February, and if not distracted by travelling to Spain would normally have set my alarm bells ringing immediately.

"Clive

The KPMG report is being presented to the HBOS Group Audit Committee on 8 March 2005.

We will be able to resume our discussions immediately after then and I do not see why they could not then be concluded very quickly.

On the basis of the above, I would hope you would be able to let the process run its course rather than commence legal proceedings.

I look forward to hearing from you.

Best wishes, David Fisher"

See www.crashbankwallop.co.uk/library/8-19-2 to read the whole email trail.

As I said, Fisher's email was really significant, and the clue was in the opening sentence. It revealed that Fisher had already been told that the KPMG report was going to be completed prior to the 8 March Audit Committee meeting. I suppose that this made sense, because HBOS would have wanted the investigation wrapped up before the time limit for me issuing legal proceedings, so as to kibosh my case.

However the fact was that – without HBOS and KPMG engaging in unfair tactics – finalising the report by 8 March was impossible. I'd only had chance to read the copy of the transcript of my second interview with KPMG late on Monday 7 March on my return from Spain. It was nearly 100 pages long and, given the appalling way in which the questioning had been conducted, it would take some considerable time to respond.

Once in receipt of the transcript, proceedings moved fast. At 9.27am on 7 March I wrote to Howard and Hamilton:

> *"We obviously need to decide next steps quickly. The one thing we may want to do today is to re-emphasise that the investigation cannot be completed until we have provided our final input following our recent meeting... and that any update to the Audit Committee should be prefaced as such."*

See www.crashbankwallop.co.uk/library/8-20

I followed this up with another email to them both at 11.45am to which I attached a detailed analysis of the 18 February KPMG interview transcript. Although I was still in the process of preparing further clarification notes, I summarised the main areas for attack.

After having read the transcript twice, I upgraded my initial "stumbling and introverted" description of my interview performance to a five or six out of 10. However, the obvious aggressive tone of the investigators' "quizzing" of me called into question the validity of the terms of reference, which of course we still hadn't been given the opportunity to formally comment upon. The transcript also demonstrated that the inquiry seemed much more about whether GRR and I had followed proper protocol and process in doing our jobs than if Crosby, Ellis and Dawson had cases to answer of regulatory breach. I wrote:

> *"It almost feels as if the whole idea was aimed at undermining my credibility in order to bring the whole 'Outline of Case' down like a pack of cards."*

I also recommended to Howard and Hamilton that we draw up a plan of action to deal with the various possible outcomes from the investigation.

My analysis can be read here:

www.crashbankwallop.co.uk/library/8-21

Later that day at 1.26pm, Bates sent me an email which is yet more clear evidence of what KPMG was up to. As Maureen and I were travelling back from Spain that day, I did not see it until nearly 8.30pm that evening.

He wrote:

> *"Paul*
>
> *As requested we have arranged for two copies of the transcript of our meeting of 18 February to be sent to your solicitors. We are now in the process of pulling*

together our conclusions in order to report back to HBOS against our terms of reference. I know that we touched upon this during our meeting, but feel that it is appropriate to again ask if there is any more evidence that you would like us to consider before we finalise our conclusions. We aim to pull together our report next week. Please could you let me know whether or not you would like to offer additional evidence by close of play Monday 7 March and if so provide an estimated timeframe for delivery.

Regards

Adam"

I wrote back at 8.45pm:

"Adam,

I have only read this email just now (8.29pm today) and cannot respond to you by close of play today as your email requests.

As we told Tony Hobson in writing, I have been out of the country until today and have only today had the first opportunity to read the transcript of my meeting with you on 18th February. I have not yet had a chance to digest matters sufficiently to be sure as to whether or not there are other items of evidence which I need to provide to you. In addition, I will need to discuss the position with my legal advisers, one of whom has only been able to read the transcript today and the other is also out of the country until tomorrow morning and will not be able to read the transcript until tomorrow at the earliest.

The only point that I would make, therefore, is that, if you are intending to provide an early briefing to the HBOS audit committee tomorrow, it would be advisable to proviso that briefing with the fact that it is likely that my advisers and I will wish to provide the investigation team with clarification / amplification of the matters raised in my meeting with you on 18 February. In these circumstances, I do not think that it would be appropriate to brief the audit committee that the investigation is to all intents and purposes complete in case any areas of amplification / clarification which we provide resulted in any substantive change to KPMG's opinion.

Regards

Paul"

See www.crashbankwallop.co.uk/library/8-21-1

All the evidence was stacking up to indicate they were working towards a cover-up. The KPMG investigators were on a mission to brief the Group Audit Committee the following day with the good news story that HBOS was in the clear.

By this stage, I was well and truly in a fight for my life zone. I could feel what was happening but I was not going to give up.

On Wednesday 9 March the day after the Audit Committee had met, I dispatched my first email salvo to Bates.

(See www.crashbankwallop.co.uk/library/8-22). In it I put him on clear notice of the risks he was facing if he did not do his job properly:

"Adam,

My advisers and I are hoping to meet in London on Friday morning and should be able to get back to you fully by the middle of next week.

In the meantime, just a few initial points:

It would be helpful in answering whether there may be more evidence you need for us to have a list of interviewees – for example, have you interviewed Steve Kaplan to establish his corroboration that I raised the Jo Dawson threat with Jackie Moore – of course, if Jo Dawson admits the threat this would not be necessary.

You also raised issues relating to my confidential Upward Feedback report. Although I do not see what relevance this has to the investigation which should be focused on establishing whether there is evidence of the regulatory breaches set out in the Outline of Case, it does seem to me that if it is going to form any part whatsoever of the evidence leading to KPMG's conclusions, it is only appropriate to interview Steve Kaplan who compiled it; not only that, Steve Kaplan has been involved in working closely with me throughout my time at HBOS and before and so his evidence of what was happening during the relevant period should be quite important.

I think it would also be appropriate, as I suggested in my first meeting with you, for you to speak directly to Peter Hamilton himself who, as a barrister has reviewed the evidence and has advised me on my regulatory obligations.

I have not discussed these points with my advisers yet, so you should not, at this stage treat them as formal requests.

Kind regards
Paul Moore"

The next day, Thursday 10 March I went down to London with Maureen to meet my lawyers on the following Monday in Hamilton's chambers at 4 Pump Court, Temple. We stayed with Maureen's aunt and uncle, Gloria and Peter Barton, the same house in Fulham where I'd gone to live during our separation period. Once we'd settled in I sat down to write a briefing for the crucial meeting with Howard and Hamilton on Monday.

I knew that producing a detailed response was going to be an arduous job in just a few days over the weekend but I was in a highly threatening situation so just got on with the job. This was the last chance to get the KPMG "mouse in the corner". I sat for hours at Gloria's dining room table thinking and writing. The words flowed easily but it was very tiring and I only finished my paper and sent it off to Hamilton and Howard at 5.36pm on Sunday evening. It was more than 12,000 words long and covered 24 pages of A4 paper. It is set out in full here: www.crashbankwallop.co.uk/library/8-23

Basically, having spoken to Hamilton and Howard first, I set out our response to each element of the KPMG investigation team's line of attack during the second interview, and the evidence provided in support. This would form the basis for what Hamilton described should be a written "re-examination in chief" conducted in the same tone as court proceedings.

The next morning Peter Hamilton, Clive Howard, Steve Kaplan and I all met at 4 Pump Court. The

Temple is one of the so-called Inns of Court used by the barrister profession for centuries. It is a special place just south of the Strand in London right next to the Royal Courts of Justice. Hamilton was a "tenant" (that's what they call a member of a set of Chambers) of 4 Pump Court. The Temple is all olde worlde and a lovely oasis of peace in the middle of the hustle and bustle of central London.

During our meeting we used the initial draft of my response as the basis for our discussions. My lawyers requested "further and better particulars" in some areas and important amendments in others. In particular, they wanted all the evidence of when and how Ellis had failed to support me.

We also agreed to send a hard-hitting letter to Hobson following his response on 28 February to the accusations we made in our letter of 24 February that the investigation was not being conducted appropriately or fairly.

Over the next few days I adjusted the document until we had all agreed a final version and at 1.54pm on Friday 18 March I sent our response by email to Bates. I was satisfied that we had done everything we could. My email and its two attached documents can be read here: www.crashbankwallop.co.uk/library/8-25

We had dealt pretty much conclusively with every single point of questioning that had come my way on the 18 February, and more. The main document ran to 11 pages and almost 5,000 words. Here is one short extract:

It is suggested that my input to the June Audit Committee was 'extraordinary'. I have asked for an explanation as to in what way my performance was regarded as extraordinary.

- *Until such time as those details are provided. I cannot comment further. With respect, I do not believe I should have to make a request for details of such a serious potential allegation. Those details should have been provided to me at the outset.*

There was one line of attack that KPMG had taken in the meeting that was particularly below the belt and that was the use of my confidential upward feedback report to try and discredit me. It was absolutely outrageous and a breach of ethics that the HR department at HBOS had agreed to disclose this information to the KPMG investigation team. That is why I insisted that KPMG interview and take evidence from Steve Kaplan, because the "360-degree feedback" provided strong evidence that in most respects I was doing a good job. KPMG, on the other hand, was seeking to pick out the negatives from the report and use them as weapons against me and as the excuse for Crosby firing me. This was totally unethical in itself but what made it even worse was that the positives far outweighed the inevitable negatives. It was nothing less than immoral.

As a result, in preparing my 18 March response (I might even call it "my defence") to KPMG, I asked Steve to prepare a report specifically dealing with my feedback and, in particular, my relationship with Ellis.

On the matter I wrote this:

> *"Mike Ellis rated me significantly lower than the average score on many of the competence and DNA areas e.g. he only rated me 5 out of 10 on integrity. In a meeting to discuss my upward feedback, he actually laughed at the negative comments as if they corroborated his view without giving proper support for the positives. What was I supposed to think?*
>
> *"On this whole issue of my upward feedback, I would like to add that its use in supporting any conclusion that I acted technically incorrectly is wrong and inappropriate. Most importantly, this type of feedback must always be guaranteed to be treated almost in as confidential a manner as one's doctor's records. I assumed that this strict duty of confidentiality applied in my case.*
>
> *"In any event, upward feedback of this type is not carried out for performance management purposes but for personal development purposes. It is, in fact an indication, of a person's good faith and desire to improve. If either I, or the person who wrote the report had ever believed that it might be used as the basis to challenge my competence and professionalism, he would never have advised me to share it with others. I am very disappointed indeed that any one from the HR community would release the document in this way.*
>
> *"Notwithstanding all of that, the feedback is extremely positive in many respects. As I said in my email to Adam Bates recently, if there is any intention whatsoever to use this feedback in KPMG's Report, I insist that KPMG interview Steve Kaplan who will be able to provide a proper balance."*

I sent Steve's new witness statement to Bates along with the main document. The whole document is here: www.crashbankwallop.co.uk/library/8-25-1 but here are a few extracts:

> *"The feedback indicated that Paul was seen by the vast majority of those interviewed to offer tremendous value to the bank. He was a breath of fresh air and much admired. They recognized they needed people like him to change things. This was first demonstrated in IID where he had developed a number of strong relationships and was starting to gain a track record of delivering results. As was always the case with Paul, there was always a 'but' relating to his style and personality. He turned some people off and confused others with inconsistent behaviours at times."*

Another section said:

> *"Throughout this period I had seen Paul make a genuine and concerted effort to improve in all of the behavioural areas which had been identified. Though not always successful — Paul would be the first to agree that there was still much room for improvement in some key areas — he nevertheless had made a genuine attempt and steady and considerable progress toward becoming a better manager and, dare I say, person."*

On the relationship between myself and Ellis, Steve had highlighted a number of points. From Ellis's side he had observed a "*natural dislike*" and "*failure to understand Paul's fundamental personality traits and style*" while having a "*need to 'be right' in his viewpoints (thus making the other person 'wrong')*".

However Steve said I had a responsibility for what occurred.

"He [Paul] can be a challenge to manage and will often be seen as a 'handful'. It is true that Paul should have been expected to understand how to manage upwardly as well, but my understanding is that Paul had asked for Mike's input in a variety of ways and on many occasions with no result.

"Having said that, I believe that the majority of the responsibility for the dysfunctional nature of the relationship falls to Mike. As the senior person, it was his responsibility to: ensure the right relationship was established up front; help create an environment in which Paul could succeed; support Paul in that effort. I am not aware that Mike did any of these.

"Instead he seemed to take great delight in pointing out Paul's foibles — he laughed in the meeting Paul and I had with him to review the feedback report — yet I do not believe he ever acknowledged the major shift that was occurring in the way the regulatory function was being carried out and in which it was beginning to be viewed by many of its customers? The results of the MORI poll must have totally astounded and befuddled him.

"Mike may have been an excellent accountant, but from my interactions with him on several occasions I would not think he would score very high in Emotional Intelligence or understanding and/or managing people.

"There is no doubt in my mind that Paul honestly and genuinely wanted to establish an effective working relationship with Mike. It would have been silly for him

not to want to make that happen. At the same time, Paul had his own views on regulatory affairs — of which he is arguably an expert and about which he had far greater knowledge and experience than Mike. (When Paul was about to move from IID to GRR in an interview with Phil Hodkinson he remarked that 'Mike didn't care about risk management' ...'and that James Crosby thought he knew more about regulatory affairs than Paul'.) A healthy debate in which substantive issues were bottomed out and a common front going forward was established is what should have been the norm. I believe Paul would have done anything in his power to make that happen. I believe he tried everything he could think of to bring this about.

"My sense was that Mike might have wanted to establish an effective relationship, but one that he had created in his mind — not necessarily one that would have been possible and workable in the real world with Paul — or someone like him. Mike seemed to feel very 'right' about his viewpoints — most probably fuelled by others within the organisation who held similar views. He seemed determined to kick Paul into shape and / or teach him a lesson — or both. He obviously had no idea who / what he was dealing with, for (if I have it right) when he tried to reign Paul in, he only got a (predictably) even more forceful and deliberate push back. I do not believe Paul was arguing his corner to hear himself speak. I believe he was genuinely trying to do his job in the best possible manner."

Steve's report continued:

"Mike appears to have been unwilling to genuinely listen. He often had different views and arrived at his

own (different) conclusions, thus undermining Paul. I got the sense that there seemed to be constant undertow of another (hidden) agenda. This situation had to be a completely untenable for Paul. For Mike et al at the top of the organisation, one can only speculate that they had to come to the growing realisation that in Paul they had someone who would not be made to comply with their way of operating if to him it meant the dereliction of his duties — which he was legally required to perform. This had to be considered quite dangerous.

"So what's the bottom line? Whether by intention or circumstance, this relationship was probably doomed from the outset. Paul clearly annoyed Mike in a variety of ways — and vice versa — all of which probably would make perfect sense depending who you were talking to. I would think that Mike expected Paul to figure out how to fit in and work effectively with him and other key players at the centre and across the organisation. (The fact is Paul did do this in many instances and had many excellent relationships in the bank).

"I also believe there was always only one possible way of operating: Mike's. As I indicated previously, I believe he was determined to 'break' Paul. I also believe there is a strong element of unfairness in what occurred. Paul is inherently a very fair and open person. From what I have heard I do not believe Mike made an honest attempt to really meet him halfway. Paul would have gone considerably more than halfway to find a way of working together."

With these comments from Steve I felt we had now well and truly hit that idea out of the stadium for six.

Thank you very much, Steve, for having the courage and conviction and ethics to write this witness statement. Not many people have the personal integrity to do something like this, especially when it might affect business opportunities.

On 21 March, Howard sent a "Sidewinder" missile to Hobson. Here is part of the email:

> *"In respect of all the matters raised in the Outline of Case, is there prima facie evidence of HBOS treating Paul Moore adversely as a result of protected disclosures which are relevant to the FSA? If there is such evidence does this mean that HBOS is in breach of The Principles for Business and, in particular, Principles 1 (Integrity), 2 (Skill, care and diligence), 3 (Management + control) and 6 (Customers' interests)?*
>
> *"I know from the earlier correspondence with you that you share our wish to ensure that the investigation deals with these points and hopefully you will recognise our concerns that the approach adopted by KPMG seems to have been focused on Paul Moore and not the issues outlined above."*

And that was it: we could do no more. Irrespective of the odds, I still felt confident. Even if KPMG wanted to do the wrong thing, we had now well and truly put it in a position where to do so would be a very serious risk indeed. Now, at least, I would have time for some rest and relaxation while our input was processed into a final KPMG report.

The children broke up from school on Tuesday 22 March and we flew off *en famille* to Chile the following day. We were met at Santiago Airport by the whole Oats clan. It's fair to say that I was well and truly knackered. The stress of being dismissed, the final weeks at HBOS, the writing of the Outline of Case and the KPMG investigation had been enormous since November 2004. It was not only intellectual stress, it was severe emotional stress as I tried to defend my good name, professional career and, most importantly, the financial wellbeing of my family.

I have never really been very ambitious or interested in money but I did take my responsibilities to my family in "bringing home the bacon" very seriously indeed and being out of a job, quite frankly, scared me. I badly needed a rest. I could, however, relax in the knowledge that the hard fight would soon all be over and hopefully I would be vindicated. I even ventured to wonder, what would happen to Crosby? He would be in serious trouble and would probably have to resign from HBOS.

When the KPMG investigation report came out in my favour, this would mean that Crosby's status as the most senior approved person at HBOS would be under scrutiny by the FSA and, if it stuck to its own rules, it would withdraw its approval and he would have to stand down. I pondered whether, when that happened, I could return to HBOS as I had always wanted.

Santiago, with my family, in autumn was the perfect place to wind down and take my mind off the HBOS affair for a while. We were staying as usual with Leonor and Peter at their house in the beautiful and peaceful tree-lined city district of Providencia. We all just relaxed and basked in the sun. We had the numerous noisy family gatherings and the children had all their first cousins to play about with. Maureen had catch-up time with her parents and two brothers and sisters. It never mattered how long Maureen lived in the UK, she was always in essence South American by nature and culture and she eased her way back into that way of life in an instant. She also had all her old school, college and work friends with whom to reconnect and we were always going out for dinner or to some get-together. It was a lovely life there.

Despite the relaxation something was still niggling away in the back of my mind and after about 10 days into our holiday, in early April, it started to bother me why I'd received no news about publication of the KPMG final report. So I contacted Clive Howard. No sign of it. I told him to let things be.

On 11 April, at the beginning of the week we were due to fly back to the UK, I followed up again but there was still no report. Good, I thought; it must be that HBOS doesn't like what it's seeing and is trying to get KPMG to change the report in the bank's favour. This time I asked Howard to step up the pressure.

We flew into Heathrow on 16 March at the end of the school holidays and, after dropping Emily off at Ascot, drove back to Wass. It was chaos and cold. We had embarked on a major refurbishment and building project for the cottage in January and the place was still as if a bomb had hit it. We had hoped and prayed that the new kitchen would have been completed by the time we arrived back but it wasn't. So we cooked on two camping gas rings and with a microwave – in what was to be "the snug" – on concrete floors. We had no living room because that was full of all our furniture but we did have an oasis in our bedroom and bathroom which we'd had finished before we embarked on the rest of the ambitious construction project. Anyway, progress was being made and we could see that in the next few months we might be back to normal. Of course, it took longer: building projects always overrun on time and budget. The boys, Daniel and Oliver, returned to Gilling Castle while Maureen and I made do with our half-built home, with no central heating and tarpaulins keeping the rain out of one of the upstairs bedrooms.

And guess what? Still no KPMG report. After more conversations with my lawyers I finally got the call from Clive Howard on Thursday 28 April.

"I've just received the final KPMG report." He hesitated. "I always told you it would be bad but it's even worse than I expected. But don't worry, we will get you a fair settlement. I have already sent it to you by courier and you will have it tomorrow."

The settlement wasn't at the centre of my focus. What I really cared about was truth and justice. I think Howard had been clear in his own mind, from the word go, that there was no chance of a fair hearing from the KPMG investigation but I don't think I ever really believed him. I had also genuinely thought that I'd be able to prevent a cover-up by the strength of my responses. I was wrong. And all of a sudden I was frightened and in a terrible state. I couldn't face asking Howard on the phone what the report said and I waited through that day in a state of shock and fear.

An A4 brown envelope containing the KPMG report duly arrived the next day. It wasn't until the Sunday 1 May after going to Mass as usual at St Benedict's Parish Church and praying hard for courage, that I decided it was time to open the package and read the dreaded document. It was a beautiful, sunny spring day with a deep-blue sky interspersed with puffy white cumulus clouds, the sort of clouds I used to love to see when I was flying hang-gliders as they indicated strong thermals which we could use to gain altitude. I took the papers out of the envelope and went outside in front of the brown "pic fence" and stood in the beautiful lane in front of our stone cottage.

I read the report very quickly. It was obvious from the start that KPMG was out to get me. Far from approaching the investigation as one in which the actions of Crosby and others were under scrutiny for dismissing someone who had made whistleblowing claims, it was an inquiry into me and my actions. It was dedicated to proving that, not only had I failed to do my job properly but that I deserved to be fired. The report concluded that Crosby was perfectly within his rights to appoint Dawson as Group Risk Director.

I got to the *coup de grace* – the death blow – on page 20 after only about 10 minutes of reading. The tears had been rolling down my cheeks almost from the start. But, when I read this, the flood gates really opened.

"Mr Moore's performance

Numerous negative comments have been made regarding Mr Moore's performance in the role of Head of GRR. Whilst his technical abilities were generally recognised as strong, consistent reference has been made to Mr Moore:

- *not inspiring confidence in GRR's stakeholders;*
- *not having sufficiently strong influencing and relationship skills;*
- *being overly verbose and full of self-importance;*
- *not being on top of the detail; and,*
- *over-stating matters in an overly dramatic and theatrical way.*
- *In particular his behaviour on the following occasions was highlighted:*
- *16 September 2003 IID Risk Control Committee — Mr Moore criticised the way the meeting was chaired. A number of individuals considered this behaviour to be inappropriate;*
- *26 May 2004 Retail Risk Control Committee — Mr Moore was perceived as lecturing the committee in a patronising manner and offended individuals present with his style; and,*
- *8 June 2004 Group Audit Committee meeting — Mr Moore expressed strong views in an overly aggressive manner, he was emotional and not reasoned, measured or coherent. His behaviour was described in different ways ranging from prickly to ranting to extra-ordinary*

> *to outrageous. Mr Moore's behaviour at this meeting was the subject of a private meeting of the Audit Committee on 23 July 2004.*

In addition, reference was made to a number of private meetings that Mr Moore held with the non-Executives in which it was felt that his approach, his behaviour and the manner in which he escalated issues was inappropriate.

In contrast he did not have a private meeting with the Chairman of the Audit Committee until late 2004, although requests were made by the Chairman of the Audit Committee for such a meeting to be scheduled.

Loss of confidence

It is clear that senior executives and non-executive directors interviewed lost confidence in Mr Moore over a period of time and for different reasons. Some individuals expressed surprise that Mr Moore was appointed Head of GRR in 2003.

The whole of KPMG's report is here:
www.crashbankwallop.co.uk/library/8-28

I bent over as I cried so hard over the deep internal pain of the dishonesty and unfairness of it all. I went into that paroxysm, which most of us have experienced as a child, when you are crying so hard and, at the same time, you breathe inwards in short gasps and pants making a noise that sounds like hiccupping and you almost choke.

The definition of the word paroxysm sums up what happened to me perfectly: *"A sudden attack or outburst of a particular emotion or activity e.g. "a paroxysm of weeping"; a spasm, attack, fit, burst, convulsion, seizure, outburst, eruption, explosion or flare up.*"

It was a mixture of such deep emotional hurt and physical response that the physical and the metaphysical just blended into one.

Crash! Bang! Wallop! Yet again.

My soul ached and, in the end, it's taken me 10 years, finally, to work my way through it all and overcome the hurt of those days. That's why it took me so long to write my memoirs because up until the end of 2014 I was still too caught up in the emotion of the experience to be able to put it down in words without too much pain and the risk of unkindness and vindictiveness to those who hurt me.

In 2011 I experienced my first serious attack of clinical depression. I had never suffered from this awful and real disease before. Again, in 2012, I had such a deep depression that I developed serious suicidal thoughts. Since then, I have had two further lengthy bouts of the "black dog". There will be more about this in part two of my memoirs.

I loved HBOS and that's why I did all the things I did, but the bank shot the messenger. The trouble was I wasn't dead but I wanted to be. Many times I've wished I really had been shot. The headline to Dina Medland's *Financial Times* article on June 5 2013 about my HBOS experience summed it up: "Whistleblowing almost killed me".

Today I honestly thank God for everything that has happened and what is to happen. In a strange way, I can almost thank all the people who harmed me because if it wasn't for what took place, I wouldn't be the person I am now.

Looking back to that May day in 2005, however, I was smashed, bashed and completely crushed. I simply didn't know what to do next. With the great name and reputation of KPMG on its side, HBOS might even decide to pay me nothing in settlement on the grounds of my being fired for misconduct.

It took me quite a few days to climb out of the deep, deep hole that the KPMG report had flung me into but I had huge resilience in those days and I never gave up. I forced myself to read the report again, carefully and more dispassionately and I realised that the evidence was still very flimsy. So I sat down at my desk and wrote a draft of a first rebuttal letter.

The words just flowed out onto the keyboard. It was easy. I felt that the report was incompetent, ridiculous and, to my mind at least, a cover-up. The FSA would never accept it. My courage began to return.

The whole five-page letter is here:

www.crashbankwallop.co.uk/library/8-29

I said the KPMG report *"materially failed"* to take into account key evidence given to the investigation team.

> *"In our view, therefore, the Report is imbalanced and has arrived at conclusions which, if reviewed by an external independent tribunal, would not be supported."*
>
> *The mere fact that the report states that its findings*

are consistent with the oral briefing given to the March Audit Committee which took place a full ten days before Paul submitted his final eleven page written evidence to KPMG is strongly indicative that KPMG had already 'made up their minds' and did not take into account any of the subsequent and important evidence given to the investigation team by Paul.

It also demonstrates that the concerns we raised in our letter to Tony Hobson on the 24th February about the appropriateness of the adversarial approach adopted by KPMG in a case involving serious allegations of whistle-blowing were, in fact, justified even though, at the time, they were totally rejected.

We are also very concerned to understand why, if KPMG had already made up their minds as to the outcome of the investigation by the March Audit Committee, why it took two months for them to finalise their short report?"

My rebuttal letter went on to say that most of the issues raised in the Outline of Case had not been addressed, including the lack of support from Ellis, and that new evidence revealed in the KPMG report about the holding of private meetings to discuss GRR's business plan, only further supported our position. Information about Jo Dawson's development needs also backed up our claims.

I added:

"The Report paints a picture of Paul as wholly incapable of building and maintaining relationships with key stakeholders. This not only fails to take account of

Paul's previous history of having demonstrated his strength in this area over many years in industry and professional services but it also fails completely to take account of the very strong relationships he and his team built at the operating division level throughout the whole of the rest of HBOS."

"The section dealing with KPMG's views on Jo Dawson's appointment and how that 'juxtaposes' with the criticisms of Paul's style and approach is frankly nothing short of bizarre. In our view, it is also technically the least appropriate interpretation of the FSA's Rules and against standard principles of statutory or regulatory interpretation.

"On the one hand, Paul is criticised for not being able to build relationships with key stakeholders and is dismissed. But, on the other, Jo Dawson who is explicitly recognised as having significant style and personal behavioural issues (a bit abrasive at times can inhibit her ability to build deep relationships, inflexible, lack of warmth, demanding to work for, track record of confrontations within HBOS, not a diplomat) and who has no technical knowledge or experience is appointed as GRD.

"KPMG's conclusion that none of this, or the fact that she effectively admitted the threat she made to Paul, matters is simply wrong.

"In addition, the notion that any properly drawn-up competence framework for the GRD role would exclude the requirement for technical knowledge and skills is also wholly unbelievable and wrong. Although

for some roles, it is possible that basic management skills would be sufficient, this simply cannot be the case for roles which are primarily technical such as the role of GRD. In any event, anyone with the development needs which Jo Dawson had, far from being the "lead candidate", would not even get a first interview."

I sent the draft letter to Howard and Hamilton and they didn't recommend changing a single word. So it was typed up and fired off to HBOS: on Friday 13 May! HBOS would be legally bound to send a copy of the letter to the FSA which when compared alongside the KPMG report would scotch any ideas it might have of putting the matter to bed. The FSA would not be able to accept the KPMG report "as read" and would have to call me back in to hear my side of the story.

HBOS's response was no surprise. The bank came at us immediately and strongly in a way that clearly demonstrated that it wanted to agree a financial settlement with me as soon as possible. It requested a meeting but we refused to talk until a number of demands had been met.

Howard drew up a letter setting out our stall for the value of a full year's total remuneration package, plus the bonuses due for the previous year, plus my legal expenses. HBOS agreed without debate to the bonuses amounting to about £245,000 (actually the share options awarded ended up being worth a very great deal more than this because I was able to sell them in advance of the 2008 crash in the HBOS share price). I set out the value of a year's remuneration package on a spreadsheet as follows:

Paul Moore - value of total remuneration		
Item	**Value**	**Notes**
Base Pay	257,000	
STI	102,800	Assumes payout at 40% of base pay
Sharekicker entitlement	30,840	Assumes bonus taxed at 40% and then multiplied by 50%
LTI	111,949	Assumes an average payout rate of 200% every three years
Pension	128,500	Assumes the cost of the 1/45th scheme including the life and disability cover equals 50% of base pa.
		This matches the value as shown in the accounts to Phil Hodkinson who is same age - 46
Car cash	7,992	Equals 666 monthly payment multiplied by 12
Other	3,000	Bupa and other flex benefits
Total	**642,081**	

STI stands for Short Term Incentive, LTI for Long Term Incentive. These were the "bankers' bonuses". The total value of my package at reasonable estimates of the STI and LTI payouts came to £642,081. It took no time to negotiate this. HBOS just fell over and we settled at one very short meeting in Old Broad Street. We got everything that Howard advised me to go for. Also, instead of paying the value of the pension, HBOS agreed to give me another year's actual pension which meant it would be tax free and therefore worth more to me.

As a result, with the 2004 bonuses and the financial settlement for my dismissal, I received about £760,000 in cash and shares, a year's extra pension (worth about £128,000) and legal fees of about £75,000 (paid directly to Howard and Hamilton). This made a total value of my settlement of £963,000. Of this, after an initial £30,000 which was tax free and a very small part of the cash settlement which was expressed to be for hurt feelings which was also tax free, the rest was subject to full income tax: so I suppose British society gained from my suffering at the hands of HBOS to the tune of about 40% of all of that, which is more than £280,000. That year, what with the sale of other earlier HBOS shares that had crystallised plus the settlement, I seem to remember that my tax return said I'd had a total income of £920,000.

Most people would probably think that's a huge amount of money and I would agree, but actually the settlement I received never compensated me and my family for what I lost in earnings over the coming years, which I conservatively estimate to be between £3 million and £4 million. This is because I became and will remain, until such time as the laws of protection change, a marked man in the financial services sector: a whistleblower not to be touched with a barge pole.

We received a draft settlement agreement within a few days setting everything out in strict legal terms and including a standard "gagging" clause committing me and my family to confidentiality on everything to do with HBOS generally and our dispute in particular. In other words, if I spoke up HBOS could sue for all the money it had paid me and more.

I met with my lawyers in Hamilton's Chambers on a balmy day in the last week of May for a final discussion before agreeing to the formal settlement. It was the room on the basement floor of 4 Pump Court, down the corridor on the right. It had bright new furniture and modern boardroom-style chairs. The room had a high ceiling and big windows looking out onto an inner court yard of the Temple.

We were at the tipping point. Similar to Frodo in *The Lord of the Rings*, I just didn't really want to do what I had come there to do. One part of my head and heart wanted to settle, take the money and move on and put this horrendous saga behind me. The other yearned and cried out for truth and justice and felt dirty at the idea of accepting the "30 pieces of silver".

I said to Howard and Hamilton: "Even though we are so far down the line and have agreed a settlement in principle, I feel very strongly that we just should not do this. The KPMG report is outrageous and it's easy to prove that. We need to go back to see the FSA and tell them it's all wrong. They should have contacted us anyway to ask what our views of the KPMG report are. "

"No, Paul," they both said almost in harmony.

"But, I have a duty to tell the FSA that they can't rely on the KPMG report."

Hamilton spoke: "Paul, you are no longer an approved person; you have no obligation to make any further regulatory disclosures. You have done what you had to do when we met them in December. You really must take the settlement and move on."

I came back again: "Why don't we go to the press and tell them what's happened?"

"Because they won't listen especially with the existence of the KPMG report," said Hamilton. "And if you do, HBOS will withdraw the settlement offer and they have unlimited financial resources and will fight to the death and with the KPMG report they could easily win. You and your family may end up with nothing and no chance of a further career if you take this public."

Then Hamilton, my long-term friend, colleague and trusted adviser delivered the coup de grace in that soft and persuasive voice that he used so effectively.

"Paul, you just must settle and move on – for your family's sake."

I was beaten. My mental and emotional health was battered and bruised. I simply could not think straight anymore. My armpits sweated profusely almost all the time. I was drinking like a fish. I wasn't sleeping. I was a train crash.

It was over. I couldn't take anymore. I capitulated to the advice of lawyers and my friend.

The KPMG report had done the trick for HBOS and in the process made me and my family disappear.

CHAPTER 9

Intermission

Less than four months after signing my "gagging" order with HBOS in late June 2005, I was hitting the headlines. Since being forced out of the bank on the back of the KPMG investigation whitewash, I'd managed to achieve something that most whistleblowers rarely do, which is to get another job in the sector of their expertise.

Marsh, the world's largest general insurance brokerage, had hired me as Head of Compliance and made a big song and dance in the newspapers about having recruited me. My introduction to Marsh had arrived completely out of the blue at a time when I was still struggling to put behind me the deep trauma of the HBOS saga. The bank, supported by KPMG, had well and truly crushed me. Together, they had covered up the truth and made it abundantly clear that anyone at HBOS, however senior, who raised their head above the parapet would be summarily executed.

Of course, unless I was mad, it is a self-evident truth that I only did what I did at the bank because I cared more about the other HBOS stakeholders than myself. Above all, I cared deeply about the millions of HBOS customers and tens of thousands of employees. But I also cared about the shareholders, the Board and even Stevenson, Crosby, Hornby, Ellis and Dawson. Indeed,

I would say that what I did was an act of love and not the opposite.

Dwight Eisenhower, the late American President, once said, "Never confuse honest dissent with disloyal subversion". Well, HBOS had done that alright.

The history of mankind is literally and metaphorically littered with the corpses of people who from conscience, competence and courage chose to take the risk of speaking truth to power. The expression, "Don't shoot the messenger" came from Shakespeare's *Henry IV Part 2* and was also used in *Antony and Cleopatra*. The idea originated in Sophocles' *Antigone* as, "No one loves the messenger who brings bad news".

Famous examples of people who spoke truth to power, or as we call them these days, whistleblowers, include the Old Testament prophets, Jesus Christ, Francis of Assisi, Galileo, Copernicus, Thomas a Becket, Thomas More and William Wilberforce. In more modern days, they include Mahatma Gandhi, Martin Luther King, Nelson Mandela, Sherron Watkins (the Enron whistleblower), Joe Darby (abuse of Iraqi prisoners in Abu Ghraib jail), David Kelly (Iraq weapons of mass destruction), Dr Kim Holt (UK NHS and Baby P) and Michael Woodford (Olympus).

It turns out that the reason the Court Jester was dressed up as a lunatic was so that he could make a joke out of delivering difficult messages to the King. That's why the Joker in the pack of cards wins the trick!

So, there I was, yet another whistleblower who had been metaphorically executed. At that stage I knew very little about this whole topic, but I was to learn a lot more over the coming years about the common experiences of whistleblowers.

All that was left for my solicitor Clive Howard to do was finalise the settlement in accordance with our negotiations. Now we had agreed the deal, I felt a huge sense of relief and also the need for a holiday in the sun. By coincidence, my friend Glynn Thompson was going on a sailing trip to Majorca only a couple of weeks later so I decided to join him and a couple of other chums.

Apart from a very nasty jellyfish sting (the scar of which I still have on my left elbow), we had a wonderful time and it was a great way to de-stress. On 25 June, while we were sailing off the south coast of the Balearic Islands, I got a call on my mobile phone from Howard to say that the agreement was ready for my signature. I just said, "Sign it for me". He warned that it contained the strongest possible gagging clause that any of the "Magic Circle" firms of solicitors in London could devise and that I'd have to keep my mouth tightly shut about the whole affair or HBOS would sue me for everything I was worth. So, it really was over. The End. *Finito*. I could start to put the whole sorry episode behind me.

Yet even then, I still couldn't fully let go and I spent the rest of the sailing trip half hoping the FSA would contact me for my views on the KPMG report. The rebuttal letter we'd sent to HBOS should by now have been disclosed as a regulatory requirement and the FSA would know that KPMG had failed to follow proper protocol. But the FSA never did contact me. It simply accepted the KPMG report "as read". On one analysis, it was mere incompetence. On another, it was something worse. Crosby was a non-executive Director of the FSA. There was a strong inference of undue influence going on here.

The Majorca high-seas adventure certainly helped to kick-start the healing process and on my return home I threw myself back into overseeing the building work on our cottage. While the dispute with HBOS had been going on, I'd distracted myself by project managing the renovation with a friend of mine, David Read, who lived in the village. We employed two excellent sub-contractors, a carpenter and a builder, and my main job was to keep morale up by making them bacon and egg sandwiches every morning with plenty of HP sauce. By June, we'd made great progress and had an almost fully functioning kitchen.

Maureen and I had also decided that as soon as the summer holidays began we would go to Spain. The whole family needed a good rest and we'd been invited by our friends, Miguel and Mercedes, to spend the summer with them in the Spanish resort of Almería on the Costa del Sol. As we'd be away from early July until the end of August, we drove there by taking the ferry from Portsmouth to Bilbao, in northern Spain. We were still driving the trusty old Mercedes E 300 turbo diesel estate that I had purchased when I was a partner at KPMG. I would drive down with Daniel and Oliver, Maureen's niece Connie and her friend Francisca. Maureen and Emily would fly down to join us later.

The advance party set off from North Yorkshire mid-morning in a happy holiday mood to catch the ferry. About halfway to Portsmouth, my mobile started ringing. It was James Davies. Everyone in the car politely fell silent while I chatted with him on hands-free, as we motored on down the M40. We spoke briefly about the injustice of the KPMG report before he gave me some uplifting news.

"Paul, the main reason I called you is I've just been phoned by a headhunter who's got the absolutely perfect job for you." James was referring to an opening at Marsh, part of the Marsh McLennan Corporation (MMC). Buoyed by James' call, I was on a high by the time we boarded the ferry. We had great fun on the two-night boat trip to Bilbao, taking in, amongst other passenger entertainment, two rather cheesy variety shows. Some people took the trip as a mini-cruise and returned to the UK on the same boat to continue their carousing.

We disembarked in Bilbao at 7am and drove the 1,060km to Almería in 11 hours. During the journey the temperature topped 43C but the air-conditioned Mercedes kept us cool and we sang, hummed and nodded along to Shania Twain, Van Morrison and Abba. We were all happy, but I was even happier thinking that I was now possibly on the road to a new job, and with a large financial settlement from HBOS in my pocket.

The summer in Spain with the whole family was a wonderful period. The only problem was that the house we'd rented had no air-conditioning and it was extremely hot. I'd go fishing with Miguel very early in the morning. We ate lunch at about 3pm and only started dinner around 10.30pm. At one dinner party that Miguel and Mercedes organised, we didn't start eating until 11.30pm, but this was the way of life and with Maureen's mother tongue being Spanish, we all integrated quickly. One negative was that I did find myself drinking a great deal. In fact, I realised that I probably had a drink problem which I was going to need to deal with at some stage. But, not yet.

After a lengthy interview process, I started work at Marsh on Monday 10 October, 2005 and left the company on 6 July, 2006. I'm not at liberty to explain why.

I spent most of summer 2006 at home in North Yorkshire where the building work on our house was now finished. However, we did go to Spain for a couple of weeks in July, just after the children broke up from school, and we came back in time for Maureen's parents to visit us from Chile. In August, I completed one of the best risk management decisions I ever made in my life, by re-mortgaging Keeper's Cottage with Barclays bank.

At the end of August that year, I met a man called Robert Toone, a successful barrister and devoted Catholic. We were both attending our local parish barbecue and we hit it off immediately. Robert now lives two doors down the lane from us and he and his wife, Amanda, are the most wonderful people and put into practice everything for which the Christian story stands. He has come to be a very important person in my journey in faith and it was Robert who introduced

Maureen and me to an association called Teams of Our Lady. This association supports small groups of husbands and wives meeting together, once a month, to share their experiences as Christian families, pray and help one another to cope with the day-to-day stresses and strains of marriage and children. It creates exactly the sort of atmosphere needed for marriages to succeed.

Once, when driving down to London with Maureen, Robert gave us a set of CDs entitled *Believing God*, by an American Christian preacher called Joyce Meyer. We finished listening to the fourth and final CD as we parked at Maureen's aunt and uncle's house in Fulham. Those recordings were not only a key moment in my own journey of faith, but they also turned out to be the spiritual inspiration that finally led me to breach my gagging order with HBOS and blow the whistle publicly in September 2008. The title of the fourth CD was, *You can't defeat Goliath with your mouth shut!*

In September 2006, once the children were back at Ampleforth and St Mary's, Maureen and I drove down to Spain with Maureen's sister and partner. We stopped in the Dordogne, and went to see how building work was progressing on our Spanish villa near Marbella. It was nearly complete and by October was finally ours to enjoy. We spent the half-term school holidays there for the first time and the views over the Mediterranean to the African coast were spectacular.

Maureen had kept saying to me that we should take the developer up on his offer to buy the building contract back from us. Obstinately, I had refused on the basis that we would be giving up the huge capital gain on the villa. At that time, it was worth at least €1.75 million. However, immediately after our trip, we agreed to sell it the following spring. It turned out that we didn't get our act together, and by the time we did the property market was plunging in 2007. A banking crisis was looming. We should still have sold the property then but we didn't. It was May 2013 before we finally got a sale and we made a significant loss. It was uncomfortable but did me a lot of good. It was the biggest financial blunder of my life. Maureen was right all along but I was in the iron grip of greed.

Failing to sell the villa was all the more ridiculous given the fact that I had been advising all my friends that we were about to have a major correction in asset prices. I remember telling Robert Toone, who was living in rented accommodation at the time, to wait and watch the markets for a while before buying a house. He did and it saved him a good deal of money.

Towards the end of 2006, I invested £100,000 of working capital in a small voice and data communications business called Complete Networks Ltd, which we later affectionately referred to as Complete Nitwits Ltd. I became the Chairman and CEO, and from early 2007 threw myself into helping set up the business development strategy, structure, culture and people. I left in 2008, given other priorities in my life, in particular what happened when I went public about the HBOS affair. However, the business has gone from strength to strength picking up a major contract with the NHS Ambulance Service to design and implement its communication systems. Now that's what I call a "life or death" contract. My childhood friend, Tim Hughes, who I introduced to the business, is still involved and doing well.

By the summer of 2007, it was clear to me that we were getting close to a financial crisis. As we still owned the villa in Spain we went to stay there for the entire summer. Maureen designed the layout and it was truly beautiful, with travertine marble throughout, pool and sunbathing terraces. It was a memorable time for the family.

Although my official links with HBOS had been severed, I still had my contacts there, and had reconnected socially with my former boss Phil Hodkinson. We loved to go for a curry in Twyford near his Holyport home and at first we made a pact not to discuss the HBOS affair. By the end of the summer of 2005, Phil had been appointed CFO of HBOS when Mark Tucker left to become the CEO of the Prudential.

On 14 August, while we were at the villa in Spain, I received an email from Phil. He'd told me, confidentially, some considerable time before, that he would be retiring on his 50th birthday, in April 2008, to spend more time on charity work and to take up some non-executive positions. Consequently, HBOS was going to have to find a new CFO well in advance of that date. Phil wrote:

"Hi Paul. My retirement has now been announced ... much to my relief I can tell you, although you may be as surprised as I to hear, that my successor is one Mike Ellis! As I don't leave until April next year, I'm not really sure what to expect of the next 8 months..."

What? Ellis, coming back to his old job? This was seriously bad news and made me very suspicious indeed. I knew that Phil would have been doing his pragmatic best to keep HBOS on the straight and narrow. I wondered whether the reason that Ellis had been re-recruited was because, unlike Phil, he would have been easier to manipulate, so the CEO and the other executives got what they wanted.

I replied to Phil a couple of days later:

*"Well done for being a person who can give up the position, power and possessions associated with being the FD of a top company. But, your moving on is bad news for us shareholders! I am glad I got my risk management right and sold all my LTIS shares at £10.99....**I am not sure ...the decision on your successor was such a good idea as you can imagine.**"*

I spoke to Phil by phone after this and we were both equally appalled at the idea of Ellis returning.

By this stage in August 2007, the banking crisis had begun. BNP Paribas, one of the largest banks in the world, had frozen several of its hedge funds. On 9 August, the *Financial Times* (*FT*) reported:

"Investment funds on both sides of the Atlantic were affected by recent market turmoil on Thursday. BNP

> *Paribas shocked European markets by freezing three funds exposed to the stumbling US subprime mortgage market.*
>
> *BNP Paribas, one of Europe's biggest banks, blamed a 'complete evaporation of liquidity in certain market segments of the US securitisation market' for the temporary decision to stop redemptions from the three funds, and further investments.*
>
> *Collapse of demand for some forms of securitised debt made their assets impossible to value, the bank said.*
>
> *Freezing the funds, which invest in asset-backed securities, was the best way to 'protect the interests and ensure the equal treatment of our investors'.*
>
> *Shares in BNP Paribas fell 3 per cent to €82.57 by the close on Thursday."*

This was the first proper red flag of the gathering financial storm.

In early September, I started to do some more formal volunteer work with Robert Toone and a charity he'd set up called xt3 Media. Among other things, xt3 (which is short for "Christ in the third millennium") had published a bestselling book called *From Gangland to Promised Land* by born-again Catholic, John Pridmore. It was an amazing story about a gangster from London's East End who had become a devoted Christian and went around the country giving talks to thousands of young people about his experience. At the Pope's World Youth Day in Sydney, Australia, in 2008, John spoke for nearly 30 minutes to more than 300,000 people.

Robert and his brother John wanted to use xt3 to build a social networking platform – similar to early versions of Facebook – for use at a World Youth Day, an event initiated by John Paul II and contrary to its title actually lasts a whole week. Robert, one of the best and most honest sales people I have ever met, had visited Rome and convinced Cardinal Pell, the most senior cleric in the Catholic Church in Australia, to launch xt3.com in Sydney. It was a complex IT project that would be used by tens of thousands of people and when Robert asked me to help I become an xt3 trustee in September 2007.

A couple of weeks later on 14 September – just over a month since the BNP Paribas debacle – Northern Rock had to seek emergency liquidity support from the Bank of England, to enable it to stand behind and pay its depositors. It had borrowed far too much money on the wholesale markets and was simply not able to refinance the debts that became due.

By 17 September the Bank of England was forced to guarantee all depositors money in Northern Rock. This happened after a full-on run on the bank with huge queues of customers trying to withdraw their money.

Eventually, Northern Rock was nationalised on 22 February 2008 after aborted attempts by Lloyds Banking Group and others to acquire it. This, I knew, was the beginning of the end but I never imagined the coming banking crisis would be as catastrophic as it turned out to be.

I was still working hard on my investment in Complete Networks, but at the same time I had thrown myself into the deep end with the xt3.com project.

By mid-November I was getting very worried about the scheme, so I recruited a top-class programme manager called Nigel Clark. Without him, the project would never have succeeded. Robert, though, was making good progress on the fund-raising side of the equation and, in the end, he raised well over £1.5 million in less than six months. He did this with the massive assistance of Oliver Pawl, an ex-Deputy Chairman of Credit Suisse and a devoted Catholic. Robert had met him by complete chance in the queue outside the Vatican after the death of John Paul II.

Around early December, I started to get the first inklings, tickles and nudges that the HBOS saga may not be completely over for me but I put those thoughts to one side, remembering what my professional advisers had told me. I was sure that nobody would really believe me even if I did try to go to the media. I also had to consider my gagging order very carefully.

Just before Christmas the Teams of Our Lady organised a pre-Christmas Mass, followed by a bit of a shindig. This was the first year that Maureen and I had been involved and we didn't really know many of the people from the other teams in the area. Robert and Amanda lived in Wetherby, prior to moving to Ampleforth, and the get-together was in someone's house there.

After the Mass, I was milling around meeting people when I bumped into Danny Savage. He was the northern correspondent for BBC News and I'd often seen him reporting on the main national news as well as the local news channel, Look North. I got talking to him and we started to discuss the situation in the banking world. For some reason I started to tell him about my HBOS nightmare and suggested we did a story about it. I'm not entirely clear what Danny thought, except probably that I was a lunatic. In any event nothing came of it.

As 2008 got underway it was all systems go with Complete Networks and xt3.com. I wasn't being paid for either role, even though they were consuming a great deal of my time and energy. However, the hard work paid off and by March we had Complete Networks under control and xt3 was moving along nicely under its slogan Connect With Millions, Share Your Experience, And Build A Better World.

Then on 14 March, the next big explosion went off in the banking crisis – the multi-billion-dollar failure of US investment bank Bear Stearns. Its collapse sent shockwaves around the world's financial markets and resulted in a Federal Reserve Bank of New York bailout and fire sale to JP Morgan Chase.

At the end of April, as the aftershocks continued to reverberate, Royal Bank of Scotland (RBS) announced a rights issue to raise £12billion from its shareholders to shore up its balance sheet. By this stage it had made the disastrous decision to acquire ABN Amro for €71billion, a move which should never have been permitted by the regulators. The BBC News reported:

"The bank [RBS] said it had seen a 'severe and increasing deterioration in credit market conditions, the worsening economic outlook and the increased likelihood that credit markets would remain difficult for some time'."

It was another major signpost to the global financial meltdown about to take place.

In early June RBS completed its rights issue, the largest ever seen in European markets. At the time of writing, the bank is being sued in a "class action" by a large number of its shareholders who allege that RBS misrepresented its financial position in the prospectus for the rights issue.

On Tuesday 29 April 2008 HBOS followed RBS's lead by announcing its need to raise £4billion through its own rights issue. The *FT* quoted HBOS's Andy Hornby as follows:

"'It's the right time in the cycle to build really strong capital ratios for the long term. Banks that don't have strong capital ratios will find it harder,' Mr Hornby said.

'I believe we are taking the right call for the next four years,' he said.

The move was a sharp contrast to the bank's stance eight weeks ago when it announced its results, and comes just days after a £12bn cash call from rival Royal Bank of Scotland.

Mr Hornby denied HBOS had bowed to pressure from regulators or politicians to strengthen its capital ratios.

However, the Financial Services Authority recently held a series of high-level meetings with senior executives of leading banks to stress the importance of strong capital reserves."

The HBOS rights issue completed on 21 July 2008 by which time its share price was 6p lower than the price of the rights issue shares, so it's hardly surprising that only 8% of existing shareholders took up their rights. The remaining 92% had to be taken up by the underwriters. They would have pre-sold many of these rights in the market place before completion harming their counterparties financially.

This is how reporter Robert Peston summed up the situation:

"***HBOS HUMBLED***

HBOS's £4bn rights issue has been an absolutely colossal flop.

It is, in fact, the quintessence of a flop.

The deal will probably enter the City lexicon as the phrase 'doing an HBOS', to mean how not to raise money – though that would be unfair, because HBOS is the victim of a rights-issue system that is cumbersome and slow (and should therefore be reformed).

But here's the important point.

HBOS has got its money, some £4bn.

So this is not a case of an important bank being deprived of vital capital.

What's happened is that its own shareholders don't want the new shares, or at least they want only 8% of them.

Shareholders cold-shouldered the sale because the price of HBOS shares (and other banks' share prices) plummeted at the make-your-mind-up moment last week, after the woes of Fannie Mae and Freddie Mac took investors to the brink of a nervous breakdown.

The remaining 92% of HBOS rights shares will go to the underwriters, unless they can be placed in the market over the next couple of days.

That means about £2.2bn of stock will be shared between just two investment banks, Morgan Stanley and Dresdner Kleinwort.

Here's what's irksome for HBOS.

Underwriters like Morgan Stanley and Dresdner are reluctant buyers of shares in these circumstances, not long-term investors – even though both have hedged their exposure to HBOS and are therefore not facing colossal losses.

The market knows that the underwriters would want to sell their stock at the earliest opportunity, which would keep HBOS's shares under downward pressure at a time when the weak housing market is doing quite enough to depress its shares.

So HBOS is keeping its fingers and toes crossed that investors who actually want to hold its shares can be persuaded to buy in the coming hours."

It now turns out that the HBOS rights issue was based on what appear to be deliberate misrepresentations to the market which could well amount to various criminal offences.

Whenever a public company launches a rights issue, it is obliged, both in its prospectus and at an extraordinary general meeting of shareholders, to disclose to potential investors any material risks facing the company. Evidence now proves that HBOS failed to do so. I watched the whole of the extraordinary general meeting of shareholders via a webcast and can testify that at no point did Lord Dennis Stevenson, Andy Hornby or Mike Ellis make any mention to shareholders of the massive "liquidity risks" faced by HBOS, or other key risks. Yet it was the crystallisation of the liquidity risk that led to the bank's failure.

The term liquidity risk is best described as the risk that a company has that it may not be able to refinance the money it has borrowed on the wholesale markets to fund its lending growth. In this regard, at the apex, HBOS had borrowed close to £270billion on the wholesale markets. About 60% of this money had to be repaid and re-borrowed within 12 months. This meant that in order to remain solvent HBOS needed to borrow £162billion over a 12-month period. To put that in perspective, in the same year that this occurred, the total net cost of the NHS UK, the largest non-military organisation in the world, was under £100billion. On a monthly league table always sent to the HBOS Board of all the largest global borrowers in the wholesale credit markets (banks as well as sovereign governments), HBOS was more often than not in the top 10. In one year, it is reputed that HBOS borrowed more on the wholesale markets than the Italian government.

As one very senior HBOS treasury executive put it to me: "We all knew we had a massive liquidity risk. But, we all hoped we could jump off the merry-go-round before anyone else and before it span out of control."

In the summer of 2014, my colleagues and I discovered the smoking gun. At the very time that HBOS was selling the rights issue to the markets, it was taking massive emergency liquidity support from the Bank of England. This wasn't disclosed in the prospectus or at the extraordinary general meeting. HBOS's auditors, KPMG, and its corporate finance advisers, knew this but chose to do nothing about it, thereby facilitating the misrepresentations and harm towards shareholders. KPMG almost certainly had a statutory duty to report this to the regulators and the criminal justice system. Worse still, the Bank of England, the FSA, the Treasury, Chancellor Alistair Darling and almost certainly Prime Minister Gordon Brown, all knew about it.

Tom Harper of the *Independent on Sunday* had this to say on 31 August 2014:

> *"Documents published on the Bank of England website reveal the Labour government was 'fully aware of the vulnerabilities of HBOS' from at least September 2007 and was receiving 'daily liquidity reports' on HBOS from the Financial Services Authority. Despite the turmoil behind the scenes, in December 2007 the then HBOS chief executive Andy Hornby announced the bank was 'set to deliver a good full year outcome' and its 'capital strength' continued to 'underpin confidence and support for HBOS in the wholesale funding markets'.*
>
> *Problems escalated, and on 21 April 2008 the Treasury and the Bank of England launched the 'special liquidity*

scheme' (SLS), which lent HBOS an estimated £40bn over the following months. But one week later, HBOS published its £4bn rights issue, failing to mention the state support on which it was reliant.

In summing up the bank's position, the prospectus told investors that there had 'been no significant change in the financial or trading position of the Group since 31 December 2007' – failing to mention the massive support it was receiving from SLS.

At a meeting in June 2008, HBOS shareholders were persuaded to vote in favour of the rights issue. During that meeting, Lord Stevenson said: 'Performance will be satisfactory and resilient. Armageddon may happen and we should be prepared for it and we are.

'We are telling the truth; we are truthful people. But if we weren't, there's an army of regulators, auditors, etc, to make sure we are.'"

In the same article I was quoted as follows:

"Paul Moore, a former HBOS executive whose warnings over the bank's finances were suppressed by his superiors, said: 'This is an extremely serious matter. The state support was clearly a material fact that should have been disclosed to the markets in the rights issue. In fact, as the Bank of England is the 'lender of last resort', this essentially means that HBOS were tantamount to insolvent when they launched and completed the rights issue. Failures have been made by HBOS, the Bank of England, the FSA and the Treasury. We need to know what former Prime Minister Gordon Brown and his Chancellor, Alistair Darling, knew about this.'"

Two stories written by the journalist Ian Fraser (author of *Shredded: Inside RBS, The Bank That Broke Britain*) on the subject of the HBOS rights issue, had appeared in the *Independent on Sunday* on 8 November 2009. They were headlined 'The unanswered questions around the emergency HBOS cash call' and 'Inquiry asks if HBOS misled over rights issue'.

It also turned out that Lord Dennis Stevenson had been in direct written correspondence with the Chairman of the FSA, Sir Callum McCarthy, even earlier than that. Here is an extract from a letter from Stevenson to McCarthy dated 18 March 2008:

> *"How would we fare if liquidity completely dried up, you asked? Does that keep me awake at night? Well yes of course one worries about everything, but the answer is no! First, our close monitoring of those who supply the lines of credit leads us to the view that the circumstances in which ours would be withdrawn would either be the 'freak' circumstances outlined above (but even that is judged to be unlikely) or where the world has collapsed to an extent that all bets of all kinds are off. The commonsense of the situation is that we are dealing with lenders looking to lend money to a highly conservative institution.*
>
> *Incidentally, this may be the context to make the point that the time may have been reached where it will be a sensible precaution for the BOE [Bank of England] to find a way of making it plain that it will accept the high quality assets we are talking about as collateral. In the same spirit – and I suspect there are other voices on this subject – I do think it would be helpful if the BOE made it clear that the*

three month repo facility will be provided for as long as is necessary and will be unlimited as to amount.

This takes me a little way away from your question as to how I am feeling! Thank you, by the way, for asking it even if it was only meant in a corporate sense! To repeat, the bottom line is that without wishing to be the slightest bit complacent, we feel that HBOS in this particular storm and given its business characteristics is in as safe a harbour as is possible while at the same time feeling commercially rather frustrated!

Yours sincerely

Dennis Stevenson"

There is a juxtaposition here. On the one hand, Stevenson assures Callum McCarthy that HBOS is a highly conservative institution that does not have or foresees liquidity problems. On the other, he makes an apparently off-the-cuff appeal to McCarthy to encourage the Bank of England to provide liquidity support.

The entire letter and earlier correspondence between Stevenson and McCarthy is here:

www.crashbankwallop.co.uk/library/9-1

The upshot of all this is clear. Contrary to the rule of civil and criminal law and the provisions of the FSA's rulebook, the directors of HBOS, its professional advisers, the regulators and politicians all conspired to support a rights issue based on deliberate misrepresentations of the financial position of HBOS. This is worse than scandalous but, to date, it has not been subject to a proper investigation or accountability, notwithstanding the fact that this matter has been reported in detail, along with all the evidence that supports the allegations to regulators and to the Treasury Select Committee. My guess is that this matter will be investigated following the publication of the final HBOS report.

The excuse would no doubt be that, at the time, they thought that what they were doing was the greatest good for the greatest number of people. Nonetheless if, in a democracy, the rule of law does not apply to everybody equally, you haven't got a democracy. Utilitarianism does not permit breaking the law.

The fact is that when HBOS completed its rights issue, it would have been insolvent had it not been for the Bank of England's support. Furthermore, on any sensible risk analysis, the idea that the £4billion of capital HBOS raised was ever going to be sufficient to save it was ludicrous.

Towards the end of May 2008, Phil Hodkinson came to stay with us in Wass so that we could go walking together in the North York Moors. I have some lovely photographs of the two days we spent. As we hiked, we both mused over what was going to happen in the banking markets over the coming months and Phil expressed his huge relief that he was no longer part of it.

About a month later, during the course of the HBOS rights issue, I wrote an email to Phil asking for his take on risk scenarios for HBOS shares. He sent me a detailed response which painted a bullish picture. He said HBOS shares were undervalued *"due to funding issues and the pending house crash"* but that in the longer term, about three years, *"the gain should be good"*. He even predicted that within 12 months the bank's shares, *"will be measurably better than the rights issue price (350p?)"*.

So, here we had the recently retired CFO of HBOS who was still clearly caught up in the "group think" of the moment. Phil's risk analysis of the HBOS situation really couldn't have been further from the reality.

As it happened, I still had some HBOS shares which had been allocated to me on a conditional basis in March 2005 at a share price of about £10. I wasn't permitted to sell them until March 2008 by which time they were worth about £5. With the HBOS share price in freefall I never did take up any rights. In the end, my shares that were at one point notionally worth more than £200,000, finished up valued at about £5,000 on Lloyd's acquisition of HBOS. I still own the shares in case I want to attend an AGM of Lloyds Banking Group or to take legal action as a shareholder.

So, the HBOS share price – having once stood at the dizzy heights of more than £11 – finally hit its Nemesis at 70p when the Lloyd's sale completed in January 2009.

By amazing coincidence, I bumped into Andy Hornby at York railway station around about this time. "You must be having fun?" I said to him. He clearly wasn't. He looked terribly stressed and told me it wasn't a pleasant time. I haven't spoken to or seen him since.

In June I met with Danny Savage again at another Teams of Our Lady get-together, in Wetherby, and tried once again to get his interest in doing a story. This time, I think he was beginning to realise that perhaps there was some method in my madness. Once again nothing came of it, which was probably a good thing as I potentially stood to lose everything if I spoke publicly.

Maureen, Oliver and I flew out to Sydney on 8 July to work with xt3.com at World Youth Day there and we stayed in Australia until 22 July. By the grace of God and some jolly hard work by a whole load of people, we had managed to launch the xt3.com social networking platform successfully by the end of June. It was definitely one of the highest-risk projects I had ever been involved in but pretty much the whole development team was in Sydney for its launch. Within a few days there were tens of thousands of people using xt3.com on their mobile phones and laptops – and the network never crashed once.

It is still used as one of the key communication tools of the diocese of Sydney which acquired it from xt3 Media. Cardinal Pell has since been appointed the Vatican's equivalent of the Chancellor of the Exchequer. Perhaps he needs a new head of risk management? I can't imagine that the Vatican Bank could be any more difficult to handle than HBOS.

We attended the final Mass said by Pope Benedict XVI at a racecourse just outside Sydney and more than 650,000 people were present. After Sydney, we flew to Cairns and spent a week at a resort in northern Queensland. We went on a tropical forest cable-car trip and a sailing boat on the Great Barrier Reef.

When we arrived back in the UK, the crisis in the banking sector seemed to be worsening almost daily and by the end of August 2008 the markets were in turmoil. Time and again my conscience pricked me to step out of the shadows and reveal my story. It was worse at night, my mind working overtime and flipping me in and out of sleep. I took guidance from the prayers of my dad's Catholic inspiration, Blessed Cardinal Newman, and listened again to the Joyce Myers CDs. But I was still in a dilemma as to what to do.

Then, the tsunami came thundering in on 15 September 2008. Lehman Brothers, one of the largest investment banks in the USA, run by Dick "the Gorilla" Fuld, filed for bankruptcy. Christine Lagarde, the French Finance Minister, had advised Hank Paulson, the USA's chief Secretary of the Treasury, in the strongest possible terms not to allow Lehman Brothers to fail if he wanted to avoid complete meltdown of the global financial system. He disregarded her advice and, later, she described him as watching the financial tsunami coming towards him, without thinking of anything else, except which pair of swimming trunks he should wear.

At 2.13am on 16 September, I woke up and decided, there and then in bed, that I was going to go public and blow the whistle to the media, irrespective of my gagging clause or any risk to the compensation I had received from HBOS. I drifted back into a deep sleep and got up the next morning revitalised. I powered up my computer and at 9.31am sent an email to the BBC's Danny Savage that would change the direction of my life for ever. This is what it said:

"Danny,

What has really caused the banking crisis and what should be done about it to make sure it doesn't happen again?

We have spoken briefly a couple of times about my experience as Head of Regulatory Risk and Compliance at HBOS.

I think (but am not 100% sure!) that, given recent events in the banking world, the time may now have come when someone who has been there / done it / and wears the T shirt ('I was the Senior Compliance Officer who was fired for trying to slow down the bank') speaks out again on what has gone wrong in the financial system and what needs to be done to make sure it does not happen again.

My agenda is simple – to try to get the re-vamped system to work properly from a policy perspective taking into account the practical experience of someone like me and what can be learned from my story. There are quite a few key things that need policy changes in my view to make it work. I have not really heard any of these proposed yet. As you can imagine, it would also be good to feel vindicated, although this is not really that important – it's a fairly lonely business speaking out as the stories of the prophets tell us! But I want to avoid revenge at all costs!

The sort of thing I would like to consider is an article and input to TV interview. It is difficult to know how to raise things without reference to the specifics...but no doubt you are good at that.

What has happened here is nothing short of a complete failure of the entire system of corporate governance in banks. In short:-

- *Executive management / directors have failed (but none have been fired yet) and been remunerated to fail. Either they knew the risks they were taking and were reckless (because there was no downside for them) or they did not know the risks and were incompetent.*
- *Internal risk and compliance officers have failed or have been too frightened to speak out.*
- *The non executive have failed adequately to oversee the executive.*
- *The institutional shareholders have failed to oversee their investments.*
- *The FSA has failed.*
- *As I say a good deal needs to change:*
- *Regulation of the remuneration systems of management must be far more intrusive.*
- *Risk and compliance systems cannot solely rely on internal staff. Substantive performance needs to be audited formally by an external expert that can be sued.*
- *The scope and depth of the annual audit must be signed off by the FSA. The only thing that will keep the auditor honest is the risk of being sued.*
- *Likewise, the scope and depth of the financial audit needs to be formally signed off by the FSA.*

- *Involvement by the FSA in the selection and oversight of the non executive must be much greater. The fact is that the Executive is in reality in control of the non executive and far too close to it. My case proves this conclusively. The week before Crosby removed me from office, Tony Hobson (Chairman of Group Audit Committee) told me what a good job I was doing... and then Crosby removed me because Hobson did not protect me as he should.*
- *Internal risk and compliance officers must not report to the Executive but must report to the new type of non executive and potentially also to a Council of Shareholders only. The test of fitness and properness for their role must be much more strongly regulated. Institutional shareholders must be required to take a much more active role in the oversight of the businesses they own. I suggest a policy of a formal Council of shareholders which is paid for by the company it oversees.*
- *The regulator must impose much more rigorous regulatory requirements in a whole range of areas.*
- *There must be new rules about whistle blowing which prevent companies / regulators sweeping what happened under the carpet by misusing shareholders funds. When HBOS settled with me I was always schizophrenic about being paid off to keep quiet about what had happened.*

Regards
Paul

PS As you might imagine, I did sign a gagging order in my settlement agreement with HBOS but I believe it is unenforceable."

The financial tidal wave had most definitely hit shore but without realising it, my electronic message to Danny that morning was about to combine to create the perfect storm.

CHAPTER 10

"You can't defeat Goliath with your mouth shut"

It was 17 September. The breaking news on the BBC took my breath away.

I was passing through the snug with a fresh cup of coffee when Robert Peston's exclusive report flashed onto the television screen.

Lloyds TSB had agreed to take over HBOS for £12 billion. British Premier Gordon Brown's government had waived all competition laws to allow the purchase to take place.

It was a shotgun marriage – arranged and forced. I was flabbergasted.

The BBC's website on that 17 September reported the news as follows:

> *"BBC business editor Robert Peston said the government had opted to push through the Lloyds TSB-HBOS tie-up after HBOS voiced concerns that depositors and lenders had begun to withdraw their credit from the bank.*
>
> *'There were growing concerns in the HBOS boardroom that a climate of fear was being created about its future that could have led to a funding crisis, or a Northern Rock-style run - on steroids,' he said.*
>
> *The deal was negotiated at the very highest level, with Prime Minister Gordon Brown telling Lloyds TSB*

Chairman Sir Victor Blank that it would be helpful if Lloyds could end the uncertainty surrounding HBOS by buying it.

'It was not in the government's interest for there to be the faintest risk that it would have another Northern Rock on its hands,' our business editor added."

Without the support of Lloyds, HBOS would have gone bankrupt and, similar to Northern Rock, it would have had to have been nationalised. My mind spun back to that boardroom meeting on 27 July 2004. QED.

That evening, at just after 9.30pm, I couldn't hold back from writing an email to Mike Ellis. I simply said:

"You should be ashamed of yourself personally and of yourselves as a board. Read this correspondence when, as usual, you failed to do what you should have."

I was referring to the correspondence I'd had with him following the Board meeting when he failed to support changing the minutes to reflect what I had actually said.

The next day, 18 September, as the bank's takeover news made global headlines, I emailed Clive Howard and Peter Hamilton, and then sent a message to James Davies, headed QED:

"James,

I know I should not rake over old ground but I just could not resist sending you this extract from the correspondence I had with Ellis about the board minutes when I talked to them about the sales culture review. Including this choice comment which I made:

- *That from a strategic perspective, very careful consideration should be given in the development of Retail's operating and strategic plans as to exactly what level of sales growth is achievable, given current capacity, without putting customers and colleagues at risk.*

After hubris indeed comes Nemesis! It is ineluctable, as my Greek philosophy teacher told me when we studied the Greek tragedies! How the mighty fall!

Paul"

Over the following weeks I became so absorbed in Complete Networks and xt3.com that I more or less forgot about my email to Danny Savage. I'd also just picked up my first piece of consulting work with a firm called Curzon Consulting, owned and run by a friend of mine, Andrew Morgan. I'd gone back too on my personal pledge never to work in financial services again, and had applied for a job at Northern Rock as Head of Compliance. It would be based in Newcastle-upon-Tyne, only an hour's drive from Wass, and I had the perfect credentials.

With all this going on, I was caught a little on the hop when TV producer Jacqui Farnham called me on Tuesday 21 October. She'd got my name and telephone number from Danny and wondered if I'd agree to be featured in a *Money Programme* special the BBC was making about the HBOS affair. The programme was to be called *HBOS: Breaking the Bank*. I sent Jacqui a copy of the email I'd written to Danny, along with a few key documents, but told her that I needed to take legal advice before I went public. However, I wrote:

"But maybe now is the time to get this stuff on the table."

Joyce Meyer's CD kept ringing in my ears and my soul, "You can't defeat Goliath with your mouth shut".

Clive Howard told me that although there were legal doubts as to whether the gagging clause was enforceable, I should still treat it as though it was. He said I'd be taking a major risk of being sued by HBOS if I went public. It was sobering advice but these were exceptional circumstances, and so I agreed to meet Jacqui the following day in the BBC Media Centre just up the road from the BBC Television Centre in White City, London.

Almost immediately after I'd left the Media Centre meeting, I received an email from Paul Mason, the highly respected Economics Editor of BBC *Newsnight*. He was going to be the presenter on *The Money Programme* and said he'd like to do an interview with me on camera. I told him that I wasn't going to do that but that I would provide him with all the documentation that he needed. His email read as follows:

"Dear Paul,

We spoke just now about The Money Programme *special HBOS: Breaking the Bank. I am writing to outline what an on-screen interview by you would involve. We would record an on-camera interview covering the following:*

1. *What was in the report submitted to the FSA regarding HBOS's compliance? What was its key point? What did the FSA do in response?*
2. *How did the Group Audit Committee react when you presented your concerns to them about a 'cultural indisposition to challenge'?*
3. *What do you think are the systemic lessons of the failure of HBOS?*
4. *What was the culture within the bank with regard to sales? How were people incentivised and did this put the bank at risk of treating customers unfairly?*
5. *Anything else you think it is vitally necessary to say about the culture of the bank.*

I think this would form a powerful core of the piece, which would make people finally sit up and listen to what's been wrong in banking and regulation.

We would obviously have to put critical points and allegations to those involved: HBOS and the FSA.

I really hope we can make this happen.

Paul Mason

Reporter, The Money Programme

Economics Editor, BBC Newsnight"

I had never, in my life, been involved in a media interview, let alone in front of a TV camera. I didn't want to do it. I didn't think there was any reason for me to do it. I replied to Paul Mason, by sending him the key documents and directing him where to look. At the end of my email, I wrote:

> *"I think you may find that when you have read the materials you might be in a better position to decide what line you would like to follow and I do think it may still be possible to get the key messages across without putting me in front of the camera."*

I was staying at Maureen's aunt and uncle's house in Fulham that night and I have to admit that I'd had rather too much to drink. The next morning, 23 October, Mason and Farnham launched a concerted campaign to persuade me to go on screen. I refused.

Shortly after, I received a personal telephone call from Dominic Crossley-Holland, the BBC's head honcho for "non-news factual" which covered documentaries including *Panorama* and T*he Money Programme*. Dominic told me that it was a crucial matter of public interest that I should appear on camera in the programme. Without further ado, he told me he was sending a car around to pick me up in Fulham to take me to meet him. I capitulated to this request for a meeting but emphasised it would not guarantee that I would appear on camera.

The car arrived 15 minutes later. I hadn't even had enough time to take a shower and put on some smart clothes but I thought if I did end up giving an interview I'd be able to come back and freshen myself up.

I was driven to the BBC Television Centre, directed into the lift and then ushered into a dingy meeting room. Dominic, Paul Mason and Jacqui Farnham were all in there waiting for me.

Dominic told me that there was a huge difference in the impact of a documentary if the person providing the key evidence was interviewed on camera. He said the documentation I'd provided was good – but the human factor was key. Similar to many people, I was suspicious of the media and wasn't sure if I could trust them.

We got talking about our backgrounds, and I mentioned to Dominic that I'd gone to Ampleforth College. He asked me if I knew Cardinal Basil Hume and I said that he was the Abbot at Ampleforth Abbey when I was in the school and had been in the same house there as my father in the Forties. It turned out that Cardinal Hume had been Dominic's mentor for some time, and this broke the ice between us.

This all led to me agreeing to appear on camera subject to consulting my trusted adviser Maureen first. A conference call was set up and we rang her. I outlined the situation and Dominic explained to her why it was so important that I appeared on camera. After a few moments of reflection, Maureen said I should do it because there was such high public interest in someone who had been at a senior executive level in a failed bank speaking out.

After the decision was made, I felt a great sense of calmness. I just knew I was doing the right thing. I'd never wanted to sign the HBOS gagging order and from the outset I was only after truth, justice and reform. Speaking up would give me an opportunity to achieve these goals.

I turned to Dominic and asked when they would want to do the interview. "Immediately," he said. I was shabbily dressed and desperately needed a shower but they insisted on doing the interview straight away to give time to put the programme together before it was broadcast. So we moved to a dark rectangular room where there were a group of camera and sound technicians and within 10 minutes it was all over. I felt dumbfounded. I was still not sure I should be doing this. It all seemed very surreal. Me? Doing an interview with the Economics Editor of *Newsnight*. It was all a bit like what Joyce Meyer had said when she reminded us that *"David ran quickly towards Goliath."*

The interview itself was all a blur and I had no idea how I would come across. I just remember Paul Mason asking me what it was like at HBOS and replying: "I felt like a man in a rowing boat, trying to slow down an oil tanker." After the main interview, we took some additional location shots with me walking along talking to Paul and then footage of me leaning on the balcony railings around the top of the BBC Television Centre.

Shortly after this, I was told that the programme would be broadcast on 30 October – my 50th birthday. So on the day, instead of the normal celebrations, the whole family gathered around the screen to watch my maiden TV appearance. I was on tenterhooks but after watching it we were all surprised at how well I did. The only embarrassing bit was the shot of me on the balcony showing my big tummy and scruffy jeans. The excessive drinking wasn't doing my waistline any good, let alone anything else.

I felt good about what I'd done but it was an odd sort of birthday present.

Apparently, HBOS had attempted to prevent the programme going out by threatening to take out an injunction. It didn't and the broadcast made a big splash. I was quoted in hundreds of articles for the "rowing boat" comment. The programme can be watched here: www.crashbankwallop.co.uk/library/10-1

Following the transmission, I started to get a bit of a public profile. Friends and strangers reassured me that I'd done the right thing and I became known as the HBOS Whistleblower. The epithet has followed me everywhere since.

About a week later, a reporter from the *Daily Telegraph* asked me to write a letter to the paper. Knowing nothing about the media, my first draft was far too long but here's most of what was printed:

"Sir

I have been a specialist in financial sector regulation, compliance and risk management since it all began in 1986. Among other senior roles, I have been a partner at accountants KPMG and head of group regulatory risk at HBOS between 2002 and 2005. You could say that I've been there, done it and got the T-shirt!

In my opinion, what has happened to the banks calls into question the effectiveness of the whole system – executive management, internal risk, compliance and audit functions, non-executive governance, regulatory and political oversight. Putting it bluntly, there have been failures in all key areas.

One key change I believe needs to be made is for internal risk management and compliance functions – whose formal role is to oversee the activities of the executive – to report primarily not to the executive (as almost invariably all do) but directly to the non-executive.

Reporting into the executive creates an inherent conflict of interest – on the one hand their job is to rein in the executive, on the other, if they do so they may become less than flavour of the month. By changing the reporting lines in this way, the staff carrying risk management and compliance roles will feel much more protected.

Any decision as to the appointment, performance or dismissal of these functions should be determined by the non-executive board. I also strongly believe that the work of the internal risk and compliance functions should be covered by a formal opinion as part of the annual statutory audit.

Yours
Paul Moore"

I also contacted Paul Mason again and congratulated him on the programme. I said there was much more detail that needed to come out – including names. This is what I said:

"Paul,
Hope all goes well with you...have a look at the email trail below... The Telegraph will be publishing the shorter re-draft of the letter which Philip Aldrick assisted with....and covering it with a brief story... It was Philip who picked up on The Money Programme story...see the article I sent you earlier.

Might there be any mileage in using the Money Programme work you did to try to feed some of the policy ideas I have into a Newsnight commentary or some other programme? The letter to The Telegraph covers one or two key points but there are others... (I have included the points in the letter for completeness)...we could allude to my experiences in a general sense to bring the points to life??....will need more thinking but here are the basic ideas:-

- *Remuneration and performance management of exec...e.g. regulatory sign off, bonuses held in a trustee account over longer time frames to ensure short termism does not take hold.*

- *Formal qualifications and competencies for risk managers and compliance professionals so that the Jo Dawsons of the world cannot be appointed to this type of role whilst on the conveyor belt to an executive role which naturally gives them a conflict of interest...these roles are becoming as important as CFO role and need something like the ICA [International Compliance Association] to regulate training and competence...*

- *Formal audit of risk management, compliance and internal audit functions to keep them honest (in the letter but can be expanded on).*

- *Risk management and compliance reporting to non-exec with sufficient time and profile to balance the exec (in the letter but can be expanded on)....Hector Sants made a huge noise about managing conflicts of interest before he became CEO of FSA in a Dear*

CEO letter in September 2004...this is directly in point here...I will try to find what he said and get it to you... it make a really good spring-board for the point I am making....as well as many of the other points.

- *Even more focus on competence and independence of non-executives, e.g. register of non-work social meetings, pre-appointment investigation of 'links' / potential conflicts of interest, e.g. cross-board connections... I'm on your remuneration committee if you're on my audit committee, pre-appointment record of reasons why a person is competent for a particular committee....to prevent the Dunstone... 'Well they got that appointment wrong'.*
- *Much much more rigorous and prescription of the regulation of affordability and suitability requirements for the sale of credit products...to prevent ordinary people who cannot resist the temptation of getting into excessive debt.*
- *Further development of Whistleblowing rules to make sure that those who raise legitimate issues are not just 'bought off' with shareholders money.... The case should be reviewed by the regulator and action taken if necessary to ensure those responsible cannot get away scot-free.*

Not sure whether I am barking up the wrong tree? Let me know what you think.

Regards

Paul"

However, nothing more came of this, which was a disappointment as I felt we had only just covered the tip of the iceberg. The devil was in the detail but it didn't look as though the media had the determination and attention span to dig any deeper into the story. So how was I going to complete the job that I started?

A couple of weeks later, Maureen flew on her own to Santiago, to spend time with her family before the rest of us flew out. That year, as on so many previous occasions, we wanted to take advantage of the summer weather in Chile. The children and I arrived there on the morning of Friday 12 December. There was the normal raucous welcome from almost the entire Chilean family. It's a big shock to the system, flying from a cold, wet, dark England to the dazzling sunshine and heat of Santiago, but it doesn't take long to get used to.

A few days later, back in the UK, the then Leader of the Opposition David Cameron MP made a keynote speech at Thomson Reuters on 15 December on the banking crisis. This received international publicity.

Just before Christmas, I was asked to do a pre-recorded interview for the BBC World Service. I did this with Gideon Long, the BBC correspondent in Santiago. The interviewer was Rob Young, a business reporter and presenter on Radio 5 Live and the BBC World Service. It was a good interview and made some waves.

The next day, 23 December, having begun to give the whole media issue a bit of reflection, I wrote to Rob:

"I enjoyed the opportunity to get involved in your programme yesterday and I am prepared to be further involved if you would find that useful. I got the sense that I may be able to help you navigate the topic that you are covering even better, if we spent a little more time off-the-record and then potentially re-record the interview in the most focused and effective way. I am prepared to put in the time if you can cover my expenses only.

I am new to this media game but am keen to stick my oar in to the current debate as I have been involved in the regulatory scene in the UK since it began, and I felt as though some of the input I gave yesterday could have been more effective had it been a little more prepared. It's a fairly fine line that I am trying to tread between 'spilling the beans' and not being interested in revenge – and coming across as sour grapes.

The only thing that interests me is getting some of the lessons learnt on the table so that policy changes can be made for the future. But one has to reference some specifics of one's experience to bring the policy points to life. For instance, the appointment of someone with no experience as Group Risk Director. By the way, in settling my whistleblowing claim, of course, I entered into a gagging order which puts me at some legal risk – although the timing is such, as I said yesterday, that I can no longer be accused of damaging HBOS as they are already so damaged as to be irrecoverable. Therefore I shall be ignoring this risk."

Attached to my email, I sent Rob a blog that I had written but had not published. I wrote this sitting on a sofa in my sister-in-law's partner's house, overlooking the dunes and the Pacific Ocean. Here is part of it:

"The 2008 financial crisis: will the pride and prejudice of the past lead to a brave new world – or just more great expectations?

Introduction – will we ever have the courage to find out what happened and learn the lessons, or will vested interest resist a thorough investigation?

One of the most extraordinary things about the 2008 financial crisis and its aftermath is that it has been so big, has cost developed economies so much money and has involved so many vested interests – powerful and rich executives, their powerful and rich non-executive friends, powerful but ineffective regulators and powerful but ineffective politicians – that no-one powerful wants anyone to find out exactly what did happen, who was accountable and what should be done about it to make sure it does not happen again. It might be just so embarrassing for all the 'great and the good' involved.

Let's just have a look at two examples.

At the very top of the tree, Gordon Brown swaggers around holding himself out as the economic saviour of the world for his post financial disaster response with a level of hubris that defies belief. But does he ever acknowledge, let alone apologise for the fact that it was he, as Chancellor of the Exchequer who presided functionally over the economic strategy that got us into this mess in the first place? No more boom and bust, he promised; he guaranteed! And, yet, it very much looks like he will have presided over the biggest boom (what he calls 'the longest sustained period of economic growth') in the history of the country – as well as one of the biggest busts. Surely, you don't need to be an economic rocket scientist or mathematical financial risk management specialist to recognise that economic growth based almost solely on excessive consumer spending, based on excessive consumer credit, based on massively increasing property prices which were caused by the very same excessively easy credit could only ultimately lead to disaster. No, in Gordon's mind it was all caused by global events beyond his and anyone else's control. But that is just what the Greek tragedies taught us – hubris brings a kind of blindness and Nemesis will be the result.

To be fair on Gordon, his post crisis actions have been impressively bold – Northern Rock nationalisation, Special Liquidity Scheme, recapitalisation of the banks, massive increase in the PBR [Public Sector Borrowing Requirement] to stimulate the economy. But this does not exonerate him anyway for being at the helm when he hit the iceberg.

Somewhere further down the tree of 'the great and the good', and just to pick one other impresario, let's talk about the performance of Sir James Crosby, the CEO of HBOS until July 2006. It is probably fair to say that it was James Crosby and not Andy Hornby, the current CEO of HBOS, who was the original architect of the bank's rapid growth strategy (growth with no controls some would say) which, when liquidity dried up following the exposure of the US sub-prime scandal, ultimately led to the forced and humiliating merger with its hitherto underperforming cousin, Lloyds TSB. Crosby called his approach the 'customer champion strategy'! Funny sort of customer champion whose business ends up being merged with another huge retail bank only because the Prime Minister overrides the competition rules!

After his retirement from HBOS (and you have to give him credit for his timing), James Crosby was knighted for his fine contribution to financial services. He is currently the deputy chairman of the FSA and, to boot, the expert adviser to Gordon Brown on how to solve the mortgage crisis! His fine contribution to financial services will include hundreds of thousands of customers struggling to repay the debts they were sold by HBOS, tens of thousands of employees with no jobs, and even more shareholders whose balance sheets will have taken a massive hit as the share price tumbled from over £11 to under £1. In hindsight the HBOS story seems very much the same as the story of the emperor's new clothes! But anyone who spoke up and said so wouldn't last long.

Yes, politicians and regulators alike are saying that something must be done and focusing on executive pay. But no one seems to be up for a proper investigation of how we got ourselves into this mess in the first place – and it's not really surprising when you think about it. There are too many powerful and rich people who have been involved in getting us into this mess.

Surely someone, somewhere must have recognised that we were indulging in two of the cardinal sins which lead to disaster – greed and pride.

What is 100 per cent clear is that the developed world, and especially the USA and UK, has still not got its policy act together in overseeing the excesses, incompetencies, unethical, and often illegal (sometimes criminal) activities of the financial services industry. Maybe the latest debacle being the most serious and tantamount to the greatest example of what some people would call 'authorised organised global crime' should be the final catalyst for finding out what has happened and doing something about it. And I would like to be a part of that, if I can, having spent my whole career as a regulatory specialist witnessing the problems since 1984."

The entire blog, including a list of recommended policy changes, is here:

www.crashbankwallop.co.uk/library/10-2

We had a fabulous time that Christmas in Chile (family photo, above). Straight after New Year we all went out riding as a family over the dunes and onto the long empty Pacific Beach near Con. Daniel, who had never ridden a horse, took to it instantly. In less than 10 minutes, he was galloping and sitting in his saddle as if it was an armchair.

I was supposed to be flying back with the children to the UK on Saturday 3 January. Maureen was staying in Santiago for another 10 days with her family. However I was enjoying myself so much that I extended my visit to return with Maureen on 14 January. This meant sending the children "home alone" but Emily turned 18 on 10 January and was quite old enough to manage the trip with her younger brothers.

On 5 January I received an email from Karen Kiernan, an investigative journalist with the BBC, who asked if I knew anything about a suspected large fraud at HBOS. Ultimately, this became known as the HBOS Reading Fraud, but this was the first I had heard of the matter and I read the detailed documents Karen sent to me before responding. In the first paragraph, I wrote:

> *"Although I don't really like the 'style' of the complainants and think the facts need some more rigorous 'forensic analysis', I do think the story is really quite interesting even though I personally have no knowledge of the specifics. If the central core of the story is accurate, there clearly seems to have been cover up."*

My analysis was later to prove correct (more about this in part two of my memoirs). In particular, I have uncovered clear evidence that suggests HBOS Chairman Lord Dennis Stevenson and others should be investigated for conspiring to pervert the course of justice – a serious criminal offence. In layman's terms, they sought to cover up the fraud. The entire email is here: www.crashbankwallop.co.uk/library/10-4

Maureen and I flew back to the UK and landed at Heathrow on 15 January. From Chile to chilly is the only way to describe it. Snow lay on the ground and it took us a while to reacclimatise. I was still continuing to deal with the financial management of Complete Networks, which had become a bit of a nightmare, but my mind and heart and soul were really focused on how I could get the full HBOS story out there in a way which might do some good.

On 20 January, I wrote again to Jacqui Farnham at the BBC with some more details of the story, trying to persuade her to pick up where *The Money Programme* had left off. In the final paragraph of my email I wrote:

> *"I still think there is more to do in this area both in terms of finding out how it all happened... I am convinced that if we dug hard enough we would find dishonesty... allocate proper accountability... and make sure new policy fits the bill... this is not going to be done by the Establishment as the vested interests caused it in the first place and they will do anything to cover the mess up...... I could come and work with you lot at the BBC on this!"*

There was little in the way of interest and I began to wonder how I was going to get the media's attention.

On Sunday 1 February, our great family friend Fr Matthew Burns, a Benedictine monk and priest from Ampleforth Abbey, came to stay with us for a few days respite to recover from a bad cold.

I'd known Fr Matthew, a tall, good-looking chap with sharp features and tidy white hair, since I was at Ampleforth College. When we had returned up North after I took the HBOS job, I reconnected with him. He has helped our family more than anyone can know and I gave my first full confession to him on my return to the Catholic faith – and there was a lot to tell him. At a surprise 40th birthday party for Maureen that year at the whitewashed old Wombwell Arms in Wass, I announced that Fr Matthew was going to carve her a Madonna and child from wood. I'd never even mentioned the idea to him but Fr Matthew took up the challenge and created the most beautiful, rustic and life-size sculpture that now takes pride of place in the corner of our kitchen.

While Fr Matthew was with us, at his request I purchased a copy of the *Daily Telegraph* on my way back from morning Mass in Ampleforth on Tuesday 3 February. Buying the newspaper that day was the turning point in my blowing the whistle on the full HBOS story. Fr Matthew was sat down at the table in our slate-floored, oak-beamed cottage kitchen when I walked in from Mass. I sat directly opposite him, put the *Daily Telegraph* on the table and pushed it towards him. As I did so, the business section slipped out of the main paper. On its front cover was a picture of Lord Dennis Stevenson, Andy Hornby, Fred Goodwin and Sir Tom McKillop, the chairmen and CEOs of HBOS and RBS. I read the article quickly. It reported that on the following Tuesday 10 February, the four bigwigs from the world of banking were going to be formally interviewed by the Treasury Select Committee.

Crash! Bang! Wallop!

It was like being hit over the head by a baseball bat. That's it. It was the final call to witness. It was crystal clear. Forget the media. Tell the full story to the Treasury Select Committee (TSC).

I started to rant about what had happened at HBOS but Fr Matthew gave me a good dressing down and warned: "If you're going to tell the story to the committee, don't you dare behave in an angry way. Hatred will get you nowhere. Ultimately, forgiveness is the key." He was right. If I was going to give evidence, I had to be calm and collected. This was not an exercise in revenge but in the truth setting everyone free.

The TSC is described on its website as follows:

"It is appointed by the House of Commons to examine the expenditure, administration and policy of HM Treasury, HM Revenue & Customs, and associated public bodies, including the Bank of England and the Financial Conduct Authority."

The website adds:

"When the Committee has chosen an inquiry it normally issues a press notice outlining the main themes of inquiry, and inviting interested parties to submit written evidence. It may also identify possible witnesses and issue specific invitations to them to submit written evidence.

The House has given the Committee the power to send for 'persons, papers and records'. It therefore has powers to insist upon the attendance of witnesses and the production of papers and other material. These formal powers are rarely used."

The committee had launched an investigation into the banking crisis and had decided to use its formal powers to insist on the attendance of Stevenson, Hornby, Goodwin and McKillop.

It was obviously the right and proper place for me to lay out my detailed evidence about what had happened at HBOS. In a sense, the TSC was the most senior tribunal in the land; the best place to take and analyse my evidence. It was the perfect answer to my prayers.

I left the kitchen and went to my little office. I calmly opened my laptop and "Googled" the Treasury Select

Committee. I found the telephone number and dialled it.

There was an answer almost immediately: "Treasury Select Committee, how can I help you?"

"My name is Paul Moore and I think I may have some important evidence to give you in advance of your meeting next Tuesday with the ex-chairmen and CEOs of HBOS and RBS," I said. "I was the Head of Group Regulatory Risk at HBOS and was dismissed by James Crosby for trying to prevent the bank from taking excessive risks. I had a whistleblowing claim at the time. I think you will find my evidence useful in understanding some of the key causes of the banking crisis and the kind of policy response that is required to ensure that the same thing doesn't happen again."

The response was positive: "Oh that sounds very interesting. Perhaps you could send me a short summary of your evidence in writing? We can then decide next steps."

"Yes, that's fine. You'll get it tomorrow morning."

That afternoon I wrote to Paul Mason and Jacqui Farnham again.

"Paul and Jacqui,

I read in The Telegraph today that the Treasury Select Committee proposes to interview various top bankers next week about the financial crisis, and their part in causing it. Attendants will include Fred Goodwin, Sir Tom McKillop, Andy Hornby and Lord Stevenson.

Might this not be a time for the BBC to suggest that the committee puts to the HBOS witnesses – especially

Lord Stevenson (on behalf of Sir James Crosby) the following?:

- *Wasn't it actually Sir James Crosby who was the architect of the disastrous 'grow assets at all costs' strategy that led to HBOS's [collapse], and the humiliating demise by the forced acquisition by Lloyds? If it was, how could Sir James still be the Deputy Chairman of the FSA, advise Alistair Darling on how to solve the mortgage crisis and justify his knighthood for his fine "contribution to financial services" when this will have included millions of people in debt misery? People who were oversold credit, tens of thousands who will lose their jobs, and many more whose balance sheets have been trashed by the precipitous fall of the HBOS share price?*

- *Why did Lord Stevenson and the rest of the board think it was it was okay for James Crosby to appoint someone as Group Risk Director in 2005 who had no experience of risk management at all? This looks like incompetence at best and was more like gross recklessness. Why should people who make such foolish appointments in key internal control posts be allowed to keep their bonus? Was it not true that the person appointed was actually on track for an executive position as head of the Insurance and Investment Division, which meant that she was conflicted from challenging the executive fully?*

- *Why did they think Charles Dunstone was the right person to chair the Risk Control Committee (i.e. audit committee) overseeing the activities of the Retail Division (i.e. the Halifax) when he had no banking experience, was rather too friendly with Andy Hornby and admitted to me that he was not sure that he knew how to do the job?*

- *It might also be an idea to ask why the FSA permitted someone who had no experience of risk management to become the Approved Person for this role. Might it have been because James Crosby at the time of the appointment was a non-exec of the FSA?"*

This time the media took the bait.

Some people might say all this was pure serendipity. I prefer to quote from Shakespeare's Hamlet.

"There's a divinity that shapes our ends, rough-hew them how we will."

CHAPTER 11

"Your group risk manager said you were selling too fast, too much and it was very risky and you sacked him"

George Mudie MP, Leeds East –
UK Treasury Select Committee 10 February 2009

I've always loved the music of Annie Lennox, and just the way she is. So to hear the Scottish singer and social activist waxing lyrical on national television about how important she thought whistleblowers, like me, were to society, was both humbling and uplifting.

It's weird and wonderful happenings such as this that ensue from suddenly finding yourself under the glare of the media spotlight. I'd been a normal bloke (actually, I'd been an abnormal bloke!) just doing my job and now Annie Lennox from one of my favourite bands, Eurythmics, was talking about me on British prime-time TV's *The One Show*. What was going on?

The fact is that when the media moves, it moves *en masse* and the storm I'd created, without realising it, had reached hurricane proportions.

It had all begun on Thursday 5 February when I got down to the serious business of marshalling my evidence for the Treasury Select Committee (TSC). Firstly, I wrote a draft email to send to the committee.

The opening of my email said this:

> ***"Strictly Private and Confidential***
>
> ***To disclose this information publicly I shall need to be required to do so by law to avoid being in breach of a "gagging order" in a compromise agreement to settle a whistleblowing claim which HBOS settled with me.***
>
> *Dear Sir,*
>
> *I understand that you have decided to cross-examine key executives and non-executives of RBS and HBOS next week to try to understand more about the part they played in the current banking and financial crisis.*
>
> *As the ex Head of Group Regulatory Risk at HBOS (2002 to 2005) who had responsibility for overseeing executive management's compliance with FSA regulation (including its requirements for banks to have adequate risk management systems and control), I have some very specific information which, as a matter of public interest, may assist the committee in understanding what went wrong at HBOS and the type of changes to the governance and regulatory system that might help prevent the same things happening again."*

You can see the rest of the email here:
www.crashbankwallop.co.uk/library/11-1

But, instead of sending it immediately, on the advice of my barrister Peter Hamilton, I rang the Clerk of the TSC, John Benger, to find out the procedures for providing evidence.

Benger was extremely helpful. He listened carefully to what I had to say and said my evidence could be very important indeed. But I'd have to get it to him by the end of play on Thursday and it was now midday on Wednesday. Also, it could be no more than 5,000 words long. At the end of our call, I said to him: "John, just out of interest, what about my gagging order?" He replied instantly: "Oh, don't worry about that Paul, you've got Parliamentary privilege!"

I nearly fell off my chair. Of course, as a lawyer myself, I should have realised. Evidence accepted in the Houses of Parliament provides legal immunity and therefore I'd be protected.

I immediately set about writing my submission and although I thought it was going to be very difficult, it wasn't. The words literally cascaded from on high into my head like a waterfall, down into my fingers and onto the keyboard of my laptop like a torrent. It was as if I had divine assistance. I managed to write 5,198 words before midday on Thursday. Benger agreed to extend the deadline until the following morning to allow me to have my submission checked by Hamilton and by 6pm my lawyer had confirmed it to be accurate and fair. On Friday I made some further minor amendments and sent it to Benger at 10.46am with the following covering email:

"Dear Sir,

As discussed with you on Wednesday and then again yesterday, please find enclosed a memorandum of evidence relating to the banking crisis. This has been very specifically prepared in advance of the committee meeting on Tuesday at which Lord Stevenson, the former Chairman of HBOS and Andy Hornby, the former CEO of HBOS will be questioned.

It relates to my personal testimony from the time when I was Head of Group Regulatory Risk at HBOS. I believe it will be of particular relevance to Tuesday's meeting and will assist the committee in understanding the causes of the crisis and how to prevent such an event happening again.

I have discussed the question of Parliamentary privilege with you and you have told me that if the evidence is relevant it will obtain that privilege but that if it is not you will return the document to me so that it may remain confidential. As the document makes clear, much of the information in my testimony is subject to a gagging order in a settlement agreement I entered into with HBOS following a whistleblowing claim I made against them. Therefore, the issue of Parliamentary privilege is important.

If the evidence is relevant and you intend to pass it to committee members and publish it, I would be grateful if you would give me permission to release the document to Paul Mason who is the economics editor for the BBC's Newsnight programme and to my own lawyers.

Please confirm to me by email or phone your intention or not to use this evidence and, in any event, safe receipt.

I should add that my evidence totals 5,203 words...but that each paragraph is numbered as requested and this has added quite a number of "words" to the total.

If required I am prepared to testify."

I rang Benger to tell him that I'd sent it and 45 minutes later he phoned me back. He sounded breathless and excited. He said my evidence was highly relevant and would definitely be used to cross-examine Lord Dennis Stevenson and Andy Hornby the following Tuesday. He went on: "Your evidence is explosive and we won't be releasing it to the full committee and witnesses today because it will be leaked to the media over the weekend." He told me that the members and witnesses would be given copies immediately before the meeting on Tuesday started.

Frankly, I was taken aback and began to wonder what I had unleashed. Being a non-political animal, I hadn't given a moment's thought to the close relationships between Stevenson, Crosby and the PM Gordon Brown. All I wanted was the truth to come out so that it could be used to rebuild a more robust governance and regulatory system to avoid another global banking crisis.

I sent copies of the document to Hamilton, Clive Howard and the BBC's Paul Mason. This is what I said to Paul Mason:

> *"I sent a 5000 word detailed Memorandum of evidence to the TSC this morning. They are delighted with its content and said it was exactly what they were looking for as it was so unusual to find someone with inside knowledge of compliance and risk management who was prepared to speak out. They are adding specific questions in their briefing to members relating to my testimony. They have confirmed that their lawyers have advised them that*

my evidence will be fully protected by parliamentary privilege.

As they consider the material so explosive, they have decided not to give it to members today as they are sure it will be leaked. They will be giving it to them on Monday. The material will become public on Tuesday at 9.45 at which time they have authorised me to brief you.

I am extremely happy with the way the document I wrote came out but it will certainly 'put the cat amongst the pigeons' and I think that it would be advisable for us to talk about how you and the BBC could make use of it."

This is what I said to Hamilton:

"They have received and read the document they told me that it is definitely relevant and will be privileged. They said it is exactly what they wanted and that they have briefed the committee to ask specific questions about its content. They said that they will not release it to members until Monday because it will just get leaked to the press and that I can brief Paul Mason on Tuesday and discuss it in the media after that.

Alea iacta est [the die is cast]...I wonder if it will be Veni, vidi, vici [I came, I saw, I conquered]?

This version has some amendments from the one you read. In particular I inserted a paragraph about having no interest in blame.

Tell me what you think about the final version.

Best wishes and thanks for all your support through these years. We can now finally tell the whole story under privilege. Let's hope it helps for the future."

Hamilton replied:

"Great stuff, Paul.

I will read it again but I am sure it will be as good as the version I read last night. Please keep me in the picture as things develop. With a bit of luck, not only will veni, vidi, vici be appropriate, but Stevenson and Hornby will be in tres partes divisi sunt [divided into three parts].

Best wishes, Peter"

A bit later, I got confirmation from Benger on the question of Parliamentary privilege:

"Dear Paul

Further to our telephone conversation, I can confirm that no action could be sustained against you in respect of the evidence you gave. It would be a contempt for HBOS to seek to punish you in any way on account of your evidence. It would also be a criminal offence under the Witnesses (Public Inquiries) Act 1892. I have checked this advice with the relevant House authorities who have confirmed its accuracy.

With best wishes, John"

"Wow," I thought. "Thanks be to God! I wonder what's going to happen next?"

I can't remember much about that weekend. I know that I read and re-read the evidence I had written and was very happy with the way it had come out.

On the Monday, the day before the TSC meeting, I was due to drive down to my mother Jean's home near Bristol with our son, Oliver. It was half-term and Emily and Daniel had public examinations coming up in the summer and needed to revise. It would be best if Oliver was out of the house to avoid distractions.

I hadn't heard from Paul Mason, so I sent him another email:

> *"Paul,*
>
> *I have not heard from you, yet. Shall I use another route to get this into the public arena e.g. Peston? [television journalist Robert Peston] Will be on road from about 12.30 on mobile [provided].*
>
> *I really do think you will find the additional detail in the evidence highly newsworthy.*
>
> *Paul"*

He responded quickly.

> *"I am very keen to get this out – can it be reported before the embargo? I did send you a reply but maybe it got lost. Either way are you available tomorrow for interview on Newsnight (pre-recorded?). I think we should get it to the widest possible audience."*

As Oliver and I drove down the M1, Mason phoned and asked for a copy of the document. He insisted that I come to London early the following morning to be interviewed for the BBC *Newsnight* programme. I tried to resist but he wasn't going to be put off. I told him that the BBC would have to pay my expenses of a first-class train ticket and, after some persuasion, he agreed. He said he would send a car to pick me up from Paddington Railway Station to take me to the BBC Media Centre and I committed to be there before 9.30am.

As soon as Oliver and I arrived at my mum's house in Bristol, I sent my submission to Mason with the following covering email:

"Paul,

Here is the document. This is on the strict condition that it is not reported until after the commencement of the hearing at 9.45 tomorrow. I will be on my mobile [provided] to speak to you at any time this evening or a landline [provided]. Give me a ring once you have read and digested it in any event so we can discuss where to meet in London tomorrow and when.

My objective is simple – now it's out there, the widest and deepest coverage possible so that my experiences can be used in the public interest and to feed into the public policy debate – as well as the investigation just announced to be led by Walker [Sir David Walker]. I guess that if you think this should go to other parts of the news in the BBC (e.g. News at 6.00 / 10.00) you will pass it on with the same condition attached.

Paul"

Also that evening, I emailed my only other media contact Philip Aldrick at the *Daily Telegraph*.

"You will recall that we corresponded following your article after I appeared on The Money Programme and you published a letter from me – see email correspondence below.

Last Friday following discussion with the Treasury Select Committee I lodged a 5,000-word memorandum of detailed evidence 'spilling the beans' on exactly what happened at HBOS which will be provided to members for the cross-examination of Stevenson and Hornby tomorrow. My testimony has parliamentary privilege which overrides the gagging order I signed when I settled my whistleblowing claim against HBOS.

As you helped in the past I thought it was appropriate to offer The Telegraph the story first. The clerk of the TSC commented that my evidence was highly relevant, unique and explosive. It has only been as a result of obtaining parliamentary privilege that I have been able to speak out fully...and I am sure The Telegraph will find the material fascinating."

It wouldn't be long before I had more media contacts than I could possibly have imagined or wanted.

The next morning I caught the train from Yatton, near Bristol, at 7.30am and sat comfortably in my first-class seat. I re-read my evidence once again and I wondered what all of this was leading to.

I was picked up as agreed at Paddington station and arrived at the BBC Media Centre on time to meet Paul Mason. We talked about my evidence and he told me it was going to be a very big story. After chatting for about 30 minutes, he took me into a small recording studio and interviewed me to camera, which took half-an-hour. It was all a bit of a whirlwind and I can't really remember the whole content of the interview. However, the key section went as follows:

Moore: "I was Head of Group Regulatory Risk at HBOS. I realised that the bank was moving too fast and

I raised those challenges very strongly at Board level."

Mason: "When you raised concerns with the boss of HBOS James Crosby, what happened to you?"

Moore: "Well, ultimately, I was removed and dismissed."

Mason: "Why?"

Moore: "Well, I believe because I raised challenges which he was not comfortable with. He said, of course, it was because I didn't fit in."

Immediately we had finished the interview, Paul took me into the main *Newsnight* office. He put me in front of the TV monitor and said: "Now, just have a look at what's been going on at the Treasury Select Committee." By then, it was about 11.15am. A technician set the monitor to the moment that committee members Andrew Tyrie, the Conservative MP for Chichester and George Mudie, Labour MP for Leeds East, started to question Stevenson and Hornby about my evidence. What follows is the Hansard (the official edited verbatim report of Parliamentary proceedings) transcript from the exchanges.

Q1759 Mr Tyrie: Mr Hornby, you have said that you listened very carefully to siren voices, although presumably you shouldn't listen to siren voices but perhaps to air raid sirens. Lord Stevenson, you have said that you exercised good countercyclical caution. You have also said, Mr Hornby, that HBOS had very elaborate risk testing systems in place, or perhaps it was Lord Stevenson. Your ex-Head of Group Regulatory Risk tried to use those very systems to protect the bank and, when he tried, he says that he was subject to "threatening behaviours". Is that true?

Mr Hornby: Absolutely not.

Q1760 Mr Tyrie: He has made it up, has he, when he says, "My team and I experienced threatening behaviours by executives when carrying out our legitimate role . . . "?

Mr Hornby: I have absolutely no recognition of what he might be referring to. I assume you are referring to the period way before I was chief executive. I really do not know what is being referred to. All I can say is that in my experience of watching HBOS executives interacting with risk professionals both before and after I was CEO, I saw people in a constant dialogue and really trying to face head on into issues. I do not recognise that behaviour.

Q1761 Mr Tyrie: He says that board minutes failed to record his expressions of concern that the bank was going too fast. Is this true, Lord Stevenson?

Lord Stevenson of Coddenham: No, it is not true.

Q1762 Mr Tyrie: He has made that up as well, has he?

Lord Stevenson of Coddenham: I think that is using an emotive phrase. People say things. I am familiar with the episode and the issue. I think I am right in saying that as a result of the allegations we commissioned a very extensive independent study of everything together with the FSA which clarified this, which is the basis on which you are getting such a robust response from us. If I am right about that, I think it would be absolutely in order, though I shall check, for that to be made available to you.

Q1763 Mr Tyrie: So all these completely unsubstantiated allegations the FSA themselves would not recognise, is that what you are saying?

Lord Stevenson of Coddenham: The allegations were made.

Mr Hornby: If you go back to 2005, there were a whole series of reviews that we were constantly doing internally often with external help and always in conjunction with the FSA. The FSA personally reviewed the sales culture you are referring to and we made sure that we implemented all the recommendations with very close co-ordination with the regulator. It is as simple as that. That would be the case with all the various risk management reviews that have been done over the last eight years.

Q1764 Mr Tyrie: Did the FSA uphold your repudiation of all his allegations?

Mr Hornby: The FSA — this is before I was chief executive so I cannot speak for every point of detail here — were very clear that our action plans that we put in place on the back of all the various risk reviews that had been done were logical and they monitored our performance against them.

Q1765 Mr Tyrie: Is it not the case that the FSA in their report wrote, "There is a risk that the balance of experience among senior management could lead to a culture which is overly sales focused and gives inadequate priority to risk"?

Mr Hornby: That clearly is in the report. We went through everything with them in huge detail. If you look at the balance of the senior team, we had colossal banking experience, an average of 35 years.

Q1766 Mr Tyrie: I am not challenging that there are experienced people there; I am challenging that they used this experience effectively. I am not suggesting that your bank could have possibly escaped the crisis, all banks have been hit; I am challenging the view that you did not take reasonable steps in light of very clear warnings that were being made from within your bank.

Mr Hornby: As we outlined in our submission, we did try and make radical changes. We have all accepted the fact that the balance sheet growth that had been built up over many, many years meant that we did end up over-reliant on wholesale funding. We would have liked to have predicted an even greater contraction in wholesale funding markets. I think it would be difficult. I accept the fact we did not fully prophesize it. I do not believe that was because we were not listening to the risk function.

Lord Stevenson of Coddenham: We are talking here about our retail business. At any point in time, of course, we are reviewing our risk management and the balance between sales and caution at any point in time. Just to be absolutely clear and we would be happy to supply backup on it, we did a clear review of it, at the end of which the FSA regarded the matter as closed. We are very happy to give you all the information you need to back that up.

Q1767 Mr Tyrie: So it is the FSA that also got it wrong, is that your suggestion? I hope you do not disagree with the view that the statements of caution he was making on the points of substance were wrong, that you should have gone hell for leather with all these sales and that the balance of risk that you took at the time was right. You began with an apology today.

Lord Stevenson of Coddenham: I do not disagree with that at all. It is the right frame of mind for any banking. It is a balance.

Q1768 Mr Tyrie: So you got it wrong but in your defence you are saying the FSA got it wrong as well, is that right?

Lord Stevenson of Coddenham: No. What you have referred to were some allegations that were made which were independently investigated and the FSA were satisfied with them. I am very happy to provide you with all the backup to that.

Q1769 Mr Tyrie: I will just ask the same question again. You agreed that you got it wrong, that you did not correctly assess the risk. Everyone is agreed that banks did not do that. You are therefore presumably agreeing that Mr Moore correctly identified one of these risks to which due attention was not paid. Is that correct?

Lord Stevenson of Coddenham: I would say it is not correct. I understand the thrust of your question. The fundamental mistake, if that is the word, that HBOS along with many other banks in the world made was failure to predict the wholesale collapse of wholesale markets. Mr Moore's allegations were nothing to do with that. They concerned a perfectly reasonable area for concern which I and my colleagues have been constantly concerned about, which is the balance between the sales culture on the one hand and caution and integrity on the other. The area, as we have said in our submission, which has caused HBOS problems has been the collapse of wholesale markets.

Q1770 Mr Tyrie: You are saying that even with the advantage of hindsight you got the balance between the sales culture and the risks that it might generate correct. You are unrepentant about the judgments you made even with the advantage of hindsight. Is that correct?

Lord Stevenson of Coddenham: You are forcing me into a corner.

My Tyrie: I was just trying to get a straight answer.

Lord Stevenson of Coddenham: The truth is that there is no absolutely correct balance in any part of our business or any other bank's business. I think if you were to examine our retail business over the last few years you would find that we had not got it very wrong, particularly the thing you are talking about. Just to be absolutely clear, going right back to what both Andy Hornby and I said at the beginning, we fully accept that we failed to predict what happened in wholesale markets.

Q1771 Mr Tyrie: You said that you had not got it very wrong which must mean that you got it roughly right. Is that right?

Lord Stevenson of Coddenham: Right. The other side of which is —

Q1772 Mr Tyrie: Why are you apologising if you got it roughly right? I am left bewildered now.

Lord Stevenson of Coddenham: It is apples and lemons. We are apologising for what happened to our business and we have made it plain that the key factor that affected what happened to our business was the collapse in the wholesale markets. That is not the issue that Mr Moore is raising and you are raising.

Q1773 Mr Mudie: There are shades of Adam Applegarth here, ie there was nothing wrong with you, it was the market and the extreme credit crunch, the breakdown of wholesale markets. Is that what you are saying?

Lord Stevenson of Coddenham: No.

Q1774 Mr Mudie: What are you saying? We did not bring you here, contrary to what the press think, to cause you public humiliation. We brought you here to find out what happened, to hear how we avoid it happening and what steps we should take. There are two chairmen here. What is causing the anger in the public's mind is that you are in denial. Your group risk manager said you were selling too fast, too much and it was very risky and you sacked him. You come to this Committee and you say to Andrew, "He got it wrong. We got it right." You are the ex-chairman and he is the ex-chief executive officer who got it right. Why are you the ex-chief executive and ex-chairman if you got it right?

Mr Hornby: What our submission clearly says is that the balance sheet growth that had been put on over many years, from the inception of HBOS in 2001, meant that we were overexposed to wholesale funding when the wholesale funding markets closed. That is indisputable.

Q1775 Mr Mudie: That is Adam Applegarth.

Mr Hornby: The balance sheet growth that we put on, no one is taking away responsibility for that and we are very clear on that in our submission. I think the point which Denis is making and which I completely comply with is about the complete closure of wholesale markets in the way that they did completely close. We did take a lot of premeditated actions in order to try and reduce our reliance on those markets. Clearly if we had seen the fact that they were going to close entirely coming we would have done even more even earlier and even quicker. We do accept the fact that the building up in the balance sheet over many, many years meant that we were reliant on wholesale funding. The contrary point is that we did try. We would have liked in retrospect to have done even more. We did take action to recognise the risk there.

Q1776 Mr Mudie: Nobody is suggesting you did not. You ran a business in a way that got caught out when the market conditions changed. I interrupted you and said Adam Applegarth. He got abused right, left and centre for his extreme model. You ran not exactly the same sequence but a flawed model. You ran something that when the market conditions changed your business is in a very bad way and you are an ex-chief executive officer.

Mr Hornby: Yes. It actually goes back many, many years in that the former Bank of Scotland business was largely reliant on wholesale funding that did not have a retail deposit base in the UK.

Q1777 Mr Mudie: I know that. We are all aware of that. Just accept it. Do not try and equivocate, et cetera, et cetera. You did something that was applauded whilst you were making a lot of brass. It turned out to be dodgy when the market conditions changed. We can move on when you say that is it to decide how we can adjust external factors or even internal factors to prevent this sort of thing happening again. Is that not the way forward?

Mr Hornby: I completely agree. We have already said that the building up of reliance on wholesale markets was what has left us vulnerable.

Q1778 Mr Mudie: That means risk. What Andrew is questioning is the fact that you sacked a barrister, a fella who had been complimented at various times by various people. A senior figure prevented him from putting something in the board minutes which said you were running a risk here. He says in his memo to us, "When I was Head of Group Regulatory Risk at HBOS, I certainly knew that the bank was going too fast (and told them), had a cultural indisposition to challenge (and told them) and was a serious risk to financial stability . . . and consumer protection (and told them)." That is what he is saying. You equivocated when Sally asked you and you further equivocated when Andrew asked you. You sacked this fella. He took you to an industrial tribunal and he won. We are told you paid him undisclosed damages and put a gagging order on him. In fairness to a bank learning lessons, it seems to us in the Committee with this document that you did not want anybody being blunt with you about the risks you were running.

Lord Stevenson of Coddenham: I understand exactly what you are saying. First of all, I remember the incident very well. It was taken very seriously by the Board at the time, with the Chairman of the Audit Committee, Tony Hobson, doing it. We commissioned an independent study into it. I am very happy to provide all the materials to the Committee about it. I do think that in a number of areas it is a fact that very carefully arranged risk management systems developed over the years with our regulator did not spot scenarios coming out that have come up. The stress testing did not stress test adequately. I am being very open. There is nothing in denial about that. I am just being very open about it. How that is changed in future is a hugely important issue.

Q1779 Mr Mudie: Not only did you sack him, the person you appointed in his place had never carried out a role as a risk manager of any type before. The individual had primarily been a sales manager and was a personal appointment of the Chief Executive Officer and was against the wishes of other directors. Does that not worry you, if that is true?

Lord Stevenson of Coddenham: It is not true. The board took it very seriously. It was a major preoccupation. The board was briefed on it by the chairman of the audit committee with personal responsibility on it. We delayed the appointment of the person you are talking about, who is an outstanding executive, until the independent review had been carried out and until the FSA and ourselves were happy with it.

Q1780 Mr Mudie: Andrew made the point that, at the end of the day, you sacked your group risk fella for the warnings he gave you. Now, four years later, it turns out he was right and you were wrong.

Mr Hornby: This incident you are referring to was with the former chief executive back in 2005.

Q1781 Mr Mudie: You were on the board then.

Mr Hornby: I was on the board. When James proposed the appointment, as he did, of Jo Dawson to take on that role, I, along with many others, thought it was a very good appointment. She had huge banking experience built up over many years.

Q1782 Mr Mudie: In risk?

Mr Hornby: In many matters very pertinent to risk management.

Q1783 Mr Mudie: We are arguing about risk. You sacked this fella and then you appointed someone else who this gentleman is suggesting had no — and I did not mention a girl or her name in fairness to the individual — risk experience of any kind. Your chairman says that the individual who gave us this is telling lies on this point. Can you just confirm that you are saying she had risk experience?

Mr Hornby: No. What I said was she had many years of working in the banking industry, including in risk management.

Q1784 Mr Mudie: How come your chairman said she did?

Mr Hornby: She had not had a formal risk title, but she had many years of working in the banking industry within risk. If you talk to the chief executive who took the decision, he made sure he strengthened the risk function alongside in response to the report and in response to all the other actions.

Q1785 Mr Tyrie: You have made specific denials on a wide range of issues raised by Mr Moore which taken together appear to challenge all the substantive points that he has made, that the risk culture was out-of-kilter in your bank and you appear to be blaming everything on the collapse of the wholesale markets. You will correct me if you think I have misinterpreted what you have just been saying. His allegations are very specific and detailed. He said at paragraph 2.13, for example, "I told the Board they ought to slow down but was prevented from having this properly minuted by the CFO. I told them their sales culture was significantly out of balance with their systems and controls." Is it true that he was prevented from having his concerns properly minuted?

Lord Stevenson of Coddenham: I am not aware of that communication. We took it very seriously. We had over a nine month exercise investigating it. May I suggest that we make that available to the Committee? You would be free to talk to the FSA about it who were involved in it. The one thing I can assure you, there is no denial, anything to do with risk is taken very seriously by the board.

Q1786 Chairman: Paul Moore said that prior to HBOS, from 1995 to 2002, he was a Partner with KPMG's Financial Sector Practice specialising in regulatory services and advised a number of FTSE100 companies. He says in paragraph 3.19 that he was dismissed by the then Chairman, James Crosby, who said, "The decision was mine and mine alone" but refused to explain why. He then goes on to say that what this has led to is ". . . millions of people in excessive debt, 10,000s who will lose their jobs and many more whose balance sheets have been impacted by the precipitous fall of the HBOS share price . . . " That is his accusation which is on the record. To be fair to yourselves, if we engage in this correspondence it will help us because we want to be fair to everyone.

Lord Stevenson of Coddenham: Yes.

My jaw dropped. I couldn't believe what I had seen and heard.

As I watched the TSC meeting, I finally realised the enormity of what I had done, but I didn't truly understand what was going to happen next. I really had put the cat amongst the pigeons. I still didn't appreciate the political ramifications that were about to unfold. At one point I popped out of the office to have a cigarette and was accompanied by a young woman who wasn't smoking. I asked her why she'd followed me outside and she said she was under strict instructions to ensure I wasn't "kidnapped" by other parts of the BBC for their own broadcasts. Later, I discovered that there's a lot of infighting at the "Beeb" and news stories are hot property not always to be shared with others.

I went back into the *Newsnight* office and did another camera interview with Paul Mason while actually watching the monitor of the TV coverage of the TSC meeting.

By the time the meeting was over at about 1pm, I started to get bombarded by requests for TV, radio and newspaper interviews. Simon Duke from the *Daily Mail.* Tom Bawden at *The Times.* Dan Hewitt at ITN. *Channel 4 News.* John Kenchington at City A.M. etc. And this was only the start of the media maelstrom.

I refused to speak to any of them. As far as I was concerned, I'd done my job and wasn't going to make any further comment. If the media wanted to write articles all they needed to do was to read my evidence, the whole of which can be read here:

www.crashbankwallop.co.uk/library/11-2

Here are some key extracts:

2. Executive summary of the main points I wish to make

2.1 My evidence relates to all sections of the Committee's Terms of Reference but is drawn specifically from, and relates specifically to, my personal experiences at HBOS.

2.2 The main points I wish to make are these:

2.3 I believe that there are important general lessons to be learned from my personal experiences as a risk and compliance professional at HBOS and elsewhere that could assist the Committee and others in the public policy debate about what needs to be changed in the governance and regulatory system to help to ensure that the same risks are mitigated in the future.

2.4 *In order to draw out the general points that need to be made, it is necessary to tell at least a part of the rather complex personal story that occurred at HBOS and I request the Committee's forbearance with this because it draws into sharp focus the lessons about the crucial importance of really effective governance. I give a short summary of the key facts of my story at HBOS in this section (2.12 to 2.19 below) and add some further factual information that I would like the Committee to consider in section 3 below.*

2.5 *The key general points I wish to make are these:*

2.6 *In my view, as an experienced risk and compliance practitioner, the problem in finding the real cause of the banking crisis is being made more complex than it needs to be.*

2.7 *I believe that we are missing the wood for the trees and that the key solutions to prevent such an event happening again are simpler than we think. In relation to policy changes, I make some short recommendations that the Committee may wish to consider in section 4 below.*

2.8 *But let's start with the cause and this fairly obvious proposition: even non-bankers with no "credit risk management" expertise, if asked (and I have asked a few myself), would have known that there must have been a very high risk if you lend money to people who have no jobs, no provable income and no assets. If you lend that money to buy an asset which is worth the same or even less than the amount of the loan and secure that loan on the value of that asset purchased and, then, assume that that asset will always rise in value, you must be pretty much close to delusional? You simply don't need to be an economic rocket scientist or mathematical financial risk management specialist to know this. You just need common sense. So why didn't the experts know? Or did they but they carried on anyway because they were paid to do so or too frightened to speak up?*

2.9 *What my personal experience of being on the inside as a risk and compliance manager has shown me is that, whatever the very specific, final and direct causes of the financial crisis, I strongly believe that the real underlying cause of all the problems was simply this* ***– a total failure of all key aspects of governance. In my view and from my personal experience at HBOS, all the other specific failures stem from this one primary cause.***

2.10 *In simple terms this crisis was caused, not because many bright people did not see it coming, but because there has been a completely inadequate "separation" and "balance of powers" between the executive and all those accountable for overseeing their actions and "reining them in" i.e. internal control functions such as finance, risk, compliance and internal audit, non-executive Chairmen and Directors, external auditors, the FSA, shareholders and politicians.*

2.11 As I recently commented on the BBC Money Programme called HBOS: Breaking the Bank, "Being an internal risk and compliance manager at the time felt a bit like being a man in a rowing boat trying to slow down an oil tanker." If we could turn that man in the rowing boat into a man with a tug boat or even the Pilot required to navigate big ships into port, I feel confident that things would have turned out quite differently.

2.12 When I was Head of Group Regulatory Risk at HBOS, I certainly knew that the bank was going too fast (and told them), had a cultural indisposition to challenge (and told them) and was a serious risk to financial stability (what the FSA call "Maintaining Market Confidence") and consumer protection (and told them).

2.13 I told the Board they ought to slow down but was prevented from having this properly minuted by the CFO. I told them that their sales culture was significantly out of balance with their systems and controls.

2.17 At this point ***I want to stress in the strongest possible way that I am simply not interested in blame and I don't think it really ever works****. I was ultimately fairly compensated by HBOS. What I am* *very interested in is the future. As I wrote once to my boss at HBOS itself, what we need this crisis to do for us is "to create a watershed here so we can move on from the issues of the past (from which we can learn but not blame) to the brave new world of the future." Although, key people at HBOS did do wrong, I am also sure that their intentions were usually good and, in a sense, they were also caught up themselves in what the Greek tragedies would call the "ineluctability of fate".*

2.18 *Returning to my story: after I was dismissed and to prove just how seriously HBOS took risk management, I was replaced by a new Group Risk Director* ***who had never carried out a role as a risk manager of any type before****. The individual concerned had primarily been a sales manager and was a personal appointment of the CEO against the initial wishes of other Directors. You can't blame her for accepting the job as it got her on the Group Management Board and shortly afterwards the main Board.*

2.19 *On any reasonable interpretation, this appointment could not have met the FSA's "fit and proper" requirements for the roles of CF 10 (Compliance Oversight) and CF14 (Risk Assessment) which are as follows:*

"In determining a person's competence and capability, the FSA will have regard to matters including but not limited to.....whether the person ***has demonstrated by experience and training*** *that the person is able, or will be able if approved, to perform the controlled function."*

2.20 *All these matters were reported to the HBOS Non-Executive Chairman of the Audit Committee as well as the FSA. I was given no protection or support. A supposedly "independent report" by HBOS's auditors said HBOS were right but failed even to interview key witnesses.*

2.21 *I believe that, had there been highly competent risk and compliance managers in all the banks, carrying out rigorous oversight, properly protected and supported by a truly independent non-executive, the external auditor and the FSA, they would have felt comfortable and protected to challenge the practices of the executive without fear for their own positions. If this had been the case, I am also confident that we would not have got into the current crisis. I believe that my personal story of what happened at HBOS demonstrates this exactly.*

2.22 *To mix a few well known similes/metaphors/stories, the current financial crisis is a bit like the story of the Emperor's new clothes. Anyone whose eyes were not blinded by money, power and pride (Hubris) who really looked carefully knew there was something wrong and that economic growth based almost solely on excessive consumer spending, based on excessive consumer credit, based on massively increasing property prices which were caused by the very same excessively easy credit could only ultimately lead to disaster. But sadly, no-one wanted or felt able to speak up for fear of stepping out of line with the rest of the lemmings who were busy organising themselves to run over the edge of the cliff, behind the pied piper CEOs and executive teams that were being paid so much to play that tune and take them in that direction.*

2.23 *I am quite sure that there were many, many more people in internal control functions, non-executive positions, auditors, regulators who did realise that the Emperor was naked but knew if they spoke up they would be labelled "trouble makers" and "spoil sports" and would put themselves at personal risk. I am still toxic waste now for having spoken out all those years ago! I would be amazed if there were not many executives who, if they really examined their consciences closely, would not say that they knew this too.*

2.24 *The real problem and cause of this crisis was that people were just too afraid to speak up and the balance and separation of powers was just far too weighted in favour of the CEO and their executive.*

In section three of my submission I went on to discuss the appointment of Dawson as Group Risk Director and the FSA's role in allowing this to happen. I also made an anecdotal reference to Charles Dunstone and his position as Chairman of the Retail Risk Control Committee, an area of business he admitted himself to having no experience in.

I then gave a short summary of some of the policy points I considered should be debated.

3.22 *As referred to in section 2 above, on my unfair*

dismissal a person was appointed as Group Risk Director who was an ex-sales manager who had no experience of risk management or compliance. I have already referred to this in some more detail in section 2 above. This was a personal appointment of James Crosby and some might question whether this fulfilled his fiduciary duties as a Director under Company Law or Principle 2 and 3 of the FSA's Principles for Business set out above.

3.23 My concerns on this appointment were reported to the FSA but despite the clarity of their guidance on assessing fit and properness (see section 2 above) they permitted the individual concerned to become an Approved Person. It is extraordinary in my view that the FSA permitted this, when this role is so important to the fulfilment of their statutory objectives. Maybe they felt constrained as James Crosby was a non-executive director of the FSA at the time?

3.24 One final interesting but telling anecdote of my personal story relates to Charles Dunstone (founder of the Car Phone Warehouse). Charles was a non-exec director of HBOS which made good sense given their strategy of turning the bank into a retailing operation. He is clearly an outstanding business leader. But, strangely, he was also appointed to be the Chairman of the Retail (Halifax) Risk Control Committee (a divisional audit committee). He admitted to me that he was very friendly with Andy Hornby and that they met quite often socially. Of course, he was supposed to be challenging Andy Hornby. He obviously had no technical competence in banking or credit risk management to oversee such a vital governance committee. Another HBOS non-exec said to me one day of him and his role "Well, they got that appointment wrong, didn't they". Even more extraordinary than this, Charles Dunstone himself admitted to me and my colleague one day words to the effect that he had no real idea how to be the Chairman of the Retail Risk Control Committee!

3.25 *This just shows how little real regard HBOS had for the importance of the non-executive roles. It is also probably in breach of Principles 2 and 3.*

4. *Some recommendations for policy analysis and development*

4.2 *Remuneration and performance management of exec..., e.g. regulatory sign off, bonuses held in a trustee account over longer time frames to ensure short-termism does not take hold.*

4.3 *A more detailed policy and rules which allow the FSA to test the cultural environment of organisations they are supervising, e.g. tri-annual staff and customer survey. There is no doubt that you can have the best governance processes in the world but if they are carried out in a culture of greed, unethical behaviour and indisposition to challenge, they will fail. I would now propose **mandatory** ethics training for all senior managers and a system of monitoring the ethical considerations of key policy and strategy decisions within the supervised firms.*

4.4 Much more formal qualifications and competencies for risk managers and compliance professionals so that only fit, proper and competent people can be appointed as CF10, CF11 and 14 – Compliance Oversight, Anti-Money Laundering and Risk Assessment. These roles are becoming as important as CFO role and need something like the ICA / Institute of Actuaries to regulate their training and competence.

4.5 Regular formal independent audit of risk management, compliance and internal audit functions to keep them honest – and to make them feel they will be backed up / protected if they do their jobs properly and cause a bit of inevitable friction.

4.6 Risk management and compliance with at least an equally weighted reporting line to a non-exec with sufficient time and profile to balance the executive. The non-executive need to be "executive" in relation to their primary accountability of overseeing the executive. No person responsible for a key internal control function can be dismissed without a full and minuted meeting of the non-exec and the incumbent must be given a right of reply. The FSA should formally approve such decisions.

4.7 Much, much more focus on competence and independence of non-executives, e.g. register of non-work social meetings, pre-appointment investigation of "links" / potential conflicts of interest e.g. cross-board connections - I'm on your remuneration committee if you're on my audit committee, pre-appointment record of reasons why a person is competent for a particular committee.

4.7 *Much more involvement of the regulators in the terms of reference of the statutory auditors – the level of cost associated with formal independent audit is inadequate and needs to be radically increased. How can a firm like HBOS be audited for £5m or less?*

4.8 *Much more rigorous prescription of the regulation of affordability and suitability requirements for the sale of credit products...to prevent ordinary people who cannot resist the temptation of getting into excessive debt.*

4.9 *Further development of whistleblowing rules to make sure that those who raise legitimate issues are not just "bought off" with shareholders money....the case should be reviewed by the regulator and action taken if necessary to ensure those responsible cannot get away scot-free.*

4.10 *Much, much better pay for senior regulators so that the FSA can recruit the best – pay twice as much, get four times as much done at eight times the quality.*

5. *A final observation*

5.1 *One final observation I would make about the HBOS disaster is this; wasn't it actually Sir James Crosby rather than Andy Hornby who was the original architect of the HBOS retailing strategy? At first this was good in that it purported to be a*

"Customer Champion" strategy. The problem was that a reduced margin strategy is predicated on the need for improvements in cost control and at the same time massive increases in sales. It is now clear that this disastrous "grow assets at all costs" strategy was what led to HBOS's downfall and humiliating demise by the forced acquisition by Lloyds.

5.2 *Sir James is still the Deputy Chairman of the FSA and advises the government on how to solve the mortgage crisis. Some might now also question what his "contribution to financial services" has in fact been, when this will have led to millions of people in excessive debt, 10,000s who will lose their jobs and many more whose balance sheets have been impacted by the precipitous fall of the HBOS share price – apart from the reduction in competition in the retail financial services market threatened by the new Lloyds Group?*

5.3 *Shouldn't the Committee be asking him to testify?*

As I got on the train at Paddington to return to the calm of my mum's lovely cottage in the flatlands between Flax Bourton and Clevedon, west of Bristol, my head was in a spin. I collapsed into my first-class seat and exhaled deeply. "Well, that's over," I thought.

As I sat there slumped in my seat, one of the train stewards walked past and asked me if I would like a copy of the *Evening Standard* newspaper. I said yes. I put the paper down in front of me and looked at the headline (See www.crashbankwallop.co.uk/library/11-2-1):

The day I gave my evidence

WEST END FINAL

Evening Standard

TUESDAY 10 FEBRUARY 2009 LONDON'S QUALITY NEWSPAPER 50p

AS **SCOLARI** GOES, CHELSEA PLOT TO TEMPT **ZOLA** BACK

● SPORT BACK PAGE ● NEWS PAGE 5

Brown's adviser 'sacked banker who got it right'

It didn't mean anything to me. I read on.

HBOS executive tried to raise alarm over risk-taking

PAUL WAUGH AND NICHOLAS CECIL

ONE of Gordon Brown's key City advisers was today accused of sacking a whistleblower who warned that risky bank practices would "lead to disaster" years before the financial meltdown.

Sir James Crosby was named in bombshell evidence submitted to a Commons committee investigating the near collapse of the banks.

He is currently deputy chairman of the Financial Services Authority, the chief regulator of the industry, and one of the Prime Minister's favourite private sector advisers.

But it was revealed today that as chief executive of HBOS, one of the banks crippled by the credit crunch, he allegedly dismissed a senior official who raised fears that the bank was growing too quickly and putting itself in danger.

The whistleblower was Paul Moore, former head of group regulatory risk at HBOS, and the official directly responsible for assessing the correct balance between risk and safety.

Mr Moore's account of his warnings and his alleged treatment by Sir James was disclosed in a public session of the Treasury select committee this morning, where bankers including former HBOS chiefs Andy Hornby and Lord Stevenson were giving grovelling apologies for their actions.

Mr Moore claimed that "anyone whose eyes were not blinded by money, power and pride" would have realised problems were building up for HBOS and other banks.

In a letter to the committee, published by chairman John McFall, he said: "I certainly knew that the bank was going too fast (and told them), had a cultural indisposition to challenge (and told them) and was a serious

CONTINUED ON: PAGE 2 ▶

Goodness gracious me! I turned over the page.

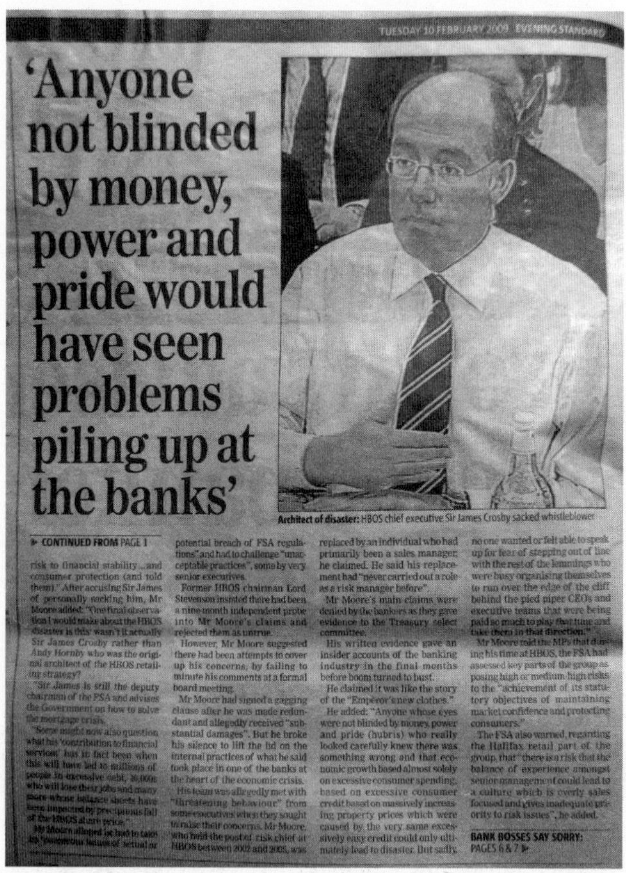

TUESDAY 10 FEBRUARY 2009 EVENING STANDARD

'Anyone not blinded by money, power and pride would have seen problems piling up at the banks'

Architect of disaster: HBOS chief executive Sir James Crosby sacked whistleblower

▶ CONTINUED FROM PAGE 1

risk to financial stability ... and consumer protection (and told them)." After accusing Sir James of personally sacking him, Mr Moore added: "One final observation I would make about the HBOS disaster is this: wasn't it actually Sir James Crosby rather than Andy Hornby who was the original architect of the HBOS retailing strategy?

"Sir James is still the deputy chairman of the FSA and advises the Government on how to solve the mortgage crisis.

"Some might now also question what his 'contribution to financial services' has in fact been when this will have led to millions of people in excessive debt, 36,000s who will lose their jobs and many more whose balance sheets have been impacted by precipitous fall of the HBOS share price."

Mr Moore alleged he had to take up "numerous issues of actual or potential breach of FSA regulations" and had to challenge "unacceptable practices", some by very senior executives.

Former HBOS chairman Lord Stevenson insisted there had been a nine-month independent probe into Mr Moore's claims and rejected them as untrue.

However, Mr Moore suggested there had been attempts to cover up his concerns, by failing to minute his comments at a formal board meeting.

Mr Moore had signed a gagging clause after he was made redundant and allegedly received "substantial damages". But he broke his silence to lift the lid on the internal practices of what he said took place in one of the banks at the heart of the economic crisis.

His team was allegedly met with "threatening behaviour" from some executives when they sought to raise their concerns. Mr Moore, who held the post of risk chief at HBOS between 2002 and 2005, was replaced by an individual who had primarily been a sales manager, he claimed. He said his replacement had "never carried out a role as a risk manager before".

Mr Moore's main claims were denied by the bankers as they gave evidence to the Treasury select committee.

His written evidence gave an insider accounts of the banking industry in the final months before boom turned to bust.

He claimed it was like the story of the "Emperor's new clothes."

He added: "Anyone whose eyes were not blinded by money, power and pride (hubris) who really looked carefully knew there was something wrong and that economic growth based almost solely on excessive consumer spending, based on excessive consumer credit based on massively increasing property prices which were caused by the very same excessively easy credit could only ultimately lead to disaster. But sadly, no one wanted or felt able to speak up for fear of stepping out of line with the rest of the lemmings who were busy organising themselves to run over the edge of the cliff behind the pied piper CEOs and executive teams that were being paid so much to play that tune and take them in that direction."

Mr Moore told the MPs that during his time at HBOS, the FSA had assessed key parts of the group as posing high or medium-high risks to the "achievement of its statutory objectives of maintaining market confidence and protecting consumers."

The FSA also warned, regarding the Halifax retail part of the group, that "there is a risk that the balance of experience amongst senior management could lead to a culture which is overly sales focused and gives inadequate priority to risk issues", he added.

BANK BOSSES SAY SORRY:
PAGES 6 & 7 ▶

I couldn't bloody believe it. What WAS taking place? Me, on the front page of the *Evening Standard*? That's ridiculous.

I looked across the table at the man sitting opposite me. He was reading the *Evening Standard* too. What an extraordinary feeling. There I was. The person making the headlines in the *Evening Standard*. There he was, sitting directly opposite me reading the same headlines but not knowing that he was reading about the person sitting opposite him. It was surreal.

I couldn't resist it. I said to him: "You won't believe this but it's me they're referring to in those headlines." He couldn't believe it but then we got talking and he realised that it was true.

My mobile phone hardly stopped ringing on that train ride to Yatton. The journalists had found my number and were after me. I kept telling them that I was going to make no further comment.

I can't recall what time I got to my mum's house but she'd begun to hear the media reports of what had happened at the TSC and said she was very proud of me. She told me that I was going to make a difference to the way banking worked in the country. I poured myself a stiff drink or five. The evening whizzed by, I was featured on BBC *Newsnight* and got an email from Paul Mason:

> *"Hi Paul, you are setting the whole news agenda here: Crosby is possibly toast now." He asked me for the written evidence that Crosby had actually fired me. At about 11.30pm he emailed me again: "Every front page leads with your story. Congratulations. A pleasure to meet as always. McFall [Labour MP John McFall, Chairman of the TSC] wants to talk to you." I replied: "Thank you. I have also enjoyed getting this out with you... Let's carry on!"*

At 6.35pm the next morning, I sent Paul Mason the Crosby memo in which he had said that "... the decision was mine and mine alone".

An hour later a friend of mine, Gary Brandon, emailed to say that I was on the front page of Metro, the main free London morning paper given to everyone as they got onto the Tube or bus. As the morning went on, I got a constant stream of telephone calls asking for interviews. I turned them all down and I didn't even bother to buy the newspapers. Another message that landed in my inbox was from Danny Savage, to say I'd been on the BBC 6 o'clock news the night before. I hadn't seen it and I asked him to pray for me. I also got a personal message from a family friend in Ampleforth, which meant a great deal to me:

"Dear Paul,

WELL DONE, WELL DONE.

What a wonderful, measured and responsible witness you have been to the Christian values of truth, integrity and courage.

I thank God for your gifts. You are the reason that parents like me send our children to Ampleforth.

Thinking of you and praying for you,

Peace,

Kit"

Late morning, I was sitting in a bit of a daze on my mum's sofa having a cup of coffee when her home telephone rang. At least I knew it wouldn't be journalists calling. I answered and it was my sister-in-law, Anne.

"He's resigned!," she said.

"Who's resigned?," I replied.

"James Crosby," she said.

"I can't believe it."

"Turn on the television," came Anne's reply.

I put the phone down and switched on to the BBC. There in front of me, the reporter was announcing that Sir James Crosby had resigned as the Deputy Chairman of the FSA and had issued a statement which included the following: "… Whilst I am totally confident that there is no substance to any of the allegations, I nonetheless feel that the right course of action for the FSA is for me to resign from the FSA board which I do with immediate effect."

This was beyond comprehension. Why would he resign if he denied my allegations?

At 11.14am an email pinged in from *Channel 4 News.* It was the first channel off the blocks:

> *"Good morning, I hear from Jacqui Farnham that you've been forwarded several requests for interviews following yesterday's Treasury Select Committee hearing. I am Jon Snow's producer at Channel 4 News and without wanting to add to your pile, would like to let you know that he is extremely keen to speak to you on the programme tonight, if there's any chance you can fit us in.*
>
> *The interview would be a one to one sit down with Jon and would be the top of our programme, which is 7pm. We would also be able to do a pre-record this afternoon if you're unable to make it live tonight."*

I never had time to reply. I regret that because I'm a

huge fan of Jon Snow and *Channel 4 News*. I would have loved to have done a one-on-one with him.

Suddenly, I realised it was Wednesday: Parliamentary Question Time was about to start. I watched the BBC live coverage from the House of Commons with my mouth wide open and jaw on the floor.

Prime Minister Gordon Brown was referring to me by name. He was coming under heavy fire from the Opposition's David Cameron.

Here is the Hansard transcript from that day's Prime Minister's Question Time (PMQT). My story top of the agenda of PMQT: it was like an out-of-body experience. Labour MP Khalid Mahmood was speaking:

> ***Mr. Mahmood***: *My constituents are fed up with irresponsibility from the bankers and the mistakes that are costing the country millions. Does my right hon. Friend accept that those allegations, including the most recent against Sir James Crosby, must be fully investigated to restore confidence in our banking sector?*
>
> **The Prime Minister**: *It is right that we investigate serious allegations that are made about the banking system. These are serious but contested allegations; in relation to Sir James Crosby, these are allegations that he will wish to defend himself against, so it is right that he has stepped down as vice-chairman of the Financial Services Authority. It is important that the Financial Services Authority shows at this time that it is operating to the best standards possible. The Walker review that is being set up will look at exactly these matters – risk management, remuneration and the performance of boards – and I*

believe that the system of regulation in this country can and will be improved.

Mr. David Cameron (Witney) (Con): *They can even plant questions at short notice. Let us be clear about what has happened. In the last half hour, Sir James Crosby, the man who ran HBOS and whom the Prime Minister singled out to regulate our banks and to advise our Government, has resigned over allegations that he sacked the whistleblower who knew that his bank was taking unacceptable risks. Does the Prime Minister accept that it was a serious error of judgment on his part to appoint him in the first place?*

The Prime Minister: *The allegations that were brought before the Select Committee on the Treasury were investigated by the independent KPMG in 2005. The allegations made by Mr. Moore were found not to be substantiated. That was an independent review, which was done by KPMG and reported to the Financial Services Authority. However, it is right that when serious allegations are made, they are properly investigated. No doubt the Treasury Committee will want to look at them; and no doubt the Conservative party will want to wait to see how that investigation takes place. The Walker committee will look at every aspect of banking regulation, which we know can be improved. The unfortunate thing is that every time we have called for more regulation, the Conservative party has called for less.*

Mr. Cameron: *The Prime Minister talks about the KPMG investigation, but it was after that investigation that the bank virtually went bust. Taxpayers have poured billions* *of pounds into the bank. Not only was Sir James Crosby appointed as one of the top regulators in the country – and, I have to say, knighted by the Prime Minister for his services – but the Prime Minister has been relying on him for economic advice. Sir James Crosby was the man who was going to sort out the mortgage market, so will the Prime Minister confirm that, as well as standing down from the Financial Services Authority, Sir James Crosby is no longer one of his advisers? Is that the case?*

The Prime Minister: *Sir James Crosby did two reports: one for the Chancellor on mortgages, and one for me, when I was Chancellor, on security issues. He has completed these reports. He is no longer an economic adviser to the Government – [Hon. Members: "Ah!"] And he has only been so in the context of doing two reports. If I may say so, we are facing very big issues in the economy at the moment, and the way in which the Conservative party wants to trivialise them does it no merit.*

Mr. Cameron: *There is nothing trivial about asking the Prime Minister about the man he appointed to regulate the banks. Why cannot the Prime Minister just admit, for once, that he made an error of judgment? Is this not a big part of the Prime Minister's problem? Sir James Crosby has had the decency to resign. Why cannot the Prime Minister have the decency to admit that he got something wrong? Is this not part of the problem? There has been no apology about boom and bust, and no apology about Britain being better prepared. Even the bankers have apologised – when is the Prime Minister going to? Won't you just admit, one more time, that it was a misjudgement to appoint him to all those roles?*

***Mr. Speaker**: Order. I must tell the Leader of the Opposition that the term "you" is not permissible. He should not use it — [Interruption.] Order. Be quiet! I have said this time and time again, and I will not say it again.*

Finally, I realised the political ramifications of what I'd done.

Sir James Crosby had been a long-term political ally of Tony Blair's New Labour and Gordon Brown, as was Lord Dennis Stevenson. He had been appointed as the Deputy Chairman of the FSA by Gordon Brown's Treasury department when he was Chancellor of the Exchequer. His resignation was great ammunition for the Conservatives.

My mother, Oliver and I sat there completely dumbfounded at what was going on and then the phone really started ringing.

Before long, I'd been sent copies of the full media statements made by both Sir James Crosby and the FSA.

Sir James Crosby's statement

"In the light of recent media coverage I have decided to issue a short statement.

Just over three years ago I resigned my position as CEO of HBOS. Towards the end of my time as CEO of HBOS, as part of a wider restructuring of group functions, the Risk Function was elevated to report direct to the CEO. As part of this I asked one of our risk managers, Paul Moore, to leave HBOS. At the time he made a series of allegations. These were independently and extensively investigated on behalf of the Board, the results of which they shared with the FSA.

That investigation concluded that Mr Moore's allegations had no merit. Last autumn (on a BBC programme) and again yesterday at the Treasury Select Committee he repeated substantially the same allegations. HBOS has reiterated its view that his allegations have no merit. Questions have also been raised about my independence from government.

During the last two years I have devoted considerable time to producing two reports for the Government; the first on identity assurance and ID cards (published last March) and the second on mortgage finance (published last November).

I am confident that anyone who either worked with me on the reports or indeed anyone who has read them will conclude that they are the work of someone who is genuinely independent of government.

In addition I want to emphasise that I have absolutely no political connections or affiliations.

I am full of admiration for my colleagues at the FSA and the work they are doing under extreme pressure.

As a non-executive director I have an absolute responsibility to ensure that I do not make their task any more difficult.

Therefore, whilst I am totally confident that there is no substance to any of the allegations, I nonetheless feel that the right course of action for the FSA is for me to resign from the FSA Board which I do with immediate effect."

The FSA's statement

The Financial Services Authority (FSA) can confirm that specific allegations made by Paul Moore in December 2004 regarding the regulatory risk function at HBOS were fully investigated by KPMG, which concluded that the changes made by HBOS were appropriate. The chairman of the FSA will write to the Chancellor of the Exchequer by the end of today, setting out the details.

Sir James Crosby has decided to resign from the board of the FSA, for the reasons he has set out in his public statement, and we would like to thank him for his very significant contribution to the FSA over the past few years.

Hearing these denials by Crosby and the FSA, as well as the reliance on the KPMG report, I couldn't keep silent any longer. I decided to issue my own media statement by way of rebuttal:

To whom it may concern – statement by Paul Moore in response to the resignation of Sir James Crosby as Deputy Chairman of FSA

I have decided to make a written statement in response to Sir James Crosby's resignation statement and to distribute it through Newsnight to the widest possible media audience.

I read with interest that Sir James continues to refute the allegations I made in my evidence to the Treasury Select Committee and I want all those interested to know that I continue to stand firmly and confidently behind what I have said.

I have a significant body of detailed additional evidence which will corroborate what I said. I am confident that the "independent report" to which Sir James has referred will not bear up to any proper independent scrutiny. I described that report as "supposedly" independent in my evidence to the committee and I strongly stand behind that statement. No doubt I shall be given the opportunity at an appropriate time to disclose my evidence and demonstrate what I am saying is true. Today I have had countless messages of support from the very many people who have always known the truth of what happened at HBOS.

By way of comment, I would simply say this: I am not interested in blame even though many people will think that this is what my agenda is. People who know me will testify to this but I have to say that I do find it sad that people in such important fiduciary positions find it so difficult to admit their mistakes and to say that they are sorry. Fighting to the bitter end is always worse for all concerned.

From a personal perspective, I feel very peaceful and ready to be challenged about what I have said. As you will be able to tell from my evidence I strongly believe in culture which is open to challenge. I have a strong personal faith which is with me now.

I shall repeat the above statement on camera to the main news channels.

Paul Moore

2.00 pm Wednesday 11th February 2009

I then agreed to do interviews to camera with the BBC and the other main TV news channels. As I was in Bristol, I went to the BBC studios in Whiteladies Road where BBC natural history programmes were made. As I had been to Bristol University I was on familiar ground.

I arrived at the studios at about 3.30pm and did an on-camera interview with BBC Look North who I'd promised to talk to first as I lived in Yorkshire. I then spoke to Nick Robinson, the BBC's Political Editor and then I did an interview with *Sky News Live* on the pavement outside the Whiteladies Road studios. On my way to driving to see my friend Glynn Thompson, I gave a telephone statement to Channel 4 News live.

In every interview to camera, I said pretty much the same thing. This is what I said to the BBC:

"I was surprised that he [James Crosby] resigned so quickly and I was interested to hear him denying the allegations that I made in my evidence and I want to make it absolutely clear that I firmly and confidently stand behind everything that I have set out in my evidence, that I have detailed corroborative evidence to support that and that the report on which he relies will not subject itself to proper independent scrutiny without falling down like a house of cards."

While all this was going on, I was getting lots of emails from friends pledging their support including one from Peter Lytton-Cobbold whose family own Knebworth House in Hertfordshire and whose grandfather Cameron "Kim" Cobbold was the Governor of the

Bank of England. Peter had gone to Eton College public school in Berkshire and was in the same year as David Cameron, later to be Prime Minister. Peter wrote:

> *"Doesn't look like you need an introduction to David Cameron anymore!! Well done for being brave – I was worried when I first heard that they might get at you for taking a settlement – but from what I heard on the news you have been totally open and upfront with them. Timed to perfection giving evidence to the Commons Select Committee and quite right that it is in the public interest and what happened should be in the public arena. It can't have been an easy decision for you and you have all our respect and admiration. Just received Kit's email while writing this – our prayers are also with you and the family. I imagine it might be a couple of hard days as they kick back at you but you have public sentiment behind you and more importantly your friends, and more importantly than that your family."*

By about 6pm, I was starting to get requests from overseas media and, in particular, the USA. I was approached by *The Wall Street Journal* first and then *The New York Times*. It was becoming a global news story.

Paul Mason contacted me again and asked for the evidence that proved that the KPMG investigation report into my allegations was a cover-up, so I sent him the rebuttal letter.

I received my first approach from a "red-top" newspaper, the *News of the World* but was too occupied to phone back.

It was 8pm and I was a bit of a wreck when I got to my

mum's. I'd been operating as a one-man press office and when one telephone call ended, another started. Emails were arriving with a pinging sound every minute or so on my Blackberry mobile phone.

However one call came in at 8.30pm that stood out from the rest. It was from Jennifer Hughes at the *Financial Times*. She said: "We've got the KPMG report and want to discuss it with you."

It had been leaked to the *FT*, presumably with the intention of putting the kibosh on me. Stevenson had promised to send the report to the TSC when he had used it in HBOS's defence at the Tuesday meeting, but Committee Clerk Benger hadn't received it, even though the *FT* had. I'd already dealt with the KPMG report in my evidence and made it quite clear that it was a cover-up. In fact, on that very day I had phoned Benger and offered to send the committee my copy but protocol said we had to allow Stevenson to send it in before I responded with my detailed evidence.

I was pleased the *FT* had the report and I said to Jennifer: "Good, if you'd phoned me earlier I would have sent you a copy myself."

There was some laughter and then she said: "The KPMG report says that you were, 'overly verbose and full of self-importance', 'over-stating matters in an overly dramatic and theatrical way', that your behaviour was described as, '... ranging from prickly to ranting to extraordinary to outrageous'. What have you got to say about that?"

"Well," I replied very calmly and slowly. "I...

am…prepared…to accept the description that I was 'extraordinary', after all, it must have seemed extraordinary that someone like me was challenging the business strategy of someone as powerful as James Crosby. But, so far as all the other descriptions are concerned, I can only reply to you in the famous words of Mandy Rice Davies [of 1963 Profumo affair fame], 'Well, they would say that, wouldn't they?'"

More laughter.

I sent Jennifer a copy of our rebuttal letter and she replied at 11pm saying:

> *"… we've reflected the thrust of your points in our story."*

Half-an-hour earlier my pal Gary Brandon sent me another email:

> *"Paul, I am getting fed up, as much as I love you, I do not want to see your face in every paper or hear your name on every news broadcast. Did you know that The Sun said you were 61?"*

By that stage, I had finally sat down to watch BBC *Newsnight* with mum and Oliver. The story was the top of the programme and covered nearly 10 minutes. They did an outstanding job in summarising the whole story. I have used this *Newsnight* coverage ever since in all my keynote speeches. You can watch the entire section here www.crashbankwallop.co.uk/library/11-3 It shows the BBC door-stepping Crosby at his home in North Yorkshire, a key clip from the TSC meeting, my interview with Paul Mason, the interchange between Gordon Brown and David Cameron in PMQT and my final statement to camera where I stated I stood behind everything I'd said.

The clip also commented on a more detailed statement that the FSA put out later on that day:

FSA statement re: HBOS

Further to our earlier statement, the Financial Services Authority (FSA) has issued the following fuller account of the issues relating to the risk function at HBOS, raised at the Treasury Select Committee on 10 February 2009.

Having examined carefully the files relating to this issue, the FSA can confirm that specific allegations made by Paul Moore in December 2004 regarding the regulatory risk function at HBOS were fully investigated by KPMG and the FSA, which concluded that the changes made by HBOS were appropriate. This statement gives an account of the actions taken by the FSA in relation to concerns expressed in 2004 by Mr Moore, former head of Group Regulatory Risk at HBOS. It is focused on these specific concerns rather than providing a complete description of the regulatory relationship with HBOS.

Risk assessment

2. *As background to the specific set of allegations made by Mr Moore, we set out below relevant developments in relation to the HBOS risk framework:*

- *the FSA conducted a full risk assessment of HBOS (known as an ARROW assessment) in late 2002 which identified a need to strengthen the control infrastructure within the group;*

- *we then decided to commission a "skilled persons report" from PWC on the HBOS risk management framework, using formal information gathering powers under section 166 of the Financial Services and Markets Act 2000: their extensive report revealed a need for improvements in the HBOS risk management environment;*
- *the FSA then conducted a further full risk assessment of the HBOS group to cover all of the group's business, formally recording its assessment in December 2004, the assessment was that the risk profile of the group had improved and that the group had made good progress in addressing the risks highlighted in February 2004, but that the group risk functions still needed to enhance their ability to influence the business, which we saw as a key challenge.*

Changes at HBOS

3. Other key events took place in 2004:

- *following the departure of the Chief Financial Officer, who had been responsible at Board level for regulatory risk, and as part of a wider restructuring, HBOS decided to upgrade the risk function by appointing a new group risk director as the senior executive responsible for regulatory risk in the group;*
- *following that appointment, the then head of group regulatory risk, Paul Moore, was informed on 8 November that he would leave as part of this restructuring; he subsequently approached FSA to*

express concerns about HBOS and in particular about the suitability of the new appointee as the group risk director;

- *in his view, the new group risk director was not 'fit and proper' to be approved by the FSA to hold that post, by reason of lack of integrity, lack of experience in risk management, and of general attitude and approach;*
- *he also made other allegations about HBOS's overall risk framework.*

Action taken by the FSA

Urgent action was taken to follow up these specific allegations:

- *following consultation with the FSA, the HBOS Group Audit Committee commissioned an external review on the fitness issues from its auditors KPMG: the FSA satisfied itself about the skill and independence of the individuals selected to conduct the report for KPMG and about the scope of the report;*
- *KPMG undertook around 80 hours of interviews and meetings with 28 individuals including the HBOS CEO, CFO, and then Head of Retail, as well as the former head of regulatory risk himself;*
- *the FSA suspended its decision on whether or not to approve the appointment to the new role, pending receipt of the results of the KPMG investigation;*
- *the FSA approved that individual only when it had received those results, which indicated that KPMG 'did*

not believe that the evidence reviewed suggested that the candidate was not fit and proper', that 'the process for the identification and assessment of candidates for the GRD position appeared appropriate', and that 'the structure and reporting lines of Group Regulatory Risk are appropriate';

- *the KPMG report also indicated that there was no evidence in the report that Mr Moore was dismissed due to being excessively robust in the discharge of his functions. (It should be understood that the KPMG report concerned the allegation that the new director was not fit and proper rather than the more general issue of HBOS' risk control framework identified in the skilled persons report. The KPMG report did not extend to these issues.)*
- *The FSA also followed up Mr Moore's concerns by meeting him independently and separately discussed the KPMG report directly with KPMG.*

Subsequent relevant events

5. *The FSA continued to pursue concerns about the risk management framework. As a consequence, we wrote to HBOS again on 29 June 2006 with a further interim ARROW risk assessment. In that letter we made clear:*

- *that whilst the group had made progress, there were still control issues. We made clear that we would closely track progress in this area;*

- *the growth strategy of the group posed risks to the whole group and that these risks must be managed and mitigated.*

Conclusion

In conclusion, the FSA confirms that the allegations made by Mr Moore were taken seriously, and were properly and professionally investigated. It should also be noted that the FSA's concerns about HBOS' risk management framework considerably pre-dated the allegations by Mr Moore.

There are two extraordinary aspects of this statement. Firstly, the FSA said it carried out the Arrow assessment in 2002 – its full assessment was actually in 2003. Secondly, in section 5 of the statement, the FSA admits it carried out further work in June 2006 and continued to have concerns that "*the growth strategy of the group posed risks to the whole group and that these risks must be managed and mitigated*".

I had raised the red flag in 2004 and been fired for it, yet, by as late as 29 June 2006 the FSA was continuing to have serious concerns about HBOS. So why didn't the FSA do anything about it? Was it because of the influence of James Crosby on the Board of the regulator?

I went to bed that night full of alcohol and with an even greater sense of surreality than before. I felt like I was hallucinating. I prayed for reconnection with reality.

The next day, Thursday 12 February, the media storm continued. I was approached by *Good Morning Britain*, the *Daily Mail,* ITN, CNN, the *Press Association*, *The*

Times, the *FT*, the *Daily Telegraph, Bloomberg News, The Sunday Telegraph, The Sunday Times, The Independent on Sunday* and more. BBC Radio 4 wanted me to do an interview with Michael Buerk for a show called *The Choice*. I simply couldn't satisfy demand but I managed to do key interviews with CNN (Quest), ITN, the *Daily Mail, The Sunday Times, The Sunday Telegraph* and *The Independent on Sunday*.

I think all the other publications (and there were literally hundreds of them) relied on the existing materials and their own thoughts.

To this day I have still not managed to collate a scrapbook with everything in it but some can be read, seen or heard here:

www.crashbankwallop.co.uk/library/10/additionalmedia

I did both the CNN Quest and ITN interviews in my mum's cosy little sitting-room with the cameras, lighting and sound engineers all around.

Throughout, Oliver sat watching from the sofa opposite and during one short interlude he gave me a good talking to for being a bit too hard and self-righteous. From the mouths of babes!

On that Thursday, I phoned Benger and left a voicemail offering to send him all the evidence that proved the denials of Stevenson, Crosby and the FSA were misrepresentations but he replied by email to say

I should wait until HBOS had said what it had to say. This made sense because it would put me in the picture of its entire defence to which I could then respond.

This is what he said:

"Dear Paul

Thank you for this. I think the best approach from our point of view is to wait until we hear directly from HBOS. We will then forward that response to you for you to reply by means of a separate memorandum. I would suggest if you want to include your lawyer's appraisal but exclude salary details etc you simply include the relevant extracts in your submission (perhaps indicating that the final paragraph of the letter deals with salary details and is for that reason excluded).

Best wishes
John"

In any event, I decided to send him the rebuttal letter to the KPMG report as well as supporting statements from my lawyers:

From: *Peter Hamilton*
Sent: *12 February 2009 17:09*
To: *'BENGERJS'*
Subject: *Paul Moore*

Dear Dr Benger,

I am a barrister in practice at 4 Pump Court, Temple, London EC4Y 7AN. I have been asked by Paul Moore to write to you as I represented Paul Moore in his whistleblowing case.

I have been surprised that it has been reported that the KPMG Report was independent. In my view since KPMG were the auditors of HBOS, KPMG could not have been regarded as independent of HBOS. It follows that the FSA should not have regarded it as independent.

The Report was not only of limited scope (as KPMG and the FSA, in their statement issued today, say) but reached conclusions that a properly independent tribunal would not have reached.

For both those reasons it is disappointing that the FSA have appeared to accept it.

The FSA should not have approved the appointment of Ms Dawson to such a senior and important position on the basis of the evidence available to them at the time.

In the light of these points the significance of Sir James Cosby's position at the time as both CEO HBOS and Non-Executive Director of the FSA should be investigated.

Yours sincerely,
Peter Hamilton

Dear Sir,

RE: PAUL MOORE

We acted as Solicitors to Paul Moore in his whistleblowing claim against HBOS and are instructed to write to you on his behalf.

The KPMG Report was relied on by HBOS and the FSA to justify the dismissal of our client. We do not accept that Report should have been.

KPMG wrote the Report at the same as they were acting as Auditors of HBOS. That immediately raises issues of potential conflict. The relationship with KPMG was managed by the Chief Financial Officer of HBOS and to whom our client directly reported. Again, this raises issues of potential conflict.

The KPMG Report itself was limited in it scope. Indeed KPMG have accepted this themselves, so we would argue that it never covered the essential issues raised by our client.

In this context it was very disappointing that the FSA simply accepted the Report.

Moreover, our client believes the FSA should not have approved the appointment of Ms Jo Dawson (who we believe did not have compliance or regulatory experience) to take on key aspects of our client's role, without at the very least, carrying out a rigorous review.

At the relevant time, Sir James Crosby (who dismissed our client and, we understand, appointed Jo Dawson) was both CEO HBOS and Non Executive Director of the FSA.

In these circumstances, our client asks for an investigation by the Committee as to whether the position of Sir James Crosby in the FSA at the relevant time influenced the approval by the FSA of the KPMG Report and the approval of the appointment of Jo Dawson.

Yours faithfully,

Russell Jones & Walker

Our rebuttal letter to the KPMG report was a powerful Exocet-like missile or should I say missive. It was the one written document that I drafted which my solicitor, Clive, allowed to be sent to the other side pretty much verbatim. Here are a couple of extracts:

First extract

The KPMG Report

In our negotiations, you should be aware that we consider that the KPMG Report has materially failed to take into account the evidence given by Paul to the investigation team in key areas. In our view, therefore, the Report is imbalanced and has arrived at conclusions which, if reviewed by an external independent tribunal, would not be supported.

The mere fact that the report states that its findings are consistent with the oral briefing given to the March Audit Committee which took place a full ten days before Paul submitted his final eleven page written evidence to KPMG is strongly indicative that KPMG had already "made up their minds" and did not take into account any of the subsequent and important evidence given to the investigation team by Paul. It also demonstrates that the concerns we raised in our letter to Tony Hobson on the 24th February about the appropriateness of the adversarial approach adopted by KPMG in a case involving serious allegations of whistle-blowing were, in fact, justified even though, at the time, they were totally rejected. We are also very concerned to understand why, if KPMG had already made up their minds as to the outcome of the investigation by the March Audit Committee, why it took two months for them to finalise their short report?

Second extract

- The section dealing with KPMG's views on Jo Dawson's appointment and how that "juxtaposes" with the criticisms of Paul's style and approach is frankly nothing short of bizarre. In our view, it is also technically the least appropriate interpretation of the FSA's Rules and against standard principles of statutory or regulatory interpretation.

  On the one hand, Paul is criticised for not being able to build relationships with key stakeholders and is dismissed. But, on the other, Jo Dawson who is explicitly recognised as having significant style and personal behavioural issues (a bit abrasive at times can inhibit her ability to build deep relationships, inflexible, lack of warmth, demanding to work for, track record of confrontations within HBOS, not a diplomat) and who has no technical knowledge or experience is appointed as GRD.

  KPMG's conclusion that none of this, or the fact that she effectively admitted the threat she made to Paul, matters is simply wrong. In addition, the notion that any properly drawn-up competence framework for the GRD role would exclude the requirement for technical knowledge and skills is also wholly unbelievable and wrong. Although for some roles, it is possible that basic management skills would be sufficient, this simply cannot be the case for roles which are primarily technical such as the role of GRD. In any event, anyone with the development needs which Jo Dawson had, far from being the "lead candidate", would not even get a first interview.

These are just a few of the key points about our views of the KPMG Report which we would draw to your attention at this time.

The rebuttal letter can be read in full here: www.crashbankwallop.co.uk/library/11-4

That day, I was also invited to appear on ITV's *This Morning* programme with Phillip Schofield and Fern Britton but I was so busy I didn't even notice the email. I needed a press office.

I did however speak to ITN newsreader Julie Etchingham, a friend of a friend.

On Friday morning, during prayer, the scripture reading was powerful and very relevant to what was going on. It was from St Paul's letter to the Ephesians 4: 29-32:

> *"Do not use harmful words in talking. Use only helpful words, the kind that build up and provide what is needed, so that what you say will do good to those who hear you. And do not make God's Holy Spirit sad; for the spirit is God's mark of ownership on you, a guarantee that the day will come when God will set you free. Get rid of all bitterness, passion, and anger. No more shouting or insults. No more hateful feelings of any sort. Instead, be tender-hearted to one another, and forgive one another, as God has forgiven you in Christ."*

I took these words to heart. Hate the sin not the sinner became my motto and, apart from the odd blip, I have tried to stick by it in all my subsequent speeches and media interviews.

I did my main print media interviews with Helen Weathers of the *Daily Mail*, Maggie Pagano writing for *The Independent on Sunday,* Louise Armitstead from *The Telegraph* and Claire Newell at *The Sunday Times*.

Here is a selection of "clippings" (See www.crashbankwallop.co.uk/library/11-4-1):

Daily Mail - 14th Feb 09

EXCLUSIVE: The whistleblower who, to the embarrassment of Gordon Brown, triggered the fall of a leading financial regulator reveals the full extraordinary story of how he was sacked for daring to tell the truth about greedy, reckless banks

Sunday Telegraph - Main Story - 15th Feb 09

Independent on Sunday - Front Page - 15th Feb 09

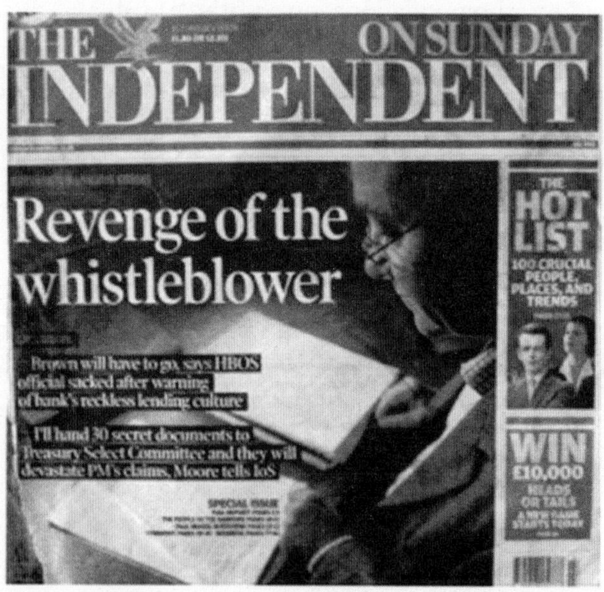
THE INDEPENDENT ON SUNDAY

Revenge of the whistleblower

Brown will have to go, says HBOS official sacked after warning of bank's reckless lending culture

I'll hand 30 secret documents to Treasury Select Committee and they will devastate PM's claims, Moore tells IoS

SPECIAL ISSUE

THE HOT LIST
100 CRUCIAL PEOPLE, PLACES, AND TRENDS

WIN £10,000
HEADS OR TAILS

I wasn't at all happy with the article that appeared on the front page of *The Independent on Sunday* headlined "Revenge of the whistleblower". I had made it absolutely clear during my interview with Maggie Pagano that revenge had nothing to do with it and I never said, "Brown will have to go..." I made a bit of a hullabaloo about it and Maggie apologised to me formally, in writing, when I threatened to refer it to the Press Complaints Commission. I really don't think it was her fault but this was a sharp lesson in the pitfalls of dealing with the media.

When I had been briefing Maggie for the article, she got under my skin good and proper. I liked her, trusted her and opened up completely to her. At one point we were discussing Tony Hobson and the positive feedback he'd given me. I suggested that Maggie ring him at home and try to discover why it appeared he'd turned turtle on me. Later, she told me that he had explained what had happened by saying, "I only meant to say that Paul was doing his job well technically".

Inevitably it wasn't long before the massed ranks of the media had found out where I lived and become encamped in the village pub, the 17thcentury Wombwell Arms. Sky News and other stations door-stepped Maureen and Emily early on the Thursday morning and hung around in the narrow lane outside our cottage for much longer. Of course, I wasn't there. I was in Bristol with my mum where they couldn't find me.

As the weekend approached, I managed to come up for air long enough to realise that Lord Dennis Stevenson would be providing the KPMG report to the TSC, so I decided that I'd better get on with the job of collating my corroborating evidence. On Saturday morning I wrote to Benger:

"John,

I did not get time to collate everything yesterday so apologies....I will do so this week end...but I think there is going to be a bit of problem here as the level of detail will be just too much for the committee to digest unless they take a law degree!

This is what I suggest...I collate the papers and email them to you...you have your top analytical person (preferably a good lawyer) and then I or my Barrister / Solicitor could meet up for a conference with you to clarify anything that is unclear.

With the greatest deference, I am not entirely sure the TSC is the right forum to test the veracity of my allegations... and if we are not careful, we are going to end up with trial by media.

Regards, Paul"

The media interest in my story just wouldn't die down and later on Saturday morning I was contacted by Sally Roberts, the producer of *Channel 4 News,* who asked if I could do an interview on Sunday about the additional documents I proposed to send to the TSC. Again, I was too preoccupied to respond.

Out of the blue I also received an email from Anthony Smith, a former member of my staff from HBOS, telling me an amazing revelation about Jo Dawson. Apparently she had admitted to him on the way to a meeting with the FSA that she knew nothing about risk or regulation. I'll return to Smith's story very shortly.

In the wake of the weekend's media coverage, I got together with my next-door neighbour, Roger Statham, to prepare a press release. Roger was chief probation officer for the North-East of England and was used to dealing with journalists and politicians. On Monday 16 February we issued the following statement to the *Press Association* news agency:

"I have read with interest this morning for the first time the full version of the article in the IoS called 'The revenge of the Whistleblower'.

I had already commented to Sky News on Saturday evening that if the main body of the article did not provide a fair balance to what I had said to the journalist that I would set the record straight. My primary goal is to ensure that everything I say is fair.

Although I think much of the article is good and sound, it has definitely exaggerated what I said to some material degree in places and I would like to make the following key points:

- *I have no political affiliations at all and have no recollection of ever having spoken to a politician of any party. If I have, I never discussed politics. I have in fact voted for both the Conservatives and Labour in the past and have great regard for the Liberal Democrats.*
- *I did not say, 'Brown must go. He cannot remain in office'.*
- *I had a very lengthy conversation with Maggie Pagano about the whole affair and aimed many of my comments at the KPMG report on which Gordon Brown, the FSA, Sir James Crosby, Lord Dennis Stevenson, Andy Hornby and the rest of the HBOS Board at the time are relying to deny the veracity of my allegations to the Treasury Select Committee.*
- *I told Maggie that I have detailed evidence – and, yes, it does amount to many dozens of documents – which will rebut the independence and veracity of the KPMG report and corroborate the veracity of what I said in my now public testimony. I said that if my allegations are proved truthful, which I am confident they will be,*

this would raise very serious questions for all those who are relying on the KPMG report.

- *My agenda here from the start, and as I made very clear in my original testimony, was not aimed at blaming individuals but at helping to see a marked improvement in regulatory procedures and governance in the financial sector. I am sad that the affair has developed in such a way that I have no choice but to contest the truth of what I have said when I believe it is clear to most ordinary people what has happened.*
- *My focus now is to concentrate on compiling the evidence I have in such a way that it can be of most use to the Treasury Select Committee. I hope to send it to the Committee in the next few days while the Committee is in recess along with all Members of Parliament.*

Later that day, I wrote to Helen Weathers at the *Daily Mail* thanking her for the article she'd written and finally got around to accepting an invitation from BBC Radio 4's Dawn Bryan to do an interview with Michael Buerk on *The Choice*. I emailed Louise Armitstead, who had written *The Sunday Telegraph* piece, saying what a good job she'd done. I'd also been approached by Will Hutton and I agreed with him to appear on Channel 4's *Dispatches*.

As I was doing it, I felt the interview with Will was a good one. I said that HBOS, in order to fund its rapid lending growth, was more often than not in the top 10 wholesale borrowers in the world, including sovereign governments and that, in one year, it borrowed more money on the wholesale markets than the Italian government. I went on to say that a massive change was needed in the world and that it was completely wrong that in Western Europe more money is spent on ice-cream every year than it would cost to feed all the starving people on the planet. When the cameras stopped rolling, I was pleasantly surprised to receive a round of applause from the crew and congratulations from Will on my TV performance.

Now back to the Anthony Smith story. On Tuesday 17 February, he also blew the whistle on HBOS. Anthony had worked with me and my department when I was head of GRR and was a manager based at Clerical Medical in Bristol, part of HBOS's Insurance and Investment Division.

He accused senior executives at the bank of turning a deaf ear to employees who tried to raise concerns. Here is an extract from the BBC online news website:

HBOS risk control 'dumbed down'

By Anthony Reuben
Business reporter, BBC News

Risk managers at HBOS were discouraged from challenging business decisions, a former employee has told BBC News.

Anthony Smith said the risk group's culture changed in 2005 after his boss Paul Moore was replaced by someone with no experience of risk or regulation.

"There was definitely a dumbing down of the risk function and challenging the business... was not welcome," he said.

Risk team member Anthony Smith (right) with former HBOS chief executive Sir James Crosby

The entire report is here:
http://news.bbc.co.uk/1/hi/business/7892079.stm

In the Mail Online on 18 February, *Daily Mail* reporter James Chapman wrote:

> *"He [Anthony Smith] described an occasion when Miss Dawson was asked to speak at a dinner attended by FSA bigwigs, including then chief executive John Tiner. Mr Smith said he was asked to prepare a four-page summary of regulation for her because she did not want to look foolish at the function. He said he thought it was strange for someone in such an elevated position, who was advising members of the board on risk, to have 'no knowledge at all about risk and regulation'."*

The Telegraph's online story relating to Anthony's allegations, quoted Shadow Chancellor George Osborne, as saying:

> *"This is yet more evidence of systemic failure to control irresponsible lending at HBOS."*

Anthony's story went global and was extremely helpful to my own cause. I sent him an email: "Well done and thanks for the support; it means a huge amount. The article is excellent on the website...r u on tele?"

He was on the telly, the BBC 6 o'clock News! Recently, I asked Anthony to write up his story.

Here it is: www.crashbankwallop.co.uk/library/11-5

On 18 February, I travelled to London and met a group of people for lunch in the private members Reform Club on Pall Mall, including Prof Amin Rajan and Prof Andrew Kakabadse who specialised in corporate governance at Cranfield Business School. Andrew is probably the world's leading academic expert on corporate governance and has become a highly-respected friend, and later in 2009 helped with a major survey of risk management professionals into the causes and implications of the banking crisis. There will be more about this in the sequel to this book about the long march for truth and justice.

Just before the lunch, I met up with Chris Ship who is now the Deputy Political Editor of ITV News. I gave him much more detail about the additional evidence that I would be presenting to the TSC after it had received the KPMG report.

Towards the end of the week the media frenzy had begun to die down; thank goodness. This gave me time to get stuck into preparing my additional evidence for the TSC. I sent my first draft plus accompanying documents to Peter Hamilton on Monday 23 February.

The next day I received an email from Danny Savage forwarding another email from BBC producer Deborah Hawkes, inviting me for an interview on the HARDtalk news programme. Danny said:

> *"Now then Paul.. Have a look at this email below. They are quite a serious and responsible bunch and guests are usually really big hitters so you've made it to the A list!! I think if you agreed parameters with them it would be quite good and they seem to be after what we have talked about. It gets broadcast on the BBC News channel and then repeated often in the dead of night! Have a think about it and I'll see you on Wednesday. Over and out. Danny."*

By now, two weeks had passed since my evidence to the TSC had gone live, but there was still no sign of the KPMG report being sent by "the other side" to the Committee. I was becoming suspicious that there was some monkey business going on, so I emailed John Benger:

From: *Paul Moore*

Sent: *24 February 2009 09:12*

To: *'BENGER, Dr John'*

Cc: *'Peter Hamilton'; 'Clive Howard'*

Subject: *Paul Moore and HBOS*

Dear John,

I must say that I am getting quite curious / concerned / suspicious about why we have still not received any evidence supplied by Sir James Crosby, ex HBOS executives and the FSA. After all Stevenson and Hornby said that they could provide it pretty much immediately. Crosby referred to it when he resigned nearly two weeks ago.

The FSA referred to it in their first statement on Wednesday pm / Thursday am also nearly two weeks ago. What is more, a leaked copy of the famous KPMG report was in the hands of the FT by Wednesday evening which forced me to send them a copy of our first rebuttal letter which you now have as well. Surely, if they all rely on the KPMG report, they could just send you an immediate copy. I repeat my offer of providing you directly with a copy of the KPMG report and continue to maintain in the most vigorous way that it will not withstand public independent scrutiny.

I have not been pushing hard to complete my additional evidence simply because we agreed that there was no point in sending it in until Crosby et al had sent in their evidence. Nevertheless, I have nearly completed my detailed resume of additional evidence and am pretty confident that there is nothing that HBOS / Crosby can add which I will not have dealt with. I expect to complete my document today.

I think the thing that concerns me most now that I have taken the step to speak out in the public interest is this - surely, the Committee needs my evidence before it questions the FSA? Is the delay by HBOS etc intended in any way to avoid the FSA having to answer questions relating to my additional evidence?

Kind regards

Paul

PS See attached email from you to Peter Hamilton on Friday confirming that still there was no evidence from the other side.

John Benger replied as follows:

From: *BENGER, Dr John*

Sent: *24 February 2009 09:15*

To: *Paul Moore*

Subject: *RE: Paul Moore and HBOS*

Dear Paul

Thank you for this. I think the Committee has a huge number of questions to ask the FSA in any case and they do of course have your original submission. I suspect the delay may be caused by the fact that we have asked all the banks to supply us with additional evidence on a wide range of topics and I assume that Lloyds/ HBOS are incorporating this material within that evidence. I will of course let you know once we have received this but when I checked yesterday it had still not arrived.

With best wishes

John

On Wednesday 25 February, I had to go to a meeting in Leeds of the trustees of xt3 Media. As I was driving along the M1, my mobile rang. It was Benger. With my phone on hands-free, he told me that the TSC had finally received the KPMG report and that I was now authorised to send in my additional corroborative evidence. It had been done on the day the FSA was going to be interviewed by the Committee, so I'd have to act swiftly to get my evidence to the Committee in time for it to be used to question the FSA.

I drove to the xt3 meeting room, which overlooked the Leeds and Liverpool canal, as fast as I could and explained that I had to do something before we could start.

It was 1.23pm when I sent my additional evidence:

From: *Paul Moore*

Sent: *25 February 2009 13:23*

To: *'BENGER, Dr John'*

Cc: *'Peter Hamilton'; 'Clive Howard'; 'Paul Moore'*

Subject: *RE: Paul Moore and HBOS*

John,

Following our earlier lengthy conversation, I now enclose my additional evidence in its final form by 1.30 as agreed. There is only one supporting document attached but you already have the detailed rebuttal letter to the KPMG report.

I formally request immediate permission to brief the press on this evidence of vital public interest; please could you respond to this request immediately?

Kind regards

Paul Moore

He replied as follows:

***From:** BENGER, Dr John*

***Sent:** 25 February 2009 13:34*

***To:** Paul Moore*

***Subject:** RE: Paul Moore and HBOS*

Dear Paul

Thank you for this. At present I have still not received a submission from the FSA or HBOS along the lines of our earlier conversation.

I am afraid it would not be appropriate for you to release your memorandum to the press at this time nor to make any wider use of it. The Committee has to take a decision that it is accepting your evidence as evidence before its inquiry and obviously is not in position to do so at this time. I will let you know as soon as this decision has been taken (which should be no later than tomorrow).

The issues of confidentiality and privilege which attach to it means that the Committee must take such a decision formally rather than informally.

Best wishes

John

Hugh Pym, the BBC's Economics Editor at the time, was present at the TSC for this session.

He contacted me on my mobile and then sent me this email:

From: *Hugh Pym*

Sent: *25 February 2009 16:10*

To: *Paul Moore*

Subject: *RE: Contact*

Your name was mentioned at the committee - Lord [Adair] Turner said that, given the philosophy at the time, the HBOS handling of the process was "appropriate"

I replied immediately:

Yes. I disagree!

My entire additional evidence and all the accompanying documents are available here:

www.crashbankwallop.co.uk/library/11-AdditionalEvidence

Here's an extract:

MEMORANDUM OF ADDITIONAL EVIDENCE TO THE TREASURY SELECT COMMITTEE RELATING TO THE BANKING CRISIS

PREPARED BY PAUL MOORE - EX HEAD OF GROUP REGULATORY RISK, HBOS PLC

25TH FEBRUARY 2009

Introduction and important preliminary points

1. I provided my initial evidence to the Treasury Select Committee (TSC) on Friday 6th February 2009 and before I set out my substantive additional evidence, I need to make some important preliminary points.
2. The purpose of my original testimony was not (as some of the media reports have suggested) to reek a personal vendetta against those who acted to my detriment (see 2.17) in dismissing me from HBOS. Nor was it to obtain a re-hearing of the fairness or otherwise of that dismissal. It was solely to provide what I considered to be relevant evidence to assist the TSC and Parliament to learn the lessons from my personal experience because, as I said, I believe "....it draws into sharp focus the lessons about the crucial importance of really effective governance" (see 2.3 and 2.4) in the financial sector.
3. Unfortunately, it has turned out to be impossible to deal with the policy points that can be learned without also dealing with the personal even though I would have preferred to have avoided that.
4. **The allegations I made** in my original testimony have been denied by Lord Dennis Stevenson, Andy Hornby, Sir James Crosby and the FSA.
5. **All parties have relied on a report produced by KPMG to deny the truth of what I said in my original testimony.**
6. The Committee will recall that I did not seek to avoid the issue of the KPMG report and actually referred to it myself in sections 2.20 - 3.21 of my original testimony. For ease of reference, I repeat what I said there:-
   a. 2.20 "A supposedly "independent report" by HBOS's auditors said HBOS were right but failed even to interview key witnesses."
   b. 3.21 "As I stated above in section 2, a **supposedly "independent report"** by **HBOS's auditors said HBOS were right but failed even to interview** key witnesses. No doubt they and the FSA would rely upon this report. In relation to this report, you should be aware that, following the very first response to the report from my lawyers and me which challenged it vigorously, HBOS settled within a very short time."
7. Notwithstanding the vigorous denial of my allegations, I made the following statement last Wednesday at about 2.00pm and repeated it to ITN, BBC and Sky News on Thursday to camera.

> "I read with interest that Sir James continues to refute the allegations I made in my evidence to the Treasury Select Committee and I want all those interested to know that I continue stand firmly and confidently behind what I have said.
>
> I have a significant body of detailed additional evidence which will corroborate what I said. **I am confident that the "independent report" to which Sir James has referred will not bear up to any proper independent scrutiny.** I described that report as "supposedly" independent in my evidence to the committee and I strongly stand behind that statement. No doubt I shall be given the opportunity at an appropriate time to disclose my evidence and demonstrate what I am saying is true."

8. This Memorandum of additional evidence is provided in response to the evidence now produced pursuant to a request by the **Clerk of the TSC, Dr John Benger** to provide the TSC with the additional evidence to which I referred in this statement and elsewhere.
9. At first, the intention was to provide the TSC with all relevant corroborative documents. However, following correspondence and discussions with the Clerk of the Committee last week, it was agreed that it would be impractical, confusing and, (having regard to the specific terms of reference of the TSC) unnecessary to provide the Committee with all the documents.
10. To put this in perspective, on an initial tally by myself and my advisers, the minimum number of relevant documents totalled 53 and amounted to approximately 4.5 megabytes of written material i.e. literally hundreds of pages.
11. In these circumstances, my advisers and I have agreed with the Clerk of the Committee that the most useful approach to the provision of additional evidence is to write a detailed resume and history of events which are relevant to the terms of reference of the TSC but without supplying all the underlying corroborative documents.
12. I have already said in my original testimony that I strongly believe that the prime or underlying cause of the banking crisis (i.e. what permitted **the symptoms of over-lending (including sub-prime), excessive credit and liquidity risk to occur without** adequate restraint) was **a completely inadequate "separation" and "balance of powers" between the executive and all those accountable for overseeing their actions and "reining them in"**.
13. When I refer to "...all those accountable for overseeing their actions and "reining them in", I want to be absolutely clear that I mean **every constituent that has a part to play in oversight** i.e. internal control functions such as finance, risk, compliance and internal audit, the non executive directors, external auditors, The FSA, the shareholders and the analysts **and, very importantly, the politicians.**
14. The terms of reference of the TSC state that - "The Treasury Committee is **seeking** to **identify** lessons that can be learned from the banking crisis." **In particular, it seeks to identify lessons relating to securing financial stability, protecting the taxpayer, consumers and shareholder interests.**
15. I strongly believe that a detailed resume of my personal story from HBOS, without supplying all the underlying documents, is the most appropriate approach for all key stakeholders and will draw out the key lessons for all these areas which are the subject of the TSC's enquiry. I also believe that it will show the importance of the points I made in section 4 of my original testimony - **"Some recommendations for policy analysis and development".**
16. Finally, it may very well be that it is in the public interest for there to be a more detailed enquiry / investigation in a different "tribunal" than the TSC into what happened in the lead up to the current crisis and who did or did not do what and what it teaches us about what the future policy should be.

After watching some of the TSC proceedings on the Parliament TV programme early the next morning, I sent a further email to Hugh Pym:

> **From:** *Paul Moore*
>
> **Sent:** *26 February 2009 08:57*
>
> **To:** *'Hugh Pym'*
>
> **Subject:** *RE: Contact*
>
> *From viewing some of the committee it seems to me that the FSA said:-*
>
> - *If we met the same things now we would not handle it the way we did then i.e. with our new "philosophy" Moore would be right*
> - *But in the "bad, bad old days" it was OK to be bad.*
>
> *It won't come as any surprise to you to know that the key FSA Principles, Rules and Guidance was exactly the same then as it is now....so why was it OK then?.....spin I guess...also FSA are trying to protect government as well...*

On the same day, I received an email from Helen Weathers, and also Maggie Pagano forwarding an email from Alexis Hood, producer of *The One Show*, the BBC's early evening daily talk show. I was wanted for yet another interview and I said yes. It was conducted the following week with Paddy O'Connell who also presents, on the 42nd floor of Broadcasting House, on BBC Radio 4 on Sunday mornings. The interview was filmed as we sat talking on high chairs in the

NatWest Tower – which was renamed Tower 42 – on Old Broad Street, a few doors down from the HBOS offices in London. Our backs were to the window and the cameras were set so that they could look out over the City of London. Just before the cameras started rolling, one of the crew asked me to do a sound test i.e. speak so that they could test that the sound levels were right for the recording. I had done these quite a few times over the previous week and decided to tell a limerick:

"There was a young monk from Siberia,
Whose morals were rather inferior,
He did to a nun, what none should've done,
And now she's Mother Superior!"

Paddy O'Connell, who was sitting next to me, piped up: "I've got a better one than that!
There was a young woman from Spain,
Who liked it now and again,
Not, now and again, now and again,
But NOW and AGAIN and AGAIN!"

The whole crew laughed and so did I. The broadcast went out as a report at the top of *The One Show* that evening and it just so happened that one of my favourite songwriters Annie Lennox from the famous band Eurythmics was the main guest. I watched later in disbelief as she made some very empathetic and kind comments about what whistleblowers had to go through. Annie, if you should read this book, I would love you to get in touch. You could really help with this important aspect of how our society needs to change.

Getting back to the email exchanges on the 26th, I received the following one from Benger:

Dear Paul

Just to confirm that the Committee will be accepting your revised evidence and that this will appear on our website soon. The KPMG report will also be accepted as evidence in the same way.

Best wishes

John

As my evidence would be protected by Parliamentary privilege I could safely share it with the media, and so I did. My additional evidence was 13,288 words and proved conclusively that the allegations that I had made, in summary, in my initial evidence were true and, in particular, the claim that the KPMG report was a cover-up.

Within a few minutes, Louise Armitstead from the *Daily Telegraph* sent me the following email:

From: *Louise Armitstead*

Sent: *26 February 2009 15:50*

To: *Paul Moore*

Subject: *RE: URGENT: Paul Moore and HBOS*

Paul – if you can resist releasing all this, we will make it The Telegraph's main story tomorrow..... the more exclusive it is, the bigger the editor will go. I have read the whole thing. Deal?

Louise

I had to tell her that the evidence was now publicly available on the TSC website and, therefore, could not be exclusive. No story appeared the next day. I was beginning to understand the way the media worked.

In fact, it turned out that almost none of my media contacts could be bothered to publish anything, even though this was far more important information than the evidence that I had originally given to the TSC. In that case, I thought, I'll issue another press release. My neighbour Roger Statham's excellent judgement came into play again.

PRESS RELEASE RELATING TO MY ADDITIONAL EVIDENCE TO THE TREASURY SELECT COMMITTEE RELATING TO THE BANKING CRISIS

PREPARED BY PAUL MOORE - EX HEAD OF GROUP REGULATORY RISK, HBOS PLC

26TH FEBRUARY 2009

1. I have now presented my second tranche of evidence to the Commons Select Committee and it has been accepted and published by them.

2. It fully supports my initial evidence and vindicates my concerns about regulation in the Banking industry and from my own experience HBOS in particular.

3. The handling of my evidence is now a matter for this Select Committee aspect of government. However as my previous comments have raised so much public interest and comment I would like to put on record the precise nature of my concerns in simple terms.

4. In my role in HBOS as Head of Group Regulatory Risk I instigated, and was part of, a number of exercises which gave clear insight into culture and behaviours within HBOS. My role was to interpret the findings of these exercises and to advise of their implications in terms of risk and regulatory requirements.

5. Understanding risk at all levels all levels is a key part of ensuring appropriate strategic business decisions and maintaining ethical practice in a way which sustains public confidence and the long term viability of the company.

6. As I undertook these exercises it became clear that there were some serious issues emanating from the developing culture in HBOS. One was the potential for miss-selling.

7. For example, we questioned and reviewed the sale of Corporate Bond Funds. A corporate bond fund is a collective investment scheme which uses investors' money, as its name suggests, to purchase bonds i.e. corporate debt. Depending on the debt purchased it can be higher or lower risk and the capital value of an investment can go up or down depending on a range of factors including the view taken by the market of the risk relating to the bonds held by the fund as well as the direction in which interest rates move.

8. As the yields went down on standard deposit accounts, many customers were switched into CBF and GRR and I were not confident that customers who were switched out of deposit accounts into CBFs would really understand the additional capital risks they were taking on and we wanted to ensure they did. What was clear was that the advisers were strongly targeted to sell CBFs to deposit account customers whose deposits matured and the margin HBOS made on CBFs was very much higher than on deposit accounts. This obviously increased the incentive to sell them. We discovered that a material percentage of clients did not understand the risks.

9. We also began to question the suitability of creditor insurance sales (also known as PPI or Payment Protection Insurance) sold along with personal loans and mortgages. The potential miss-selling here comes in various forms. Because there is such significant profit generated by creditor insurance (say 10% of group wide profits), I witnessed a huge amount of management attention in HBOS GI and in Retail paid to hitting sales targets in this area.

10. This type of sales pressure drove front line staff towards marshalling clients towards taking on personal a loan rather than say a short term overdraft, or use of revolving card facility. It can also potentially drive staff to 'encourage' customers to take out larger loans than they really needed, wanted or should take on because that way the creditor premium is larger as well. Apart from this, creditor premiums were incredibly high and paid up front so that even if a personal loan was repaid half way through its term no premium was refunded. Also it appeared that many customers who bought PPI were never able to claim as they were in an excluded class.

11. These illustrations arise directly from the sales culture.

12. The overall implication of the sales culture being out of balance with risk management and compliance controls is twofold.

    a. The risk to customers is that they are miss-sold/oversold credit of all types - credit cards, personal loans, excessive mortgages, creditor insurance, and investment products such as Corporate Bond Funds which are not necessarily suitable to their needs or affordable.

    b. The risk to colleagues (which is a reference to the bank as a whole) is that for every loan made above the deposit base, more wholesale funds are required with the consequential increased credit and liquidity risks. Ultimately, of course it was the liquidity risk in the wholesale markets that crystallised, but the underlying cause of this was a whole market place in which the sales culture got out of balance with the controls and risk management.

13. I raised my concerns at the most senior level in the company and I was dismissed unfairly by James Crosby who said the decision was "mine and mine alone". Neither, the non executive directors, nor the FSA supported or protected me and the supposedly independent KPMG report will not withstand any fair public scrutiny. I deal with this in detail in my evidence.

14. I believe that what my evidence demonstrates is what I said in my original testimony. In simple terms this crisis was caused not because many bright people did not see it coming, but because there has been a completely inadequate separation and balance of powers between the executive and all those accountable for overseeing their actions and reigning them in. That is internal control functions such as finance, risk compliance and internal audit, non-executive Chairmen and Directors, external auditors, the FSA, shareholders and politicians.

15. For the future I hope that some rigour can be applied to analysing these issues; both by Parliament, appropriate regulatory bodies and academic institutions. It is also proper that the media should retain oversight of what are bound to be long-term exercises. Ultimately I would hope to play a part in this because the FSA and politicians need to involve professionals like myself and others with real practical in depth on the ground experience in the construction of new robust and morally defensible governance frame works.

16. I was pleased to hear yesterday that the FSA is now going to adopt a more rigorous approach to supervising its members.

The 26 of February 2009 was a very long day. I pressed the "send" button on my final email to Caroline Binham at *Bloomberg News* at 5.18pm on that dark, cold late-winter evening. I was exhausted. I sat at my desk with a cup of tea and a cigarette and took a deep intake of breath. Then my business landline phone rang. That was unusual as most people contacted me on my mobile. I let it ring for a while and almost didn't answer: but it might be someone interesting. I picked up the receiver.

"Paul Moore speaking."

"It's Ken Clarke here," the caller said.

"I'm sorry, I don't know anyone called Ken Clarke."

"Ken Clarke, the MP," he replied.

"Oh, THE Ken Clarke?"

"Yes."

"Oh, I rather like you, especially the fact that you drink beer and smoke. In fact, you're one of my favourite politicians, and I don't like many!" I said.

We both laughed.

The Conservative MP went on: "Well, I'd very much like to meet with you and discuss the evidence you have given to the Treasury Select Committee."

Wow, I wasn't expecting that. "Good, because I'd very much like to meet you as well and discuss it."

Ken Clarke was the Shadow Business Secretary and had a very important role indeed in relation to challenging what the Labour government was doing about investigating the causes and implications of the banking crisis.

"Excellent," said Ken.

"But," I said, "I have to say that I am not prepared to meet you unless you read my entire evidence in detail and it's very long. You're a QC [Queen's Counsel] and you should be able to digest that in a couple of hours maximum. The devil is in the detail and you need to read it. I can't get the media to read it because they haven't got that attention span. And I should say that if we do meet, I'll test you on it."

Again we broke into laughter.

"Paul, that's fine. I'm going to Northern Ireland this weekend but perhaps you could speak to my assistant Debbie Sugg and organise a convenient date next week and send her the documents you need me to read."

He gave me her telephone number and asked me to ring her immediately.

We said goodbye and I put the phone down.

I immediately picked it up again and phoned Debbie Sugg. We organised the meeting with Ken for the following Tuesday 3 March at his house in Kennington near to The Oval cricket ground where he loves to go to watch his favourite sport.

I took her email address and agreed to send her the documents immediately. It was 5.42pm when I dispatched the data into the ether.

Good, I thought. We might, now, be getting somewhere. My end-game was to persuade the powers that be that we needed a full-scale independent judicial enquiry into the 2008 banking crisis and, in particular, into what had happened at HBOS. Ken Clarke, a lawyer, was the perfect person to enlist to lead the charge of the opposition. The government would never call for such an enquiry, for obvious reasons.

I tidied my desk, put the lights off, closed the office door and went into the snug. I poured myself a large drink, sat down and let the warm feeling of the alcohol flood through my body. I was relaxed. Things were looking up. With a proper independent enquiry it would be all over within a year and the economy could be rebuilt on a solid foundation of banking propriety. Annie Lennox's song *There Must Be An Angel* sprang to mind.

CHAPTER 12

Meeting The "Big Beast"
"Paul, your evidence demonstrates at least civil wrongdoing and probably criminal wrongdoing"

Kenneth Clarke, Shadow Business Secretary Of State
3 March 2009

Taking morning coffee with the "big beast" didn't scare me at all. Actually, Ken Clarke the MP came across as extremely urbane and charming, far removed from his media moniker.

Sitting with the Tory grandee in the comfort of his front room, I couldn't help but feel that at last someone in a position of authority was prepared to look at the detail and hopefully act on it.

The vastly experienced Conservative politician had served as both Education and Health Secretary in Margaret Thatcher's government in the late Eighties and early Nineties and was Home Secretary and then Chancellor under Prime Minister John Major between 1992 and 1997. Now he was the Shadow Business Secretary and if anyone knew their way around the Houses of Parliament it was Clarke.

I'd travelled by train to London on Monday 2 March for an 11am interview with Will Hutton for Channel 4's *Dispatches*. My meeting with Ken Clarke would take place the following day at his home in Kennington. The Channel 4 filming went well but despite my best efforts the media's interest in the HBOS story had waned and the news agenda moved on – something I found perplexing.

In the present day, after many years of experience dealing with the press, I have come to expect this kind of behaviour. With the world moving apace and many stories to cover, it's extremely difficult to get journalists to focus on the nitty gritty. So I was pinning my hopes on Mr Clarke, as a barrister himself, to delve into the detail.

On the Monday afternoon, after the *Dispatches* interview, I met up with my old friend and KPMG colleague Marcus Sephton. Back in February when everything kicked off in the media, he'd been extremely supportive and had sent me a text which simply said, "Brilliant exposé; brilliant exposure." He knew what KPMG had done was totally unprofessional and, in his role at the firm, had refused to have anything to do with the investigation. It was good to see him and catch up.

Afterwards, I went for a drink with another mate, Louis Jordan, who is now one of the most senior vice-chairmen at accountancy firm Deloitte. We went to a pub near Trafalgar Square, drank too much and reminisced about our days at KPMG. We laughed about the night he took me to Annabel's nightclub in Berkeley Square, London, where we rubbed shoulders with the rich and famous and even bumped into Prince Andrew's older daughter Princess Beatrice. During our boozy reunion,

Louis said that what I needed was an agent like him. I still hope that one day it happens.

I went to my meeting with Mr Clarke on the morning of 3 March filled with hope and anticipation.

His house looked smart from the outside, and Mr Clarke answered his front door to me with a firm handshake before showing me into his unostentatious and somewhat shabby chic home. I'd always looked upon the three-time party leadership contender as a man of the people. Seeing him in the flesh, with his heavy jowls and jolly looks, he reminded me somewhat of my old boss Ellis. There was no doubt about it, though, that Mr Clarke was a big hitter. He was a key member of the "powers that be" and also the elite Bilderberg Group of world political, industry, finance and media leaders. The real question was whether he'd be joining the "powers for me"!

Before we sat down to talk I asked to borrow the loo, and was directed upstairs while Mr Clarke made coffee. When I returned from the bathroom he was seated on a small sofa in his living room with his back to a window which looked out onto the street. I sat in an armchair directly opposite him, with an occasional table between us on which he'd placed our coffees.

I knew he was a director of British American Tobacco and asked him if I could smoke. He agreed, and I rolled a cigarette with my Golden Virginia tobacco. He took out a small cigar. We both lit up, drew on our respective smoking equipment and relaxed into our chairs. After the normal niceties, including me flattering him a little, we got down to business.

I reminded him that when we spoke on the phone I had expected him to read my entire evidence in detail. Furthermore, that I'd promised I would test him on it. He nodded and so I did.

"Ken, what happened on 1 October 2004?" I asked.

"That was the day when you wrote to Mike Ellis telling him that the Board minutes of the meeting you attended did not reflect what you'd said," he said.

"Yes, that's right. Good, it's clear you've read my evidence. Now I want to ask your opinion, as an eminent QC, on the evidence and what it demonstrates."

"Paul, your evidence demonstrates at least civil wrongdoing and probably criminal wrongdoing; breach of regulatory requirements and probably breach of fiduciary duties of the directors."

"You got it in one, Ken," I said, "and I am absolutely confident, as a barrister myself, that if I was entitled to conduct a detailed forensic inquiry into what happened at HBOS, I would find evidence of dozens of criminal offences."

"I'm sure you would," he responded.

I relaxed even more.

I'd got his full attention and pressed on: "So, what we now need is an independent judicial enquiry to get to the bottom of this cesspit of wrongdoing. It's absolutely impossible for the Treasury Select Committee to do the job properly. They neither have the powers nor the competence. A properly constituted independent judicial enquiry can require witnesses to disclose confidential documentation and give oral evidence under oath. The devil is in the detail here, and we need to get deeply into that detail in order to be able to understand what happened, who did what, who didn't do what, and why." Mr Clarke was nodding his head gently in agreement.

I took a sip of coffee and continued: "We will only be able to rebuild the appropriate policy response once we know the detail. In addition, people need to be held to account for their wrongdoing and a lot of very senior people have engaged in very serious wrongdoing. They made a great deal of personal wealth in the process. It is a matter of extreme public interest to get to the bottom of all this and, if necessary, put some people in prison.

"It would be completely wrong for the FSA to conduct such an investigation because they are conflicted. They are part of the problem, and may well have engaged in wrongdoing themselves, either deliberately or through incompetence."

"I agree," Mr Clarke said.

I felt myself slumping back into my chair. It was comfortable and soft. All the tension that had built up inside me over so many years just seemed to disappear, there and then in the MP's sitting room. And that was the end of the business conversation for the day. For the rest of my visit, we exchanged further pleasantries and I talked for a while about the time I'd met with the General Counsel of British American Tobacco, when it owned Allied Dunbar.

When the meeting came to an end Mr Clarke walked with me onto the pavement outside his home. Just as I was about to leave him, I said: "Would you like me to come and meet David Cameron and George Osborne because I obviously know all the evidence back to front, which proves that what I said is true?"

"No, Paul, that's not necessary. The evidence you've already given me is absolutely clear."

"So, I'll be hearing from you soon?"

"Yes," said Mr Clarke.

We shook hands again and I walked away calmly and slowly with a great sense of peace overwhelming me. "A good job, well done", I thought. I had achieved my objective.

In our meeting he promised he would sort things out for me. Not long after, he was appointed Justice Secretary, when the Conservative party won the General Election in May 2010.

On 8 March 2009 I sent my final evidence to the Treasury Select Committee calling, as agreed with Mr Clarke, for an independent judicial enquiry, not just into HBOS but into the whole banking crisis.

This is what it said:

MEMORANDUM OF FURTHER ADDITIONAL EVIDENCE TO THE TREASURY SELECT COMMITTEE RELATING TO THE BANKING CRISIS

PREPARED BY PAUL MOORE – EX HEAD OF GROUP REGULATORY RISK, HBOS PLC

8TH MARCH 2009

Introduction and summary

1. *I provided my initial evidence to the Treasury Select Committee on Friday 6th February 2009. I also offered them more detailed evidence on 25th February 2009.*

2. *This further additional evidence is provided following correspondence with the Clerk of the Committee, to deal with outstanding points that have not been covered in my earlier evidence.*

3. *In particular, this evidence deals in more detail with the denials of my allegations by Gordon Brown, the FSA, Sir James Crosby, Lord Dennis Stevenson and Andy Hornby. It also deals in some detail with my response to the FSA's detailed statement dated 11th February.*

Summary of my further additional evidence

4. *In summary, I now say as follows:-*

a. *The relevant parties stated that my allegations were fully and properly investigated and claimed that they would provide further evidence, including the "so called independent" KPMG report which would prove that my allegations held no merit.*

b. *The Prime Minister stated in the House of Commons:-*

"However, it is right that when serious allegations are made, they are properly investigated. No doubt the Treasury Select Committee will want to look at them and no doubt the Conservative Party will want to wait to see how that investigation takes place."

c. *Despite the vocal and high profile denials of the parties, in fact, no further evidence other than the KPMG report has been received by the Committee.*

d. *I stated on numerous occasions, after the denials of my allegations that I had detailed additional evidence which would corroborate all my allegations and which would prove that the KPMG report would not withstand truly independent public scrutiny.*

e. *I have now provided a detailed resume of additional evidence, which proves overwhelmingly the veracity of my original allegations, and deals conclusively with the KPMG report. No-one now believes that the report was independent and my additional evidence demonstrates that it cannot be relied on in any way.*

f. *Following the provision of my additional evidence, over a full week and half ago, no additional evidence has been provided by any of the parties to rebut what I have said.*

g. *The Treasury Select Committee should now accept my allegations and pay due regard to them in writing its report.*

h. *The Treasury Select Committee should propose that the recommendations I made for policy changes (demonstrated by the allegations I made) should be considered by the appropriate fora including the FSA.*

i. *Finally that, as my evidence demonstrates potential wrongdoing by the parties (see 18 below), the Treasury*

Select Committee should recommend in its report that such matters should be dealt with in the appropriate tribunals and by the appropriate authorities.

Further additional evidence

5. *Lord Dennis Stevenson and Andy Hornby both denied my allegations in their interviews with the TSC and relied on the "KPMG Report".*

6. *When Sir James Crosby resigned as the Deputy Chairman of the FSA, Gordon Brown told Parliament in Prime Ministers Questions, on 11th Feb 09: "The allegations that were brought before the Treasury Select Committee were investigated by the independent KPMG in 2005. The allegations made by Mr Moore were found not to be substantiated. That was an independent review that was done by KPMG and reported to the Financial Services Authority.* ***However, it is right that when serious allegations are made, they are properly investigated. No doubt the Treasury Select Committee will want to look at them and no doubt the Conservative Party will want to wait to see how that investigation takes place.****"*

7. *Gordon Brown also said: "It is right that we investigate serious allegations that are made about the banking system. These are serious but contested allegations. In relation to Sir James Crosby, these are allegations that he will wish to defend so it is right that he has stepped down as vice chairman of the Financial Services Authority."*

8. *The FSA issued a long statement on 11th February which included the following:- "Having examined carefully the files relating to this issue, the FSA can confirm that specific allegations made by Paul Moore in December 2004, regarding the regulatory risk function at HBOS were fully investigated by KPMG and the FSA, which concluded that the changes made by HBOS were appropriate......In conclusion, the FSA confirms that the allegations made by Mr Moore were taken seriously, and were properly and professionally investigated."*

9. *I wish to tell the Committee that, apart from the obvious general point that I disagree with their conclusions, there are a number of specific parts of the FSA statement with which I am at odds.*

a. *In particular I would say that, although the FSA responded that the specific allegations made by me were "properly and professionally investigated" and "that the changes made by HBOS were appropriate", the FSA themselves also say in the same statement that in June 2006 "there were still control issues" [at HBOS] and "the growth strategy of the group posed risks to the whole group and that these risks must be managed and mitigated".*

So in these circumstances, how can they genuinely say that the changes made were appropriate?

Also, when Lord Turner gave evidence to the Select Committee he said that Jo Dawson would not now have been approved by the FSA. Since there has been no change to the relevant rules relating to the approval of approved persons, Lord Turner's evidence amounts to an admission that the changes made by HBOS in 2004-5 were not appropriate.

I also disagree with what the FSA said, at the Committee, which is that actions taken then were appropriate under the "philosophy" that applied then. The rules were the same.

b. *In their statement, the FSA say:-*

"The FSA conducted a full risk assessment of HBOS (known as an ARROW assessment) ***in late 2002*** *which identified a need to strengthen the control infrastructure within the group".*

In fact, the Arrow assessment was conducted in 2003 and it did not cover the whole of HBOS. It covered all divisions apart from the Strategy and International division.

c. *In their statement, the FSA also say:-*

"The FSA then conducted a further full risk assessment of the HBOS group to cover all of the group's business, formally recording its assessment ***in December 2004****. The assessment was that the risk profile of the group had improved, and that the group had made good progress in addressing the risks highlighted* ***in February 2004****, but that the group risk functions still needed to enhance their ability to influence the business, which we saw as a key challenge."*

They did not carry out a further full risk assessment in December 2004, and the risks were not highlighted in February 2004 but in December 2003.

d. *These simple errors relating to dates demonstrate a lack of care and attention at the FSA which is telling in itself.*

e. *In their statement, the FSA say:-*

"Following that appointment, the then head of group regulatory risk, Paul Moore, was informed on 8 November that he would leave as part of this restructuring; he subsequently approached FSA to express concerns about HBOS and in particular about the suitability of the new appointee as the group risk director."

This is not fully accurate. I approached the FSA with a long and detailed list of concerns including the allegation that I was dismissed by James Crosby for raising many issues of actual or potential breach of the FSA requirements (i.e. that I had a whistle blowing claim). In fact that was the post serious allegation of all. The issue of the new appointee was only one of the many issues raised. It was certainly not the most serious as the statement suggests. All the allegations were set out in a detailed Outline Case demanding a full and independent investigation. A full copy of this Outline case can be provided if required.

f. *In their statement, the FSA state:-*

"The FSA satisfied itself about the skill and

independence of the individuals selected to conduct the report for KPMG and about the scope of the report."

The investigation did not cover all the areas that should have been covered, and we complained about this at the time to HBOS. We also complained at the time about the conduct of the investigation. It is not clear that HBOS passed these criticisms on to the FSA as they should have. I have detailed documentary evidence of each of these complaints and I have copied one letter in my earlier evidence.

Secondly, on the so-called independence of the KPMG report, it is worth repeating that my solicitor and counsel have both written to the Select Committee and stated publicly that the report could not have been regarded as independent, since KPMG were the auditors of HBOS. It follows that the FSA should not have regarded it as independent. In fact I am not sure anyone now really accepts that the report was independent.

g. *In their statement, the FSA say:-*

*"The FSA approved that individual only when it had received those results, which indicated that KPMG '**did not believe** that the evidence reviewed **suggested** that the candidate was not fit and proper', that 'the process for the identification and assessment of candidates for the GRD position **appeared appropriate**', and that 'the structure and reporting lines of Group Regulatory Risk are appropriate'*

Words such as "did not believe...suggested" and "... appeared appropriate" are hardly the most unequivocal.

In any event, we sent the strongest possible rebuttal of all the points made in the KPMG report to HBOS, within a short period of time of receiving the report. The Committee has seen a copy of this letter.

An important question is whether HBOS sent this rebuttal letter to the FSA. Under the FSA Principles for Business they were required to do so. Even if they did not, why did the FSA not call me back to ask me about my view of the report? There is no doubt that they should have done so and not simply accepted the report "as read". This simply suggests that they wanted to close the file without properly completing the work of investigating all the serious allegations that were made.

Perhaps this was convenient as James Crosby was a non-executive director of the FSA at the time?

h. *In their statement, the FSA say:-*

The FSA also followed up Mr Moore's concerns by meeting him independently, and separately discussed the KPMG report directly with KPMG

This suggests that I met the FSA after the KPMG report. This is not true. They should have done so. In fact, I only met them before the report was commissioned from KPMG in December 2004. They should have called me in to find out my response to the report.

10. Sir James Crosby's resignation statement said:-

"Towards the end of my time as CEO of HBOS, as part of a wider restructuring of group functions, the Risk Function was elevated to report direct to the CEO... As part of this I asked one of our risk managers, Paul Moore, to leave HBOS....At the time he made a series of allegations....These were independently and extensively investigated on behalf of the Board, the results of which they shared with the FSA. That investigation concluded that Mr Moore's allegations had no merit....Last autumn (on a BBC programme) and again yesterday (Tuesday) at the Treasury Select Committee he repeated substantially the same allegations. HBOS has reiterated its view that his allegations have no merit.....I am totally confident that there is no substance to any of the allegations."

11. Subsequently, Sir James Crosby said in a newspaper interview that he would bring forward detailed evidence to rebut my allegations. I believe he also told you this.

12. I issued a press release on the 11th February in which I said as follows:

"I have a significant body of detailed additional evidence, which will corroborate what I said. I am confident that the "independent report" to which Sir James has referred will not bear up to any proper independent scrutiny. I described that report as "supposedly" independent in my evidence

to the committee and I strongly stand behind that statement. No doubt I shall be given the opportunity, at an appropriate time, to disclose my evidence and demonstrate what I am saying is true.

13. *Had all relevant parties not denied my allegations, I believe we could all have moved on to deal solely with the question of future policy construction. However, this has not happened and the Prime Minister himself has said that such serious allegations need to be investigated.*

14. *As you know, I have now provided my detailed resume of additional evidence to the Committee but Sir James Crosby, Lord Stevenson, Andy Hornby and the FSA have not provided any additional evidence other than the KPMG report which, as you know, I had already offered to send to the Committee before the week ending 13th February.*

15. *My additional evidence proves my allegations unequivocally and that the KPMG report bears no weight. It was effectively a "whitewash".*

16. *I assume that as no further evidence to rebut my allegations has been received that this means that my allegations are now accepted and the Select Committee will be able to conclude that this is the case.*

17. *I believe the public interest demands this conclusion, as well as my reputation. I have all the underlying documents, which support the detailed resume of additional evidence if these are required. I have referred to these in my detailed resume.*

18. *I believe that my allegations raise important questions of potential wrong-doing / incompetence by the relevant parties which should be followed up.*

    They raise questions as to the actions and omissions of the FSA. It should be noted that the Principles and rules which applied then are the same as now, and that it is not appropriate to say that everything done then was permitted because the "philosophy was different".

    My allegations also raise questions of potential breach of company law fiduciary duties of the relevant HBOS directors, as well as their potential breach of the FSA's Principles for Approved Persons. [In particular principles one and two which require an approved person to act with integrity in carrying out their controlled function as well as with due skill, care and diligence.]

19. *My allegations also support the important recommendations for policy changes, as set out in my first memorandum of evidence, which should be accepted by the Committee for further detailed consideration. My advisers and I are prepared to be involved in any discussions to this end. We have more detailed points which we believe would add value to further discussions.*

20. *If the Select Committee feels it is impossible under its terms of reference to achieve what Gordon Brown said in the House of Commons it may that it should recommend an investigation in another appropriate tribunal e.g. a judicial enquiry. If it does so, as I have*

already recommended in my evidence, I would suggest a broad-ranging investigation into the banks as a whole, not just HBOS.

I expected to hear from Ken Clarke and the Conservative Party a loud and public demand for the independent judicial enquiry that we had agreed upon. Nothing happened. I followed up Mr Clarke numerous times with no response. I finally got a response from him on 14 May:

"Dear Paul,

I am sorry – that I have not been getting back to you since you have been sending me e-mails and messages in recent weeks. Everything you have provided me with since we met has shown the enormity of the problems at HBOS and the failure of the regulators to respond properly to your complaints.

The difficulty is that I have no control over the Treasury Select Committee and you have been unable to persuade them to take further evidence or to go further into their inquiries into the behaviour of Crosby and others. This must be causing you enormous frustration, but they give the impression of taking the view that this is now a private dispute and that they have taken it as far as they are justified in doing in the public interest. The Committee have also ceased to take a close interest in events at HBOS before the crash and things have moved on.

I do of course appreciate that events have not moved on as far as you are concerned and that you are understandably left with a deep sense of pressing grievance.

Our conversation and your documents were of great use to me in giving me an insight into the worst features of banking salesmanship and lack of compliance at the height of the banking boom. If an occasion occurs in which I can take it further or draw on your expertise further, I will of course do so. At the moment, however, I do not think that I can.

Yours sincerely,

Kenneth Clarke

The Rt. Hon. Kenneth Clarke, QC, MP"

Disingenuity in a nutshell. Mr Clarke was the Shadow Business Secretary. Dealing with the banking crisis and the HBOS affair was slap, bang, wallop in the bull's-eye of his accountability. But, of course, the Conservative Party received well over 50% of its political funding from the banking and financial services sector. It wasn't in its interests to make a big hoo-ha that could annoy its rich donor friends.

Between May 2010 and September 2012, Ken Clarke (whose wife Gillian sadly passed away in July 2015 aged 74) served under David Cameron as Lord Chancellor and Justice Secretary. During this time while he was in the government, I wrote to him again several times reminding him of his responsibilities for the administration of justice. I had to follow him up for a response. Here is my final request for a response and a meeting on 20 April 2011:

"I re-copy below what I wrote some time ago now. If I do not hear anything from you relating to a meeting with

Ken within a few days, I will be obliged to consider other avenues without reverting to Ken. Please confirm that you have told him this. I do think it is simply wrong that, in relation to such an important matter of justice, the Justice Minister does not have the courtesy to respond in a fair and reasonable timeframe to me, especially after the valuable help and time I gave him in 2009. As we approach Easter, I just wanted to let you know that I am available to discuss this matter (subject only to my regular visits to Church!). Please phone my landline below and, if I am not there, leave a couple of times when you will ring and I will do what I can to be at home at that time.

<u>Email dated 9 April following up my email of 27 March</u>

I am truly disappointed and surprised that I have had no response whatsoever to my email below either from you or Ken.

I think that after Ken openly admitted to me that the evidence I gave to the Treasury Select Committee demonstrated at least civil wrong-doing from a regulatory perspective that he did nothing about it at the time. It seems even worse now that he is the Justice Minister. It was never a private dispute between James Crosby and me; it was a set of allegations that demonstrated breach of The Principles for Business under the FSA regime or even breach of fiduciary duties under S172 of The Companies Act 2006.

<u>I want to meet with Ken to discuss this</u>*. If this cannot be arranged then I may need to resort to alternative methods to achieve truth and justice."*

He did nothing.

Why?

Here is his explanation.

/05 2011 11:07 FAX 002/002

From: The Rt. Hon. Kenneth Clarke, QC, MP

HOUSE OF COMMONS

LONDON SW1A 0AA

19th April, 2011

Dear Mr. Moore,

Thank you very much for you further emails. I am afraid that I do receive hundred of emails each week and we were simply not able to respond to yours as quickly as you would have wished. I also do not think that a further meeting between us would serve very much purpose at the moment, as I am now Lord Chancellor and these matters really no longer come remotely within my responsibilities.

I have read your letter to Andrew Tyrie and I do remember being very impressed by what you told me at our meeting. You were clearly alleging complete failure to give the proper priority to regulatory and risk control requirements at HBOS when you were there. I seem to recall however that at the time, I indicated that I had no powers as a Member of Parliament and Shadow Business Secretary to produce any further remedy. I await the outcome of the Treasury Select Committee's enquiries and the claim by Sir John Crosby and the FSA that they would continue to contest your allegation.

You are obviously once more in touch with the Treasury Select Committee and really this is a matter that falls completely within their remit. I know Andrew Tyrie well and I will try to take the opportunity to discuss it with him after the Recess, but I really do not think that I can get involved publicly in this matter. The new Government has obviously already addressed regulatory changes for the future in the light of experiences at HBOS and other banks.

I am sorry that I cannot be more helpful.

Yours sincerely,

Mr. Paul Moore,

Just over a year after sending me this missive, Britain was rocked by a double whammy of banking scandals: serious failings by banks in the sale of financial products to small businesses and the Libor rate-rigging affair at Barclays.

Suddenly it seemed Justice Secretary Ken Clarke was on the warpath. Speaking about the two outrages, on BBC Radio 4's *Today* programme in June 2012, he insisted that bankers who had committed crimes must be prosecuted.

Mr Clarke said:

> *"We are very bad at prosecuting financial crime in this country. I suspect financial crime is easier to get away with in this country than practically any other sort of crime. This is still being investigated, no doubt, but once these investigations are complete, if they have committed criminal offences they should be brought to trial."*

And what did Clarke and the Government do this time?

Nowt!

EPILOGUE

Democracy, capitalism and freedom in crisis; where shall we go from here?

Part I

It is 20 September 2015. I am sitting here looking out of my little office window in our lovely old (1790) Keeper's Cottage in North Yorkshire. It is a beautiful bright early autumn day with the leaves starting to turn golden. I feel calm and peaceful. All the pain and suffering and tribulation of the past 10 years has finally "thawed, melted and resolved itself into a timeless dew". What once seemed to be a complete and utter disaster for my family and me has literally transformed itself into Amazing Grace. My wife Maureen was right. It was all part of God's plan for my life. Now I understand. As Rick Warren, the author of one of the world's bestselling books, *The Purpose Driven Life*, wrote, "*We get transformed by trouble*".

Robert Toone, my great friend and spiritual adviser on my journey in faith, was also right when, at my very lowest point, he said to me, "Just remember what Blessed Mother Teresa said, 'Well, if I lose my reputation, that's at least one less thing to worry about.'"

However the story has not yet ended and there is much to tell about what happened after my meeting with Conservative MP Ken Clarke on 3 March 2009. Yes, there is still more to do to bring about Truth and Justice but it needs to be done with a great deal of Love. If it is, it will set us all free, in the end. Greed enslaves us. It looks like freedom but it isn't. It's slavery.

The plain fact of the matter is that the vast majority of people working in banking and financial services (and anywhere for that matter) are good and honest people trying to do a good job. The trouble is that we have all been caught up in a "system" that has encouraged us to do things that we know are not right.

This "system" is one in which profit, power and celebrity take precedence over principles and people.

When these powerful human temptations are the only measuring sticks in our lives, we become enslaved to pride, greed, envy, vanity and all the other "deadly sins" that may look like happiness but which, in the end, lead to the destruction of our real freedom.

Desire is suffering say the Buddhist masters, and they are right. St Paul, maybe the greatest human ideologist in the history of mankind, wrote in his first letter to Timothy:

> *"Those who want to be rich are falling into temptation and into a trap and into many foolish and harmful desires, which plunge them into ruin and destruction. For the love of money is the root of all evils, and some people in their desire for it have strayed from the faith and pierced*

themselves with many pains. But, you man of God, avoid all this. Instead, pursue righteousness, devotion, faith, love, patience and gentleness."

After having watched our now Prime Minister David Cameron deliver a speech on the banking crisis at Thomson Reuters in December 2008, I went on to write to the Treasury Select Committee a couple of months later. It was only thanks to the matter being raised by the then committee member Andrew Tyrie MP, that my evidence was ever revealed and that I came to be known as the "HBOS Whistleblower" in the subsequent media storm. It has now been more than six-and-a-half years since my meeting with Ken Clarke.

During that period Mr Clarke did briefly break his silence on the issue of bankers and their irresponsible actions, when as the Justice Secretary he was interviewed on BBC Radio 4's *Today* programme. Referring to his comments, *The Mail Online* reported on 30 June 2012:

"Asked about the two major scandals that have rocked the City this week, Mr Clarke acknowledged that financial crime was 'easier to get away with' than virtually any other misdemeanours, but he said there should be criminal prosecutions where crimes have been committed. 'We are very bad at prosecuting financial crime in this country. I suspect financial crime is easier to get away with in this country than practically any other sort of crime. This is still being investigated, no doubt but once these investigations are complete, if they have committed criminal offences they should be brought to trial'."

Sadly, and partly because of his inaction, we still have not achieved final Truth and Justice (let alone repentance and a just making of amends), for the obvious wrongdoing that led to the banking crisis and the misery it caused to billions of people around the world.

It's been a long march. For our team of steadfast volunteers on this journey and me, it's been a marathon and we've still got the last three miles to run. The story goes on.

The final report into the HBOS disaster and its protagonists, has yet to be made public after nearly four years of detailed investigation by the Prudential Regulation Authority (PRA) on behalf of the Financial Conduct Authority (FCA). I have been giving detailed evidence to this investigation since autumn 2011 and have provided the inquiry team with access to unedited versions of key chapters of this book and additional material.

As has now become commonplace, the report has been inappropriately delayed by those being criticised as they scrabble around abusing the "Maxwellisation Process" to try to avoid the truth which they must know is inevitable. This is exactly the same reason why the Chilcot report into Britain's role in the Iraq war is also being held up. Publish and be damned, we say. The "defendants" have been given easily enough opportunity during the course of the investigation to present their defences and mitigations. Any further delay to either report is wrong and against the public interest.

Having said that, and with a genuine desire for reconciliation with all those who have harmed my family and me and so many others, my advice to the key executives and non-executives at HBOS who have done wrong is simple. Do what former Conservative MP Jonathan Aitken did after his well-publicised fall from grace for serious perjury. Deeply examine your consciences, have a confessional moment, say sorry to everyone whom you have harmed and spend the rest of your days making amends for your wrongdoing. Freedom for you and your families and friends from the horrors through which you are going can only be based on the following idea: "Forgiveness races towards repentance at Godspeed". Set yourselves free by facing up to the truth. The truth will always set you free… But it isn't free. I know that. Jonathan Aitken has proceeded with grace to rebuild his reputation as a person who, having made a mistake, has been able to rise from the ashes.

Andrew Tyrie MP has been a stalwart in standing up for Truth and Justice in relation to the banking crisis and other wrongdoing in the financial sector. He has been the Chairman of the Treasury Select Committee (TSC) since 2010 and from 2012 has also chaired the Parliamentary Commission on Banking Standards (PCBS) which was set up after the Barclays Libor scandal in the summer of that year. His extremely high competence and integrity shines through a melee of the exact opposite. He should be applauded and rewarded for the extraordinary work he has done. Thank you,

Andrew. Well done.

Andrew and a few others continue to make good progress on many fronts in the work that he has led both in the TSC and the PCBS. In particular, investigation by the PCBS into HBOS (as an example of the culture and standards in banks) has proved that it does not need to take years to get things done. In fact, the PCBS has shown that it is possible to conduct a detailed inquiry into a complex set of facts and, by applying the right people to the job, can get to the bottom of things quickly. That investigation (about which I was the very first witness to give oral evidence on 30 October 2012) including the writing of its report, took less than seven months from start to finish. The report published on 5 April 2013 into HBOS was called "'An accident waiting to happen': The failure of HBOS". It was and is, without doubt, the best report of its kind that I have ever read in my professional career spanning more than 30 years. The news release which accompanied the report wrote as follows (www.crashbankwallop.co.uk/library/E-1):

NEWS RELEASE

Under strict embargo until 00.01, Friday 5 April, 2013

Failure of HBOS linked to "colossal failure of senior management and the Board", says Banking Commission Report

The Parliamentary Commission on Banking Standards has today published its Fourth Report - *'An accident waiting to happen': The failure of HBOS.*

Epilogue

Commenting on the publication of its Fourth Report, the Chairman of the Parliamentary Commission on Banking Standards, Andrew Tyrie MP, said:

"The HBOS story is one of catastrophic failures of management, governance and regulatory oversight.

"The sums would never have added up: the Commission has estimated that, taken together, the losses incurred by the Corporate, International and Treasury divisions would have led to insolvency, regardless of funding and liquidity problems, had HBOS not been bailed out by both Lloyds and the taxpayer.

"The Commission concluded that primary responsibility for these failures should lie with the former Chairman of HBOS, Lord Stevenson, and its former Chief Executives, Sir James Crosby and Andy Hornby.

"Only Peter Cummings has faced regulatory sanction for HBOS' failures. The Commission was surprised by this.

"It is unsatisfactory that the FSA appears to have taken no steps to establish whether the former leaders of HBOS are fit and proper persons to hold the Approved Persons status elsewhere in the UK financial sector. The Commission has therefore asked the regulator to consider whether these individuals should be barred from undertaking any future role in the sector.

"For the future, more needs to be done. Those responsible for bank failures should be held more directly accountable for their actions and face sanction accordingly. The Commission will return to this issue in its Final Report.

"The regulators also have a lot of explaining to do when it comes to their role earlier in the HBOS debacle. From 2004 up until the latter part of 2007, the FSA was 'not so much the dog that didn't bark as the dog barking up the wrong tree'.

"The FSA responded favourably to a Treasury Committee request for a comprehensive report, similar to that prepared on RBS, not just into the failure of HBOS but also into the FSA's own conduct. The Treasury Committee has appointed specialist advisers whose job will be to ensure that this work is done thoroughly."

The lead member of the Banking Commission's Panel on HBOS, Lord Turnbull, added:

"As a result of our work on the failure of HBOS, light has been cast on an issue that had previously received very little public scrutiny.

"The evidence we have gathered is of singular importance to the Commission's consideration of banking standards and culture. It will also help the new regulators as they conduct their own investigation into HBOS

"In 2001, two well established organisations were brought together with a combined market capitalisation of around £30 billion. Just seven years later all that value had been destroyed.

"This is a story of a retail and commercial bank, rather than an investment bank, brought down by ill-judged lending, poor risk control and inadequate liquidity. Its strategy was flawed from the start.

"In evidence to the Commission, its leaders consistently refused to acknowledge the extent to which HBOS contributed to its own demise, preferring to present it as a victim of circumstances.

"There are lessons too for the regulators, who briefly identified the key shortcomings – poor credit control and excessive reliance on external funding – but who subsequently shifted their focus to the processes of risk management and large scale models rather than on asset quality and liquidity."

On the day of the publication of this news release and the "Accident waiting to happen" report, I conducted numerous media interviews with all major broadcasters; Sky News, BBC News, ITV, Channel 4 News, Channel 5 News, CNN and CNBC. I was also quoted in numerous print media publications and did several radio interviews as well.

On 13 April 2013, Sir James Crosby (as he then was) on the day that former British Prime Minister Margaret Thatcher died, attempted to bury the news, with her, that he was giving up his Knighthood and 30% of his £580,000 per annum pension. It was on that evening that I sat next to Jeremy Paxman, reading his autocue before he spoke, when he opened BBC *Newsnight* as follows:

> *"Well, it's certainly a contrast to the not unfamiliar spectacle of people discovering that by making themselves filthy rich a grateful nation will delightedly offer them in the express lift to the upper floors of the class system or a key to the executive washroom of the constitution that is the House of Lords.....Sir James Crosby, the prominent incompetent, who wrecked the HBOS bank wants to give up his Knighthood and a bit of his near £600,000 a year pension...but only a bit...It might save him some of the embarrassment that surrounded his fellow cowboy Fred Goodwin who wrecked another perfectly good bank. ... But is it enough though?"*

This was Paxman at his English sardonic best. You can only imagine how that felt from a personal perspective. I must admit to having had a moment when my human temptation to revenge got the better of me but I held back because Truth without Love is cruelty.

It was only yesterday that I wrote again to Andrew Tyrie about the final HBOS report by the PRA, attaching a copy of a press release I had issued two days after Crosby gave up his Knighthood, which said this:

PRESS RELEASE
(Embargoed to 12.00 hours Thursday march 15)
HBOS whistleblower calls for GORDON BROWN to be questioned under oath

Speaking at the Centre for Investigative Journalism's Whistleblowing Conference at London's City University on Thursday March 15 at 12 noon, Paul Moore HBOS's former Group Head of Regulatory Risk called for a Public Open Inquiry into the global banking crash, with the powers to subpoena witnesses, including senior politicians, and to question them under oath.

He said: 'The banking crash was more than a financial disaster. Following public apologies by both President Clinton and Gordon Brown, the leaders of the two nations at the epicentre of the crash, we now know that it arose from the virtual hijacking by bankers of the political and regulatory process. As Jesse Norman MP put it "Lobbying is a canker on the body politic". And it means we have never got to the bottom of what happened, who did what, held people to account and reformed the banking sector properly.

Brown apology:

In a keynote speech to the Institute for New Economic Thinking at the Bretton Woods conference in New

Hampshire on Saturday April 9 2011 Mr. Brown said that he had come under "relentless pressure" from banks not to over-regulate. The previous April he had said in a television interview that "we should have been regulating them more".

Clinton Apology:

President Clinton said in an ABC television interview he said, 'I think if I had tried to regulate the Republicans would have stopped it. But I wish I should have been caught trying. That was a mistake I made.'

Welcoming the FSA's recently announced formal enforcement action and public censure of HBOS, Mr. Moore, said:

"This action and report by the FSA is long overdue. It vindicates the clear warnings I gave to the Board of HBOS, under the Chairmanship of Lord Stevenson of Coddenham, as long ago as 2004. Had the board heeded those warnings the bank could have been saved but, driven by their own greed and pride, the board chose to ignore them and dismiss me.

'It was James Crosby, a friend and close confidant of Gordon Brown, who fired me and then went on to be appointed by Gordon Brown as the Deputy Chairman of the FSA even though the FSA knew he was running a highly risky bank. He, more than anyone else, was responsible for attempting to sweep my warnings under the carpet and when I gave my evidence to the Treasury Select Committee he was forced to resign from the FSA. He has not commented on the matter since.

'We now know that the FSA was hamstrung by conflicting objectives and by the presence on its board

of conflicted people, like Sir James Crosby. We must now use the FSA's report into HBOS as a lens through which to peer into the detailed inner machinations of the banking elite that not only forced their way into the very organisations that were supposed to be regulating them but also infected and affected Government and regulatory policy itself.

That is why it is vital that the former Prime Minister Gordon Brown and other politicians and regulators must be called to describe in full, the pressures they came under at the highest level.

In the process of a proper public enquiry the full scale of the wrongdoing at HBOS (including the clear inference of non-disclosures on the Rights Issue and the Lloyds Acquisition) will be properly exposed to the bright light of day and those responsible finally held to account. It is essential, in this and every respect, that the enquiry is held in public to inhibit the "behind closed doors" fixing that has become such a destructively systemic feature of British political life.

For example, there are few people in this country who have held more of the reins of power than Lord Stevenson of Coddenham, the former Chairman of HBOS. He is a personal friend of both Tony Blair and Gordon Brown. Such people are able to whisper in the ears of our leaders but the public nature of an enquiry would go a long way towards neutralising the secret powers of such people.

Lord Stevenson has been Chairman of Pearson, publishers of the hugely influential Financial Times and chairman of the equally powerful Economist magazine. He has been at the centre of establishment life as Chairman of the Trustees of the Tate Gallery and the Aldeburgh Music Festival. He has been 'kingmaker' as Chairman of the House of Lords Appointments Commission among many some 20 other influential appointments.

Protection for whistleblowers:

The effectiveness of such an Inquiry would be massively increased by proper protection for whistleblowers. I know from a lifetime either in or associated with the banking industry that most people who work in banking are good and decent people. They are angry that the industry they serve has been brought into disrepute by their bonus driven leaders. These people know exactly what went on and are burning to lift the lid on practices that have disgusted them for many years but their duties to their families prohibit them from doing so. As I know to my cost, the penalties for taking a stand are dire; so, to encourage people to come forward, we need much better protection for whistleblowers.

We should all also understand that the banking collapse was human as well as a financial disaster. According to the UN, the global banking crisis drove more than 100m people into poverty worldwide. Mortality and morbidity statistics relating to the effect of poverty indicate that it is likely that more than 10m people died as a result.

Note to Editors:

I am travelling in the USA but can be contacted by email [provided]. I shall be speaking at the Centre for Investigative Journalism's Whistleblowing Conference at City University from 11.00 until 1.00 on Wednesday March 15th.

So, we still await the final chapter of this long and arduous journey; this long march to Truth, Justice and Freedom. It won't be long, I hope, that the final report into HBOS will, after more than four years, be published and opened to scrutiny by the media and the general public who have paid the price in numerous ways for the HBOS disaster.

In my email, yesterday, to Tyrie I also wrote as follows:

> *"It is absolutely wrong, as a matter of extreme public interest, that this crucial report should be delayed any further. It is four years since I gave my initial evidence to this review to Grant Thornton [accountancy firm]. Moreover, two days ago it was seven years to the day when Robert Peston announced the news that HBOS was to be taken over by Lloyds, a deal which was approved by Gordon Brown and which has led to reduced competition and nearly 40,000 people losing their jobs... By a banking group which has now paid well over £12 billion (partly taxpayers money) for PPI compensation at the same time as paying its CEO £11 million of this last year and it's Chief Risk Officer over £5 million!*
>
> *This report into HBOS **must** be published within the next month or two.*
>
> *Frankly, it is totally wrong that I, personally, have had to spend nearly all of the last period of my and my family's life acting as an unpaid officer of the rule of law having been dismissed unfairly by HBOS, covered up by KPMG, unsupported by the FSA and then treated like toxic waste by the industry in which I had great expertise because I was a whistleblower, leading to mental health problems not only for myself but my family too.*

Above and beyond this, when one of the most senior and experienced politicians in the United Kingdom at first tells you that your evidence demonstrates at least civil wrongdoing and probably criminal wrongdoing and, then, proceeds to do absolutely nothing about the matter, it calls into question whether the rule of law does, in fact, apply in the United Kingdom which is the oldest Parliamentary democracy in the world and looked up to by the Commonwealth and most other countries to act as an example to the rest of the world."

Earlier in the email, I wrote: "In my view, the principle that should be adopted here, subject to some final tidying up... should be, 'publish and be damned'."

Let's wait and see what happens.

The rest of the story of how we got from the Ken Clarke meeting to today will be told in the sequel to this book. There's a great deal still to tell and some of it is amazing.

Part II

I want to end this book by writing about the big picture; where this world of ours and humanity finds itself, how it got there and what we can do about it.

It seems to me and almost everybody I meet, that mankind has got into a right old muddle and that we need to do something about it.

Our democracy, our capitalism and, even our freedom in the developed world is in crisis.

So far as the developing world is concerned, the ideas

of democracy and capitalism are just a pipe dream. In many of these places, water, shelter, food, basic medical care and the smallest modicum of personal security are almost non-existent. So, the idea of freedom might as well be as far away from these countries as the Americans are from landing a man on Mars.

The most obvious physical signposts of the problems the world faces are being planted in our countries, at the border crossings, this very moment. The war refugees and the economic migrants are walking, running, boating, swimming and stowing themselves away even in freezer containers (cum morgues), in the belief and hope that they will find a new life worth living.

Their risk appetites are so high that they are prepared to put their lives and those of little children at risk day in day out and night in night out. So far, we have only seen the gentle ripples before the tsunami, but when it hits shore no fence, no border control, no security guard, no banning from trains, no Nigel Farage, no UKIP, no nothing will stop the deluge. We will be overrun by humanity fleeing from places and situations which make it safer to put their lives on the line than to stay where they are.

It's all very, very frightening and the right-wing politicians appeal to that fear to turn people from being good and kind to being bigots at best and downright racists and armed gatekeepers at worst. We become the Adolf Hitler's of the modern world. But you can't blame ordinary people for this fear. It's only natural. They blame the migrants for the problems in their own countries.

Yet here's the rub: the Truth is that it's actually our fault that they put their lives at risk to come to our countries. When I say "our", I mean the political and economic leadership of this world because it is they who have treated the developing countries as places to be exploited by the "Corporatocracy" for the financial benefit of their rich Western shareholders.

So, if the problems we face are actually the accountability of our supposedly free, democratic and successful capitalist world, we are not going to have any choice but to pick up the pieces and stick them back together with something a bit more permanent than strong glue or immigration quotas.

This accountability is exactly the same that we face if we fail to love our children enough and turn them into hopeless adults with no self-esteem, no decent education and problems with mental health, drink and drugs. We might want to blame them for being layabouts living off the state but, actually, it was our fault – those of us in leadership positions.

In fact, the problems of our world are pretty easy to explain. Before I do so, I want to preface my "polemic" by making some very important preliminary remarks.

Firstly, I'm not a loony lefty. I do believe in capitalism but just not the sort of capitalism that we've got right now. At the same time, I don't believe that the only way to solve the problems of the world is to do it through poverty, asceticism or mass redistribution of wealth or on the lines of the Communist manifesto. Yes, St Francis of Assisi instigated some major changes by approaching it from the perspective of poverty and so did Jesus. However, William Wilberforce was a rich man and he led the campaign to abolish the slave trade from a position of power and wealth. Yet he didn't focus that power and wealth on himself, but on others. Abundance which does and should include physical wealth is good but, in my world view, it's more about wellbeing than materialism or consumerism. It's okay to have a reasonable amount more than we actually need. On the other hand, we should not have so much "stuff" that it enslaves us and takes away our freedom at the same time as exploiting others.

The thing about greed is that it damages others as we exploit them for our own benefit. It damages ourselves as we forget what life is all about and also our planet as we over-consume our way into environmental degradation.

As the Dalai Lama put it so beautifully just recently: "Man sacrifices his health in order to make money. Then he sacrifices money to recuperate his health. And then he was so anxious about the future but he does not enjoy the present; the result being that he does not live in the present or the future; he lives as if he is never going to die, and then dies having never really lived."

My simple explanation of the state of our planet today is set out below using the ubiquitous PowerPoint to make it as easy and as quick to understand as possible. Interspersed between the slides are some comments I have written.

The state of democracy and capitalism

- **Democracy captured by big business**
  - Oil, weapons, banking, pharma, agrochemicals, retailing, (Walmart, Amazon), Technology (Google, Facebook, Apple, Microsoft) gambling, drinking, illegal drugs.
- **Capitalism has gorged itself to death like the caterpillar**
  - Big business puts profit before principles and people.
  - Company law was not designed for corporate entities with balance sheets the size of sovereign states.
  - Gross Domestic Product, the Key Performance Indicator of capitalism, measures revenues of prostitution and illegal drug sales.
  - See Paul Mason's book , *PostCapitalism: A Guide To Our Future*

We don't really live in a democracy. We live in a "Corporatocracy"; a "Greedocracy"; an Elitocracy; in fact a "Corruptocracy".

In the famous words of an American newsreader: "It's official. The cause of the Iraq war was a three-letter word. Not WMD. But OIL." This was let slip by the previously worshipped Chairman of the US Federal Reserve, Alan Greenspan.

American politician Robert Kennedy said in 1964 that Gross Domestic Product (GDP) – the monetary value of all the finished goods and services produced in a country in a specific period of time – measures everything except what makes life worth living. He was right then, and the case is open and shut now. When GDP, the key measure of our society's performance includes sales of illegal drugs and prostitution, you know that you're in an absolute mess. There are some images which sum it all up here:

www.crashbankwallop.co.uk/library/E-2

To truly understand the historical, economic and other analytical context, read the prophetic and game-changing book *PostCapitalism: A Guide to Our Future* written by Paul Mason, the Economics Editor at *Channel 4 News*. I agree with pretty much everything he says in it and would recommend it to anyone who has even the remotest interest in solving the problems the world faces. Mason's book follows on from his earlier publication *Meltdown: The End of the Age of Greed*.

The other thing that explains everything in our developed world today is our culture. I call it a culture of "MEEE, MORRRE, NOWWW!" But, let's not forget, our culture has been led by the rich and powerful and celebrities; so don't blame ordinary people for picking up on it and making themselves miserable as well. It is summed up below.

The culture of our world

- **3,000 adverts hit us (our children) every day telling us that happiness means money, power, celebrity, good looks and sex**
  - "Take the waiting out of the wanting"
  - "You're worth it"
  - "Barclays – Best for Fixed Rate Mortgages"
  - Retail therapy – lead to same chemicals in brain as cocaine!
- **We live in a culture of "Me, More, Now". G Me P! Mammon and stuff**
  - Materialism, secularism, consumerism and ethical relativism
  - We have been "ismed" to death
  - **Having and Doing NOT Being and Relating**

Those 3,000 adverts that bombard our children every day in every way from every communication platform on the planet, remind us of the famous lyrics of The Rolling Stones song, *(I Can't Get No)* Satisfaction and Depeche Mode's, *Just Can't Get Enough*.

The adverts sell our children and ourselves on the idea that happiness is about what you have and how you look and how much sex you can get away with. We call it, "Retail Therapy" when we go out to make ourselves happy by buying stuff. Have we gone mad?

Eminent psychiatrists and psychologists can tell you that Retail Therapy is a bit like alcoholism. Each time a purchase is made, it releases additional chemicals in the brain similar to the result of taking cocaine.

Greed is an addiction. It's not just about having more than you need. It's about having a dysfunctional relationship with the material world. It's often driven by fear of economic insecurity which drives us to be miserly and terrified about the future. Charles Dickens', *A Christmas Carol* portrays this very well. It also portrays how much happiness giving and focusing on others can bring, even when you're rich. The fear of economic insecurity along with the addiction to stuff is at the heart of greed and we are all wrapped up in it to one degree or another. Of course, some people say that fear stands for, "false evidence appearing real".

The overall situation is beautifully rendered in the incredible film *The Age of Stupid*. This was the last movie that Pete Postlethwaite, the famous actor, ever made. At the time, he was in the final stages of dying of cancer.

He said that it was the most important film he ever made in his life.

It's often only dying that brings us to our senses when we finally realise what life was supposed to be all about.

It was in *The Age of Stupid* that a child who is doing the voiceover in an animated section of the movie says, "With profit the only measuring stick, destroying the planet is built into the system." Out of the mouths of babes comes the Truth.

The upshot of all this is that it has led to the most horrendous inequality; inequality which is increasing every day, every month and every year.

The consequences

- **Inequality as bad as 100 years ago**
  - Top 1% own 45%; bottom 50% own 1%......AND GETTING WORSE!
- **"The Spirit Level" proves inequality causes all social ills**
  - Infant mortality, teenage pregnancy, obesity, addiction, mental health, morbidity, mortality, number of prisoners etc.
  - **Japan spends 1/3 per capita on health as USA but has 50% less infant mortality and lives eight years longer"**

No Love, Truth, Justice = SLAVERY

There are so many statistics about horrendous inequality in the world that I don't really know where to start.

After 400 years of capitalism, well over 40% of the world's wealth is owned by one per cent of its people, leaving only 1% of the wealth for the poorest 50% of its people. We spend more money on ice cream in Western Europe than it would cost to feed the entire world, and I believe that the same is true of pet food. The three richest people in the world own more assets than the one-billion poorest.

Here are some other key statistics from:

www.inequality.org which is a project set up by the Institute for Policy Studies in the UK.

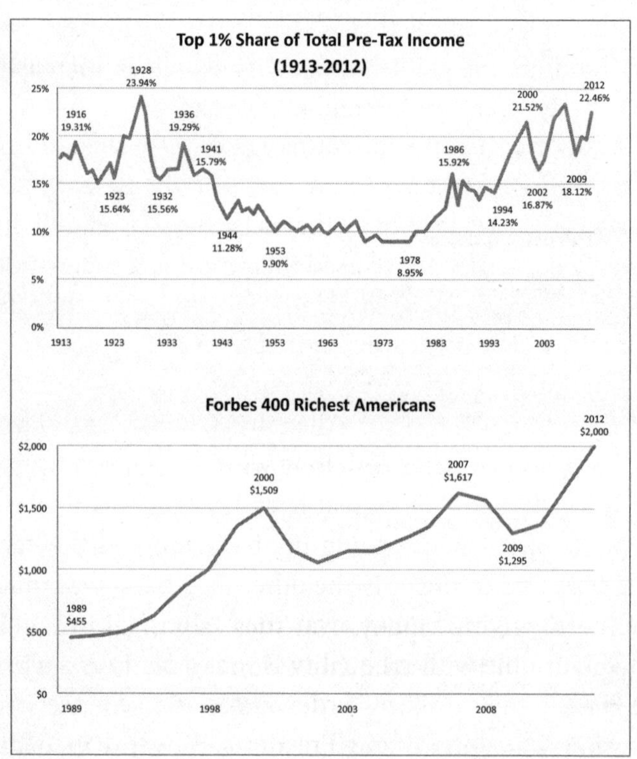

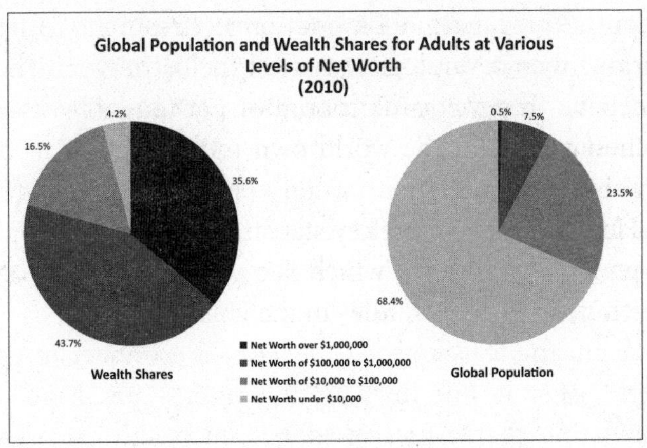

Many rich people, of course, like Bill Gates and his wife Melinda are an example to us all. The couple know that it's the love of money that is the root of all evil, not money itself. They have used their money for enormous good and much more efficiently and effectively than any sovereign state could dream to do.

On the other hand, apparently Gates' famous Microsoft partner Paul Allen has chosen to build a private motor yacht 220m long with its own submarine.

A wealthy and very great friend of mine with whom I shared a flat while doing my bar exams in the early Eighties said to me only the other day that it was much better fun giving money away than making it.

The trouble with inequality is that it leads to a world in which the "pecking order" takes precedence over Love, Truth, Justice and Freedom. A world in which people feel that they are useless and less valuable than others, is a world that will fall to pieces.

In the prophetic book *The Spirit Level*, two North Yorkshire epidemiologists prove conclusively that ALL social ills, in developed economies, are caused by levels of inequality.

This includes; infant mortality, childhood pregnancy, obesity, morbidity (levels of illness), numbers of people in prison, levels of mental health problems, addictions etc etc and, of course, how long people live.

Japan, the least unequal developed economy in the world, spends one-third of the money per head of population than America spends on health care. The result is Japan has half the infant mortality and its people live eight years longer than Americans.

What is probably more extraordinary to the radical right-wingers is that Japan doesn't achieve this by high tax rates and mass redistribution of wealth. It achieves it simply because there are much lower income differentials between the bottom and the top.

So, what is the answer to all this misery?

Shall we just dig ourselves a bunker in our back gardens fill it up with baked beans, Marmite, Yorkshire tea bags, AK 47s and ammunition, like the "preppers" we see on those marvellous reality TV programmes coming to us from the USA? Or shall we try to do something about it?

Well, I know what I think but it's not just me. Almost all of us believe that the "zeitgeist is upon us". French writer Victor Hugo summed it up beautifully when he said: "The most powerful force on Earth is an idea whose moment has come."

Albert Einstein put it another way when he said: "And the world is a dangerous place. Not because of the people who are evil; but because of the people who don't do anything about it."

To summarise, the fundamental problem in our world today has arisen because society's leaders – political, business, celebrities and the mass media – have led us to believe that peace, joy and wellbeing are all about a culture of "Me, More, Now", or what I call G Me P.

The love of money and me is at the centre of everything we do. We (and I include myself here) have become mesmerised by and addicted to the deadly sins of pride, greed, vanity, envy, gluttony and lust. GDP measures everything except what makes life worth living.

My volunteer team and I feel enormously energised by the sentiment expressed by the people we meet every day who want a massive change in the world. If we really want to solve the problem of banks and bankers, it is time for us all to work together for this change.

We believe that all people of goodwill, whether of faith or not, have had a dream for many years that if we share our experience, strength and hope, as well as our combined knowledge and skills, we really can reach out and start a new popular movement that will build a better world.

If the zeitgeist is upon a moment in history, it is not so much about making the technical argument as about joining all the dots and starting a popular, peaceful movement for reconciliation, recovery, renewal, reformation and renaissance. If we all work together we can build a new Earth. We can free ourselves from the slavery of greed and the damage it does to others, ourselves and the planet.

In one way, this is political but it's absolutely not party political. In fact, we need to move on from the politics of Left and Right to the politics of plain old right and wrong.

There are countless organisations on the same journey (some people estimate the number at nearly 1,000,000). And, of course, there are millions and millions of ordinary people who yearn for the change.

We all need to work together to provide leadership and join them around one common agenda for change.

In finishing this book, my own fervent prayer for this moment in history is that this year will mark the time when we all start working together to build a popular movement for change to help abolish our modern-day slavery, the spiritual slavery of "me, more, now".

A movement is born
– The NEW WILBERFORCE Movement –
Integrity in Action

With a clear sense of direction we have built a powerful initial plan and we would like everyone to be involved in developing it further.

William Wilberforce was one of the world's greatest politicians and social and moral activists. He worked tirelessly for the abolition of the physical slave trade. He also set up the Royal Society for the Prevention of Cruelty to Animals (RSPCA) as well as other causes at the heart of social justice.

In the confident hope of receiving William Wilberforce's inspiration and action-focused approach to leading major change, a team of us are about to unveil a big idea. And we want you all to be part of it.

We will soon be launching The NEW WILBERFORCE Movement which will become a mass peaceful movement of individuals and organisations that seeks to free us all from the slavery of greed and the damage it does to others, ourselves and the planet. We will achieve this by seeking to restore values and ethics in society and by living by the core watchwords of Love, Truth, Justice and Freedom.

The NEW WILBERFORCE Movement's strategy will focus on: Communicate. Connect. Campaign. It will be highly action-focused and will shortly launch its first campaigns in which you and everyone you know can get involved. It will only work with your involvement.

The NEW WILBERFORCE Movement will have three strings to its "bow"; a thinking arm which concentrates on research, debate and influencing key public policy, a campaigning arm called The NEW WILBER FORCE and, finally, there will be an enterprise arm called The NEW WILBERFORCE ENTERPRISES which will prove that, in business, you can be good, do good and create abundance for all on a "Win Win Fair Share" basis. The enterprise arm will do what it says on the tin.

Watch this space to read, see and hear all about it. It will be a unique organisation combining thought leadership, peaceful but powerful campaigning and collaborative economics in action.

There will obviously be a lot to do; like William Wilberforce we will be up against virtually the entire Establishment of vested interest. The "Corporatocrats", the "Greedocrats" and the "Elitocrats" won't like it but some things, like Love, Truth, Justice and Freedom are worth fighting for.

To get this done, once and for all, we are all going to need to work together, cooperate together, everyone together. That way we can connect with millions, share our experience, strength and hope and build a better world – together.

Please join The NEW WILBERFORCE Movement.

Go to www.newwilberforce.co.uk Help us build a better world.

Final food for thought:

> *"Development is impossible without upright men and women, without financiers and politicians whose consciences are finely attuned to the requirements of the common good. Both professional competence and moral consistency are necessary. When technology is allowed to take over, the result is confusion between ends and means, such that the sole criterion for action in business is thought to be the maximisation of profit, in politics the consolidation of power, and in science the findings of research."*

Once profit becomes the exclusive goal, if it is produced by improper means and without the common good as its ultimate end, it risks destroying wealth and creating poverty.

It's funny how everyone considers honesty a virtue, yet no one wants to hear the truth.